HANDBOOK OF RESEARCH ON LEADERSHIP

Handbook of Research on Gender and Leadership

Edited by

Susan R. Madsen

Orin R. Woodbury Professor of Leadership and Ethics, Woodbury School of Business, Utah Valley University, USA

EE Edward **Elgar**
PUBLISHING

Cheltenham, UK • Northampton, MA, USA

Published by
Edward Elgar Publishing Limited
The Lypiatts
15 Lansdown Road
Cheltenham
Glos GL50 2JA
UK

Edward Elgar Publishing, Inc.
William Pratt House
9 Dewey Court
Northampton
Massachusetts 01060
USA

Paperback edition 2018

A catalogue record for this book
is available from the British Library

Library of Congress Control Number: 2016959924

This book is available electronically in the **Elgar**online
Business subject collection
DOI 10.4337/9781785363863

Printed on elemental chlorine free (ECF)
recycled paper containing 30% Post-Consumer Waste

ISBN 978 1 78536 385 6 (cased)
ISBN 978 1 78536 386 3 (eBook)
ISBN 978 1 78811 974 0 (paperback)

Typeset by Servis Filmsetting Ltd, Stockport, Cheshire
Printed and bound in the USA

Contents

Contributors

Karlygash Assylkhan is a PhD student in the Organizational Behavior Program at the Weatherhead School of Management, Case Western Reserve University, USA. She is interested in investigating temporal dynamics and time-based characteristics (for example, time perspectives and time discounting), and their impact on individual, team, and organizational behavior. She holds an undergraduate degree in Business Administration from the University of International Business and Economics in China and a master's degree in Economics from KIMEP in Kazakhstan. She has worked as an auditor and consultant at PricewaterhouseCoopers and as a governmental project manager for the transit of energy across Central Asian countries to China.

Ann M. Berghout Austin is a professor at Utah State University (USU), USA, and Founding Director of USU's Center for Women and Gender. She received her PhD in Child Development from Iowa State University, USA, in 1981 and has been at USU since then. She directs an active research program focusing on girls' and women's leadership development, child care quality and availability, and children's early mathematics concepts. She has served as a major professor for more than 40 doctoral and master's students. In December 2015, *Statesman*, the USU student newspaper, listed her as one of the "Top Ten Most Influential People at USU."

Amy L. Bartels is a doctoral student in Organizational Behavior at Arizona State University, USA. She holds a Master of Education in Higher Education Administration and Juris Doctorate from the University of Nebraska, USA. Her current research focuses on understanding the dynamics of leadership and other work relationships, stress and well-being both within and outside the workplace, and the relationship between engagement and stress appraisals.

Judith Baxter is Emeritus Professor of Applied Linguistics at Aston University, UK. She specializes in the fields of sociolinguistics, gender and language, leadership discourse, feminism, and poststructuralist discourse analysis. She has published several books on the language of women leaders, including *Double-Voicing at Work: Power, Gender and Expertise* (2014), *The Language of Female Leadership* (2010), and *Positioning Gender in Discourse: A Feminist Methodology* (2003), all published by Palgrave Macmillan. Her latest book, with co-author Haleema Al A'ali *Speaking as Women Leaders: Meetings in Middle Eastern and Western Contexts*, was published by Palgrave Macmillan in September 2016. Her research regularly features in the international press, TV, and radio, such as the BBC Two series *Hilary Devey's Women at the Top*.

Laura L. Bierema is Associate Dean and Professor, University of Georgia College of Education. Her academic program is in Learning, Leadership, and Organization Development. Prior to a career in higher education, she held a variety of human resources management and executive positions in the automotive industry with AlliedSignal, Inc. (now Honeywell). Dr. Bierema's research interests include women's leadership, workplace learning, career development, organization development, executive coaching, and critical human resource development. Dr. Bierema holds both bachelor's and master's degrees from Michigan State University, USA, and a Doctor of Education degree from the University of Georgia, USA. She has published seven books and over 80 articles and book chapters. Dr. Bierema's research and publications have received multiple honors and awards, including two book-of-the-year awards for her co-authored book, *Adult Learning: Bridging Theory and Practice.*

Diana Bilimoria, PhD, is KeyBank Professor and Chair and Professor of Organizational Behavior at the Weatherhead School of Management, Case Western Reserve University, USA. Her research focuses on gender, diversity, and inclusion in the leadership and governance of organizations, particularly women's career and leadership development; the composition of corporate and non-profit boards of directors and top executive teams; and organizational transformation by enhancing diversity and inclusion. She is the author of several books and has published extensively in leading journals and edited volumes. She has received several awards for her research, teaching, and service contributions.

Michelle Bligh is a professor of Organizational Behavior and Leadership at NEOMA Business School in France. She also serves as Academic Director of the Center for Leadership and Organisational Effectiveness (CLEO). Prior to joining NEOMA, she was a professor at Claremont Graduate University (USA), where she served as Associate Dean. She has been published in over a dozen academic journals, and she was recognized by the *Leadership Quarterly* as one of the top 50 most-cited authors of the last decade. She also serves on the review board of the *Leadership Quarterly* and as Associate Editor of *Leadership*. Dr. Bligh has taught and consulted on the topics of leadership and change management around the globe, including in Europe, Asia, North America, and Latin America.

Debbie Lamm Bray has spent more than two decades helping people discover and utilize their calling. Her particular passion is facilitating women's development in their gifts, strengths, and passions. Lamm Bray was ordained in 1993 as a minister with the Assemblies of God denomination, and she recently served on the national-level General Presbytery. In addition, Lamm Bray was the first woman to have voting privileges on the Oregon Ministry Network Presbytery. She holds a Master of Arts in Theological Studies from George Fox Theological Seminary and a PhD in Higher Education from Azusa Pacific University, where her dissertation research focused on the experiences of undergraduate women in developing a sense of calling. For most of her career, Lamm Bray has served in Christian higher education; she currently directs academics and student life at the Salem, Oregon, extension campus of Northwest University, USA.

Ronald J. Burke is Professor Emeritus of Organizational Studies, Schulich School of Business, York University in Toronto, Canada. A native of Canada, he received his PhD from the University of Michigan in Organizational Psychology. He is the editor or co-editor of 53 books with two more in process, has published over 500 articles and book chapters, and has presented over 500 papers at academic conferences in several countries. Burke is a fellow of the Canadian Psychological Association and the Founding Editor of the *Canadian Journal of Administrative Sciences*; he has served on the editorial boards of more than 20 journals. His current research interests include work and health, the sandwich generation, human frailties in the workplace, and women in management. He has participated in numerous management development courses and consulted with both private- and public-sector organizations regarding human resource management issues.

Constance Campbell is the W.E. Carter Distinguished Chair in Business Leadership at the College of Business at Georgia Southern University. Her research focuses on leader identity theory and gender, and on the experiences of women who hold formal leadership positions in science, technology, engineering, and mathematics (STEM) fields. With undergraduate and master's degrees in Psychology, Constance worked for several years as Director of Counseling before completing a PhD in Management at Florida State University, USA. In over two decades of university teaching, she has won awards for her face-to-face and online teaching of leadership and management courses. Constance also enjoys conducting training with adult learners in leadership development programs for working professionals.

Cathleen Clerkin is a research faculty member at the Center for Creative Leadership (CCL), USA. She is an interdisciplinary researcher whose areas of expertise include women's leadership, social identity management, holistic leadership development, and creativity and innovation. Prior to joining CCL, Cathleen led a number of research initiatives both in the US and overseas and has won multiple awards and honors for her research, including recognition from the National Science Foundation. Cathleen graduated Phi Beta Kappa from the University of California, Berkeley, and earned her MS and PhD degrees in Psychology from the University of Michigan, Ann Arbor, USA. She completed a postdoctoral fellowship at the Center for Creative Leadership before joining as a faculty member.

Lynne E. Devnew is on the associate faculty for the doctoral program at the University of Phoenix, where she chairs dissertation committees and is a senior research fellow leading the Women and Leadership Research Group. She is also a visiting research fellow at Bentley University, conducting collaborative research for their project, Overcoming Challenges to Gender Equality in the Workplace. Devnew has her DBA in Strategy from Boston University, MS from the Master's Degree Program for Executives at Columbia University, and BS from Simmons College, USA. She was a senior middle manager at IBM. Her research efforts are focused on developing women's leader identities and women's influence on decision making on corporate boards of directors. She is currently co-editing a book to be published in 2018, *More Women on Boards of Directors: An International Perspective*, and she serves as Program Chair for the Women and Leadership Affinity Group of the International Leadership Association's 2017 conference.

Amy B. Diehl is Associate Vice President of Technology and Library Services, and Director of Systems and Applications, at Shippensburg University of Pennsylvania, USA. Amy has a PhD in Administration and Leadership from Indiana University of Pennsylvania. Her doctoral dissertation focused on how women leaders in higher education make meaning of adversity. Amy is a frequent speaker at international, national, and regional conferences on challenges women leaders experience. She also guest lectures and consults on unconscious gender bias, helping individuals and organizations learn how to identify and eliminate such bias. She received the 2016 Women and Leadership

Affinity Group Outstanding Scholarship for Emerging Scholars Award from the International Leadership Association. Her research has been published in academic journals: *Human Resource Development Quarterly* and *Advancing Women in Leadership.* She also contributed a chapter to *Women and Leadership in Higher Education*, the first volume in the International Leadership Association's Women and Leadership series.

Leanne Dzubinski is an associate professor of Intercultural Education at Biola University in La Mirada, California, where she teaches and mentors doctoral students in all stages of their careers. She is chair of the graduate department and Program Director for the PhD in Intercultural Education. Her research has focused on women in evangelical non-profit organizations. She does organizational consulting and presents at conferences on women's leadership, adult education, and international non-profit work. Her writings appear in both scholarly and practitioner journals, including *Human Resource Development Quarterly, Online Learning, Journal of Transformative Education*, and *Adult Learning.*

Chrys Egan holds a Communication PhD from Florida State University and is an associate professor of Communication and Gender at Salisbury University (SU), USA. She published chapters in *Family Communication: Theory and Research, Advancing Theories of Women and Leadership, Communication Theory and Millennial Popular Culture: Essays and Applications*, and *Communication and Global Engagement across Cultural Boundaries.* Textbook ancillaries include *Communication Research Instructor's Manual* and *The St Martin's Guide to Public Speaking: Student Workbook, Testbank, and Instructor's Manual.* She has published in the following journals: the *Free Speech Yearbook, Studies in Popular Culture, Journal of Popular Culture, Iowa Journal of Communication*, and *Gender in Management: International Journal.* She was Conference Co-chair for Popular Culture in the South, and Women and Leadership Affinity Group (WLAG). She is the International Leadership Association's WLAG Communication Chair. She received SU's Outstanding Faculty Award and President's Diversity Award.

Carole Elliott is Professor of Human Resource Development at Roehampton Business School, University of Roehampton, UK, and Visiting Fellow at The George Washington University in Washington, DC, USA. She is Editor-in-Chief of the Taylor & Francis journal *Human Resource Development International* and Principal Investigator for the Economic and Social Research Council (ESRC) seminar series "Challenging Gendered Media (Mis)representations of Women Professionals and Leaders." Recent collaborations with Valerie Stead have resulted in the research monograph *Women's Leadership* (2009) and scholarly articles in journals such as *Management Learning and Leadership.* Elliott recently co-edited a special issue of *Management Learning*, "Critical and Alternative Approaches to Leadership Learning and Development" (2013), and an issue of *Advances in Developing Human Resources* titled "Using Creative Techniques in Leadership Learning and Development" (2015). Carole is Co-editor of the volume *Gender, Media and Organization: Challenging Mis(s)Representations of Women Leaders and Managers*, a volume in the series Women and Leadership, published by Information Age Publishing.

Wendy Fox-Kirk is an assistant professor in Management at the Goddard School of Business & Economics at Weber State University, USA. She was previously Deputy

Director of the MBA program at the University of Birmingham in the UK, where she also completed her PhD in Business. Her research interests focus on identity issues and power in relation to disadvantage in the workplace. Her latest research uses Bourdieu's Theory of Social Action to examine women's leadership journeys in higher education and to critique authentic leadership theory.

Rita A. Gardiner is an assistant professor in Critical Policy, Equity, and Leadership Studies at the Faculty of Education, The University of Western Ontario, in London, Ontario, Canada. Her research interests include exploring authentic leadership through the lens of existential phenomenology, and intersectional approaches to current ethical and political problems in leadership. Rita teaches courses on theoretical approaches to leadership and leadership ethics. Her recent publications include *Gender, Authenticity and Leadership: Thinking with Arendt* (Palgrave Macmillan, 2015). In 2014, she was awarded the Paul Begley Award for her outstanding contribution to postgraduate research in the study of values and educational leadership by the University Council for Educational Administration Consortium for the Study of Leadership and Ethics in Education. Rita received her PhD in Women's Studies and Feminist Research from The University of Western Ontario in 2013.

Kerry Roberts Gibson is an assistant professor in the Management Division at Babson College, USA, where she currently teaches foundations of management and entrepreneurship. She previously taught both organizational behavior and human resources at Georgia Tech, USA, where she completed her PhD. Professor Gibson's primary research interest is workplace relationships. She focuses on relationship development mechanisms, such as self-disclosure and gratitude. She explores how these relationship mechanisms drive outcomes, such as organizational identification, engagement, and voice. She is published in the *Journal of Vocational Behavior* and has presented her research at the Academy of Management Annual Meeting, the Positive Relationships at Work Microcommunity Research Meeting, the Positive Organizational Scholarship Research Conference, and the International Association of Positive Psychology World Congress.

Christy Glass is a professor of Sociology at Utah State University, USA. She earned her PhD in Sociology from Yale University, USA, in 2005. Her research and teaching focus on gender inequality, race/ethnicity, and work and leadership. Her current research focuses on factors that shape promotion opportunities for women and racial/ethnic minorities and the organizational factors that shape employer perceptions of women and mothers. She has published widely in top journals in sociology and management, including *Social Forces, Work and Occupations, Gender and Society, Social Problems, Strategic Management Journal*, and *Human Resource Management*. Her research aims to inform workplace policies and practices that can reduce inequality and promote fairness. Her research has been featured by the *New York Times*, the *Guardian*, National Public Radio, *Huffington Post*, CNN, and the *Harvard Business Review*.

Elizabeth Goryunova is an assistant professor of Leadership and Organizational Studies at the University of Southern Maine. Her teaching affiliation also includes the University of Utah, Southern New Hampshire University, and Utah Valley University. Prior to academia, Elizabeth successfully led (as President/CEO and prior to that as Chief Operating Officer) the strategic development of the World Trade Center Utah. In addi-

identity, dirty work, vulnerability, and leadership. Sharon is Associate Editor for the *International Journal of Management Reviews*. She has published in journals such as *Human Relations, British Journal of Management, Organization, International Journal of Management Reviews, Gender, Work and Organization, Human Resource Development Review, Qualitative Research in Organizations and Management: An International Journal,* and *Gender and Management: An International Journal.* Sharon is Co-editor of the volume *Gender, Media and Organization: Challenging Mis(s)Representations of Women Leaders and Management,* a volume in the series Women and Leadership, published by Information Age Publishing.

Wendy M. Murphy, PhD, is an associate professor of Management at Babson College, USA, where she teaches organizational behavior for undergraduates and managing talent in the MBA program. Her research is at the intersection of careers, mentoring, and work–life issues, with particular attention to nontraditional developmental relationships and learning. Murphy has published her work in a range of journals, such as *Human Resource Management, Gender in Management, Journal of Management,* and the *Journal of Vocational Behavior,* among others. Her book with Dr. Kathy Kram, *Strategic Relationships at Work: Creating Your Circle of Mentors, Sponsors, and Peers for Success in Business and Life,* bridges mentoring scholarship and practice. In 2014, she was recognized by Poets & Quants as one of the "40 Most Outstanding B-School Profs Under 40 in the World."

Kristina Natt och Dag has a PhD in Educational Research and Policy Analysis from North Carolina State University, USA, where she earned a 2015 outstanding dissertation of the year award. She also has a master's in human rights from Lund University in Sweden. She has been working in the field of training and organizational development (both corporate and non-profit sectors) for the past two decades. With experience in a variety of sectors, such as finance, health care, and maintenance, she has extensive global experience and speaks numerous languages. Kristina is currently working with the North Carolina Medical Society, where she is the Director of the Kanof Institute for Physicians Leadership. Her specific areas of research are authentic, ethical, and global leadership. She is Chair of the Leadership Special Interest Group of the Academy of Human Resource Development and regularly presents at various conferences. She has also co-edited a recent special issue of *Advances in Developing Human Resources*.

Faith Wambura Ngunjiri is the Director of the Lorentzsen Center for Faith and Work, and an associate professor of Ethics and Leadership at the Offutt School of Business at Concordia College, USA. Her work has been published in various journals, including *Journal of Management, Spirituality and Religion, International Journal of Qualitative Studies in Education, Journal of Business Communication,* and *Journal of Educational Administration,* among others. She is the author of *Women's Spiritual Leadership in Africa* (SUNY, 2010) and co-author of *Collaborative Autoethnography* (Left Coast Press, 2013). She is Co-editor of two books, *Women as Global Leaders* and *Women and Leadership around the World,* both published by Information Age Publishing. Faith is Co-editor of two book series: Women and Leadership: Theory, Research and Practice (Information Age Publishing) and Palgrave Studies in African Leadership (Palgrave Macmillan). She earned a doctorate in Leadership Studies from Bowling Green State University, USA.

Suzanne J. Peterson is an associate professor of Leadership at Arizona State University's (ASU) Thunderbird School of Global Management, USA. She has held the same position at ASU's W.P. Carey School of Business. She is an award-winning teacher and a highly sought-after executive educator. She does a variety of speaking, consulting, and coaching for senior audiences, primarily on Wall Street and in other financial services firms. Her research centers on the behaviors that characterize remarkable executive leaders, the neuropsychological origins of leadership, and the dynamics surrounding women on corporate boards. Her research has appeared in top peer-reviewed management and psychology journals, and she has designed and delivered executive education leadership initiatives for numerous global companies.

Katharina Pick is a clinical assistant professor of Management at the Peter F. Drucker and Masatoshi Ito Graduate School of Management at Claremont Graduate University, USA. She teaches classes in organizational behavior, teams, gender and leadership, and design thinking. She currently also coordinates Drucker's Women in Supply Chain Mentoring Program and is engaged in the Executive Mind Leadership Institute at the Drucker School. Her research has examined the internal group dynamics of corporate boards of directors and board leadership. Other academic interests include gender and leadership and design thinking in organizational development and strategy. In her clinical role, Katharina provides leadership coaching to executives at the Drucker School and for programs at the Getty Leadership Institute. In coaching, Katharina integrates current models of leadership effectiveness, Drucker's Principles of Self-management, Jungian psychology, and best-practice coaching. Katharina holds a PhD in Organizational Behavior and an MA in sociology from Harvard University, USA.

Deborah L. Rhode is the Ernest W. McFarland Professor of Law, Stanford Law School and the Director of the Center on the Legal Profession at Stanford University, USA. She is the former President of the Association of American Law Schools, the former Chair of the American Bar Association's Commission on Women in the Profession, and the former Director of Stanford's Institute for Research on Women and Gender. She writes primarily in the areas of legal ethics and gender equity and is the author or editor of 27 books. Her books on gender include *Women and Leadership* (2016), *The Beauty Bias* (2010), *Women and Leadership: The State of Play and Strategies for Reform* (with Barbara Kellerman, 2009), *The Difference "Difference" Makes: Women and Leadership* (2003), and *Speaking of Sex* (1997).

Robbyn T. Scribner is a researcher and writer whose past academic work has focused on both women's leadership and careers as well as women's rhetoric and storytelling. She holds a master's degree in English with an emphasis in composition and rhetoric from Brigham Young University (BYU), USA, and a bachelor's degree (also from BYU) in European Studies. Robbyn specializes in promoting excellence in writing; she has taught university writing at all levels and co-directed a cross-curricular writing tutoring program. She has also led seminars and workshops for scholars in various fields, training them on teaching and incorporating more writing in their specific disciplines. Most recently, she has been researching and writing on issues affecting women and careers, with an emphasis on women who have taken time away from the workforce and are looking to return.

Ruth Sealy is an associate professor in Organization Studies at Exeter University Business School. As an expert on women in leadership, corporate board composition, executive careers, and role models, Ruth has worked closely with two UK government departments and the Lord Davies committee on increasing the proportion of women on corporate boards, writing reports also for the Financial Reporting Council, major listed and professional service organizations, and the European Commission. Ruth has presented research findings to academic and practitioner audiences globally. She lectures on doctoral, MBA and MSc courses and has written a number of book chapters and journal articles. Formerly, Ruth was Managing Director of a specialist holiday company, which she sold, and then worked for a number of years as a consultant. She conducted her PhD at Cranfield School of Management, UK, staying on to become Deputy Director of a research centre. Prior to her current role at Exeter, Ruth was Programme Director for the MSc Organisational Psychology at City University London, UK.

Mary Shapiro has taught for 25 years at Simmons College, Boston, Massachusetts, USA, in the School of Management, teaching organization behavior and leadership to undergraduates, MBA students, and executives. In 2014, she was appointed to the inaugural endowed Trust Professorship of Leadership Development, charged with developing a leadership platform to be infused throughout the undergraduate program. As a faculty affiliate of the Center for Gender and Organizations, she researches and publishes in the areas of women, their careers, risk-taking, and confidence. In 2015, she published *Leading Teams* with the Harvard Business School Press, and earlier she co-authored two books on interviewing and career management. Throughout her career, Shapiro has consulted with Fortune 500 companies and nonprofits to create strategic plans and develop their teams. She is First Vice Chair of the Girl Scouts of Eastern Massachusetts (GSEM) Board, USA. She received her MBA and MS Economics from Wright State University in Dayton, Ohio, USA.

Stefanie Simon received her PhD in Social Psychology from Tulane University, USA, in 2015. She is currently a postdoctoral fellow in the Department of Psychology at Carleton College, USA. Her research examines the social psychology of prejudice, stigma, and diversity. Some of her current work investigates reasons why members of different groups (for example, blacks and whites, or women and men) may disagree about whether an event was discriminatory, as well as the costs and benefits of confronting prejudice. Applied to leadership, her research explores the consequences of facing bias for nontraditional leaders (that is, women and racial/ethnic minorities) in leadership contexts. Her work is published in various psychology journals, such as the *Journal of Experimental Social Psychology*, *Group Processes and Intergroup Relations*, and *Leadership Quarterly*.

Amy E. Smith is an associate professor and MPA Program Director in the McCormack Graduate School of Policy and Global Studies at the University of Massachusetts Boston, USA. Her current research focuses on gender diversity in leadership in public organizations, career paths in public service, and issues of work–life balance. Dr. Smith also conducts research on teaching and mentoring in graduate education. Her work has appeared in journals such as the *Journal of Public Administration Research and Theory*, the *International Public Management Journal*, and the *American Review of Public Administration*. Dr. Smith serves on the editorial board for the journal *Public Performance* *and Management Review* and is active in the Public and Non-profit Division of the Academy of Management and the Public Management Research Association. She holds a PhD in Public Administration and Policy from the University at Albany, USA.

Valerie Stead is Senior Lecturer in Leadership and Management at Lancaster University Management School, UK. Valerie's research interests are in leadership and learning, and employing critical perspectives to examine women's leadership. Current research projects address the mobilization of textual and visual representations of women's leadership in the media; she examines gender, power, and leadership in family business. Valerie has published widely, including in the scholarly journals *Management Learning*, *International Small Business Journal and Leadership*, and the research monograph *Women's Leadership* (with C. Elliott, 2009). Valerie has also contributed chapters to various edited collections and most recently co-edited a volume for the International Leadership Association's Women in Leadership book series. She is Associate Editor for the *International Journal of Management Reviews*, a co-investigator for the Economic and Social Research Council's Seminar Series "Challenging Gendered Media (Mis)representations of Women Professionals and Leaders," and coordinates the Lancaster University research forum, the Academy for Women, Diversity, and Leadership.

Julia Storberg-Walker is an associate professor and Co-director of the Executive Leadership Program at The George Washington University (GWU), USA, and an Affiliate of GWU's Global Women's Institute. Julia serves as Editor-in-Chief of *Human Resource Development Review*, a theory and conceptual journal. She is also an associate at the Taos Institute. In 2015, Julia was recognized for her contributions to women and leadership theory when she received the International Leadership Association's Women and Leadership Affinity Group's Outstanding Scholar Award. She has published and presented globally on theoretical and conceptual development for applied disciplines, and she incorporates a variety of critically informed research strategies in her theorizing projects. She is currently focused on feminist theorizing as a catalyst for leading social change. Holistically, the purpose of her work is to de-center male-normed processes for generating new knowledge and to legitimate other forms of knowing in and about the world.

Chantal van Esch is a PhD candidate in Organizational Behavior at the Weatherhead School of Management, Case Western Reserve University, USA. Her research centers on the ways individuals and organizations can help diverse employees reach their full potential. She uses a multi-method, interdisciplinary approach to study careers, gender, diversity, and inclusion in management. She regularly presents her research to global audiences at the annual conferences of the Academy of Management and Southern Management Association, and has published in well-respected journals.

Jannine Williams is a senior lecturer in Human Resource Management and Organizational Behaviour at the University of Bradford, UK. From her background in working with disabled people, a PhD on disabled academics' career experiences and gender projects, Jannine has developed research interests that are broadly underpinned by critical management studies using qualitative research methods. Her research encompasses processes of organizing; categories of social relations and constructions of difference, particularly disability and gender; women's intra-gender relations and friendship at work. She has co-edited two books, *Deaf Students in Higher Education: Current Research and Practice* and *Gender, Media and Organization: Challenging Mis(s)Representations of Women Leaders and Managers*. She has published in *British Journal of Management, Studies in Higher Education*, the *International Journal of Management Reviews, Disability & Society, Human Resource Development Review,* and *Gender in Management: An International Journal*.

Meena S. Wilson is Executive Director for Genpact Centre for Women's Leadership, a first-of-its-kind corporate–academia partnership between Genpact and Ashoka University, India. A versatile 25-year veteran of the leadership development industry, her current responsibilities are to mobilize world-class resources to promote women's leadership and gender equity in India. Author of *Developing Tomorrow's Leaders Today: Insights from Corporate India* (Wiley, 2010) and many book chapters and articles, Meena also designs and delivers conference keynotes and workshops and facilitates assessment-based feedback and coaching sessions. As senior professional at the Center for Creative Leadership (CCL), she served in the US, Singapore, and India, leading multiple strategic, cross-country start-ups, such as launching CCL's first Asia–Pacific campus in Singapore and the Asia Pacific Research, Innovation and Product Development (RIPD) unit. Meena holds a PhD in Adult and Organizational Development from the University of North Carolina at Chapel Hill, USA, an MS degree from Syracuse University (USA) in television–radio journalism, and a BA from Mills College in Oakland, California, USA.

Foreword
Betsy Myers

In her introduction to this *Handbook of Research on Gender and Leadership*, Susan Madsen calls for new answers, solutions, research, and action steps when it comes to strengthening women's impact around the world. Her view, which I wholeheartedly share, is that even though women have made progress in recent years, there is still much more work that needs to be done. Indeed, according to Jason Furman, Chairman of President Obama's Council of Economic Advisers (2015), when we examine the labor forces of 24 countries, the overall proportion of working women in the United States has dropped from seventh to twentieth in a relatively short period of time. Based on Catalyst (2016) data, women today currently hold just 25.1 percent of executive and senior-level managerial positions, 19.9 percent of board seats, 9.5 percent of top-earning positions, and 4.4 percent of chief executive officer (CEO) seats. These numbers should be much higher, given that women now represent 58 percent of our college graduates.

It is true that we have more female leaders than a generation ago, but only a very small portion are sitting at the top of organizations. And, to make matters worse, the conversations we are having about gender and work today are the very same conversations we were having when I was President Clinton's advisor on women's issues in the White House during the mid-1990s. Catalyst's (2013) annual censuses of the Fortune 500 show that the gender mix at the senior levels of corporate America has changed very little in recent years. Unfortunately, this is not for lack of trying, by those with the best of intentions. However, what has historically passed for gender efforts inside corporate America has often been a series of discussions, classes, and conferences in which women find themselves talking to women. Although meaningful and productive, these strategies are often not woven into the fabric of the organization. And, on many occasions, a committed CEO and senior C-suite leaders go away believing that this support, plus periodic face-time, is sufficient.

The backdrop here, as we all know, is that the world has changed significantly. Talent is a key motivator in today's competitive global marketplace, and CEOs and savvy business leaders understand that they must have a workforce that reflects the current and future workplace and customers. They also know that the female perspective often leads to wiser decisions, and the rich relationship skills that women leaders offer frequently result in happier employees and deeper client connections. Hiring, supporting, retaining, and advancing women have become business imperatives and opportunities to be seized. The good news is that we have just about reached consensus, and the vast majority of corporate CEOs no longer ask why they should include and advance women in their organizations. So, we may understand the "why," but it is increasingly clear that what still eludes us is the "how" to include, keep, and advance women in organizations.

One of the most vital action steps is that of men mentoring women. Research shows us that men mentoring women can make all the difference to their retention and advancement. As an example, a 2014 gender parity study by Bain & Company found that nearly half of women enter the workforce with their eye on the C-suite, but their confidence and ambition levels drop 60 percent after little more than just two years on the job. One of the key findings was that marital and parental status do not significantly differ between women who aspire and those who do not. Instead, women lack the meaningful recognition, support, and mentorship from their managers necessary to shape and support their path to advancement and personal confidence. Mentorship is the essence of effective leadership, and mentoring people within an organization is a key element in the engagement and retention of top talent in today's workplace. And, because men remain the most powerful stakeholder group in most organizations, I strongly believe that men can play a powerful role in accelerating progress toward the gender equality that has eluded us for so many years.

As we work through this, it is important to remember that both women and men in organizations find themselves in a confused – and even conflicted – workplace today: confused, because gender behavior and stereotyped male–female roles in companies create uncertainty on how to be, and conflicted because we have mixed reactions, and there are judgments when we observe men acting like men, women acting like women, women acting like men, or men acting like women. We reach for programs and initiatives that might help us, and some – such as sponsorship, flexibility, and accountability – most definitely do. But corporate leaders and their teams are frustrated by the lack of gender progress as well as the gender tension (both overt and covert) that still permeates organizations. All of this drains energy and emotion – and, even worse, engagement – from our companies. So, it is no wonder that nearly two-thirds of all American workers say they are disengaged today. Reflexively promoting women into positions of greater responsibility and leadership will not immediately or necessarily boost employee engagement scores. But, as recent research from Jack Zenger and Joseph Folkman (2012) of Zenger/Folkman, a leadership development consultancy, makes clear, at every level, more women are rated by their peers, their bosses, their direct reports, and their other associates as better overall leaders than their male counterparts; and the higher the level, the wider that gap grows. These findings, as well as the insights from the contributors to this book, should be inspiration enough for us to heed Susan Madsen's urgent call for fresh approaches to women's achievement and advancement.

REFERENCES

Bain & Company (2014). Professional women lose confidence, ambition as they reach mid-career, new Bain & Company study finds. September 15. Retrieved from http://www.bain.com/about/press/press-releases/professional-women-lose-confidence-ambition-as-they-reach-mid-career.aspx.

Catalyst (2013). 2013 Catalyst census: Fortune 300 women board directors. December 10. Retrieved from http://www.catalyst.org/knowledge/2013-catalyst-census-fortune-500-women-board-directors.

Catalyst (2016). Statistical overview of women in the workforce. April 6. Retrieved from http://www.catalyst.org/knowledge/statistical-overview-women-workforce.

Council of Economic Advisors (2015). *Economic Report of the President: The Annual Report of the Council of Economic Advisers*. February. Retrieved from https://fraser.stlouisfed.org/docs/publications/ERP/2015_erp.pdf.

Zenger, J., and Folkman, J. (2012). A study in leadership; Women do it better than men. Retrieved from http://www.zengerfolkman.com/media/articles/ZFCo.WP.WomenBetterThanMen.033012.pdf.

Betsy Myers, a leadership expert, author, and advocate, also speaks at and convenes workshops around the world on the changing nature of leadership and women's leadership. Her book, *Take the Lead: Motivate, Inspire, and*

Bring Out the Best in Yourself and Everyone Around You, was released in September 2011. Her experience spans corporate, political, and higher education arenas. She is the founding director of the Center for Women and Business at Bentley University and has served as the executive director of the Center for Public Leadership at Harvard's Kennedy School of Government, USA. A senior adviser to two US presidents, the chief operating officer and chair of Women for President Obama's 2008 national presidential campaign and during the Clinton administration, she launched, and was the first director of, the White House Office for Women's Initiatives and Outreach. She also served as the director of the Office of Women's Business Ownership at the Small Business Administration (SBA). Prior to joining the Clinton administration, she spent six years building Myers Insurance and Financial Services in Los Angeles, USA, specializing in the small business and women's market. She received her bachelor's degree in business administration from the University of San Diego and her master's degree in public administration from Harvard's Kennedy School, USA, where she was also a Public Service Fellow.

Introduction
Susan R. Madsen

Although many scholars do highlight the global progress that has been made in recent decades in terms of the number of women in top positions in government, business, and education (Adler, 2015), Joshi et al. (2015) called this progress "both promising and problematic" (p. 1459). These and other researchers are quick to point out that there are ongoing, persisting challenges with efforts to strengthen women's impact around the world. For example, unequal opportunities and treatment of women (compared to men) remain concerning in nearly all countries, contexts, and sectors (Madsen et al., 2015; Yeganeh and May, 2011). The McKinsey Global Institute's (2015) "The power of parity: How advancing women's equality can add $12 trillion to global growth" stated that "gender inequality is a pressing global issue with huge ramifications not just for the lives and livelihoods of girls and women, but more generally, for human development, labor markets, productivity, GDP growth, and inequality" (p. ii). My point is that, even with some progress, there is still much more work that needs to be done.

During the past decade, research on gender and leadership has increased dramatically. In addition to my recent co-edited scholarly books – *Women and Leadership in Higher Education* (Longman and Madsen, 2014), *Women as Global Leaders* (Ngunjiri and Madsen, 2015), and *Women and Leadership around the World* (Madsen et al., 2015) – thousands of research- and theory-based books and articles have been published on various elements of women and leadership within different sectors, industries, cultures, countries, and contexts. In addition, newspaper, magazine, blog, and other social media articles (for example, stories, editorials, personal perspectives, summaries of research) are released daily within communities, states and provinces, nations, and across the globe. So, the question then becomes: why do we need another book focused on gender and leadership research? Yet, the answer is also clear: although some progress has been made, what we are currently doing is not working. We need more answers. We need more theory. We need more research that addresses questions that have not yet been investigated instead of focusing on studies that confirm what we already know. We need more change interventions based on rigorously tested women and leadership theory and research. We need new findings that get us all thinking outside the box for solutions. We need to shake things up as theorists, scholars, researchers, and practitioners so we can help change the status of women globally.

I do realize this "change the world" mentality irritates some who do not see gender issues as critical or who do not believe that true social change is possible. However, I am boldly asking for nothing less than this: let's change the world together. "Building, Bridging, and Blazing Pathways for Women and Leadership" was the title of the 2013 global women and leadership conference I chaired through the International Leadership Association (ILA, 2013). Today I still believe that we must build (through strategically expanding and deepening theory and research), bridge (through partnerships across academic disciplines, organizations, industries, communities, and others), and blaze (by becoming more informed, strengthening our voices, and increasing our courage). Of course this is no small feat, but this is what is needed. A feat is defined as "an act or achievement that shows courage, strength, or skill" (*Merriam-Webster Dictionary*, n.d.) and "a noteworthy or extraordinary act or achievement, usually displaying boldness, skill, etc." (Dictionary.com, n.d.). Yes, a feat is what is needed to make the vital changes in our world today. I believe that books like this can help. This *Handbook*, if used as I have intended, can be an important tool for scholars and practitioners to truly build, bridge, and blaze pathways for women and leadership. There are better days ahead.

THE BOOK

As a senior scholar who studies women and leadership, I used my best thinking to figure out what parts and chapters would be most useful in this *Handbook*. I based these decisions on current theory and research, and upon what we do and do not know. First, it was clear that it would be important to set the stage for the book by including a few chapters that outlined the current status of women leaders, provided insight into broad areas of work along with calls to action for enhancing women's leadership status worldwide, and explored overarching themes and metaphors that seem to guide current thinking (Chapters 1 through 3). Second, I knew it was also important to highlight some contemporary theoretical lenses that have or should frame our current scholarship. Theories centered specifically on women and leadership are so rare that it is important to understand how frameworks from various disciplines have shaped and can continue to guide our scholarship moving forward (Chapters 4 through 9). Third, there has not been another attempt to deeply interrogate the range of women's individual motivators to lead, so readers will learn a great deal as they consider the latest research on aspirations, ambition, identity, purpose and calling, power, neuroscience, and women's understandings of success and choice (Chapters 10 through 16). Fourth, although there is already a great deal of research on gender-based leadership challenges and barriers, chapters focusing on six key areas are important to the book as a whole (Chapters 17 through 22). And finally, it was important to conclude the book by focusing on the latest research on how to develop women leaders; authors of Chapters 23 through 27 fold in the existing literature discussed throughout the book and summarize current research on how to implement what we currently know about developing women so they can become leaders in companies, communities, and contexts around the world.

Part I: Setting the Stage

Part I sets the stage for the book as a whole. It includes three chapters, starting with Chapter 1, "The current status of women leaders worldwide," written by Elizabeth Goryunova, Robbyn T. Scribner, and myself, from Utah Valley University. This chapter summarizes the background and available data on the current status of women in regions and countries around the world as it relates to political leadership. The authors then provide current data on the state of women in business leadership, which includes sections on the general situation of women on corporate boards, women as chief executive officers (CEOs) (including entrepreneurs), and women in senior management roles in regions and countries. The chapter concludes with a brief discussion of gender parity and provides examples from various groups on when this parity is predicted to occur.

Chapter 2 is written by a wide variety of scholars and practitioners who are part of the Women and Leadership Affinity Group, which is hosted by the International Leadership Association (ILA). The names of these individuals were too numerous to list as authors, but they are included in the Appendix of the chapter. This chapter contains a document that was published independently in 2013 and updated again in 2015, and we are fortunate to have it included in this *Handbook* to help provide background and context. The *Asilomar Declaration and Call to Action on Women and Leadership* (Madsen and Rosser-Mims, 2015) is a guide for individual women, women's networks, and other stakeholders and organizations that actively campaign for enhancing women's leadership status worldwide. The document is designed to inspire both its authors and readers to take action in multiple ways to make leadership equality a reality. To this end, the Declaration contains strategic "calls for action" that readers may take to help change the leadership status of women worldwide. These calls for action are preceded by corresponding declarations of the existing realities to help each of us contemplate and integrate new practices into our lives.

Savita Kumra, from Middlesex University in Dubai, wrote Chapter 3 titled "Reflections on glass: second wave feminist theorizing in a third wave feminist age?" In this chapter, she sought to explore the purpose and use of metaphors in the women and leadership literature. This literature abounds with metaphors to describe, examine, and assess the various facilitators and barriers confronting women as they seek to forge their organizational careers, and "glass" has been particularly fruitful in this area. This chapter assesses the combined impact of "glass" metaphors (that is, ceiling, elevator, escalator, and walls) on women as they embark on their career journeys as well as their continued resonance with contemporary feminism. Kumra then discusses whether the "'glass'" metaphors have served their purpose and, as we progress from second wave liberal feminist ideologies to a third wave age, if it is now time to look beyond the "glass" and seek gender-based organizational analyses that aim to provide some measure of optimism and agency over one's destiny.

Part II: Advancing Women and Leadership Theory

As Kurt Lewin once articulated, "There is nothing so practical as a good theory" (as cited in Van de Ven, 1989), and Christensen and Raynor (2003) argued that sound theories can help us make predictions and interpret the present to understand what is happening and why. Yet, although there are many generalized leadership frameworks, Jogulu and Wood (2006) argued over a decade ago that the majority of models and theories were developed by men and are based on male-normed assumptions. Ely and Rhode (2010) agreed that, in terms of individual and organizational leadership theories that focus on women, there is clearly a gap in the scholarly literature. They stated: "although theory is rich on how leaders develop, we have little direct empirical evidence about how these processes may differ for women and men and less still about how they unfold in organizations" (p. 395). Ely et al. (2011) argued that "practitioners and educators lack a coherent, theoretically based, and actionable framework for designing and delivering leadership programs for women" (p. 475). And finally, Vetter (2010) supported this notion of a deficit with her extensive study of feminist theory scholarship that revealed an "alarming dearth of theoretical analysis of women as leaders" (p. 3).

The point of this background on the need for women and leadership theory is that it is a critical part to include in this book. I must admit that I came up with the idea of having chapters on different approaches or disciplinary perspectives from Nohria and Khurana's (2010) *Handbook of Leadership Theory and Practice*. They had chapters focusing on leadership theory through the following lenses: organizational behavior, psychology, clinical, sociological, economics, history, and power. I had not found a publication on women and leadership that discussed theory from various viewpoints, so I decided to organize this section similarly, and to include six chapters. I invited six prominent scholars and their colleagues to write through the following lenses: overarching, social psychology, sociology, sociolinguistics, organizational behavior, and human resource development. Of course this is not a comprehensive list of possible perspectives, but at least it is a sampling from which to consider.

The first chapter in this part – Chapter 4, "Creativity in theorizing for women and leadership: a multi-paradigm perspective" – introduces a way to understand the process of theorizing based on women's experiences and ways of knowing. Julia Storberg-Walker (George Washington University) and Kristina Natt och Dag (independent scholar) argue that this new process can serve to advance leadership theories for and by women. They conducted a theoretical analysis of the most highly cited women and leadership theories and offer it as a reflective tool for future theorizing efforts. The key contribution of this chapter is to expand theorizing from a male-dominated practice into a practice centered on women's experience and ways of knowing. To accomplish these goals, the chapter is organized into three main sections. The first section introduces the chapter and describes the importance of theorizing. The second section offers a primer on theorizing, and the third concludes by illuminating how theories from different paradigms have contributed to women and leadership theory.

Chapter 5, "Social psychological approaches to women and leadership theory," written by Crystal L. Hoyt (University of Richmond) and Stefanie Simon (Carleton College), takes a social psychological approach to understanding gender and leadership. In doing so, they explain how both the social context and people's perceptions influence leadership processes involving gender. They frame their chapter by considering the theoretical approaches taken by social psychologists that revolve around two questions: (1) Are there gender differences in leadership style and effectiveness?; and (2) What barriers do women face in the leadership domain? They argue that social psychological research helps to better our understanding of how stereotypes shape expectations people have of female leaders, as well as influence women's own thoughts and behaviors via "stereotype threat" processes. Social psychological approaches to understanding gender and leadership reveal that gender does matter in how people respond to leaders and how leaders approach their roles, regardless of whether it ought to matter.

Next, Christy Glass and Alicia Ingersoll, both from Utah State University, wrote Chapter 6 titled "Sociological approaches to women and leadership theory." They explain that few classical sociological traditions explore the experience of organizational leaders or leadership in a direct way or examine the ways in which gender relations shape access to leadership roles. As a result, there is no clear subfield related to the sociology of leadership. However, classical perspectives inform contemporary theoretical developments related to women and leadership in important ways, providing the tools with which contemporary scholars have sought to understand: (1) the factors that contribute to gender bias in leader selection and limit women's access to leadership positions; and (2) the ways in which women experience leadership and the factors that constrain women's ability to lead effectively. This chapter traces the links between classic sociological perspectives on power, status, and inequality to contemporary theories of women and leadership.

Chapter 7, "Sociolinguistic approaches to gender and leadership theory," reviews the range of theories that account for the crucial role of language in women's performance of leadership, as well as the ways women are represented as leaders in the public domain. The author, Judith Baxter (Aston University), states that first, dominance theory proposes that the social nature of language constructs men as more powerful in professional domains and women as less so. Second, difference theory argues that women and men have differently gendered linguistic styles, with men tending to prefer more "transactional" or "goal-orientated" styles of language and women preferring "transformational" or "change-orientated" styles of language. And third, discourse theory proposes that leaders construct their professional identities through the language they choose to use. However, Baxter explains that this is not a free choice, especially for women leaders: gendered discourses such as masculinization or image and sexuality can effectively restrict women's range of identities. This chapter assesses how women leaders are simultaneously enabled and constrained by the language and discourses of leadership.

Chantal Van Esch, Karlygash Assylkhan, and Diana Bilimoria, from Case Western Reserve University, have written a chapter on "Using organizational and management science theories to understand women and leadership" (Chapter 8). In this chapter the authors review several organizational and management science theories that inform women and leadership research. They offer a table of theories, relevant to women and leadership, organized by level of analysis: individual, interpersonal, and organizational. Next, they delve more deeply into select theoretical frameworks at each level to illustrate how women and leadership research may be advanced. At each level, the authors introduce the theoretical perspective, provide an overview of extant research findings specific to women and leadership, explore the implications for advancing knowledge about women and leadership, and offer guidance for future research.

Next, a prominent human resource development scholar, Laura L. Bierema from the University of Georgia, wrote Chapter 9, "No woman left behind: critical leadership development to build gender consciousness and transform organizations." This chapter interrogates prevailing understandings and practices of leadership development using a critical, feminist lens to chart a new path for developing women leaders. Bierema argues that critical feminism offers an unvarnished look at the realities of sexist, patriarchal organizations and analyzes how they perpetuate implicit bias that blocks women from full access to development experiences and advancement opportunities. This chapter embraces Mary Parker Follett's primacy of learning and the process of leadership development to draw on the fields of adult learning and human resource development to offer alternative conceptualizations and pedagogies for leadership development.

Part III: Individual Motivators to Lead

This part of the book is close to my heart, as my own research interests through the years have focused on some of these elements. In finding ways to better encourage women toward and to prepare them for leadership, one of the most important and foundational areas of emerging research focuses on understanding women's aspirations and motivations to lead (Madsen, 2008, 2009). In many cases, these driving forces appear to be different for women than for men. As I have done numerous studies through the years on understanding the lifetime development of leadership in high-profile women leaders, I have looked closely for glimpses of how they discovered and strengthened their motivations to lead throughout the years. I have also appreciated the work of my colleagues in honing new areas of discovery such as purpose and calling (Longman et al., 2011; Tunheim and Goldschmidt, 2013). As noted previously, this part of the *Handbook* delves deeply into the range of women's individual motivators to lead through considering the latest research in aspirations, ambition, identity, purpose and calling, power, neuroscience, and women's understandings of success and choice.

First, a team of authors – Lynne E. Devnew (University of Phoenix), Ann M. Berghout Austin (Utah State University), Marlene Janzen Le Ber (Brescia University College) and Mary Shapiro (Simmons College) – wrote Chapter 10, which is titled "Women's leadership aspirations." The authors recognize that how women and girls perceive leaders and leadership, how they perceive themselves, their self-efficacy in relationship to their perceptions of leadership behaviors, and what they perceive would be the rewards and punishments of being a leader, combine to shape their leadership aspirations. These perceptions are influenced by their work, relationships, and place and thus change throughout each woman's lifetime. The authors argue that raising women's and girls' aspirations is not a simple matter; changes must be made throughout the entire system to enable women and girls to see themselves as leaders, see what leaders do as having value, and see that it is possible to be a leader and still be a successful mother, daughter, partner, and friend.

Second, Chapter 11, "Women's leadership ambition in early careers," was written by two United Kingdom (UK) researchers, Ruth Sealy from the University of Exeter Business School and Charlotte Harman from Cubiks Ltd. They share a new study that looked at the recent deterioration in stated ambition levels of young female professionals, which came to their attention from UK and Irish practitioners in professional service firms who were perceiving a lack of success in the generation of women ahead of them. Sealy and Harman discuss the extant research that has tended to focus either on student perceptions of careers and aspirations or on the older age group struggling to stay in organizational life, and found a gap which they felt should be explored. Therefore, this chapter examines perceptions of women's ambition in early career stages in professional services by reviewing existing literature looking at career motivation and ambition in women, briefly outlining their empirical qualitative study with early career professional women, and then sharing the findings of the study within the context of the literature.

Next, Chapter 12, "Women's leadership identity: exploring person and context in theory," was written by three scholars: Wendy Fox-Kirk (Weber State University), Constance Campbell (Georgia Southern University), and Chrys Egan (Salisbury University). They argue that leader identity can positively or negatively impact both leader behavior and others' perceptions of leader behavior. They explain that when the dominant archetype of leader behavior is normatively and stereotypically masculine, women are faced with identity struggles and conflicts. In work contexts, dominant leader archetypes can constrain women's ability to build an effective and convincing leader identity. Despite the range of useful theories of identity construction that acknowledges person–context interactions, the focus of most theories and of most leadership development programs remains on the individual, while only minor attention is given to context. In this chapter, these authors present an overview of person–context issues in identity theory and provide a detailed examination of leader identity theories that are particularly useful to women.

Karen A. Longman (Azusa Pacific University) and Debbie Lamm Bray (Northwest University) wrote Chapter 13, "The role of purpose and calling in women's leadership experiences." They argue that over the past 30 years widespread expectations for increasing the number of women in senior-level leadership roles have been based on the highly touted "pipeline theory." Yet scholars have recently been challenging the theory as being male-normed in its assumptions of the values and rewards that motivate leadership aspirations and tenacity for those entering leadership roles. This chapter provides an overview of the literature related to purpose, calling, and leader identity development, making the case that additional, focused attention to these constructs may prove to be a more effective strategy for encouraging women to aspire to – and advance into – leadership roles.

Any discussion of gender and leadership is not complete without an examination of power. "Women, leadership, and power," by Katharina Pick from the Peter F. Drucker and Masatoshi Ito Graduate School of Management at Claremont Graduate University, is Chapter 14 in Part III of this *Handbook*. Pick argues that women's relationship to power has forever been complex and ambiguous and that there are many power-based explanations for women's leadership outcomes. Research suggests that men and women have differential access to power and differential results from trying to exercise power. She states that a question underlying various related discussions of gender and leadership is whether the relationship between power and leadership is changing, and whether women rising to leadership in increasing numbers may impact this. This chapter briefly reviews basic themes of research on gender and power in leadership in light of the most recent findings about access to power, use of power, and desire for power. Because power, gender, and leadership are not static concepts, Pick considers what conceptual changes are revealed in current research and the impact these may have.

Chapter 15, written by Suzanne J. Peterson and Amy L. Bartels from Arizona State University, focused on "Using neuroscience methods to explore gender differences in leadership." In this chapter the authors discuss current challenges associated with studying gender and leadership from a purely psychological perspective and suggest that neuromethods can complement traditional assessment methods. Peterson and Bartels review evidence derived from studies using brain imaging, endocrinology, and behavioral genetics to advance the discussion of whether gender differences are a biological reality or simply a byproduct of social or perceptual processes. They also emphasize differences related to confidence, risk taking, and leadership style in hopes of contributing to a better understanding of why women continue to face leadership barriers in today's organizations.

Finally, Sarah Leberman and Jane Hurst, from Massey University in New Zealand, wrote Chapter 16, which focuses on "The connection between success, choice, and leadership during women's careers." This chapter reviews the literature associated with women's career conceptualizations of success, notions of choice, and implications for leadership.

The authors suggest that success is valued differently by women compared with most organizations, leading to a misalignment in expectations. The discourse of choice is identified as a contested space, which has implications on the decisions women make in terms of taking on positional leadership. Leberman and Hurst present a conceptual framework linking success, choice, and leadership and conclude with a series of recommended organizational and individual strategies aimed at supporting and enhancing the careers of women as they move through the twenty-first century.

Part IV: Gender-Based Leadership Challenges and Barriers

The fourth part of the book focuses on women's challenges and barriers to leading and leadership. Although some elements of gender-based barriers are mentioned in every chapter of this book, having a specific part that summarizes the latest research and findings is critical for a few reasons. First, it is important for future studies to be crafted around questions and hypotheses that are not yet fully understood. In reviewing the literature, we continue to find studies that have explored phenomena already well comprehended. As it is vital that future research focuses on unexplored questions, this part will help set the stage for what is already known. Second, to understand how to develop women leaders, it is important to understand challenges – what is blocking women from moving forward – both internal and external. To be honest, I am sometimes shocked at how many people claim to be women's leadership experts because they can piece together content for a program, a series of lectures, or other initiatives. Some so-called leadership trainers also take the exact material they give in mixed-gender programs and just add "women" at the beginning of the title to offer a women's leadership program. The research is clear that effective women's leadership developers must have deep expertise in all of these areas, including a thorough understanding of the barriers that women face. Interventions then must be based upon this knowledge and carefully crafted into the design of any developmental initiative. The following chapters can provide this information on barriers and challenges to scholars and practitioners alike.

Chapter 17, titled "An overview of gender-based leadership barriers," was authored by Amy B. Diehl (Shippensburg University of Pennsylvania) and Leanne Dzubinski (Biola University). They argue that, despite an abundance of educated, qualified women in the workforce, they continue to be under-represented at the top of institutional leadership hierarchies. Theories of gendered organizations explain that work processes reproduce gendered structures of society in the workplace, and these processes advantage men while forming barriers to women's success. The authors' cross-sector analysis of women leaders in religion and higher education revealed 27 gender-based leadership barriers that operate at the macro, meso, and micro levels of society. They present this framework and then recommend broad strategies that will address barriers across all three levels in order to make them visible, eliminate them, and fully incorporate the potential leadership capacity of both men and women. As you will see, this chapter provides a strong, overarching framework for each of the following chapters.

Michelle Bligh and Ai Ito, while at NEOMA Business School in France, wrote Chapter 18, "Organizational processes and systems that affect women in leadership." They argue that despite the efforts to establish gender equality in organizations, intricate processes and systems hinder women's advancement into top leadership positions. In this chapter, they explore many of the organizational level barriers that impact women leaders, including hiring and selection, networking, mentoring, promotion, and negotiation. They have found that understanding each of these processes will help organizations to establish gender-inclusive strategies and gender-neutral policies that will allow women and minorities to navigate through the labyrinth more effectively.

"Individual stresses and strains in the ascent to leadership: gender, work, and family" is the title of Chapter 19, written by Amy E. Smith (University of Massachusetts Boston) and Deneen M. Hatmaker (University of Connecticut). They argue that one explanation for the limited number of women in leadership positions revolves around the tensions between family and career. Even with years of research, attention in the popular press, and the implementation of family-friendly workplace policies, professional women still struggle to navigate the path to having both a meaningful career and a fulfilling family life. In this chapter, the authors discuss the current frames for understanding gendered expectations around work and caregiving. They integrate literature on professional identity and parenthood to advance understanding of the depth and complexity of negotiating work and family. While Hatmaker and Smith focus on the stresses and strains experienced by working women in their aspirations to climb the professional ladder, they also consider the tensions faced by men.

Deborah L. Rhode from Stanford Law School and the Center on the Legal Profession at Stanford University wrote Chapter 20: "Gender stereotypes and unconscious bias." She explained that, although the last quarter-century has witnessed enormous progress for women in leadership positions, the playing field is far from even, and part of the problem is often unconscious gender bias and stereotyping. A major obstacle is the incongruity between qualities associated with women and qualities associated with leaders. Rhode argues that women are subject to a double standard and double bind. She states that what is assertive in a man seems abrasive in a woman, and female employees risk seeming too feminine or not feminine enough. In-group favoritism persists, and women, particularly women of color, are often viewed as less competent and less likely to show leadership potential. Rhode states that addressing these patterns will require both individual and institutional responses. She concludes that organizations need a strong commitment to gender equity, reflected in organizational policies, priorities, and reward structures.

Chapter 21 titled "Theorizing women leaders' negative relations with other women" was written by Sharon Mavin (University of Roehampton), Gina Grandy (University of Regina), and Jannine Williams (University of Bradford). In this chapter, the authors theorize women leaders' negative intra-gender relations with other women and call for a shift in focus from blaming individual women to fuller explanations as to why these social relations emerge. Their theory of women leaders' negative relations with other women explains how these relations take place within gendered contexts where women face gender stereotypes, can do gender well and differently simultaneously, and where homophily, homosociality, women's intra-gender competition, and female misogyny operate as complex, dialectic, dynamic interlocking gendered practices and processes. Their theory illustrates how threats to women's identity constrain and facilitate negative intra-gender behavior between women. It also illustrates how women work to negotiate, resist, and comply with these experiences and how gendered contexts exacerbate differences between women.

The last chapter in this part of the book discusses "The effect of media on women and leadership" (Chapter 22) written by Carole Elliot (University of Roehampton) and Valerie Stead (Lancaster University). This chapter examines the effect of media on women and leadership by exploring the representation of women's leadership through stereotypes and metaphors. The authors discuss the significance of the media's relationship with women and leadership and provide an overview of literature that draws attention to different ways that women's leadership is represented. They conclude that implications arising from the resilience of stereotypes and metaphors associated with women's leadership are multilayered. They discuss metaphors to draw attention to the challenges women face in achieving leadership positions. Finally, they direct our attention to an uncomfortable environment for women leaders, where gender stereotyping leads to persistent metaphors that pervade the media and popular culture.

Part V: Developing Women Leaders

All of the chapters thus far have set the stage so that we (for example, scholars, practitioners, colleagues, coaches) can more effectively be engaged in preparing women for leadership and in supporting and strengthening those who are currently leading. By clearly understanding the latest scholarship related to the current status and situation of women (Part I), the current theoretical frameworks through various lenses (Part II), the individual motivators to lead (Part III), and the gender-based leadership challenges and barriers (Part IV), I believe that we can be more prepared to develop girls and women to become leaders (Part V). The final five chapters are focused on this goal: to develop women leaders.

To begin this final part of the book, Chapter 23, titled "Advancing women through developmental relationships," was written by Wendy M. Murphy and Kerry Roberts Gibson from Babson College, and Kathy E. Kram from Boston University. They explain that over the past 30 years, research has shown that developmental relationships facilitate career success, particularly for leaders. In addition, multiple developers (for example, mentors, sponsors, or peers), rather than just one, enhance individuals' growth and advancement. The authors state that these developmental networks are essential to sustained learning and leadership growth. They draw on the literatures on leadership, identity, and positive relationships at work to provide a foundation for understanding how to advance women through developmental relationships. They argue that five specific types of developmental relationships are critical for growing women leaders (that is, mentors, sponsors, peers, executive coaches, and learning partners), and that these developers provide a range of supportive functions that both challenge and enable women to learn and thrive as they advance. The authors conclude by discussing strategies for individual women crafting these developmental relationships, and how organizations can create and sustain a climate that fosters these connections.

Chapter 24, "Gender differences in developmental experiences," was written by Cathleen Clerkin (Center for Creative Leadership) and Meena S. Wilson (Ashoka University). These authors argue that advancement to top positions in any organization requires learning from a variety of experiences. Since both leadership development and career advancement are contingent on accessing the right experiences, in the right context, at the right career juncture, an analysis of the most salient similarities and differences between women's and men's experiences is an important entry-point for expanding our understanding of gender and leadership. Clerkin and Wilson found gendered variation in access to and use of the typical developmental experiences needed to become effective top-level leaders. They explored these gender differences in regard to quantity, quality, and specific type of experiences provided to women and men. They put forward two propositions: (1) women miss out on several critical job experiences that would prepare them for senior management roles; and (2) the life experiences and capabilities that prepare women to be outstanding senior leaders do not carry gravitas in the circles in which organizational selection and promotion decisions are made. They conclude by mapping the way forward and outlining implications for future research and practice.

Of course a section on developing women leaders would not be complete without a discussion of "Women-only leadership programs: a deeper look," which is the title of Chapter 25 of this *Handbook*. Mary Ellen Kassotakis (Oracle Women's Leadership Initiative) discusses a literature review she conducted for a 15-year time period (2001 to early 2016) to explore the leadership skills needed by women, particularly in senior leadership positions in the Western world, to fill the pipeline of senior positions. In addition to development experiences in mixed gender groups, she also found that there is a distinct place for women-only programs. The results of the literature review indicate that a focus on women-only leadership development programs – whether offered by universities, corporations, or large, global consulting firms – can be a key lever in growing core talent in the quest to maximize the talent potential and profitability of organizational success.

Ronald J. Burke (York University) wrote Chapter 26, which is titled "Supporting women's career development." The purpose of this chapter was to present a variety of issues surrounding the support of women in the workplace through career development. Burke discusses women's career models and types, values of managerial women at work, initiatives supporting women's career development, and finally, implications and conclusions. Within these chapter sections, a variety of career aspects are discussed. For example, the author argues that men's and women's careers are different, with women's having more complex patterns and histories. He believes that it is also important to determine what women value at work, in order to discuss career development initiatives that organizations should consider implementing. Implications for practice are also provided with some thoughts on moving forward.

The book then concludes with a chapter that looks at "Future strategies for developing women as leaders" (Chapter 27). Faith Wambura Ngunjiri (Concordia College) and Rita A. Gardiner (University of Western Ontario) argue that as women continue to be under-represented in leadership positions, it is imperative to think and act creatively to enhance the pipeline of women available and able to take on increasing responsibilities in their organizations. In this chapter, the authors begin by engaging with what the previous four chapters in this part of the *Handbook* discussed regarding developing women leaders, then provide a succinct critical review of recent literature on women's leadership development strategies, before proposing the need for using an intersectional framework in leadership development programming for women. The authors recognize the need to engage critically with the positionality of women at the nexus of their various identities and roles, the place of identity in leadership development for women, and how women's leadership development efforts can potentially help women to overcome the barriers to their ascent to positions of authority.

CONCLUSION

I hope readers will take the time to read this book in full. Each part has valuable chapters that can provide the latest in scholarship – both theory and practice. I would encourage you to read with a reflective lens, so that you can discover findings that relate to your own as well as others' lives. I believe that many of us who do this work feel "called" to do so either by a higher power or just by feeling that we were "made" to do it: it feels right and this is where our interests and hearts lie. Frederick Buechner (1973) once asserted that true vocation joins self and service in "the place where your deep gladness meets the world's deep need" (p. 119). This is how I feel in my own work. I have found this place of gladness, and I have appreciated working alongside a wonderful set of authors who have contributed to this book – and many of you as well.

For me, this journey of strengthening each other – in so many different ways – has been transformational in my own life. As Parker Palmer (2000) once said:

> Our deepest calling is to grow into our own authentic selfhood, whether or not it conforms to some image of who we ought to be. As we do so, we will not only find the joy that every human being seeks – we will also find our path of authentic service in the world. (p. 16)

Although there are so many needs in the world related to women, I believe that we can and are truly doing our part as women and men engaged in this work. If you are new to the field of women's leadership, I encourage you to join this movement – as theorists, researchers, scholars, practitioners, and leaders – to advocate for changes that need to be made. It is our turn to stand up, step forward, and make a difference in the world. It is our turn to build, bridge, and blaze new pathways for women and leadership.

REFERENCES

Adler, N. (2015). Women leaders: Shaping history in the 21st century. In F.W. Ngunjiri and S.R. Madsen (Eds), *Women as Global Leaders* (pp. 21–50). Charlotte, NC: Information Age Publishing.

Buechner, F. (1973). *Wishful Thinking: A Seeker's ABC*. New York, NY: Harper & Row.

Christensen, C.M., and Raynor, M.E. (2003). Why hard-nosed executives should care about management theory. *Harvard Business Review*, *81*(9), 66–75.

Dictionary.com. (n.d.). Feat. Retrieved from http://www.dictionary.com/browse/feat.

Ely, R.J., Ibarra, H., and Kolb, D.M. (2011). Taking gender into account: Theory and design for women's leadership development programs. *Academy of Management Learning and Education*, *10*(3), 474–493.

Ely, R.J., and Rhode, D.L. (2010). Women and leadership: Defining the challenges. In N. Nohria and R. Khurana (Eds), *Handbook of Leadership Theory and Practice* (pp. 377–410). Cambridge, MA: Harvard Business Press.

International Leadership Association (ILO) (2013). The International Leadership Association Women and Leadership Affinity Group inaugural conference program. Retrieved from http://www.ila-net.org/WLC/WLC13/wl2013program.pdf.

Jogulu, U.D., and Wood, G.J. (2006). The role of leadership theory in raising the profile of women in management. *Equal Opportunities International*, *25*(4), 236–250.

Joshi, A., Neely, B., Emrich, C., Griffiths, D., and George, G. (2015). Gender research in AMJ: An overview of five decades of empirical research and calls to action. *Academy of Management Journal*, *58*(5), 1459–1475.

Longman, K., Dahlvig, J., Wikkerink, R., Cunningham, D., and O'Connor, C.M. (2011). Conceptualization of calling: A grounded theory exploration of CCCU women leaders. *Christian Higher Education*, *10*(3–4), 254–275. doi 10.1080/15363759.2011.576213.

Longman, K.A., and Madsen, S.R. (Eds). (2014). *Women and Leadership in Higher Education*. Charlotte, NC: Information Age Publishing.

Madsen, S.R. (2008). *On Becoming a Women Leader: Learning from the Experiences of University Presidents*. San Francisco, CA: Jossey-Bass.

Madsen, S.R. (2009). *Developing Leadership: Learning from the Experiences of Women Governors*. Lanham, MD: University Press of America.

Madsen, S.R., Ngunjiri, F.W., Longman, K.A., and Cherrey, C. (Eds). (2015). *Women and Leadership around the World*. Charlotte, NC: Information Age Publishing.

Madsen, S.R., and Rosser-Mims, D. (Compilers). (2015). *Asilomar Declaration and Call to Action on Women and Leadership*. Women and Leadership Affinity Group, International Leadership Association. Retrieved from http://www.ila-net.org/Communities/AG/Asilomar_Declaration2015.pdf.

McKinsey Global Institute. (2015). The power of parity: How advancing women's equality can add $12 trillion to global growth. September. Retrieved from http://www.mckinsey.com/global-themes/employment-and-growth/how-advancing-womens-equality-can-add-12-trillion-to-global-growth.

Merriam-Webster Dictionary. (n.d.). Feat. Retrieved from http://www.merriam-webster.com/dictionary/feat.

Ngunjiri, F.W., and Madsen, S.R. (Eds). (2015). *Women as Global Leaders*. Charlotte, NC: Information Age Publishing.

Nohria, N., and Khurana, R. (2010). *Handbook of Leadership Theory and Practice*. Cambridge, MA: Harvard Business Press.

Palmer, P.J. (2000). *Let Your Life Speak: Listening for the Voice of Vocation*. San Francisco, CA: Jossey-Bass.

Tunheim, K.A., and Goldschmidt, A.N. (2013). Exploring the role of calling in the professional journeys of college presidents. *Journal of Leadership, Accountability and Ethics*, *10*(4), 30–40.

Van de Ven, A.H. (1989). Nothing is quite so practical as a good theory. *Academy of Management Review*, *14*(4), 486–489.

Vetter, L.P. (2010). Overview: Feminist theories of leadership. In K. O'Connor (Ed.), *Gender and Women's Leadership: A Reference Handbook* (pp. 3–10). Thousand Oaks, CA: Sage.

Yeganeh, H., and May, D. (2011). Cultural values and gender gap: A cross-national analysis. *Gender in Management: An International Journal*, *26*(2), 106–121.

PART I

SETTING THE STAGE

1. The current status of women leaders worldwide

Elizabeth Goryunova, Robbyn T. Scribner, and Susan R. Madsen

The challenges and opportunities for women in countries and regions around the world continue to be topics of great interest. In fact, Joshi et al. (2015) recently reported that "gender equality appears to be at the forefront of the global humanitarian agenda" (p. 1459). Although women are now entering the workforce in higher numbers globally and gender diversity in the workforce is increasing (Ali et al., 2011; McKinsey Global Institute, 2015), this progress is "both promising and problematic" (Joshi et al., 2015, p. 1459) because the higher numbers are slow to translate into substantial changes with regard to women in the most significant positions of influence, particularly in politics and business. Yet, progress needs to be tracked and discussed so that targeted and strategic initiatives can be designed and implemented in organizations, industries, sectors, communities, countries, and regions around the world. In addition to mapping global patterns, there must also be an examination of the similarities and differences across cultures, as "traditional gender functions and distinct gender roles can also vary substantially from one society to another" (Madsen and Scribner, 2017).

It is important to understand the current status of women leaders before exploring more deeply how to advance women and leadership theory, to understand girls' and women's individual motivators to lead, to overcome gender-based leadership challenges and barriers, and to develop more women leaders. Hence, the purpose of this chapter is to set the stage for this *Handbook* by presenting background information and data on the general status of women in leadership roles, particularly in politics and business, at the country, region, and global levels. We strategically decided to go deeper into politics and business instead of providing more surface data and adding other sectors (for example, non-profit, education). In terms of politics and business, we have discovered that data are challenging to collect, particularly through peer-reviewed scholarly sources. At the same time we were able to access data from industry, government, and global organizations – such as the United Nations, the World Bank, and the World Economic Forum – that collect key demographic and economic indicators on a worldwide scale to inform global policy and economic development initiatives. In this chapter, we highlight the most critical findings, a result of our concerted effort to interpret meaningful information obtained from the available resources.

This chapter begins with some background and data on the current status of women in politics in regions and countries around the world. The second section provides recent figures on the state of women on corporate boards, followed by an overview of women as chief executive officers (CEOs) (including entrepreneurs). We then explore the current situation of women in senior management roles in regions and countries. Finally, we bring together literature discussing gender parity and predictions of when that parity may be reached, and we share some concluding thoughts.

WOMEN IN POLITICAL LEADERSHIP

Numerous studies (e.g., Catalyst, 2004; Dawson et al., 2014; Galbreath, 2011) have found a positive connection between the active participation of women in government and politics and increases in a number of democratic outcomes that address social and economic inequality. Because women tend to prioritize, engage with, and advocate issues that have positive societal implications (such as family, health, and education), their influence over public policy and budget allocation improves the quality of life for their entire constituencies, and it also strengthens parliamentary institutions.

Since 1995, when the United Nations (UN) World Conference on Women introduced the Beijing Platform for Action (United Nations, 1995), the argument for the importance of women's participation in politics has evolved. Initial notions of women's empowerment as a justice served to half the population of the world ("it is good for women") have been gradually augmented to emphasize the actual benefits of gender diversity at the political leadership level: as a resource of valuable expertise contributing to progress, innovation, and balanced decision making ("it is good for everyone"). To that end, in March 2015, UN Women declared that it had "set [its] sights on 2030 as the expiration date for gender inequality" (UN Women, 2015, p. 1), with a new global initiative: Planet 50–50 by 2030, Step It Up for Gender Equality (UN Women, 2015). Additionally, on September 25, 2015, in succession to the Millennium Development Goals, the United Nations adopted the new 2030 Agenda for Sustainable Development, which includes the gender equality goal to "ensure women's full and effective participation and equal opportunities for leadership at all levels of decision-making in political, economic and public life" (United Nations, 2015, p. 18).

In addition to strengthening parliamentary institutions with their economic and political acumen, women political leaders serve as role models for younger generations of females by influencing, increasing, and broadening their overall labor force participation. The political empowerment of women has drawn increasing attention and support worldwide, resulting in many celebrated pioneering outcomes. In the past ten years there has been a 12 percent decrease in the number of countries that had never had women appointed as a head of state, while 13 countries (including the Slovak Republic, Thailand, Denmark, and Brazil) elected their first female head of state since 2006 (World Economic Forum, 2016a). The year 2016 was commemorated, among all, with the first major-party female contender in United States (US) presidential election history, Hillary Clinton, and the second-ever female British Prime Minister, Theresa May, who took office in the aftermath of the United Kingdom (UK) decision to exit the European Union (both final prime ministerial candidates were female) (Wilkinson et al., 2016).

However, apart from a few cases of triumphant women politicians, gender parity of political leadership (50:50 gender representation) remains a distant target (Adler, 2015). While the United Nations continues to rally countries of the world in efforts to achieve gender parity, other organizations have helped to capture information about the current status of female empowerment and its global trends. For example, the World Economic Forum (WEF) monitors the worldwide gender gap in politics (that is, compares the ratios of women to men at the highest level of political leadership). In 2015, the global gap was closed by only 23 percent (9 percent improvement over 2006) (World Economic Forum, 2015). Among 145 countries surveyed for one report, the country with the

Table 1.2 (continued)

Countries	% of women in parliament (IPU, 2015b)	Country ranking of % women in parliament* (IPU, 2015b)	Legislators, senior officials, and managers rank** (WEF, 2015)	Political empowerment rank** (WEF, 2015)
Italy	31.0	36	79	24
Jamaica	12.7	125		75
Japan	9.5	142	116	104
Jordan	12.0	130	120	123
Kazakhstan	26.2	49	26	78
Kenya	19.7	86		62
Kiribati	8.7	149		
Kuwait	1.5	169	107	141
Kyrgyzstan	23.3	64	77	76
Lao People's Democratic Republic	25.0	57		84
Latvia	18.0	92	9	40
Lebanon	3.1	162	119	143
Lesotho	26.7	46	37	68
Liberia	11.0	137	96	47
Liechtenstein	20.0	82		
Lithuania	23.4	63	24	45
Luxembourg	28.3	41	94	53
Macedonia, F.Y.R. of	33.3	26	74	65
Madagascar	20.5	79	86	80
Malawi	16.7	99		95
Malaysia	10.4	140	95	134
Maldives	5.9	158	108	133
Mali	9.5	142		116
Malta	13.0	123	83	86
Marshall Islands	3.0	165		
Mauritania	25.2	55		57
Mauritius	11.6	134	90	120
Mexico	38.0	18	41	34
Micronesia (Federated States of)	0	171		
Monaco	20.8	73		
Mongolia	14.9	110	15	117
Montenegro			78	94
Morocco	17.0	96	110	97
Mozambique	39.6	14		21
Namibia	41.3	11	14	33
Nauru	5.3	160		
Nepal			99	70
Netherlands	37.3	20	84	13
New Zealand	31.4	31	19	15
Nicaragua	39.1	17	17	4

Table 1.2   (continued)

Countries	% of women in parliament (IPU, 2015b)	Country ranking of % women in parliament* (IPU, 2015b)	Legislators, senior officials, and managers rank** (WEF, 2015)	Political empowerment rank** (WEF, 2015)
Niger	13.3	118		
Nigeria				111
Norway	39.6	14	43	3
Oman			118	142
Pakistan	20.7	77	124	87
Palau	0	171		
Panama	19.3	87	6	51
Papua New Guinea	2.7	167		
Paraguay	15.0	109	52	122
Peru	22.3	67	71	67
Philippines	27.2	45	1	17
Poland	24.1	60	21	52
Portugal	31.3	32	45	41
Qatar			112	144
Republic of Korea	16.3	103	113	101
Republic of Moldova	20.8	73	13	58
Romania	13.7	115	62	113
Russian Federation	13.6	117	25	128
Rwanda	63.8	1	53	7
Saint Kitts and Nevis	6.7	153		
Saint Lucia	16.7	99		
Saint Vincent and the Grenadines	13.0	123		
Samoa	6.1	156		
San Marino	16.7	99		
Sao Tome and Principe	18.2	91		
Saudi Arabia			122	121
Senegal	42.7	7		27
Serbia			63	43
Seychelles	43.8	5		
Singapore	25.3	54	54	92
Slovakia	18.7	90	70	115
Slovenia	36.7	22	29	16
Solomon Islands	2.0	168		
South Africa	41.5	10	69	14
Spain	41.1	13	66	26
Sri Lanka	5.8	159	88	59
Sudan	24.3	58		
Suriname	11.8	132	42	90
Swaziland	6.2	155		100
Sweden	43.6	6	31	5
Switzerland	30.5	38	50	18

Table 1.2   (continued)

Countries	% of women in parliament (IPU, 2015b)	Country ranking of % women in parliament* (IPU, 2015b)	Legislators, senior officials, and managers rank** (WEF, 2015)	Political empowerment rank** (WEF, 2015)
Syrian Arab Republic	12.4	129	117	130
Tajikistan	16.9	98		103
Thailand	6.1	156	23	131
Togo	17.6	93		
Tonga	0	171		
Trinidad and Tobago	28.5	40	10	56
Tunisia	31.3	32	105	69
Turkey	14.4	112	109	105
Turkmenistan	25.8	51		
Tuvalu	6.7	153		
Uganda			85	36
Ukraine	11.8	132	27	107
United Arab Emirates	17.5	94	115	93
United Kingdom	22.8	65	44	23
United Republic of Tanzania	36.0	25	104	32
United States of America	19.3	87	12	72
Uruguay	13.1	122	65	106
Uzbekistan	16.0	106		
Vanuatu	0	171		
Venezuela	17.0	96	67	82
Viet Nam	24.3	58	87	88
Yemen	0.3	170	125	140
Zambia	12.7	125	98	102
Zimbabwe	31.5	30	97	66

Note: * Ranking of 174 countries; ** Ranking of 145 countries.

on electoral lists. Overall, according to UN Women and IPU (2015) as of January 2015, legislative candidate quotas have been implemented in 17 countries, seats are reserved for female members in parliament in six countries, and voluntary quotas have been adopted by 11 parties across the globe. The positive global trend, as observed by Adler (2015), is that the number of women leading their countries and/or governments is growing: 92 women took the office in the 2010s, exceeding the combined number of all women elected to lead their countries in the entire twentieth century.

While a number of countries over the past ten years have successfully utilized quotas as an effective stimulant of positive change, recent political dynamics have demonstrated that having quotas does not necessarily guarantee an increased number of women in parliament or ensure their strong voice as parliamentarians (Inter-Parliamentary Union, 2015a). The former Speaker of the Swedish Parliament, Birgitta Dahl, noted that a quota system alone does not solve the problem of female representation in politics because women need to be prepared and competent to enter the field, and the system needs to be prepared to embrace women politicians; in other words, countries should lay "the groundwork to facilitate women's entry into politics" (Dahlerup, 2005, p. 143).

In addition to cases of covert resistance to implementing quotas (for instance, "Juanitas" – fake female candidates in Mexico), women frequently have to deal with sexual objectification, aggression, harassment, and even violence, both during and postelection. For instance, in June 2016, Jo Cox, British Labour Party Member of Parliament, was fatally shot and stabbed after a meeting in her constituency (BBC, 2016). To mediate such issues, many countries rely on "carrots and sticks" (that is, legislative statutes, oversight, transparency, gender diversity awareness, and financial incentives). For example, in Bolivia more than 4000 incidents against women in local government – registered over a ten-year period – resulted in a 2012 law that criminalized such acts of aggression. In addition, Bolivian parties that elect more women are granted access to additional public funds (Inter-Parliamentary Union, 2015b).

Another successful measure utilized worldwide to increase the capacity and legislative influence of women in parliament is bringing them together in women caucuses and forums, thus allowing women to rally around common objectives, rise above political agendas, and collaborate across party lines, making their voices heard. According to the Database on Women's Caucuses maintained by the IPU, in 2016, 88 countries reported active women caucuses and forums (for example, Forum of Rwandan Women Parliamentarians). Historically, the first women caucuses were introduced prior to 1995 in just six countries (starting with the United States of America in 1977). Six more were added between 1995 and 2000, followed by 11 between 2000 and 2005, while the majority of caucuses and forums became active between 2005 and 2015 (Inter-Parliamentary Union, 2016).

An additional indicator of women's empowerment worldwide is the participation in leadership within national judicial systems. The World Bank and United Nations monitor the representation of women justices in constitutional courts because it can ultimately affect access to justice for the female population, especially in gender-related cases. The World Bank reports that in 2015, of 153 economies with constitutional courts, 26 economies had female chief justices, and 122 had at least one female justice. The best-performing country on this indicator was Sierra Leone, with women representing 60 percent of justices in its constitutional courts, while India closes the list at 4 percent. At the same time, the Middle East & North Africa and South Asia regions reported no women justices (World Bank Group, 2015). Central and Eastern Europe and Central Asia reported the highest regional representation of women in the justice system (approximately 44 percent), followed by Latin America (at 36 percent), while South Asia reported the lowest female representation (less than 10 percent). The United Nations estimated that women represent 27 percent of all judges worldwide (UN Women, 2011). Among international courts, as of 2011, the International Criminal Court was the only one to have achieved gender parity (approximately 58 percent of its judges are female).

Political empowerment of women is an integral component of the gender equality goal, which includes having women in top posts and leadership teams. Robert Zoellick, former President of the World Bank, declared that gender equality is not only smart economics, but it is also a resource and a right. Consequently, unless the issue of gender equality is addressed globally, the world will not be able to release the full potential of half of its population, which hampers global growth (World Bank Group, 2011). Since 1995, when the Beijing platform outlined a path toward gender equality, the efforts and strides (for example, Agenda 2030: The Sustainable Development Goals, UN Women HeforShe initiative), although uneven across the specific targets, regions, or economies, have been encouraging. However, current global socio-economic and political environments give many reasons for concern.

WOMEN IN BUSINESS LEADERSHIP

The following section provides the latest research on women on corporate boards and women as CEOs, including a paragraph on women as entrepreneurs, followed by women in senior management positions.

Women on Corporate Boards

In addition to the status of women in politics, looking at the representation of women in business settings (that is, women on corporate boards, as CEOs, and in senior management) is also important in understanding and tracking progress for women. The benefits of a gender-diverse board go beyond fair representation of the gender composition of company employees. Research continues to demonstrate positive correlations between gender diversity of the board and corporate performance (Catalyst, 2013; Dawson et al., 2014; World Bank Group, 2015). For example, the *Financial Times* reports that having at least one woman on the board of directors increases the quality of its governance and reduces the likelihood of the corporation engaging in fraudulent activities (Grene and Newlands, 2015). The more comprehensive "business case" for women on boards and in top leadership positions is summarized in a number of reports and briefs, including Catalyst (2013) and Madsen (2015). For example, Madsen summarizes a host of studies in her brief that have found the following benefits to organizations when women are on boards and in top leadership positions: (1) improving financial performance; (2) strengthening organizational climate; (3) increasing corporate social responsibility and reputation; (4) leveraging talent; and (5) enhancing innovation and collective intelligence.

These and other benefits have been utilized by global policy makers (for example, the UN, World Economic Forum, World Bank) as an argument for increased female directorship and membership on corporate and government boards worldwide. While the gender diversity of boards is beneficial to corporate performance, in 2015 the Morgan Stanley Capital International (MSCI) (Lee et al., 2015) world index showed that women held only 18.1 percent of seats on boards across private and public sector organizations. Stock index companies reported the highest number of female board members in the UK (22.8 percent), Canada (20.8 percent), the US and Australia (19.2 percent), and Germany (18.5 percent). The lowest average percentages were registered in Latin America (5.6 percent) and in the Middle East (1 percent).

Across industry sectors, participation of women in technology is the lowest: 6.8 percent for private tech and 10.2 percent for unicorn (over $1 billion value) companies (Boardlist, 2016). While current gender diversity of boards is low and improvement is slow (a 3.1 percent increase between 2009 and 2015), according to Lee et al. (2015), the numbers of women on boards and women in decision-making positions continues to climb. Additionally, the analysis of MSCI World Index companies suggests that the likelihood of female representation on boards increases in companies led by a strong female leader; as of August 2015, 57.9 percent of surveyed companies with female CEOs reported three or more female board members, as compared to 30.3 percent of surveyed companies led by male CEOs (Lee et al., 2015). Kramer et al. (2006) found that increasing the number of women in a boardroom to three or more – a "critical mass" – changes boardroom dynamics substantially and enhances the likelihood that women's voices and ideas are heard.

Other measures currently utilized worldwide to increase female representation on boards include quotas introduced by different countries for their publicly listed companies. According to the World Bank Group (2015) report, *Women, Business and the Law 2016*, such country quotas range from having at least one woman on the board (for example, Israel, India) to at least 40 percent of seats held by women (for example, Iceland, Norway, and Spain). A 2012 law adopted by the European Commission requires that by 2020 large publicly listed companies in Europe will attain a minimum of 40 percent of women in non-executive board member positions (World Bank Group, 2015). Based on its analysis of gender diversity on the corporate boards of World Index companies, Lee et al. (2015) suggests that it is quite feasible to achieve 30 percent women on boards by 2027 or earlier, if corporations were to "double the proportion of new board seats taken by women" or, alternatively, through "turnover of existing board seats" (p. 20).

Women CEOs

Despite major advancements for female leaders in several areas, women who hold the most senior positions in corporations worldwide are still in the vast minority. Recent studies have shown that women hold fewer than 5 percent of CEO positions in major corporations across the globe. An examination of some of the largest companies in the US (in Fortune 500 and 1000 companies), the UK (FTSE 100), and Canada (Financial Post 500) demonstrates this pattern at less than 5 percent (Adler, 2015). A broader study that represented almost 22 000 publicly traded corporations in 91 countries also found fewer than 5 percent of firms had women CEOs (Noland et al., 2016). Another research group has published numbers indicating a range of 9–12 percent of worldwide companies which have a woman CEO (or equivalent top position title) (Grant Thornton, 2014, 2015). These higher numbers likely stem from the inclusion of private and smaller companies. Though cited percentages vary somewhat among different studies, the overall message remains: although women are gaining significant ground in the labor market generally – and to some extent in the levels of middle and even upper management – only a small number of women are reaching the very top position in their organizations.

In their recent study of nearly 22 000 firms, Noland et al. (2016) ranked geographical regions in terms of percentage of companies with a female CEO. The highest percentages of top women leaders were found in Eastern Europe and Central Asia (8 percent), Southeast Asia (8 percent), and the Middle East and North Africa (7 percent). Southern Asia and sub-Saharan Africa were next on the list, each with 5 percent. North America, Europe, and Oceania each had 4 percent; and the two regions with the lowest percentage of female CEOs were East Asia and Latin America, each with 3 percent. Perhaps surprisingly, the top regions cited here are not typically expected to be leaders in women's rights or even general human rights, which affirms Adler's (2015) assertion that women CEOs are not located exclusively in "female friendly" countries (p. 39); they are found in every region in the world. In their exploration of why there are higher percentages of women senior leaders in Russia and Eastern Europe, for example, some point to past communist rule through the former Soviet Union, under which "leaders promised 'equal opportunity for all', best demonstrated through the promotion of women in the rapidly expanding service sectors" (Grant Thornton, 2014, p. 10). The same group attributes the relatively high percentage of female leaders in Southeast Asia and other emerging economies to the fact that many families still live in multigenerational homes or near family members who are able to provide child care, allowing women more opportunities to seek high-level leadership roles (Grant Thornton, 2014).

Although other research groups cited somewhat different numbers for how female CEO percentages break down by region, we cannot provide a direct, side-by-side comparison of the reports as they have defined world regions differently. For example, Dawson et al. (2014) reports the following percentages of companies with female CEOs: Emerging Asia (6.6 percent), Developed Asia (4.4 percent), Europe (3.5 percent), North America (3.3 percent), Latin America (2.0 percent), and EMEA[1] (1.9 percent). Though women CEOs are rare in every region, some countries and regions are consistently ranked by researchers near the bottom for having women in top leadership positions. Generally, these low percentages are greatly influenced by national culture, which, as outlined in a number of chapters in this *Handbook*, can make it difficult for both men and women to accept women as senior leaders in the workplace (Madsen et al., 2015). Many cultural perceptions inhibit women's top leadership opportunities; women will have the chance to move ahead in substantial numbers only as cultural perceptions begin to shift (Ngunjiri and Madsen, 2015).

Just as women are more likely to hold the CEO position in certain geographical regions, so more women hold the top spot in specific industries. A 2016 survey conducted by the World Economic Forum (2016b) found the greatest percentage of women CEOs in the media, entertainment, and information sector (13 percent), followed by consumer (10 percent), and mobility and professional services (both with 9 percent). Women were under-represented in other fields, such as energy (none of the companies surveyed had a female CEO), basic and infrastructure (2 percent), and information and communication technology (5 percent).

In addition to women having more leadership success in certain industries, women are also more likely to reach high-level senior positions in specific C-suite or director roles. In this section we have focused thus far only on the CEO, a position held by very few women, but women have had more success globally in other senior roles. One survey showed that women hold the position of human resource director in 27 percent of corporations worldwide, chief financial officer in 18 percent of companies, and chief controller in 14 percent of firms (Grant Thornton, 2015). Advocates for greater opportunity for women in senior leadership hope that as women hold more and more C-suite positions, they can become better positioned to move into the CEO spot. More details on women in senior positions are discussed in the following section.

Of course, not all women achieve senior leadership by working their way up the corporate ladder. According to Adler (2015), many women become the chief executive by launching their own business, and like women in established corporations, their success can also be heavily influenced by their home country. The Global Entrepreneurship and Development Institute (GEDI), in its Female Entrepreneurship Index, recently ranked 77 countries in terms of their ability to foster success in high-potential women entrepreneurs, giving each a success percentage score. Of 77 nations, the ten best countries for women entrepreneurs were ranked as follows: US (82.9), Australia (74.8), UK (70.6), Denmark (69.7), Netherlands (69.3), France (68.8), Iceland (68.0), Sweden (66.7), Finland (66.4), and Norway (66.3) (Terjesen and Lloyd, 2015). Though these scores show some bright spots globally, more than half of ranked nations (47 of 77) received a score below 50 percent, indicating significant room to improve the national climate for women who want to start a business. The five lowest-ranked nations were Iran (20.6), Uganda (18.4), Bangladesh (17.9), Malawi (15.5), and Pakistan (15.2) (Terjesen and Lloyd, 2015).

Diversity does seem to be a key component of growing female leadership at the highest levels, culminating in the CEO position. One study found that 14 percent of companies with women in senior management have female CEOs (Grant Thornton, 2013), a higher percentage than companies overall. And those companies with a larger percentage of women in upper management may also have a financial advantage. In their study of the business case for increasing female leadership in corporate settings, Noland et al. (2016) found no real effect on firm performance merely from the presence of a female CEO. However, there was a demonstrable advantage to firm performance when there were a significant number of women executives, which "underscores the importance of creating a pipeline of female managers and not simply getting women to the very top" (p. 16).

Finally, there is more evidence that even though change to women's leadership at the highest level seems to be happening at a glacial pace, such changes can begin to snowball. Adler (2015) noted that women are leading global firms in greater and greater numbers, "with the vast majority being the first woman whom their particular firm has ever selected to hold such a senior position" (p. 39). Combined with greater numbers of women in other high leadership roles, the pipeline can continue to grow, and women's voices and influence can become a stronger force within the global corporate environment.

Women in Senior Management

Just as women face many barriers to reaching the CEO position in corporations worldwide, there are also numerous challenges to women seeking to reach roles in senior management. According to a recent World Economic Forum (2016b) report, even though today's women are, on average, better educated than men across the world, and they are participating more fully in the professional realm than ever before, women are only 28 percent as likely to rise to leadership positions as men. In fact, according to Lakshmi Puri, UN Women Deputy Executive Director, 75 percent of women in the world are "trapped in informal and low paid jobs" (Puri, 2016, p. 3). Even when women enter firms at the same rate as men (which does not always happen, although their tertiary enrollment rates are higher on average across the globe) (Grant Thornton, 2014), their proportional representation at each level of the corporation decreases, dropping from 33 percent at the junior level, to 24 percent at mid-level, 15 percent at senior level, and 9 percent at CEO level (World Economic Forum, 2016b). In this section we examine how successfully women are reaching positions of senior management across the world and throughout various industries. We also explore some factors that influence women's advancement today and what leaders may need to do in the future to improve the senior leadership environment for women.

In their most recent report on women in corporate leadership, researchers at Grant Thornton (2016) found that, as a global average, approximately 24 percent of senior leadership positions are held by women, and that number has stayed fairly consistent for over a decade. This specific report showed Russia as the global leader for percentage of women in senior leadership (45 percent), and it has been at the top of those lists consistently for years. Other Eastern European countries are also highly ranked, dating back to egalitarian principles touted during the Soviet era (Grant Thornton, 2016). Researchers have also identified another region to consistently show high levels of senior leadership: Emerging Asia – with Thailand (26.5 percent), Malaysia (26.2 percent), Singapore (25.1 percent), Philippines (24.6 percent), and Taiwan (24.3) – shows relatively strong percentages of women holding senior management positions (Dawson et al., 2014). This is in stark contrast with other Asian countries, such as South Korea and Japan, which have much lower levels of female leadership (Dawson et al., 2014). Interestingly, it seems that over the past decade, countries that have traditionally had stronger economies overall are those that have consistently had lower proportions of women in senior management than many emerging nations. For example, a recent report showed that in the US, Canada, France, Germany, Italy, Japan, and the UK, women held just 21 percent of senior roles, as opposed to the 32 percent held by women in the more emerging economies of Brazil, Russia, India, and China (Grant Thornton, 2014).

Surprisingly, it can be difficult to find current and consistent data on the exact percentages of women serving in senior management roles across the world. The scope is beyond what is possible for many academic projects, and corporate and nonprofit reports often use varied criteria, making a direct comparison impossible. Yet these data are still informative, and when understood in the context of how they are gathered, can be useful in tracking trends and the most up-to-date status of women in top leadership positions. Table 1.3 charts three separate research reports, and although the rankings vary (since not all countries are considered in each report), the numbers can provide critical insights for researchers, practitioners, and policy makers.

Though women are under-represented in senior management positions in nearly every industry, some fields are more likely to have women in key roles. Noland et al. (2016) found that women had a higher share of executive roles in the financial, health care, utilities, and telecommunications areas, with fewer women leading in companies centered on basic materials, technology, energy, and industrials. The 2014 Grant Thornton report linked high levels of women's leadership to businesses that are closely allied with the public sector, such as education and social services; hospitality and professional services also have higher numbers of women executives than global averages.

As we look toward parity in female senior management, we must consider not only which industries are hiring women, but also the specific roles women are filling. As mentioned in the previous section, women are not equally represented in all C-suite roles. Female CEOs are the least common, but women are also rarely chief operations officers (COO) (one of the primary positions from which the CEO position is promoted) nor do they hold other important positions that carry profit and loss responsibilities. Women are more heavily concentrated in human resources, communications, and finance – positions that are less likely to have a direct route to the CEO role (Dawson et al., 2014).

Table 1.3   Women filling senior leadership roles by country: top and bottom

Source	Top 10 countries	Bottom 5 countries	Method used to identify top and bottom
Catalyst (2014)	China 51% Poland 48% Philippines 37% Thailand 36% Germany 31% Hong Kong 30% Turkey 30% South Africa 28% New Zealand 28% Peru 27%	UK 19% India 19% Netherlands 11% UAE 11% Japan 7%	The countries in the Catalyst tables measure their workforce using the International Standard Classification of Occupations version ISCO-88, and the relevant category. It cites data from the Grant Thornton International Business Report 2013: *Women in Senior Management: Setting the Stage for Growth.*
Dawson et al. (2014)	Thailand 27% Malaysia 26% Sweden 26% Singapore 25% Philippines 25% Taiwan 24% Argentina 22% Norway 22% Finland 19% Australia 19%	South Korea 1% Pakistan 7% Chile 7% India 7% Japan 8%	Identifying and mapping 28,000 senior managers at 3,000 companies worldwide. Percentages have been rounded.
Grant Thornton (2014)	Russia 43% Indonesia 41% Latvia 41% Philippines 40% Lithuania 39% China 38% Thailand 38% Estonia 37% Armenia 35% Georgia 35%	Denmark 14% Germany 14% UAE 14% India 14% Switzerland 13% Japan 9% (6 countries are included here because four countries are at 14%).	Data come from 6,700 interviews with senior executives from mid-market, privately held businesses in 45 countries worldwide.

The segregation of women in specific roles can lead to a simple focus on the number of women in leadership without paying heed to which roles they are actually filling, and can disguise the fact that women are rarely holding decision-making senior positions (ManpowerGroup, 2015). For women to truly achieve economic equality, they need to be fully represented at all levels and roles, including those where key business decisions are made, which will prepare women to succeed in senior management positions.

Numerous factors contribute to the unequal distribution of women at senior management levels, and many are discussed at length later in this *Handbook*. Although women are closing the education gap worldwide, some posit that women are not necessarily studying in fields that will lead them to corporate leadership (Grant Thornton, 2014). While nations are investing in girls' education, and companies are investing in junior female employees' training, the World Economic Forum (2016a, 2016b) argues that these investments are not being fully realized if women are leaving firms before reaching their full potential. This factor alone should give governments and organizations strong motivation to create more creative and effective policies and procedures.

As will be discussed later in this *Handbook*, other advocates for women's advancement assert that companies need to change the way they define leadership; recruit, hire, and promote women more effectively; support stronger work–life integration policies and practices, including flexible work time and better child care options; strengthen paternal leave policies; design women-only leadership development programs and initiatives; and implement other innovative solutions. Specific, targeted efforts will be necessary to advance women toward equality in senior management (e.g., Dawson et al., 2014; Ernst & Young, 2016; Grant Thornton, 2016; International Labour Organization, 2015; Ngunjiri and Madsen, 2015).

PARITY PREDICTIONS

The path to parity shows both progress and challenges. Information reviewed thus far indicates that, since the Beijing Platform for Action was introduced in 1995 and especially in the last decade, gender diversity efforts have become more global, prominent, focused, and fertile (Inter-Parliamentary Union, 2015b; International Labour Organization, 2015; Lee et al., 2015; UN Women, 2016a, 2016b; World Economic Forum, 2016b). However, there remain cultural, economic, and political hurdles that add to the complexity of these efforts, and there is substantial work left to be done. There is also a discourse among global economic development agencies and leaders on how long it will take humanity to achieve gender parity and how to go about reaching that destination in the most efficient and effective manner. Thus, gender leadership quotas that have been legislatively and voluntarily enacted in many countries (as a temporary measure compensating for inherent cultural and political gender stigmas) have led to an ongoing debate about their effectiveness and justification (Dahlerup, 2005; Inter-Parliamentary Union, 2015a).

For corporate boards, target quotas and dates to increase women's representation differ depending on agencies advocating for corporate gender parity. For instance, the US Government Accountability Office (2015) estimates that, at the current rate, gender parity on corporate boards will be achieved in 40 years, while Lee et al. (2015) offers two scenarios, where 30 percent female representation on corporate boards is achieved by 2027 at the "business as usual" rate, and by 2020 at an "accelerated" rate. Ernst & Young (2015) pointed out that women accounted for only 16 percent of S&P 1500 board members in 2014, a 5 percent increase over ten years. Basic modeling with mathematical functions reveals that using 16 percent as a starting point, and at a rate of 5 percent increase every 10 years, it will require 230 years to arrive at 50 percent. At the same time, Catalyst states that in 2015, 14.2 percent of companies led by a female director in the S&P 500 Index have been or are approaching 50 percent female representation on their boards (Catalyst, 2015). This shows that parity is possible.

In a more comprehensive outlook, the World Economic Forum, in its press release for the 2014 Gender Gap Report, estimated that gender parity was 81 years away (based on the data comparisons between 2006 and 2014), while its press release for the 2015 Gender Gap Report downgraded the previous prediction to 118 years, based on a mere 4 percent of the overall global gender gap being closed between 2006 and 2015 (World Economic Forum, 2014, 2015). At the same time, the Global Gender Gap Report for 2015 reveals considerable variation in the performance of individual indicators that comprise the global gender gap. Thus, gender parity is considered to be already achieved in the higher education attainment indicator, while the skilled labor indicator falls behind at 75 percent, and the leadership and political empowerment indicator is the lowest yet at 28 percent (World Economic Forum, 2015). A more optimistic (though perhaps less statistically based) opinion is revealed in a recent study of gender diversity in leadership. ManpowerGroup (2015) reported that, during interviews, 222 male and female leaders from 25 countries around the globe expressed their shared expectation that gender parity will be achieved within the Millennials' generation.

We believe that gender parity is no longer an abstract idea, that it has already become a reality in a few sectors of a few countries. In November 2015, Bloomberg reported that Canada's newly elected Prime Minister, Justin Trudeau, named 15 women into his 30-member cabinet. When asked why an equal cabinet was important to him, he famously responded, "Because it's 2015" (Kassenaar and Wingrove, 2015, para. 3). Yet we readily acknowledge that there is still substantial work to be done to achieve gender parity more comprehensively.

CONCLUSION

This chapter has summarized the background and available data on the current status of women in regions and countries around the world as it relates to political leadership. We then provided current data on the state of women in business leadership, which included sections on the general situation of women on corporate boards, women as CEOs (including entrepreneurs), and women in senior management roles in regions and countries. We then briefly discussed gender parity and provided examples from various groups on when this parity is predicted to occur. Given the constraints of this volume's chapter lengths, we summarized a limited number of sources. However, we recommend that readers study full versions of our references to gain deeper insight on this topic.

Developments of the last 20 years are genuinely encouraging. The 1995 Beijing Platform sparked dialogue about diversity and unconscious gender bias. Through the initiatives of the United Nations, World Bank, World Economic Forum – and many other global, national, and local organizations, leaders, and citizens – we have arrived at a tipping point, where the real commitment and conscientious gender inclusion begins. At the "StepItUp Global Leaders' Meeting on Gender Equality and Women's Empowerment: A Commitment to Action" (UN Women, 2016b), a number of heads of state agreed that it is indeed time for more action. Angela Merkel, Chancellor of Germany, stated, "Commitments are good. Action is better. Let us take action!" (p. 31). Prime Minister of Belgium Charles Michel exclaimed that "twenty years after the Beijing Declaration and Platform for Action, the time for balance sheets is over; we have to move toward concrete and accelerated implementation" (p. 53). Adrian Hasler, Prime Minister

holders to take measurable actions toward eliminating the inequities of women's leadership status worldwide. The document represents the collective expertise of the scholars and practitioners who attended the conferences, namely, individuals who (1) study and conduct research around the issues of women and leadership and/or (2) design and deliver leadership development/coaching programs and related consultative services for helping women to strengthen their leadership ability. Five major focus areas frame the calls for action:

1. Increasing Equality in Power and Decision-Making
2. Helping Girls and Young Women Become Leaders
3. Expanding Leadership Education and Development Worldwide
4. Advancing Women in Leadership
5. Identifying Critical Areas for Future Research

Those preparing the Declaration encourage individuals and organizations to step forward to personally accept one or more of the calls to action and to move the conversation forward even more intentionally and assertively than in the past. We are convinced the time for bringing an end to the inequality of women and leadership has come!

BACKGROUND

The *Asilomar Declaration and Call to Action (Declaration)* was first published in 2013 by attendees of the International Leadership Association's (ILA) Women and Leadership Affinity Group (WLAG) inaugural conference held June 9–12, 2013. The conference, held at the Asilomar Conference Grounds in Pacific Grove, California, USA, had the theme "Building, Bridging, and Blazing Pathways for Women and Leadership: Celebrating the Past, Present, and Future." After the second conference "Advancing Women in Leadership: Waves of Possibilities" was held in June 2015, we updated and refined the Declaration, resulting in this edition. The purpose of the Declaration is to capture and disseminate our collective ideas and challenge ourselves and the world to change the status of women worldwide. Through careful review of the United Nations' (UN) efforts to combat inequality in leadership, we designed both conferences to catalyze our collective knowledge about how we could and should assist individuals, groups, organizations, and countries to prepare and increase the number of effective women leaders. Sessions at both conferences were designed to harness the latest research and gather proven best practices in order to identify specific declarations and calls to action that we can all take to promote gender equality in leadership. This document demonstrates the continued commitment of the WLAG, the ILA, and conference participants to further the cause of women and leadership. It is also a platform for sharing the insights of leadership scholars, educators, and practitioners with other organizations also committed to advancing women's leadership.

Description of Women and Leadership Affinity Group

The WLAG is a network of leadership scholars and practitioners who work together to enhance their knowledge, expertise, and research in the area of women and leadership and to advance the standing of women in leadership. The WLAG began in 2010, when three ILA members organized a "Women in Leadership Network Luncheon" at ILA's annual conference. Approximately 100 passionate individuals gathered around interest tables for engaging lunchtime conversations. At the conclusion of the luncheon, each table provided feedback on how participants would like to create a more formal networking effort. Based on this feedback, in the spring of 2011, Dr. Susan R. Madsen founded the WLAG with an executive leadership team comprised of 12 members, who began identifying various organizational elements of the WLAG (e.g., charter, website, structure); the team convened officially at the 2011 October ILA Conference in London.

The purpose of the WLAG is to facilitate interaction and organize activities that support diverse and sustained conversations on the subject of women and leadership. The unique goals of this scholar/practitioner group include providing information, resources, and networking opportunities for those scholars and practitioners who: (1) study and conduct research around the issues of women and leadership; and/or (2) design and deliver leadership development/coaching programs and related consultative services for helping women to strengthen their leadership.

Location and Significance of Asilomar

Asilomar is a YWCA Summer Leadership Camp built in 1913 for girls and women. Known for its famous architecture, rich history, and pristine surroundings, the state park and conference center is located on 107 acres of state beach within the town of Pacific Grove, California. Asilomar is celebrated for its restored dune ecosystem and architecture designed by renowned architect Julia Morgan. In 2012, to recognize its 100 years of continual service to all citizens, and women in particular, Asilomar approached ILA about a synergistic opportunity for a women-centered leadership conference. The confluence of events was perfect, as the new WLAG was actively considering offering such a gathering. A contract was signed, and the rest, as they say, is history.

Genesis of the Declaration and Call to Action

In early 2012, the WLAG Executive Planning Team agreed that in order to move the women and leadership conversation forward globally, it was critical that a document be created and widely distributed that would highlight declarations and calls to action that would emerge from the conference. The idea came from studying the related United Nations' (UN) history. In 1975 the UN organized the historic World Conference on Women in Mexico City; subsequent UN conferences on women led to the development in 1995 of The Beijing Declaration and Platform for Action, which provided an assessment of the status of women at the close of the twentieth century and suggested paths forward. Since then, the UN has held periodic gatherings to set priorities and assess progress on The Beijing Declaration and the status of women and girls. The startup of an umbrella agency in 2012, the UN Women, provided an entity that has streamlined and further strengthened efforts for gender equality.

To build on these actions, WLAG leaders reviewed UN reports to identify leadership issues according to two criteria: (1) issues directly related to women and leadership that the UN reports confirmed need more work and research; and (2) issues in which members of the WLAG have expertise and knowledge. The five areas listed below emerged from the analysis.

Conference leaders considered the particular contributions that conference attendees could make to extend the overall global conversation; they designed processes to catalyze and capture the expertise and conference learning from participants to share in the *Asilomar Declaration and Call to Action on Women and Leadership*. The first four areas listed above became the streams for the 2015 conference to ensure that these themes remain central topics of discussion. The methods, described next, may provide other groups with innovative ways to amplify their collective voices for change.

Process

Both of the WLAG conferences were designed to maximize the exchange of ideas, facilitate conversations, and capture new knowledge regarding an array of topics related to advancing women and leadership. Specifically, the conferences became catalysts for moving the conversation forward through lively interaction and by a combination of facilitated meetings, fireside chats, developmental roundtables, facilitated mealtime conversations, and more. These different venues provided diverse opportunities for conference participants to engage in dynamic conversations on women and leadership. At the first conference, a number of session facilitators and volunteer representatives – all coached beforehand on the purpose of the event – collected notes and reflections from participants. Then, immediately following the conference, the notes and reflections were collected and compiled into one document. These notes, as well as post-conference reflections, the conference program, and the texts of all presentations and session abstracts, became the primary sources for drafting the original Declaration in 2013. Six volunteer writing teams (with a total of 28 individuals) were assigned a section of the document and were tasked with analyzing and synthesizing information from the source documents. After the full Declaration was compiled and refined by team leaders, it was sent to all conference participants for review and approval and ultimately distributed to leaders and researchers around the world. For the 2015 conference, the process was modified in order to build on to the 2013 work. At the second conference, a closing plenary session provided attendees an opportunity to share new insights and ideas that were then captured, reviewed, and analyzed by conference organizers, and then integrated into this version.

This second version of the Declaration was then redistributed to the UN Women, hundreds of key global contacts, and countless women's groups and associations around the world who are committed to advancing women's leadership. We believe that this document will provide important information and insights to organizations working on these issues and those planning future global events and efforts.

From the deliberative process started in January 2012 to the global conferences in June of 2013 and 2015, we have organized the report into five sections to represent the expertise, research, and best practices of WLAG members and other conference participants. These sections reflect our collective wisdom, passion, and commitment to women and leadership, and are presented as follows:

Section I: Increasing Equality in Power and Decision-Making
Section II: Helping Girls and Young Women Become Leaders

Section III: Expanding Leadership Education and Development Worldwide
Section IV: Advancing Women in Leadership
Section V: Identifying Critical Areas for Future Research

SECTION I: INCREASING EQUALITY IN POWER AND DECISION-MAKING

> "Equality in decision-making is essential to the empowerment of women."
> – Beijing Declaration and Platform for Action

Despite tireless work by countless numbers of women, men, girls, and boys around the globe to create a world of equality, research continues to document a persistent gender imbalance in leadership positions and key decision-making bodies in both the public and private realm (European Commission, January 2010). Following the United Nations' Womenwatch strategy, we believe we need to focus on fostering equality in three domains: (1) the social/cultural domain; (2) the economic domain; and (3) the political/civic domain. Equality in power and decision-making will likely look different in each domain, as will the strategies and tactics used to accomplish change. Further, only by addressing the structural foundations of gender inequality will true equality be achieved.

To categorize the diverse actions and strategies available to us as change makers, we adopted the AACR Model (Storberg-Walker, 2013) (see Figure 2.1). This model, adapted from Start and Hovland's (2007) "Tools for Policy Impact," illustrates a way to categorize the different beliefs and strategies that guide our actions. AACR stands for

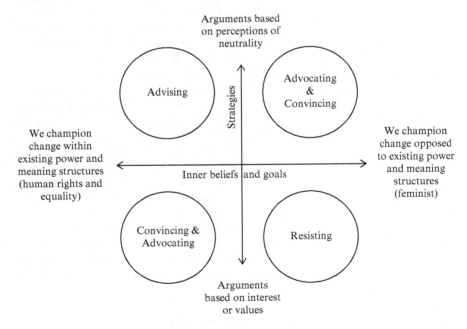

Figure 2.1   Advising, Advocating, Convincing, and Resisting Model

advising, advocating, convincing, and resisting – four tactics for change. The four tactics are archetypes or "pure forms" that can help us understand the hidden connections and shared goals of scholars building new women and leadership theories with those of practitioners protesting in the halls of Congress. The horizontal axis represents a spectrum of beliefs and goals; our ideas fall along the spectrum from the far left (advocating for human rights) to the far right (advocating for an end to patriarchy) and everywhere in between. The vertical axis represents the spectrum of rhetorical strategies we use to construct our arguments for change. Arguments based on the notion of scientific neutrality or evidence based practice are above the horizontal axis, and arguments based on values or interests follow.

The two axes create four quadrants with change tactics generated from our diverse beliefs, goals, and strategies. All four types of tactics were present in the conversations, presentations, and panel discussions at the Asilomar conferences. Scholarly social scientists presented value-free statistics that confirmed the inequality in power and decision-making across the globe. Passionate consultants/practitioners described moments of personal resistance to racism and gender discrimination. Women united in the cause debated with each other on priorities, content, and focus. Collectively, we represent a multiplicity of perspectives, and we identify ourselves at different locations within the AACR Model. We seek to align our collective interests as researchers, change makers, practitioners, mentors, students, mothers, fathers, and workers to extend our reach globally to learn, educate, and foster locally generated solutions for equality in power and decision-making. We do so with the following declarations and calls to action:

A. Declarations

1. *We declare* that the concept of neutrality – including but not limited to gender, race, sexual orientation, and ability – masks unspoken assumptions, biases, and standards that limit the self-concept of girls and women across the globe.
2. *We declare* that all claims of neutrality in practice, research, and policy are based on inaccurate assumptions and understandings; consequently, any program, policy, or research based on this claim will be insufficient to generate the structural, social, economic, cultural, and political changes needed to enhance women's global equality in power and decision-making.
3. *We declare* that the negative consequences women and girls encounter when they advocate for equality in power and decision-making vary widely in their severity – ranging from assassination or attempted assassination (for example, Malala Yousafzai) to cool indifference. We believe this range of consequences – from violent to uncivil – are a function of the advocate's race, skin color, culture, context, socio-economic status, age, and religion. We do not all suffer in the same ways.
4. *We declare* that outdated perceptions of the roles of men and women by both men and women contribute to gender disparity. Acknowledging that different cultures generate diverse experiences and perceptions, we believe that the gender disparity is generated by an unexamined belief that men should provide for the home, and women should care for the home. This belief diminishes both the possible roles for women outside of the home and the possible roles for men within it; this belief sustains the male-centered definitions of activity outside of the home, including

leadership and power; and perpetuates generation after generation of girls and women who are not able to see themselves as leaders with power.

5. *We declare* that "horizontal violence" (Freire, 1993) between women perpetuates male leadership norms, sustains gender disparity in power and decision-making, and undermines women's advancement as leaders. Horizontal violence is a recognized byproduct of the unequal distribution of power in society stemming from the relationship between oppressors and the oppressed. Funk (2002) identifies horizontal violence as dismissive, negative, demeaning, and hostile behavior caused by powerlessness and impotence; and we believe both macro (structural) and micro (individual) transformation is the only way to fully rid ourselves of these patterns.

6. *We declare* that the engine of change should operate at the local, grassroots level. While we acknowledge that an interdependent relationship exists between local, national, and global forces, we believe that sustained change – change that is safe for women across the globe and change that will shift the larger systems that perpetuate inequality – must come from the dedication and hard work of individual women, men, workers, and community leaders at the local level.

7. *We declare* that equality in power and decision-making will look different and have diverse meanings across global cultures, institutions, organizations, and communities. Consequently, we believe that statistics generated to measure the influence of women across the globe provide only a partial picture. A more complete picture must include understanding the contextual norms, cultures, meanings, and standards at the local level. To this end, we believe that collaborative and participatory approaches to scholarly research, advocacy, and activism are essential for achieving equality in power and decision-making.

8. *We declare* that even if we were to reach gender parity within existing political, economic, and social systems or structures around the world, we still would not have reached gender equality. We believe that only when these systems promote principles of inclusion, equality, and collaboration in power and decision-making will true gender equality exist.

9. *We declare* that the diversity of women and women's perspectives across the globe is a strength heretofore underutilized and under-examined. We believe that exposing our differences honestly, authentically, and respectfully will generate the collaborative space needed for accomplishing our goals.

10. *We declare* that we have the power within us to contribute to this united and compelling force for change.

B. Call to Action

1. As individual women, we must. . .
    a. Remain or become active participants in local, state/provincial, national, and global organizations pursuing strategies for gender equality.
    b. Work to be change makers in our daily lives, to lift ourselves and others from self-limiting beliefs and attitudes, and to resolve tendencies of horizontal violence.
    c. Become or remain connected to women and men across the globe working to empower women and girls.

and utilize these in expanding the training, mentoring and development of girls emerging as leaders.

3. Other stakeholders and organizations are urged to. . .

   a. Provide ample opportunity for young women to play an active role in the governance of the organizations, including positions on boards and committees.

   b. Pursue the rigorous global enlistment of young women as active participants, including international events that illustrate the leadership potential society holds for them.

   c. Target organizations around the world that work to develop girls and young women and invite them to participate and collaborate. To address funding challenges, we recommend that such organizations create alternative membership fee structures for those in countries of greatest need.

   d. Support – through in-kind donations, financial donations, or through writing and obtaining grants – a sustained research agenda that examines the diverse ways girls are educated for leadership across the globe.

   e. Develop educational programs that enhance the potential of all students and include youth in planning activities for fulfilling the promise.

   f. Provide opportunities in communities for young women to become coaches, mentors, and advisors, which will support future leadership roles for women.

   g. Create programs for young women in which they fulfill roles as civic leaders in local, regional, and national political arenas.

SECTION III: EXPANDING LEADERSHIP EDUCATION AND DEVELOPMENT WORLDWIDE

> "Ensure the availability of a broad range of educational and training programmes that lead to ongoing acquisition by women and girls of the knowledge and skills required for living in, contributing to and benefiting from their communities and nations."
> – Beijing Declaration and Platform for Action

Due largely to well-documented contextual constraints, including the demands of child care, domestic chores, and farm work as well as the inhibiting factors of tradition, ethnicity, and social class, women and girls are underrepresented in formal and informal leadership positions. We assert the need for leadership education for women and girls of all ethnicities, in all countries, all contexts, and at all levels of privilege. Our intent is not to send the message that women and girls need "fixing." We believe that girls need consistent affirmative support and encouragement from their early years to help them overcome or resist societal, cultural, and religious messages as well as self-limiting personal beliefs that can constrain goals, dreams, and attitudes about fulfilling formal and informal leadership roles. At the same time, we are compelled to send the clear message that as scholars and practitioners, we know very little about the developmental trajectory of women leaders. As women and leadership researchers and advocates, we must conduct rigorous social science research in order to best inform the development and pedagogy of leadership education programs for women and girls.

This section begins with several assertions relevant to the need for leadership development among women and girls. It is followed by a global call to action for leadership development programs that address all contexts, all ethnicities, all classes, and all parts of the world.

A. Declarations

1. *We declare* that there is an urgent need to increase leadership education and development opportunities for women and girls worldwide. We believe, however, that simply increasing the number of leadership programs and mentoring opportunities across the globe is a simplistic and ineffectual response to a complex issue.
2. *We declare* that more research is needed to understand women's leadership trajectories in multiple contexts, cultures, and societies. Research can provide the foundation of understanding how women develop into leaders, and, with that understanding, specific learning activities and frameworks can be developed.
3. *We declare* that women's and girls' leadership development programs will be successful only if the multiple contextual intersectionalities of women's lives are acknowledged, respected, and addressed. These include, but are not limited to, the intersectionalities of gender and race, faith, national and regional identity, ethnicity, lingualism, education and literacy, caste, migration, and incarceration. We assert that while men's intersectionalities may also result in their marginalization, it is women and girls who most often bear the heaviest burdens from the clash of contexts.
4. *We declare* that effective leadership development will require special attention to the intersections within intersections (i.e., roles within roles). For example, in the U.S., immigrant black women may face additional leadership challenges not typically experienced by their African-American counterparts. Women in evangelical or Muslim groups may find their leadership defined and limited by notions of gender roles and power.
5. *We declare* that the reach of leadership development programs must be extended to marginalized and underserved women populations, including working-class women, rural women, migrant women, and other groups. Privileged women are often held up as leadership role models, yet their leadership challenges are usually much different from those of women with less privilege. Leadership education models must acknowledge and honor the needs and challenges of all women.
6. *We declare* that informal leadership training begins during childhood, and that the media often play a role in perpetrating gender stereotypes. However, parents, caregivers, community members, teachers, coaches, and other early influences can have a positive and significant impact in developing women's leadership potential. We assert that young women should be encouraged to develop a clear vision about the ways they can transform their community.
7. *We declare* that women's leadership education should include a wide range of topics and skills (e.g., relationship building, communication and interpersonal skills, time management, goal setting, confidence building, risk taking, and work–life integration). We assert that while concern over work–life balance can have a dampening effect on the leadership aspirations of many women, transgenerational mentoring can help women understand and learn the skills of leadership and life from each other.
8. *We declare* that, with role models, women can envision themselves taking on formal

and informal leadership roles. We suggest that role models, as much as possible, should represent multiple intersectionalities, roles, and backgrounds. Only with these varied influences will the next generation of women leaders develop the abilities to value diverse positions and realities. We assert that as women's leadership stories are retold, their challenges should not be minimized or oversimplified.

B. Call to Action

1. As individual women we must. . .
    a. Maintain connections and networks so that we can share and learn from each other about leadership education and development for women and girls.
    b. Mentor girls and young women empowering them to become leaders in their lives and communities.
    c. Strive to empower all women to be leaders in their everyday lives, remembering that women leaders around the world have many faces (e.g., mothers, teachers, and community, business, and government leaders). While women in "informal" leadership roles may not think of themselves as leaders, they are leaders and deserve education and development opportunities to assist them in seeing themselves as such.
    d. Be sensitive to different contexts, cultures, and generations to ensure that leadership development and education do not take a one-size-fits-all approach.
    e. Harness the power of various media resources as a forum to develop and educate women and girls.
    f. Recognize the impact we can have on girls and the women around them in their homes, institutions, and communities and deepen their support and engagement in expanding development opportunities for these individuals.
    g. Combat the dominant narratives that often shape women's and girls' conception of their leadership capacity and encourage self-authorship as a form of personal leadership development.
    h. Conduct rigorous and meaningful research and evaluations, using both qualitative and quantitative methods, to assess and connect leadership education and development around the world.
    i. Design leadership education and develop curriculum to enhance women's leadership across various contexts, cultures, and groups.
2. We encourage women's networks and organizations to. . .
    a. Sustain the current momentum and host regular conferences, sessions, workshops, and gatherings that afford women the opportunity to network, share their knowledge, and continue to develop as leaders.
    b. Develop networks of support for members to share research, tools, and models of leadership development and education through online platforms to encourage learning and collaboration.
    c. Collect and consolidate resources, information, research, and tools into one online platform that is available and accessible to all who work in the area of leadership development and education of women; this will enable us to share existing knowledge and to identify gaps and needs.
    d. Re-examine the language of leadership with a goal to be more inclusive as we

develop a common language around what leadership means in different cultures, contexts, and generations and how we develop leadership around the world.

e.   Foster intergenerational connections and conversations to encourage mentorship, networking, collaboration, and leadership development and education in many contexts.

f.   Ensure that program evaluation and adequate outcome measurements are part of leadership development and education so that we can build upon the approaches that work for developing women leaders.

g.   Notice the significance in supporting the development of leadership capacities in women and girls at this point in history.

h.   Support future events to help faculty, practitioners, and others share research and best practices on different program models and outcomes.

3.   Other stakeholders and organizations are urged to. . .

a.   Investigate the factors that encourage or discourage girls and women from taking leadership roles, or from seeing themselves as leaders in their daily lives.

b.   Develop specific theories and models describing how girls and women prepare to be leaders rather than continuing to rely on male models of leadership development.

c.   Study the early childhood and youth experiences that empower and motivate women to be leaders.

d.   Consider the outcome measures that constitute best-practice markers in determining successful leadership programs for girls and women. As researchers study leadership programs, we challenge them to make a careful catalogue of contextual markers and intersectionalities so that we can begin to determine how leadership programs might be adjusted to best match with context and circumstances.

e.   Take advantage of the research to prepare more specifically targeted experiences for girls and women within the specific cultural or other contexts applicable to them.

f.   Carefully catalog demographics of groups, evaluate successful elements of programs, and report best practices so that a more comprehensive picture of leadership education can emerge.

g.   Implement workplace and school-based leadership programs specifically for girls and women.

h.   Promote the development of female leadership, whether they supervise factory workers, farm laborers, physicians, attorneys, or teachers, and so forth.

SECTION IV: ADVANCING WOMEN IN LEADERSHIP

"A woman with a voice is by definition a strong woman.
But the search to find that voice can be remarkably difficult."
– Melinda Gates, 2003

Women leaders from all over the world gathered at Asilomar in 2013 and 2015, united in thought and spirit, to deliberate the issue of advancing women in leadership. We determined that a paradigm shift is required to augment and bolster the minuscule gains made in leadership roles for women. Our increasingly complex, global challenges require a new style of leadership that models inclusive leadership practices and promotes leadership that is "fit-defined" rather than gender-defined. Our aims for advancing women in leadership include building an operational definition of effective leadership, bridging research and practice, blazing new pathways, and embracing possibilities. Our calls to action necessitate that women develop a personal leadership identity, seek challenging opportunities to explore leadership roles, and exercise constructive leadership behaviors through all stages of their lives. We affirm our commitment to Advancing women in leadership as follows:

A. Declarations

1. *We declare* that women are persistently underrepresented in leadership roles, especially at the most senior levels, despite an increasingly compelling body of evidence that supports the link between gender representation and organizational performance. We believe establishing, publicizing, and reporting targets; offering fit-for-purpose programs and activities; and addressing institutional, structural, and relational barriers will facilitate a paradigm shift that advances women in leadership.

2. *We declare* that prevailing leadership styles and patterns are predominately hierarchal, autocratic, and exclusive despite research that suggests relational, consensus-building, and inclusive styles are more effective. We believe this traditional mode of leadership is no longer fit-for-purpose in our rapidly changing world with its increasingly complex, transnational challenges. Further, we believe a paradigm shift in leadership style and approach that values and rewards behavior that models connectedness, inclusiveness, mutual respect, interdependence, integrity, and authenticity is required.

3. *We declare* that inclusivity is a moral and business imperative that facilitates the advancement of women in leadership. We believe unexamined assumptions and double standards, as well as invisible barriers embedded in organizational cultures, constrain opportunities for women.

4. *We declare* that a body of evidence is now widely available and points to strategies organizations have successfully deployed to make a difference in the representation of women at the executive table. We believe it is vitally important that change is led actively and personally by chief executive officers and senior executive teams. We assert our belief that positive role models, informal networks, sponsorship, mentoring, and other tailored developmental activities for women are vital to creating new archetypes.

5. We *declare* that fostering the advancement of women in leadership globally, particularly in countries and cultures in which women are not able to participate fully in the economy and society, increases economic and social well-being. We affirm our intention to partner with supportive leaders of both genders to bring about positive organizational and societal change.

6. *We declare* that, as women, we have it within our power to address self-limiting beliefs and inefficacious behaviors that contribute to our not fully exercising choices about our lives and careers. We acknowledge the importance of developing our own confidence, resilience, and resourcefulness to succeed as leaders.

7. *We declare* our appreciation for the extensive research being undertaken in this field

and publicized by a wide range of entities. We commit to actively collaborate with these endeavors and to build on their work. We intend to capitalize on an unprecedented opportunity to continue the dialogue in an effort to shift current paradigms.

B. Call to Action

1. As individual women we must. . .
    a. Consciously and continually develop our own authentic leadership style in harmony with personal values, belief systems, and respectfulness to another woman's right to choose a different leadership style.
    b. Proactively engage in ongoing dialogue and learning about women's leadership and support programs and activities that advance women in leadership.
    c. Explore challenging leadership roles and exercise adaptability in leadership behaviors consistent with both the requirements of each role and our own values.
    d. Examine our own biases, identify assumptions and double standards in the workplace, and question the structural barriers embedded in organizational cultures that constrain opportunities for women.
    e. Be a valuable resource for women, bridge the gap between ourselves and other informal networks, and continue to blaze pathways for advancing women in leadership.
    f. Act as positive role models, sponsors, and mentors; be mindful and intentional in exercising choices; and partner with supportive leaders of both genders to bring about positive organizational and societal change that advances women in leadership globally.
    g. Utilize qualitative and quantitative methodologies to design and conduct rigorous research on advancing women in leadership, with a focus on leadership identity, unconscious bias, and inclusive leadership skills.
    h. Acknowledge our role in supporting women and girls in their quest to build confidence, resilience, and resourcefulness. We challenge ourselves to support them in developing a personal leadership style and in addressing self-imposed barriers that hold them back.
    i. Communicate the key messages in this declaration and call to action within our respective communities.
2. We encourage women's networks and organizations to. . .
    a. Recognize our mutual interdependence, celebrate our differences, and model inclusive leadership practices that empower and advance women in leadership.
    b. Build relationships, facilitate communication, and actively collaborate with individuals, researchers, and entities that promote the advancement of women in leadership locally, nationally, and globally.
    c. Dispute mindsets that suggest leadership is gender-defined and shift the paradigm to leadership that is "fit-defined." We can do so by developing relationships with like-minded individuals and organizations, disseminating related research and best practices information, and promoting recognition or awards for individuals, organizations, and nations that embrace the new paradigm.
    d. Formalize strategic plans of action and milestones, with short- and long-term goals, to direct the advancement of women in leadership. Included in these plans

should be an outreach program and periodic assessment and reevaluation periods to allow for growth and change.

e.   Acknowledge the persistent underrepresentation of women in senior leadership roles despite an increasingly compelling body of evidence that supports the link between gender parity and organizational performance.

f.   Endorse inclusive leadership practices as a moral and business imperative that facilitates the advancement of women in leadership.

g.   Foster the advancement of women in leadership globally by partnering with supportive individual, organizational, national, and international leaders of both genders who strive to effect positive cultural change.

h.   Be a bridge between research and practice by connecting ideas and people and acting as a clearinghouse for scholars and practitioners.

i.   Capitalize on an unprecedented opportunity to influence ongoing conversations surrounding the biennial WLAG Conferences and UN Women events by disseminating the *Asilomar Declaration and Call to Action* widely.

3.   Other stakeholders and organizations are encouraged to. . .

a.   Examine their beliefs and address self-limiting behaviors that contribute to not fully exercising choices about their lives and careers.

b.   Foster and support the development of women and girls as leaders within their organizations and communities.

c.   Model inclusive leadership practices and embrace a paradigm shift that promotes leadership that is "fit-defined" rather than gender-defined.

d.   Establish "targets with teeth" and measure, report, and hold managers accountable for achieving those targets.

e.   Measure and monitor – by gender – internal promotions, development opportunities, spend levels, and pay plans.

f.   Offer targeted, fit-for-purpose, leadership development opportunities for aspiring women leaders.

g.   Implement unconscious bias-awareness programs in their organizations.

h.   Address structural barriers and facilitate flexible working practices and career paths for women.

i.   Recognize the business case for gender representation at senior levels and adopt a "small wins" approach to change.

j.   Promote educational programs and community outreach activities that advance women in leadership.

k.   Establish, promote, support, and report aspirational targets for the representation of women at all levels in organizations within their own jurisdictions.

l.   Recognize and reward leadership styles that model connectedness, inclusiveness, mutual respect, interdependence, integrity, and authenticity.

m.   Join us in capitalizing on an unprecedented opportunity to continue the conversations surrounding the biennial WLAG Conferences and this document.

SECTION V: IDENTIFYING CRITICAL AREAS FOR FUTURE RESEARCH

"A significant body of research indicates that women's empowerment and gender equality
have a catalytic effect on the achievement of human development, good governance, sustained
peace, and harmonious dynamics between the environment and human population."
– UN Women, 2013

Numerous articles, research reports, and books such as Kristof and WuDunn's *Half the Sky* document the loss to humanity when the talents and potential of women are not developed to address the major challenges facing our world. Leadership has for too long remained male-normed, with powerful but subtle forms of gender bias leading to under-representation by women in top leadership roles. One cause, discussed in the September 2013 cover story of Harvard Business Review, cites "second-generation gender bias" as "something in the water – in which women fail to thrive or reach their full potential" (p. 64). The resulting loss to organizational effectiveness – which can be a proxy for the community, nation, or society – is described by Helgesen and Johnson in *The Female Vision: Women's Real Power at Work*: "When the female vision remains untapped, both women and organizations suffer. Women are unable to translate their best observations into action. . . . Without the female vision, organizations also lose power. They undermine the full potential of their talent base" (p. 91).

This *Asilomar Declaration* identifies areas demanding action at a number of levels – individual, organizational, national, and global. Just as the 1995 Beijing Declaration and Platform challenged scholars and practitioners to focus attention and willpower on gender issues as a pressing social justice priority, we challenge future researchers to advance gender-related dimensions of leadership studies. Such research will enhance our understanding of individual, organizational, and societal dynamics and advance both inclusive and effective leadership practice. This research will need to be interdisciplinary, to address the complexities of the social construction of gender, and it will need to be multi-paradigm, to encompass and honor the multiple ways of knowing and understanding what it means to be human. The research methods used will need to be diverse – to offer a compelling alternative to the dominant (e.g., male-normed) reductionist, rationalist, and objectivist scientific method. Finally, the researcher will need to navigate the space between scholarship and advocacy, between research and practice, and between thinking and doing. We identify specific areas of research for each of the four issue areas listed in the preceding pages.

A. Increasing Equality in Power and Decision-Making

1. *Types of Power*: What can researchers contribute to our understanding of leadership by differentiating among various types of power and authority (e.g., traditional power, self-empowerment, personal authority, reciprocal empowerment)? How does context influence effective use of power? How does context influence perceptions of power and influence?
2. *Language of Power*: How can and should researchers examine the connection between the words used to describe power and male-normed perspectives of leadership? What is the connection between knowledge and power? How are contemporary leadership

Storberg-Walker, J. (2013). AACR (advising, advocating, convincing, resisting). Raleigh, NC: Author.

United Nations. (1995, September 4–15). Report of the fourth world conference on women. Declaration, B. Platform for Action. Beijing, China, UN Doc. ACONF, 177, 20. Retrieved from http://www.un.org/women-watch/daw/beijing/official.htm

The United Nations Children's Fund (UNICEF) (2007). UNICEF State of World's Children. Retrieved from http://www.unicef.org/sowc07/docs/sowc07.pdf

UN Women. (2013). A transformative stand-alone goal on achieving gender equality, women's rights and women's empowerment: Imperatives and key components. Retrieved from http://www.unwomen.org/en/digital-library/publications/2013/7/post-2015-long-paper

Womenwatch (n.d). Information and resources on gender equality and empowerment of women. Retrieved from http://www.un.org/womenwatch/index.html

APPENDIX A: 2015 REPORT CONTRIBUTORS

Report Co-Compiler: Susan R. Madsen, Utah Valley University
Report Co-Compiler: Dionne Rosser-Mims, Troy University
Conference Co-Chair: Susan R. Madsen, Utah Valley University
Conference Co-Chair: Melissa Mahan, Texas A&M University, San Antonio

Overall Document

Susan R. Madsen, Utah Valley University
Dionne Rosser-Mims, Troy University
Julia Storberg-Walker, George Washington University
Lynne Devnew, University of Phoenix
Melissa Mahan, Texas A&M University, San Antonio

Document Sections

Lynne Devnew, University of Phoenix
Renique Kersh, North Central College
Karen Longman, Azusa Pacific University
Wendy Rowe, Royal Roads University
Sherylle Tan, Claremont McKenna College
Denise Thomson, DeWitt-Thomson, LLC
Faith Wambura Ngunjiri, Concordia College

APPENDIX B: 2013 REPORT CONTRIBUTORS

Report Compiler and Coordinator: Susan R. Madsen, Utah Valley University
Conference Chair: Susan R. Madsen, Utah Valley University
Program Chair: Melissa Mahan, Texas A&M University, San Antonio

Introduction, Conclusion, and Overall Document

Susan R. Madsen, Utah Valley University
Melissa Mahan, Texas A&M University, San Antonio
Julia Storberg-Walker, George Washington University

Increasing Equality in Power and Decision-Making Section

Julia Storberg-Walker (Lead), George Washington University
Kristina Natt och Dag, Independent Scholar
Kathryn Goldman Schuyler, Alliant International University
Leah Levac, University of Guelph
Carmela Nanton, Carmel Connections Inc.

Helping Girls and Young Women Become Leaders Section

Steph Sharma (Lead), Lead The Difference
Kori Joneson, Lead The Difference
Molly McGowan, Rochester Institute of Technology
Katie Davidson, Cambridge University
Stephen Belding, University of Phoenix
Michelle Taylor, Utah Valley University

Expanding Leadership Education and Development Worldwide Section

Ann Austin (Lead), Utah State University
Lucie Newcomb, The NewComm Global Group, Inc.
Sherylle Tan, Claremont McKenna College
Shirlayne Quayle, Q3 International LLC
Maura Wolf, St. Mary's College of California

Advancing Women in Leadership Section

Denise Thomson (Co-Lead), DeWitt-Thomson, LLC
Anne Fitzpatrick (Co-Lead), Lead to Success
Elisabeth Sherwin, University of Arkansas at Little Rock
Shari Carpenter, Eastern Oregon University

Identifying Critical Areas for Future Research Section

Karen Longman (Lead), Azusa Pacific University
Mary Saunders, Texas Woman's University
Maylon Hanold, Seattle University
Rita Gardiner, The University of Western Ontario
Marcia Venegas-Garcia, California State University – San Marcos

3. Reflections on glass: second wave feminist theorizing in a third wave feminist age?
Savita Kumra

In this chapter, I will seek to explore the purpose and use of metaphors in the women and leadership literature. There is little doubt that the literature abounds with metaphors to describe, examine, and assess the various facilitators and barriers confronting women as they seek to forge their organizational careers. "Glass" has been particularly fruitful in this area. Coined in the 1980s, the "glass ceiling" provides the catch-all metaphor for the barriers confronting women, symbolizing their persistent presence while, at the same time, indicating their "invisibility" until experienced. As the nature of barriers confronting women has become better understood, the glass metaphor has been stretched to include glass cliffs, escalators, and walls.

This chapter seeks to assess the combined impact of these metaphors on women as they embark on their career journeys and assess whether they resonate with contemporary feminism. What the metaphors tend to have in common are their roots in liberal feminist discourses of the nature of systemic issues confronting women. However, times are changing and, with the rise of neoliberalism, there is evidence that many women are eschewing systemic explanations for their disadvantage. In this chapter, I thus discuss whether the glass metaphors have served their purpose and, as we progress from second wave liberal feminist ideologies to a third wave age, it is now time to look beyond the "glass" and seek to offer gender-based organizational analyses that take third wave theorizing into account.

GENDER DISCRIMINATION IN THE WORKPLACE: THE IMPORTANCE OF GLASS

One of the most dominant metaphors used to explain women's absence in senior organizational positions has been that of the glass ceiling. The glass ceiling is defined as "a barrier so subtle that it is transparent, yet so strong that it prevents women and minorities from moving up in the management hierarchy" (Morrison and Von Glinow, 1990, p. 200). There is little doubt that the glass ceiling has proven to be an alluring metaphor, and it has been utilized by countless studies to frame analysis of women's disadvantage spanning numerous national and organizational contexts. The metaphor has been expanded to more accurately reflect the nature of organizationally based gender disadvantage, and we now have literature addressing glass escalators, walls, and cliffs (e.g., Haslam and Ryan, 2008; Hewlett, 2007). This analysis will thus begin with an overview of a selection of these metaphors, identifying their definitions and development.

The Glass Ceiling

The glass ceiling, a term first introduced in the 1980s (Hymowitz and Schellhardt, 1986), provides a metaphorical description of the barriers women face as they seek to advance in their careers and the processes by which men continue to dominate the upper echelons of organizations (Bendl and Schmidt, 2010; Haveman and Beresford, 2012). The "ceiling" part of the metaphor alludes to the upper limit women can climb on the organizational ladder, while "glass" indicates the relative subtlety of these barriers, as being transparent they are not apparent to those encountering them (Barreto et al., 2009).

Countless studies have sought to examine the factors comprising the glass ceiling, with some indicating sex role stereotyping as a key influence on organizational members' perceptions of women's leadership potential (e.g., Eagly and Carli, 2003; Gorman, 2005; Powell et al., 2002). Social role theory (Eagly, 1987) is also frequently referenced as an explanation of societal constructions of the roles played by men and women in everyday life. This theory posits that behavioral gender differences are endorsed by socialization from a young age, where males are rewarded for achievement-oriented (or agentic) behavior, while females are rewarded for their emotional (or communal) orientation (see, for example, Eagly and Wood, 1999; Powell et al., 2002). This learned understanding of how men and women ought to behave directly impacts organizational processes such as selection, promotion, and reward (Agars, 2004; Powell et al., 2002). Jerlando et al. (2009) note that social role theory has been developed further to provide insight into key discriminatory processes (Frankforter, 1996; Morrison and Von Glinow, 1990). Thus, deficiency theory focuses on the ways women lack the characteristics required for leadership (Morrison and Von Glinow, 1990; Riger and Galligan, 1980), and based on these deficiencies, they receive unequal treatment. As discrimination is evident across society in general, it is unsurprising that these processes are mirrored in organizational practices (Graves and Powell, 1988; Morrison and Von Glinow, 1990).

Furthermore, consonant with role congruity theory (Eagly and Karau, 2002), women seeking advancement to executive levels are impacted by the effects of social stereotypes in two ways: firstly, they are perceived as too feminine for leadership roles; and secondly, the very fact they seek such roles undermines their femininity.

In seeking to determine whether a glass ceiling is evident or not, the work of Cotter et al. (2001) is instructional. They argue that the glass ceiling represents a specific type of inequality, which should be recognized as such. In order to distinguish the glass ceiling from other types of gender discrimination, they contend that four criteria must be met: (1) a gender difference that cannot be explained by other job-relevant employee characteristics; (2) a gender difference that has greater impact at higher levels than at lower levels of the organization; (3) a gender inequality that pertains to the chances of advancement into higher levels, not simply a reflection of the gender distribution presently at those levels; and (4) a gender inequality that increases as the career progresses.

From the preceding analysis of the glass ceiling, it is apparent that the metaphor has not been used to determine processual aspects of gender discrimination, but tends to assess discrimination from a structural perspective (Bendl and Schmidt, 2010). Consequently, the metaphor tends to depict discrimination as somewhat "static and discrete" (Bendl and Schmidt, 2010, p. 623). Since the processes of discrimination are not central to analysis, as the focus is rather on the structures within which discriminatory processes occur, the metaphor fails to consider potentially field-altering contextual factors and fluid phenomena (e.g., Linstead and Brewis, 2004). Thus, the metaphor can be viewed as a mechanism by which the status quo of discrimination in organizations is described; by concentrating on structural aspects, the centrality of "having" discrimination is emphasized (Bendl and Schmidt, 2010).

The Glass Cliff

Ryan and Haslam (2007) introduce the concept of the "glass cliff." By conducting experimental studies and archival analysis, they found that women are far more likely to be placed into risky leadership positions where the likelihood of failure is high. Their research came as a response to an article by Judge (2003) that contended corporations should be cautious when promoting women to senior board positions; her analysis showed that, of the ten companies with the highest number of women in board-level positions, six were underperforming relative to the mean performance of the FTSE 100. Conversely, the five companies with the lowest number of women represented at board level (that is, all male boards), were performing above the FTSE 100 average. Ryan and Haslam (2005) found that five of the six worst-performing companies cited in Judge's (2003) study had been underperforming prior to the appointment of a woman to a board position and, indeed, precarious organizational performance had been a key reason for appointing a woman. They provided systematic evidence to support their assertion and concluded that in crisis situations organizations may find it beneficial to depart from the old adage, "think manager, think male," and consider an alternative: "think crisis, think female." To support this contention, they cite evidence from Schein's (1973, 1975) original studies which indicate that there are some traits correlated with management success that are viewed by participants as more typical of women in general than men in general. "These included being understanding, helpful, sophisticated, aware of the feelings of others, intuitive, creative and cheerful" (Ryan and Haslam, 2007, p. 553); it is likely that many of these characteristics would be viewed as highly desirable in times of crisis.

In a study asking participants to describe the characteristics of managers best able to manage successful companies and those best able to manage unsuccessful companies, the "think manager, think male" association held for successful companies; however, for unsuccessful companies there was a very strong correlation with the female stereotype (Ryan et al., 2007). These findings also held for a number of other experimental studies conducted by the authors across a range of sectoral settings (that is, business and the legal profession), enabling them to conclude: "it is sufficient to emphasize that these experimental studies suggest that the processes that contribute to the selection of women for glass cliff appointments are not isolated to a particular context or participant group" (p. 554).

Ryan et al. (2007) draw attention to two issues emerging from the glass cliff phenomenon. Firstly, managers who offer women leadership opportunities will believe they are treating women favorably as they are providing them access to challenging and stretching assignments. Women themselves may also believe they are being offered a career-enhancing opportunity and thus feel unable to decline. Secondly, those in senior positions can deny any charge of not advancing women in their organizations, even though due to their precarity the opportunities they offer are of limited value. Seemingly, a dual success is achieved: the organization appears to be advancing the position of women, and there is little chance that gender hierarchies will actually be challenged or altered (Ryan and Haslam, 2007).

The second set of processes relates to group dynamics and in-group favoritism. The phenomenon may provide evidence that largely male power elites in organizations will reserve safer and more attractive positions for their fellow in-group members (that is, "jobs for the boys") (Balls, 1992; Gallagher, 1994; Powell and Butterfield, 2002), leaving out-group members to undertake the positions remaining. Organizational decision makers may be willing to appoint women to glass cliff positions as they make obvious scapegoats when things (inevitably) go wrong.

Glass Escalators and Walls

As glass ceiling theorizing has progressed, additional metaphors have been added to the lexicon of organizational gender discrimination. Less frequently discussed, but no less prevalent, are the concepts of "glass escalators" and "glass walls." The glass escalator (Ng and Wiesner, 2007; Williams, 1992) is a term developed to account for discrimination that women face in female-dominated occupations, and reflects the gender privilege minority males can experience through a faster promotional trajectory through the organizational hierarchy (Ng and Wiesner, 2007). Guillaume and Pochic (2009) explored the persistence of horizontal gender-based career segregation. By examining the feminization rate of careers, where women represented either more or less than 30 percent of the workforce, they found strong support for inequality on this basis, which they termed "glass walls." Because of glass walls, women tend toward certain occupations, such as human resources or marketing, which are unlikely to position them for senior positions (Miller et al., 1999).

THE PROBLEM WITH GLASS: WHY IS IT ALWAYS HALF EMPTY?

Reflecting on the origins of the "glass" metaphors aids analysis of both the reasons for their durability and the basis upon which their continued relevance is questioned. Based firmly on principles of liberal feminism, the "glass" metaphors seek to explore gender discrimination within a particular frame of analysis, based upon a number of key assumptions. Liberal feminism casts gender as an "unproblematic" categorization attaching to individuals (West and Fenstermaker, 1995), where inequality can be addressed in (what are perceived to be) gender-neutral organizations through identifying the causes of discrimination and taking action to address them.

The liberal feminist view is based upon an assumption that, as long as men and women are treated the same and women are provided with the same opportunities as men, differences in behaviors or attitudes will be eradicated (Davies, 2010). This is an individualist approach to feminism as it is based on an assumption that the actions and choices of individual women will be the catalyst to achieving equality. Within the liberal feminist perspective, gender equality does not need to be achieved by changing societal structures, as inequality is not believed to be the result of systemic discrimination. While an outcome

total devotion to work is rewarded and any hint that other factors in life are important (for example, family) is not. Sandberg's message is that those who succeed accept the status quo, take personal responsibility for adapting to the requirements of increasingly demanding organizations, fit family life around these demands (that is, never switch off even when on holiday and at weekends), and keep smiling while they do it.

Within this discourse, we thus see the "periodizing" of neoliberalism (Mann and Huffman, 2005). We sense its deeper penetration into core systems and processes and its embeddedness as a force for producing actors who are rational, calculating, and self-motivating; actors who are increasingly encouraged to interpret their individually lived experiences through discourses of freedom, autonomy, and choice no matter how constrained their lives may actually be (Rose, 1999). Questions of agency, therefore, are viewed as issues of key concern in postfeminist and neoliberal contexts that present women (particularly young women) as autonomous, agentic, and empowered subjects. The more traditional feminist vocabulary – that framed issues of inequality within processes embedded with structures, domination, and oppression – at times appears to be superseded by a more upbeat language. It is as if theorizing itself has become seduced by a postfeminist sensibility and fallen prey to the hype (Gill and Scharff, 2013). Thus, for some scholars, the direct call to personal responsibilization and individual agency (exhorted in Sandberg's book) requires consideration within the broader context of continued unequal power relations and inequality (e.g., Madhok, 2012). In addition, for others, the book is simply an extension of the deployment of the more positive and upbeat language of freedom and choice (Duits and Van Zoonen, 2006).

In the analysis of Hillary Clinton's campaign to secure the Democratic nomination and her failure to connect with younger women, who preferred her 74-year-old male rival Bernie Sanders, we see an unwillingness to identify on the basis of gender alone. This view can be attributed to a new set of perspectives developed to understand gender relations emerging from a critique of perceived inadequacies of the second wave (Mann and Huffman, 2005). From this perspective, third wave feminism arises from the observations and voices of feminists who considered themselves "against" as opposed to "after" the second wave (Koyama, 2003). These new discourses do not aim at undermining the feminist movement, but rather aim to make it more diverse and inclusive, to reposition and improve it (Mann and Huffman, 2005).

Similar to second wave feminism, the third wave encapsulates a variety of views and perspectives that combine to transform fundamentally contemporary understandings of gender. However, each approach has a number of foci in common, as each utilizes processes of difference, deconstruction, and decentering to aid analysis of modern-day feminism (Mann and Huffman, 2005). Four key perspectives most broadly represent third wave feminism: (1) intersectionality theory (Andersen and Collins, 1994; Collins, 1998), mainly developed by women of color and those from ethnic minority communities; (2) postmodernist and poststructuralist feminist approaches (Butler, 1992, 1993; Sedgwick, 1990); (3) feminist postcolonial theory, frequently referred to as global feminism (Eisenstein, 2010); and (4) a broader agenda representing the views of the new generation of younger feminists.

Within critiques of Hillary Clinton's appeal to younger women, we see elements of a number of these perspectives. Thus, in comments made about Clinton's inability to appeal to younger women on grounds other than purely gender, we see a clear reference to intersectionality perspectives. While liberal feminism has most notably been associated with white, middle-class women, intersectional approaches are able to deal with multiple aspects of individuals' identities and recognize that each element of identity encompasses elements of discrimination and privilege (Collins, 1998). By simply appealing to women on the basis of shared gender, Clinton missed the theoretical shift to a broader understanding of identity politics and a move away from the second wave reliance on essentialism and white solipsism (Mann and Huffman, 2005). She thus failed to access the support of younger women.

For younger feminists, though they frequently express their indebtedness to those who came before them (Baumgardner and Richards, 2000; Henry, 2003), their writing tends to reflect a view of second wave feminism as overly judgemental and restrictive. Findlen (1995), for example, points to a view prevalent among young women that "if something or someone is appealing, fun or popular, it or she can't be feminist" (p. xiv).

In her analysis of why younger women have rejected second wave feminism, Dent (1995) applies religious metaphors and presents the second wave as characterized by an austere "missionary feminism" that required self-policing, confession through consciousness-raising groups, and salvation through political action (p. 64). Consequently, it "puts forth its program so stridently, guards its borders so closely, and legislates its behaviour so fervently that many are afraid to declare its name" (Dent, 1995, p. 64, as cited in Mann and Huffman, 2005). In the second wave, the connection between the personal and the political required not only that personal issues should be politicized, but also that personal lifestyle choices should be reflective of and not undermine feminist political positioning. In contrast, the new generation seeks to broaden the appeal of feminism by adopting far less restrictive ideas, strategies, and ways of understanding feminism that spark condescension, disunity, and critical views from their second wave sisters (Baumgardner and Richards, 2000; Kaminer, 1995).

Within the Clinton campaign, this was most notable by the reaction to Madeleine Albright's observation that "There's a special place in hell for women who don't help each other" (as cited in Kozlowski, 2016). The widespread rejection of this assumption from younger feminists, and Albright's later retraction (Kozlowski, 2016), laid bare the rift between second wave liberal feminists and those from the third wave. To be exhorted to "fall in line" and throw their support behind a candidate they do not agree with, simply because they share gender in common, was viewed as an affront by younger women, who view feminism from a broader, more nuanced perspective.

CONCLUSION: IS THE GLASS HALF EMPTY OR HALF FULL?

In this chapter, I have explored the origins and explanations of a range of "glass" metaphors used to explain continued gender-based societal and organizational disadvantage and to explain why it might be that these metaphors require re-examination in the light of radical shifts in feminist thinking, most notably signaling a move from second wave to third wave theorizing. The "glass" metaphors share in common liberal feminist roots (Ahl, 2004; Davies, 2010) and see change coming about through sustained political and individual action. Thus, the value of the "glass" metaphors lies in their ability to identify the underlying causes of gender-based discrimination and provide a focus for collective and personal action. However, there is clear evidence that liberal feminism, as encompassed within second wave feminist perspectives, does not appeal to those forming the third wave; as discussed, this is most evident among younger women. They critique the approach on the grounds that it is narrow; appeals only to white, middle class women (e.g., Collins, 1998); establishment focused (Mann and Huffman, 2005); and undermines personal agency (e.g., Baumgardner and Richards, 2000). They can also point to the "tortuously slow rate of change" (e.g., EHRC, 2011) as evidence that the approach has made few inroads in practice, and the promised legal and political reforms have had little material impact on the lives of the vast majority of women.

However, in my view, it is important to be mindful that the alternatives also have yet to deliver material alterations in women's day-to-day lives. With little practical evidence of how this is to be achieved, they may simply represent a more attractive and optimistic offer to third wave feminists seeking to break from the perceived problems with second wave theorization (that is, lack of individual agency, freedom, choice, and empowerment) (Gill and Scharff, 2013). Although Sandberg's step-by-step guide to success may sound alluring, such efforts may do little to systemically challenge or unsettle the existing gender order. If they have an impact at all, it will likely be at the individual level. This is because the approach is based on neoliberal principles of individual responsibility and a drive to produce rational, calculating, self-motivating actors; who are required to interpret their individually lived experiences through discourses of freedom, autonomy, and choice regardless of how constrained their lives may actually be (Rose, 1999). In such an approach, we see little acknowledgement of differential power relations or adoption of the core principles embedded within broader third wave feminist theorizing, such as intersectionality, postmodernist, or poststructuralist accounts.

I would thus endorse Mann and Huffman's (2005) caution, that to ignore the exhortation from second wave feminists that the "personal is political" is not without peril. They point to the work of Dicker and Piepmeier, who refer to this approach as a "feminist free-for-all that empties feminism of any core set of values and politics" (Dicker and Piepmeier, 2003, p. 17). They contend that to challenge perceptions of what feminism is or to seek to move away from some of the more judgemental and preaching aspects of second wave feminism – by engaging in a more playful and individualistic way – has some merit. However, feminist thinking must of necessity take into account the power relations surrounding gender, race, class, and sexual orientation. Thus feminism, by definition, seeks to contain a political stance in that it aims to transform at both the individual and societal levels (Dicker and Piepmeier, 2003).

I thus believe that the "glass" metaphors have their place; however, we need to be aware of not just their strengths, but also their limitations in practice. It is important to note how disempowering these approaches can be to young women seeking to make their way in organizations and broader society. There is undoubtedly evidence that these approaches are rejected by millennials who favor third wave explanations encompassing intersectional, postcolonial, postmodernist and poststructuralist, and global perspectives. Neoliberal principles also have appeal, for the perceived optimism they offer and the personal agency they promise.

I would thus call for novel approaches, which ensure that a new generation of women are not disappointed when they take charge of their careers within the neoliberal narrative of empowerment, freedom, and choice (Gill and Scharff, 2013). An alternative narrative should be available that ensures they do not work hard to overcome barriers at a personal level which can only be countered at the societal or structural level. It may thus be time to let go of the "glass" metaphors developed to aid understanding and act as a focus for action, but which actually combine to make organizations forbidding and disempowering sites of endeavor for women simply seeking a fair chance to succeed. What we replace them with will unfold as time goes on; however, what seems clear is that we need to build in optimism and opportunity for personal agency, while ensuring that we do not separate the personal from the political.

REFERENCES

Acker, J. (1990). Hierarchies, jobs, bodies: A theory of gendered organizations. *Gender and Society, 4*(2), 139–158.

Agars, M.D. (2004). Reconsidering the impact of gender stereotypes on the advancement of women in organizations. *Psychology of Women Quarterly, 28*(2), 103–111.

Ahl, H.J. (2004). *The Scientific Reproduction of Gender Inequality: A Discourse Analysis of Research Articles on Women's Entrepreneurship.* Copenhagen, Denmark: Copenhagen Business School Press.

Alvesson, M., and Due Billing, Y. (1999). *Kön och organisation.* Lund, Sweden: Studentlitteratur.

Andersen, M., and Collins, P.H. (Eds). (1994). *Race, Class and Gender: An Anthology.* New York, NY: Wadsworth.

Balls, E. (1992). Economics of failure: No jobs for the boys. *New Statesman and Society, 5*(217) 14.

Barreto, M., Ryan, M.K., and Schmitt, M.T. (2009). Introduction: Is the glass ceiling still relevant in the 21st century?. In M. Barreto, M.K. Ryan, and M.T. Schmitt (Eds), *The Glass Ceiling in the 21st Century: Understanding Barriers to Gender Equality* (pp. 3–19). Washington, DC: American Psychological Association.

Baumgardner, J., and Richards, A. (2000). *ManifestA: Young Women, Feminism and the Future.* New York, NY: Farrar, Strauss, & Giroux.

Bendl, R., and Schmidt, A. (2010). From "glass ceilings" to "firewalls" – different metaphors for describing discrimination. *Gender, Work and Organization, 17*(5), 612–634.

Butler, J. (1992). Contingent foundations: Feminism and the question of postmodernism. In J. Butler and J.W. Scott (Eds), *Feminists Theorize the Political* (pp. 3–21). New York, NY: Routledge.

Butler, J. (1993) *Bodies that Matter.* New York, NY: Routledge.

Catalyst. (2013a). *Catalyst Census: Fortune 500 Women Board Directors.* New York, NY: Catalyst Knowledge Center.

Catalyst. (2013b). *2013 Catalyst Census: Fortune 500 Women Executive Officers and Top Earners.* New York, NY: Catalyst Knowledge Center.

Catalyst. (2014). Increasing gender diversity on boards: Current index of formal approaches. Catalyst Knowledge Center. Retrieved from http://www.catalyst.org/knowledge/increasing-gender-diversity-boards-current-index-formal-approaches.

Collins, P.H. (1998). *Fighting Words: Black Women and the Search for Justice.* Minneapolis, MN: University of Minnesota Press.

Cotter, D.A., Hermsen, J.M., Ovadia, S., and Vanneman, R. (2001). The glass ceiling effect. *Social Forces, 80*(2), 655–681.

Davies, A. (2010). Liberal feminism. In A.J. Mills, G. Durepos, and E. Wiebe (Eds), *Encyclopaedia of Case Study Research* (pp. 526–528). Thousand Oaks, CA: Sage.

Dent, G. (1995). Missionary position. In R. Walker (Ed.), *To be Real: Telling the Truth and Changing the Face of Feminism* (pp. 61–76). New York, NY: Anchor Books.

Dicker, R., and Piepmeier, A. (2003). *Catching a Wave: Reclaiming Feminism for the 21st Century.* Boston, MA: Northeastern University Press.

Duits, L., and Van Zoonen, L. (2006). Headscarves and porno-chic: disciplining girls' bodies in the European multicultural society. *European Journal of Women's Studies, 13*(2), 103–117.

Eagly, A.H. (1987). *Sex Differences in Social Behavior: A Social Role Interpretation.* Hillsdale, NJ: Erlbaum.

Eagly, A.H., and Carli, L.L. (2003). The female leadership advantage: An evaluation of the evidence. *Leadership Quarterly, 14*(6), 807–834.

Eagly, A.H., and Karau, S.J. (2002). Role congruity theory of prejudice toward female leaders. *Psychological Review, 109*(3), 573–598.

Eagly, A.H., and Wood, W. (1999). The origins of sex differences in human behavior: Evolved dispositions versus social roles. *American Psychologist*, *54*(6), 408–423.

Eisenstein, H. (2010). *Feminism Seduced: How Global Elites use Women's Labor and Ideas to Exploit the World.* Boulder, CO: Paradigm Publishers.

Ely, R.J., and Meyerson, D.E. (2000). Theories of gender in organizations: A new approach to organizational analysis and change. *Research in Organizational Behavior*, *22*(2), 103–151.

Equality and Human Rights Commission (EHRC). (2011). Sex and power report. EHRC, UK. Retrieved from https://www.equalityhumanrights.com/en/publication-download/sex-and-power-.

European Commission. (2013). National factsheet: Gender balance in boards. Retrieved from http://ec.europa.eu/justice/gender-equality/files/womenonboards/womenonboards-factsheet-uk_en.pdf.

Findlen, B. (1995). *Listen Up: Voices from the Next Feminist Generation.* Seattle, WA: Seal Press.

Fischer, E.M., Reuber, A.R., and Dyke, L.S. (1993). A theoretical overview and extension of research on sex, gender and entrepreneurship. *Journal of Business Venturing*, *8*(2), 151–168.

Frankforter, S.A. (1996). The progression of women beyond the glass ceiling. *Journal of Social Behavior and Personality*, *11*(5), 121–132.

Gallagher, J. (1994). QUANGOS: Jobs for the boys. *New Statesman and Society*, *7*(327), 16.

Garcia, V. (2013). Why I won't lean in. *Huffington Post*, July 19. Retrieved from http://www.huffingtonpost.com/vanessa-garcia/why-i-wont-lean-in_b_3586527.html.

Gill, R., and Scharff, C. (Eds). (2013). *New Femininities: Postfeminism, Neoliberalism and Subjectivity.* Basingstoke, UK: Palgrave Macmillan.

Gorman, E. (2005). Gender stereotypes, same gender preferences, and organizational variation in the hiring of women: Evidence of law firms. *American Sociological Review*, *70*(5), 702–728.

Government Statistics. (n.d.). Retrieved from https://www.gov.uk/government/ministers (accessed April 2016).

Graves, L.M., and Powell, G.N. (1988). An investigation of sex discrimination in recruiters' evaluations of actual applicants. *Journal of Applied Psychology*, *73*(1), 20–29.

Guillaume, C., and Pochic, S. (2009). What would you sacrifice? Access to top management and the work–life balance. *Gender, Work and Organization*, *16*(1), 14–36.

Halford, S., and Leonard, P. (2001). *Gender, Power and Organisations.* London, UK: Palgrave Macmillan.

Haslam, S.A., and Ryan, M.K. (2008). The road to the glass cliff: Differences in the perceived suitability of men and women for leadership positions in succeeding and failing organizations. *Leadership Quarterly*, *19*(5), 530–546.

Haveman, H.A., and Beresford, L.S. (2012). If you're so smart, why aren't you the boss? Explaining the persistent vertical gender gap in management. *The ANNALS of the American Academy of Political and Social Science*, *639*(1), 114–130.

Henry, A. (2003). Feminism's family problem: Feminist generations and the mother-daughter trope. In R. Dicker and A. Piepmeier (Eds), *Catching a Wave: Reclaiming Feminism for the 21st Century* (pp. 209–231). Boston, MA: Northeastern University Press.

Hewlett, S.A. (2007). *Off-Ramps and On-Ramps: Keeping Talented Women on the Road to Success.* Cambridge, MA: Harvard Business School Press.

Hymowitz, C., and Schellhardt, C. (1986). The glass ceiling: Why women can't seem to break the invisible barrier that blocks them from the top jobs. *Wall Street Journal*, March 24.

Jerlando, P., Jackson, J.F., and O'Callaghan, E.M. (2009). What do we know about glass ceiling effects? A taxonomy and critical review to inform higher education research. *Research in Higher Education*, *50*(5), 460–482.

Judge, E. (2003). Women on board: Help or hindrance? *The Times*, November 11, p. 21.

Kaminer, W. (1995). Feminisms 3rd-wave – What do young women want?. *New York Times Book Review*, June 4, p. 3.

Kanter, R.M. (1977). *Men and Women of the Corporation*, New York, NY: Basic Books.

Kollewe, J. (2015). Women represent less than 10% of executive directors in FTSE 100 companies. *Guardian*, December 29. Retrieved from https://www.theguardian.com/business/2015/dec/29/women-in-uk-boardrooms-executive-directors-ftse-100-companies.

Koyama, E. (2003). The transfeminist manifesto. In R. Dicker and A. Piepmeier (Eds), *Catching a Wave: Reclaiming Feminism for the 21st Century* (pp. 244–259). Boston, MA: Northeastern University Press.

Kozlowski, H. (2016). Why young women reject Hillary Clinton's brand of feminism. February 24. Retrieved from http://qz.com/623503.

Kulik, C.T., and Metz, I. (forthcoming). Women at the top: Will more women in senior roles impact organizational outcomes?. In M.A. Hitt, S.E. Jackson, S. Carmona, L. Bierman, C.E. Shalley, and M. Wright (Eds), *The Oxford Handbook of Strategy Implementation*, Oxford: Oxford University Press.

Linstead, A., and Brewis, J. (2004). Editorial: Beyond boundaries: Towards fluidity in theorizing and practice. *Gender, Work and Organization*, *11*(4), 355–362.

Madhok, S. (2012). *Rethinking Agency: Developmentalism, Gender and Rights.* New York, NY, USA and London, UK: Routledge.

Mann, S.A., and Huffman, D.J. (2005). The decentering of second wave feminism and the rise of the third wave. *Science and Society*, *69*(1), 56–91.

Miller, W., Kerr, B., and Reid, M. (1999). A national study of gender-based occupational segregation in municipal bureaucracies: Persistence of glass walls?. *Public Administration Review*, *59*(3), 218–230.

Morrison, A.M., and Von Glinow, M.A. (1990). Women and minorities in management. *American Psychologist*, *45*(2), 200–208.

Ng, E., Schweitzer, L., and Lions, S.T. (2010). New generation, great expectations: A field study of the millennial generation. *Journal of Business Psychology*, *25*(2), 281–292.

Ng, E.S., and Wiesner, W.H. (2007). Are men always picked over women? The effects of employment equity directives on selection decisions. *Journal of Business Ethics*, *76*(2), 177–187.

Powell, G.N., and Butterfield, D.A. (2002). Exploring the influence of decision makers' race and gender on actual promotions to top management. *Personnel Psychology*, *55*(2), 397–428.

Powell, G.N., Butterfield, D.A., and Parent, J.D. (2002). Gender and managerial stereotypes: Have the times changed?. *Journal of Management*, *28*(2), 177–193.

Riger, S., and Galligan, P. (1980). Women in management: An exploration of competing paradigms. *American Psychologist*, *35*(10), 902–910.

Rose, N. (1999). *The Powers of Freedom*. London, UK: Routledge.

Ryan, M.K., and Haslam, S.A. (2005). The glass cliff: Evidence that women are over-represented in precarious leadership positions. *British Journal of Management*, *16*(2), 81–90.

Ryan, M., and Haslam, A. (2007). The glass cliff: Exploring the dynamics surrounding the appointment of women to precarious leadership positions. *Academy of Management Review*, *32*(2), 549–572.

Ryan, M.K., Haslam, S.A., and Postmes, T. (2007). Reactions to the glass cliff: Gender differences in the explanations for the precariousness of women's leadership positions. *Journal of Organizational Change Management*, *20*(3), 182–197.

Sandberg, S. (2013). *Lean In: Women, Work and the Will to Lead*. New York, NY: Alfred A. Knopf.

Schein, V.E. (1973). The relationship between sex role stereotypes and requisite management characteristics. *Journal of Applied Psychology*, *57*(2), 95–100.

Schein, V.E. (1975). Relationships between sex role stereotypes and requisite management characteristics among female managers. *Journal of Applied Psychology*, *60*(3), 340–344.

Sedgwick, E. (1990). *Epistemology of the Closet*. Berkeley, CA: University of California Press.

Wallace, S. (2014). Tackling unconscious bias in banking. *HR Magazine*, September 3. Retrieved from http://www.hrmagazine.co.uk/hro/features/1146334/tackling-unconscious-bias-banking.

West, C., and Fenstermaker, S. (1995). Doing difference. *Gender and Society*, *9*(1), 8–37.

Williams, C. (2014). The happy marriage of capitalism and feminism. *Contemporary Sociology: A Journal of Reviews*, *43*(1), 58–61.

Williams, C.L. (1992). The glass escalator: Hidden advantages for men in the "female" professions. *Social Problems*, *39*(3), 253–267.

Williams, Z. (2013). *Lean In: Women, Work and the Will to Lead* by Sheryl Sandberg – Review. *Guardian*, March 13. Retrieved from https://www.theguardian.com/books/2013/mar/13/lean-in-sheryl-sandberg-review.

World Economic Forum. (2013). *The Global Gender Gap Report, 2013*. Geneva, Switzerland: World Economic Forum.

PART II

ADVANCING WOMEN AND LEADERSHIP THEORY

4. Creativity in theorizing for women and leadership: a multi-paradigm perspective

Julia Storberg-Walker and Kristina Natt och Dag

Leadership theory helps us to develop leaders (Ely et al., 2011), helps us to make decisions (Craig and Tracy, 2014), and helps us to predict events in the future (Christensen and Raynor, 2003). Paradoxically, theory is also derided for being too abstract (Schwartzman, 2006), for not producing practical knowledge (Kennelly, 2009), and for being "largely ideological prescriptions merely reflecting researchers' philosophical views" (Hannah et al., 2014, p. 599). To some, theory is dead (Swedberg, 2012), and others insist that "nothing is quite so practical as a good theory" (Van de Ven, 1989, p. 486).

Theories can generate good knowledge, but how the knowledge is interpreted is not consistent (Coder and Spiller, 2013). For example, Coder and Spiller found that one theoretical foundation undergirding women and leadership (that is, gender role stereotypes) has generated three alternative narratives: (1) leadership literature represents a male-normed reality; (2) women leaders are more effective than male leaders; and (3) there are no gender differences in leadership. These alternative narratives illustrate an example of how scholars holding different paradigms interpret theory differently. Paradigms fundamentally shape how scholars understand theory, and we illustrate how theories from different paradigms have contributed to women and leadership theory in the second main section of the chapter. What is important here, however, is to note that the wide diversity can make it difficult to discern the essence of theory and the process of theorizing. In short, the different perspectives make the process of analyzing and synthesizing theory methodologically complicated (Paterson et al., 2009).

These inconsistent and paradoxical views can and do drive people away from the topic of theory, consequently diminishing the potential for theoretically informed practice. We believe, however, and we hope this chapter convinces readers, that generating theory – a practice called theorizing – is one of the most important habits of mind for both researchers and practitioners. We make this argument as a general prescription for more impactful and relevant theory for women leaders.

We have found ways to understand and clarify some of the complex and abstract ideas pertaining to theory and theorizing, which we present in this chapter. At the same time, we illustrate the profound connections between thinking and doing, and between research and practice. To accomplish these goals, we have organized the chapter into three main sections. The first section below introduces the chapter and describes the importance of theorizing. It provides a foundation for readers on the processes of theorizing that they can apply to their current research interests and suggests that creativity and complexity are necessary ingredients for twenty-first-century theorizing. Creativity in the theorizing process is supported by a number of recognized and reflective scholars (e.g., Swedberg, 2012; Weick, 1989, 1999), and we argue that creativity is the most important skill needed for theorizing (for example, generating new theory). In the theorizing context, creativity is the ability of the theorist to make new connections; challenge internal and external assumptions; probe from multiple angles; and follow insights, hunches, and instincts. Complexity in the theorizing process is suggested by Alhadeff-Jones (2013a, 2013b) and affirmed by a George Washington University Think Tank (held in July of 2015) focused on advancing women and leadership theory. Theorizing is facing increased complexity because of the need for contextual and intersectional knowledge creation. Complexity in this context is a position adopted by the theorist to resist the scientific norm of parsimony and the pull to simplify or reduce complicated realities. We argue that reductionist social science of the twentieth century is ending, and the twenty-first century heralds a new wave of complexity in understanding the world.

In the second section of the chapter, we illuminate how research from different paradigms has contributed to women and leadership theory. We present an analysis of the most highly cited (per the Social Science Citation Index, SSCI) women and leadership scholarly articles. Through this analysis we weave together the different methods, epistemologies, and disciplines that are contributing to theorizing women and leadership. Our analysis uses Burrell and Morgan's (1979) four-quadrant paradigm model as well as Swedberg's (2012) two-context framework. In selecting the articles, we assumed that citation count was a proxy for influence: the higher the citation count, the more influence. Our assumption could be called into question, and other criticisms focused on ideological diversity and journal rankings could also be brought forward. However, we position this analysis both as a modest contribution of the state of women and leadership theory, and also as an example or template for readers to use in the future for their own theoretical analysis or theorizing process.

The third and final section of the chapter highlights how multiple paradigms have contributed to women and leadership theory. This section offers implications from the Burrell and Morgan analysis and provides suggestions for continuing to move the needle forward on theorizing women and leadership. We suggest, for example, that future theory and theorizing analysis could include a review of book chapters, journals, and articles that are not recognized by the SSCI but yet are contributing to strengthening the women and leadership theory base.

A PRIMER ON THEORIZING: MOVING TOWARD CREATIVITY AND COMPLEXITY

The topic of how to build theory has been discussed and debated in multiple disciplines in the social sciences. Whole issues of leading academic journals have been devoted to this topic (see, for example, the *Academy of Management Review* special issues on theory: Whetten, 1989; Smith, 1999). Simply put, most scholars (even today) are trained in some variation on this two-phased theorizing process: (1) create new theory; and (2) test new theory. The first theorizing phase has been labeled the "context of discovery" and phase two the "context of justification." As we describe in this chapter, these phases combine in the theorizing process and are in constant relationship to each other. At the same time, the phases demand different skills and are guided by different goals. For example, according to Swedberg (2012), "creativity is primarily what matters when a theory is devised; and scientific logic and rigor is primarily what matters in the context of justification" when a new theory is tested (p. 6).

Over the years, phase two has been the focus of theorizing efforts, and the lack of attention on phase one has generated negative consequences for theorizing (Weick, 1989). Popper (2013), Reichenbach (1951), and others, including Friedman (1999) and Merton (1967), legitimated the emphasis on the context of justification as the center of social science theorizing. Consequently, the context of discovery has been a neglected research focus in social science research ever since (Swedberg, 2012). This imbalance has generated negative consequences for social science in general and women and leadership theory in particular. For example, Harding (1987) suggested that the focus on the context of justification has "contribute[d] to partial and distorted explanations and understandings" (p. 183) and perpetuated male-normed or androcentric social theories and methods. Smith (1987) likewise illuminated how scientific thinking and conceptualizing are male-normed. Both partial explanations and male-normed approaches are clearly illuminated in the leadership literature, with a well-documented history of *he*-roic leaders.

The context of discovery is also important to women, and leadership theorists especially, since the emergence and legitimization of different ways of knowing (epistemologies) and the acknowledgement of the connection between knowledge and power. Specifically, women's ways of knowing, as presented by Belenky et al. (1986), lays the foundation for a different way of doing and learning leadership for women; and feminist theory and other critical perspectives argue convincingly of the relationship between power, language, and knowledge. Further, newer critical perspectives such as critical race theory, intersectionality theory, and post-colonial theory add multiple and alternative epistemologies and knowledge–power relations. All of these newer ideas and perspectives have increased the complexity of the research as well as the theorizing processes.

Unfortunately, however, our collective understanding of how to theorize in the context of discovery phase has continued to lag behind the empirical methods associated with the context of justification phase. Swedberg (2012) suggests there are two obstacles or epistemological barriers that have perpetuated this status quo: first, social scientists are told that "to theorize one has to proceed in a scientific or logical manner" (p. 6); second, we are told that "empirical data should enter the research process first in the context of justification . . . [in order] to steer free from 'mindless empiricism' or the production of facts without any theory" (p. 6). To overcome these two barriers, Swedberg argues strongly that theorists need to embrace non-rational, non-linear practices during the discovery phase; in fact, he values imagination, free association, and all manner of theorist-generated ideas during this phase. Further, he suggests drawing on data during the theorizing phase in order to connect the emerging theory as closely as possible to observed facts.

We agree with Swedberg's (2012) recommendations, and readers interested in learning more details are urged to read his article in full. More theorists are needed to challenge the assumptions undergirding the focus on justification, because we believe that the focus on justification has contributed to the "suppress[ion of] generative debate and the creation of new and alternative theories" (Hibbert et al., 2014, p. 278) and prevented the emergence of "new and possibly more contextualized theoretical insights" (p. 279). Further, the focus on justification does not demand that scholars be trained to wrestle with understanding the relationship between knowledge and power, nor does it require us to develop reflective and reflexive practices as social science researchers.

In sum, scholars have produced a myriad of leadership theories in scholarly articles and books grounded in the context of justification, but there are very few scholars from any discipline who have focused on the context of discovery (Karl Weick being a notable exception) or the epistemological relationship between the theorist and the theory (see Storberg-Walker, 2006, 2007). Leadership theory remains guided by the need for justification over discovery, as illustrated by Avolio et al. (2009), even though those scholars and others (e.g., Hannah et al., 2014) have begun to affirm the necessity of future-focused theory and to articulate the need for both idealism and pragmatism in developing new theories of leadership. Despite this new movement, however, the leadership field continues to wrestle with how to integrate logical and rigorous cognitive processes (that is, in the context of justification) with non-logical, creative, and inspirational processes (that is, in the context of discovery) in their theorizing practices. We address this issue next and suggest that theorizing leadership for women provides a unique and strong position for scholars to help the field of leadership to adopt a more balanced appreciation of both contexts.

Toward Creativity and Complexity

We know from the discussion above that two epistemological barriers have prevented social scientists from fully exploring and embracing the context of discovery in theorizing. What we have not fully addressed are the consequences of these two barriers. First, because social theorists have been firmly tied to the cognitive and rational focus of logical empiricism, non-logical and non-cognitive ways of knowing (that is, epistemologies) have not been viewed as legitimate ways to build new theory. Smith (1987) argued that the act of thinking and conceptualizing itself is male-normed, and that "methods, conceptual schemes, and theories [have] been based on and built up within the male social universe" (pp. 85–86). This bias has served to privilege logic and cognition over other types of knowledge and sources of evidence and data, and consequently has limited our ability to generate the leadership theories needed for women and girls based on their (our) ways of knowing and perceiving.

Second, because of the focus on justification, scholars have an unexamined reliance on complexity reduction. Social scientists seek to reduce complex realities into understandable chunks in order to explain, predict, or control them. Reducing complexity is equated to parsimony, which is one of the eight criteria for judging a good theory from a bad theory (Patterson, 1986). In this view, "parsimony . . . means that the theory contains a minimum of complexity and few assumptions" (p. xx), and Patterson's list of criteria is routinely used today as a tool to evaluate theories (Lincoln and Lynham, 2011). Theories that are not considered parsimonious are viewed as less effective or less contributory because of the unquestioned belief in the need to reduce the complexity of social theories.

We argue for the need of both non-rational thought (for example, creativity needed for the context of discovery) and complexity in theorizing. We present a different way to generate theory, and we believe that both creativity and complexity are necessary ingredients for theorists in the twenty-first century. As described by Swedberg (2012):

> what to [Reichenbach and Popper] and their followers became a reason to ignore the context
> of discovery – it only takes you away from rigor, logic, and proof – can also be seen as an

Table 4.1   Theoretical analysis of highly cited women and leadership articles

Author (Year)	Theories	Burrell and Morgan methods	Burrell and Morgan axiology	Context of discovery or justification	Theorizing
Eagly and Karau (2002)	Presenting role congruity theory	Conceptual: functionalist and interpretivist	Radical humanist	Discovery	Two forms of prejudice: women are perceived less favorably for leadership roles; evaluating leadership less favorably when done by a woman.
Hyde (2005)	Testing gender similarities; hypothesis testing	Functionalist	Functionalist	Justification	Argues that there are overinflated claims of gender differences.
Eagly and Johnson (1990)	Leadership styles theory; presenting social role theory	Functionalist	Radical humanist (for women); radical structuralist (critique of experimental research findings)	Justification and discovery	Connecting leadership styles theory with social role theory.
Eagly et al. (1992)	Gender role; congruency theory	Functionalist	Radical humanist	Justification and discovery	Theorizing the connection between evaluating leaders and gender role congruency theory.
Heilman (2001)	Gender stereotype theory	Interpretive	Functionalist	Discovery	Theorizing that gender bias in evaluations are descriptive (what women are like) and prescriptive (what women should be like).
Eagly et al. (2003)	Leadership styles (transformational, transactional, laissez-faire)	Functionalist	Radical humanist	Justification and discovery	Theorizing the connection between leadership styles and effectiveness.
Eagly et al. (1995)	Social role theory of sex differences	Functionalist	Radical structuralist	Justification and discovery	Theorizing the connection between leadership effectiveness and social-role theory of sex differences.
Heilman et al. (2004)	Gender stereotypes theory	Functionalist	Functionalist	Justification and discovery	Theorizing that gender stereotypes negatively impact evaluating women leaders.

Table 4.1   (continued)

Author (Year)	Theories	Burrell and Morgan methods	Burrell and Morgan axiology	Context of discovery or justification	Theorizing
Chattopadhyay and Duflo (2004)	Political interest	Functionalist	Radical structuralist	Justification and discovery	Theorizing role of gender in policy making.
Rosener (1990)	Interactive leadership	Interpretive	Interpretive	Discovery	Theorizing the experience of interactive leadership.
Eagly and Karau (1991)	Leadership emergence	Functionalist	Radical humanist	Justification and discovery	Theorizing the connection between leading and gender in teams.

description of these two important dimensions are urged to review the original text. For the purposes of this chapter, it is sufficient to note that the subjective/objective dimension is a way to classify theories along a spectrum from realism/positivism (post-positivism) to interpretivism/social constructivism. The regulation/radical change dimension can be thought of as a way to classify theories along a spectrum from accepting the status quo to contesting the status quo. Burrell and Morgan's (1979) model has two dimensions as crossed axes, resulting in four quadrants. The four quadrants represent four different types of paradigms, and for the purposes of this chapter, these four paradigms represent four different worldviews or sets of assumptions undergirding the research that has contributed to our understanding of women leaders. The next paragraphs provide an overview of each paradigm with general commentary about how women and leadership theorizing can be informed by considering multiple paradigms during the theorizing process.

Functionalist paradigm
Theories developed from a functionalist paradigm are not likely to resonate with women or provide routes toward gender equality in leadership positions. However, as will be described below, functionalist empirical research has generated significant findings that continue to contribute to the theorizing process. A functionalist perspective, therefore, is important for the second phase of theorizing but tends to be limiting in the first phase.

In Burrell and Morgan's four-quadrant framework, the functionalist paradigm is "characterized by a concern for providing explanations of the status quo, social order, (and) consensus" (Burrell and Morgan, 1979, p. 26). Theories classified in this paradigm are developed by theorists who "tend to be realist, positivist, (and) determinist" (p. 26). In this paradigm, order, equilibrium, and stability in society are key assumptions that are based on a realist approach applying rational explanations and knowledge.

In terms of relating the functionalist paradigm to women and leadership theory, it is important to note that Burrell and Morgan's work was first published in 1979, and our understanding of gender and leadership has advanced significantly since then. With that in mind, we interpret the functionalist paradigm in two different ways when considering

Table 4.2 *Theoretical analysis of women and leadership theories represented in Chapters 5–8*

Ch.	Discipline	Burrell and Morgan methods	Burrell and Morgan axiology	Swedberg phase	Research foci	Theories/models	Emerging new ideas and foci	View of leadership
5	Social psychology	Functionalist	Radical humanist (social psychologists work to theoretically understand and reduce inequality)	Phase one: creating (for prescriptive research) Phase two: testing (for descriptive research)	1. Leadership differences 2. Barriers facing women 3. Stereotypes 4. Boundary conditions of gender bias	Lack of fit model Role congruity theory Social role theory Stereotype threat (descriptive and prescriptive)	Intersectional research Gendering of race Situational and contextual factors of stereotype threat Identity safety	Leadership is an individual characteristic Leadership is influenced by social norms and expectations
6	Sociology (political and economic sociology subfields)	Functionalist Interpretivist	Radical structuralist (sociologists work to understand the forces that produce inequality)	Phase one: creating (for conceptualizing and theorizing) Phase two: testing (for descriptive)	1. Factors contributing to gender bias 2. Experiences of women leaders 3. Factors constraining women's ability to lead effectively 4. Cultural view of social reproduction 5. Dramaturgical and ethnomethodological view of social reproduction	Weber's theory of authority and theory of bureaucracy C. Wright Mills' power Elite Theory Bourdieu's theory of habitus Acker's gender/inequality regimes Kanter's tokenism theory Social network theory	Foci on power, inequality, and structural forces Unconscious bias Status characteristic theory Token theory (and homosocial reproduction)	Leadership is a social relationship, not a characteristic of the individual Leadership is constrained by cultural and normative beliefs
7	Applied linguistics	Interpretivist Radical Humanist	Radical structuralist (assuming language is a structure)	Phase two: testing	1. How women use language to perform leadership	Dominance theory (language constructs men as natural-born leaders)	Social constructionist orientations ("cyborg") Reclaiming archetypes	Leadership is performed through language Leadership identity is created through language

Table 4.2 (continued)

Ch.	Discipline	Burrell and Morgan methods	Burrell and Morgan axiology	Swedberg phase	Research foci	Theories/models	Emerging new ideas and foci	View of leadership
					2. How language is used to represent women leaders 3. Understanding metaphors 4. Interaction styles 5. How women are evaluated differently from men when making linguistic choices	Difference theory (men and women use language differently but complementarily when performing leadership) Discourse theory (discursive, social constructionist, or performative)	Challenging difference theory's reliance on male/female binary Gendered discourses Language is a set of resources to draw from	Language is the medium through which leadership identities are performed Language is a means to construct barriers to women leaders Discourse practices are gendered; people are not
8	Organizational science (borrows from multiple disciplines)	Functionalist Interpretivist Radical Humanist Radical Structuralist	Functionalist Interpretivist Radical Humanist Radical Structuralist	Phase two: testing (for descriptive research) Phase one: creating (for conceptualizing and theorizing)	1. Differences between men and women 2. How leadership theories are gendered 3. How social exchange theory is gendered 4. How social relationships are maintained 5. How organizations are male-normed 6. How institutional barriers prevent women from advancing to leadership positions	Emotional intelligence Leadership theories Social exchange theory Network theory Institutionalization theory	Need more research on how popular leadership theories influence leading and how they influence perceptions of women leaders Leadership development for women Gendered nature of organizational citizenship behaviors	Leadership can be researched as an individual phenomenon or as a social exchange or as a consequent of institutional structure

are either in focused one or two paradigms in general. It is clear that the scholarly contributions of these disciplines have added to our collective understanding of the issues facing women leaders; consequently, our call in this chapter for multiple paradigms is supported.

Our analysis also suggests that complexity is increasing in terms of the diversity of research questions, the multiple levels of analysis, and a proliferation of theoretical foundations. These findings support our call for diversity of research as well as our call for resisting the automatic pull for scientific reductionism. Finally, our analysis also provides a meta-theoretical view of the four chapters that would have been invisible without this analytical attempt. As reflexivity is called for as a key aspect in the first phase of theorizing (Swedberg, 2012), our analysis and resulting table may be thought of as a tool to generate future theoretical insights, ideas, and associations.

We assert that reviewing scholarly articles with the intention to theorize can generate the creativity needed for innovative new theories. In this chapter, we have presented a format for this type of analysis and described in detail how theories connect to paradigms. We suggested that the interests of the researcher should be analyzed, and we based this suggestion on the need for changes in overall theorizing as well as women and leadership theory. We offered suggestions for readers to use and modify our analytical process to meet their own theorizing needs, and we analyzed the contributions of four different disciplines to highlight the need for multi-paradigm research as well as the need to accept complexity.

We believe that, like all scholarly theories, women-centered leadership theories should be connected to evidence and crafted with rigor. Unlike previous generations of scholarly theorists, however, women-centered leadership theorists must look forward and accept the great responsibility of influencing the future of humankind. The future will not be one of consensus or homogeneity, but it can be one where women and girls are safe; where their voices have social, economic, political, religious, and environmental influence; and where men and boys stand proudly as equals. This future can be imagined through rigorous scholarly research, and it is not out of our reach. Our challenge today is to do the hard work of developing these theories and to continue to create scholarly legitimacy for this form of research.

REFERENCES

Alhadeff-Jones, M. (2013a). Complexity, methodology and method: Crafting a critical process of research. *Complicity: An International Journal of Complexity and Education*, *10*(1/2), 19–44.

Alhadeff-Jones, M. (2013b). Method and complexity in educational sciences: Introduction to the special issue. *Complicity: An International Journal of Complexity and Education*, *10*(1/2), i–vii.

Avolio, B.J., Walumbwa, F.O., and Weber, T.J. (2009). Leadership: current theories, research, and future directions. *Annual Review of Psychology*, *60*, 421–49. doi:10.1146/annurev.psych.60.110707.163621.

Bass, B.M., Avolio, B.J., and Atwater, L. (1996). The transformational and transactional leadership of men and women. *Applied Psychology*, *45*(1), 5–34.

Belenky, M.F., Clinchy, B.M., Goldberger, N.R., and Tarule, J.M. (1986). *Women's Ways of Knowing: The Development of Self, Voice, and Mind*. New York, NY: Basic Books.

Burrell, G., and Morgan, G. (1979). *Sociological Paradigms and Organisational Analysis: Elements of the Sociology of Corporate Life*. London, UK: Heinemann.

Chattopadhyay, R., and Duflo, E. (2004). Women as policy makers: Evidence from a randomized policy experiment in India. *Econometrica*, *72*(5), 1409–1443.

Christensen, C.M., and Raynor, M.E. (2003). Why hard-nosed executives should care about management theory. *Harvard Business Review*, *81*(9), 66–75.

Coder, L., and Spiller, M.S. (2013). Leadership education and gender roles: Think manager, think "?". *Academy of Educational Leadership Journal*, *17*(3), 21–51.

Craig, R.T., and Tracy, K. (2014). Building grounded practical theory in applied communication research: Introduction to the special issue. *Journal of Applied Communication Research*, *42*(3), 229–243.

DeRue, D.S., and Ashford, S.J. (2010). Who will lead and who will follow? A social process of leadership identity construction in organizations. *Academy of Management Review*, *35*(4), 627–647.

Eagly, A.H., and Johannesen-Schmidt, M.C. (2001). The leadership styles of women and men. *Journal of Social Issues*, *57*(4), 781–797. doi:10.1111/0022-4537.00241.

Eagly, A.H., Johannesen-Schmidt, M.C., and van Engen, M.L. (2003). Transformational, transactional, and laissez-faire leadership styles: A meta-analysis comparing women and men. *Psychological Bulletin*, *129*(4), 569–591. doi:10.1037/0033-2909.129.4.569.

Eagly, A.H., and Johnson, B.T. (1990). Gender and leadership style: A meta-analysis. *Psychological Bulletin*, *108*(2), 233–256. doi:10.1037/0033-2909.108.2.233.

Eagly, A.H., and Karau, S.J. (1991). Gender and the emergence of leaders: A meta-analysis. *Journal of Personality and Social Psychology*, *60*(5), 685–710. doi:10.1037/0022-3514.60.5.685.

Eagly, A.H., and Karau, S.J. (2002). Role congruity theory of prejudice toward female leaders. *Psychological Review*, *109*(3), 573–598. doi:10.1037/0033-295X.109.3.573.

Eagly, A.H., Karau, S.J., Makhijani, M.G. (1995). Gender and the effectiveness of leaders: A meta-analysis. *Psychological Bulletin*, *117*(1), 125–145.

Eagly, A.H., Makhijani, M.G., and Klonsky, B.G. (1992). Gender and the effectiveness of leaders: A meta-analysis. *Psychological Bulletin*, *111*(1), 3–22. doi:10.1037/0033-2909.117.1.125.

Ely, R.J., Ibarra, H., and Kolb, D. M. (2011). Taking gender into account: Theory and design for women's leadership development programs. *Academy of Management Learning and Education*, *10*(3), 474–493.

Fletcher, J.K. (2004). The paradox of postheroic leadership: An essay on gender, power, and transformational change. *Leadership Quarterly*, *15*(5), 647–661.

Friedman, M. (1999). *Reconsidering Logical Positivism*. Cambridge, UK: University Press.

Gilligan, C. (1993). *In a Different Voice: Psychological Theory and Women's Development*. Cambridge, MA: Harvard University Press.

Gioia, D.A., and Pitre, E. (1990). Multiparadigm perspective on theory building. *Academy of Management Review*, *15*(4), 584–602.

Hannah, S.T., Sumanth, J.J., Lester, P., and Cavarretta, F. (2014). Debunking the false dichotomy of leadership idealism and pragmatism: Critical evaluation and support of newer genre leadership theories. *Journal of Organizational Behavior*, *35*(5), 598–621.

Haraway, D. (2006). *A Cyborg Manifesto: Science, Technology, and Socialist-Feminism in the Late 20th Century*. Amsterdam, Netherlands: Springer.

Harding, S. (1987). Conclusion: Epistemological questions. In S. Harding (Ed.), *Feminism and Methodology: Social Science Issues* (pp. 181–190). Bloomington, IN: Indiana University Press.

Hartsock, N. (2004). The feminist standpoint: Developing the ground for a specifically feminist historical materialism. In S. Harding (Ed.) *The Feminist Standpoint Theory Reader: Intellectual and Political Controversies* (pp. 35–54). New York, NY: Routledge.

Heilman, M.E. (2001). Description and prescription: How gender stereotypes prevent women's ascent up the organizational ladder. *Journal of Social Issues*, *57*(4), 657–674. doi:10.1111/0022-4537.00234.

Heilman, M.E., and Okimoto, T.G. (2007). Why are women penalized for success at male tasks? The implied communality deficit. *Journal of Applied Psychology*, *92*(1), 81–92. doi:10.1037/0021-9010.92.1.81.

Heilman, M.E., Wallen, A.S., Fuchs, D., and Tamkins, M.M. (2004). Penalties for success: Reactions to women who succeed at male gender-typed tasks. *Journal of Applied Psychology*, *89*(3), 416–427. doi:10.1037/0021-9010.89.3.416.

Hibbert, P., Sillince, J., Diefenbach, T., and Cunliffe, A.L. (2014). Relationally reflexive practice: A generative approach to theory development in qualitative research. *Organizational Research Methods*, *17*(3), 278–298. doi:10.1177/1094428114524829.

House, R., Javidan, M., Hanges, P., and Dorfman, P. (2002). Understanding cultures and implicit leadership theories across the globe: An introduction to project GLOBE. *Journal of World Business*, *37*(1), 3–10. doi:10.1016/S1090-9516(01)00069-4.

Hyde, J.S. (2005). The gender similarities hypothesis. *American Psychologist*, *60*(6), 581–592. doi:10.1037/0003-066X.60.6.581.

Kellerman, B. (2012). Cut off at the pass: The limits of leadership in the 21st century. Governance Studies at Brookings. Retrieved from http://www.brookings.edu/~/media/Research/Files/Papers/2012/8/10%20leadership%20kellerman/0810_leadership_deficit_kellerman.pdf

Kennelly, J.J. (2009). Youth cultures, activism and agency: Revisiting feminist debates. *Gender and Education*, *21*(3), 259–272. doi:10.1080/09540250802392281.

Kinnunen, U. (1998). Antecedents and outcomes of work-family conflict among employed women and men in Finland. *Human Relations*, *51*(2), 157–177. doi:10.1177/001872679805100203.

Klenke, K. (2011). *Women in Leadership: Contextual Dynamics and Boundaries*. Bingley, UK: Emerald Group Publishing.

Lerner, G. (1994). *The Creation of Feminist Consciousness: From the Middle Ages to Eighteen-Seventy*, Vol. 2. Oxford, UK: Oxford University Press on Demand.

Lewis, K.M. (2000). When leaders display emotion: How followers respond to negative emotional expression of male and female leaders. *Journal of Organizational Behavior*, *21*(2), 221–234. doi:10.1002/(SICI)1099-1379(200003)21:2<221::AID-JOB36>3.3.CO;2-S.

Lincoln, Y.S., and Lynham, S.A. (2011). Criteria for assessing theory in human resource development from an interpretive perspective. *Human Resource Development International*, *14*(1), 3–22. doi:10.1080/13678868.2011.542895.

Lord, R.G., and Hall, R.J. (2005). Identity, deep structure and the development of leadership skill. *Leadership Quarterly*, *16*(4), 591–615.

Merton, R.K. (1967). *On Theoretical Sociology: Five Essays, Old and New*. New York, NY: Free Press.

Ng, T.W.H., Eby, L.T., Sorensen, K.L., and Feldman, D.C. (2005). Predictors of objective and subjective career success: A meta-analysis. *Personnel Psychology*, *58*(2), 367–408.

Ngunjiri, F.W., Hernandez, K.A.C., and Chang, H. (2010). Living autoethnography: Connecting life and research. *Journal of Research Practice*, *6*(1), 1–17.

Osteen, L., Owen, J.E., Komives, S.R., Mainella, F.C., and Longerbeam, S.D. (2006). A leadership identity development model: Applications from a grounded theory. *Journal of College Student Development*, *47*(4), 401–418.

Paterson, B.L., Dubouloz, C.J., Chevrier, J., Ashe, B., King, J., and Moldoveanu, M. (2009). Conducting qualitative metasynthesis research: Insights from a metasynthesis project. *International Journal of Qualitative Methods*, *8*(3), 22–33.

Patterson, C.H. (1986). Preface. *Theories of Counseling and Psychotherapy*, 4th edn (pp. xiii–xxvii). New York, NY: HarperCollins.

Perry, Jr, W.G. (1999). *Forms of Intellectual and Ethical Development in the College Years: A Scheme*. Jossey-Bass Higher and Adult Education Series. San Francisco, CA: Jossey-Bass Publishers.

Popper, K. (2013). *Realism and the Aim of Science: From the Postscript to the Logic of Scientific Discovery*. New York, NY: Routledge.

Reichenbach, H. (1951). The verifiability theory of meaning. In *Proceedings of the American Academy of Arts and Sciences*, *80*(1), 46–60. American Academy of Arts and Sciences.

Reinharz, S. and Davidman, L. (1992). *Feminist Methods in Social Research*. Oxford, UK: Oxford University Press.

Rosener, J.B. (1990). Ways women lead. *Harvard Business Review*, *68*(6), 119–125.

Schein, V.E., Mueller, R., Lituchy, T., and Liu, J. (1996). Think manager think male: A global phenomenon?. *Journal of Organizational Behavior*, *17*(1), 33–41.

Schwartzman, L.H. (2006). Abstraction, idealization, and oppression. *Metaphilosophy*, *37*(5), 565–588.

Smith, D.E. (1987). Women's perspective as a radical critique of sociology. In S. Harding (Ed.), *Feminism and Methodology: Social Science Issues* (pp. 84–96). Indianapolis, IN: Indiana University Press.

Smith, K.G. (Ed.). (1999). Special Issue on Theory Building. *Academy of Management Review*, *24*(4).

Steele, C.M., Spencer, S.J., and Aronson, J. (2002). Contending with group image: The psychology of stereotype and social identity threat. *Advances in Experimental Social Psychology*, *34*, 379–440.

Stone, D. (2008). Global public policy, transnational policy communities, and their networks. *Policy Studies Journal*, *36*(1), 19–38.

Storberg-Walker, J. (2006). From imagination to application: Making the case for the general method of theory building research in applied disciplines. *Human Resource Development International*, *9*(2), 227–259.

Storberg-Walker, J. (2007). Understanding the five components of theory building research in applied disciplines: A grounded approach. *Human Resource Development Quarterly*, *18*(1), 63–90.

Stryker, S., and Serpe, R.T. (1982). Commitment, identity salience, and role behavior: Theory and research example. In W. Ickes and E.S. Knowles (Eds) *Personality, Roles, and Social Behavior* (pp. 199–218). Springer Series in Social Psychology. New York, NY: Springer.

Swedberg, R. (2012). Theorizing in sociology and social science: Turning to the context of discovery. *Theory and Society*, *41*(1), 1–40. doi:10.1007/s11186-011-9161-5.

Tsoukas, H., and Knudsen, C. (2003). Introduction: The need for meta-theoretical reflection in Organization Theory. In H. Tsoukas and C. Knudsen (Eds), *The Oxford Handbook of Organization Theory: Meta-theoretical Perspectives* (p. 5). New York, NY: Oxford University Press.

Uhl-Bien, M. (2006). Relational leadership theory: Exploring the social processes of leadership and organizing. *Leadership Quarterly*, *17*(6), 654–676.

Uhl-Bien, M., Riggio, R.E., Lowe, K.B., and Carsten, M.K. (2014). Followership theory: A review and research agenda. *Leadership Quarterly, 25*, 83–104. doi:10.1016/j.leaqua.2013.11.007.

Van de Ven, A.H. (1989). Nothing is quite so practical as a good theory. *Academy of Management Review, 14*(4), 486–489. doi:10.5465/AMR.1989.4308370.

Van Stapele, N. (2014). Intersubjectivity, self-reflexivity and agency: Narrating about "self" and "other" in feminist research. *Women's Studies International Forum, 43*, 13–21. doi:10.1016/j.wsif.2013.06.010.

Weick, K. (1989). Theory construction as disciplined imagination. *Academy of Management Review, 14*(4), 516–531. Retrieved from http://www.jstor.org.prox.lib.ncsu.edu/stable/258556.

Weick, K.E. (1999). Theory construction as disciplined reflexivity: Tradeoffs in the 90s. *Academy of Management Review, 24*(4), 797–806.

Whetten, D.A. (Ed.). (1989). Special Issue on Theory Building. *Academy of Management Review, 14*(4).

5. Social psychological approaches to women and leadership theory
Crystal L. Hoyt and Stefanie Simon

As evidenced by this very book, there is a vibrant and robust scholarly interest in the study of gender and leadership. Questions surrounding gender and leadership were largely ignored in psychology until the 1970s (Chemers, 1997), when changes in both American society and the gender composition of the academy prompted researchers to ask: "Can women lead?" This naïve question soon gave way to questions focused on understanding the pervasive gender leadership gap between men and women. Although the percentage of women occupying leadership roles globally is at the highest it has ever been (Pew Research Center and Demographic Trends, 2015; World Economic Forum, 2014), women remain grievously under-represented in the elite levels of corporations and political systems (Catalyst, 2015; Center for American Women and Politics, 2015; Lawless and Fox, 2012). Much of the current scholarship on gender and leadership in social psychology is aimed at elucidating the gender leadership gap. Generally, the theoretical approaches taken by social psychologists are focused on one of these two questions: (1) Are there gender differences in leadership style and effectiveness?; and (2) What barriers do women face in the leadership domain?

ARE THERE GENDER DIFFERENCES IN LEADERSHIP STYLE AND EFFECTIVENESS?

Reflecting social psychologists' early interest in studying leadership style, one of the seminal questions researchers interested in gender and leadership asked was "Do women and men lead differently?" In a comprehensive meta-analysis, Eagly and Johannesen-Schmidt (2007) found small, but reliable, gender differences in leadership style. For example, female leaders tend to be more democratic and participative than male leaders (Eagly and Johnson, 1990), whereas male leaders tend to have a more directive, top-down leadership style than women. Additionally, in contexts that are less male-dominated, women tend to lead in a more stereotypically female (that is, communal) style than men.

More recently, scholars turned their focus to understanding whether women and men differ in their use of transformational leadership styles. Transformational leaders inspire, motivate, and develop followers and are often compared to transactional leaders who motivate followers through a system of reward-based incentives (Bass, 1998). Here again, another small but reliable gender difference emerged, such that women tend to use a transformational leadership style more than men (Eagly et al., 2003). Whereas female leaders tend to be more transformational than male leaders, male leaders tend to be more transactional than female leaders (Antonakis et al., 2003; Desvaux and Devillard, 2008, Eagly et al., 2003). Importantly, a separate meta-analysis of 87 studies revealed a positive relationship between effectiveness and transformational leadership (Judge and Piccolo, 2004). Together, these findings suggest a female advantage: women tend to use a leadership style associated with effectiveness.

Beyond leadership style, social psychologists have started to look for potential gender differences in leaders' psychology that also impact the way men and women lead. Specifically, Eagly (2013) argues that gender differences in men and women's values and attitudes likely translate to different leadership behaviors. Women tend to emphasize social values that promote others' welfare to a greater extent than men (Beutel and Marini, 1995; Schwartz and Rubel, 2005), a difference that has been shown among chief executive officers (CEOs) and board members (Adams and Funk, 2012). The fact that women emphasize more social values than men does seem to influence leaders' behaviors. For example, the proportion of women on corporate boards is related to company philanthropy and charitable giving (Williams, 2003), as well as to more positive social outcomes and greater corporate responsibility (Boulouta, 2012).

In sum, empirical research supports small differences in leadership style and effectiveness between men and women. Women experience slight effectiveness disadvantages in masculine leader roles, whereas roles that are more feminine offer them some advantages. Additionally, women exceed men in the use of democratic or participatory styles, and they are more likely to use transformational leadership behaviors and contingent rewards, which are particularly well suited to the complexity of contemporary organizations and can translate into enhanced institutional effectiveness (Eagly and Carli, 2003; Eagly et al., 2014). Women are no less effective at leading than men, and women are no less committed to their jobs or motivated for leadership roles than men. Furthermore, research shows a small gender difference such that women are more likely to focus on the welfare of others.

WHAT BARRIERS DO WOMEN FACE?

While differences in men and women's leadership style and effectiveness may be small, the barriers that women face in attaining leadership positions, as well as barriers they face while in leadership positions, are more substantial. Although gender-based leadership challenges and barriers are also discussed in Part IV of this *Handbook* (Chapters 17–22), it is important to address them in this chapter as well, given that many social psychological theoretical approaches to women and leadership revolve around questions of barriers. The majority of social psychologists who study gender and leadership focus on these barriers that women face. This focus on the disparities between men and women in leadership is not so surprising, given social psychologists' predominant focus on theoretically understanding and reducing inequality. Women navigate a complex maze of challenges along their leadership journeys. The greater difficulties that women, relative to men, encounter in leadership were originally dubbed the "glass ceiling." Two *Wall Street Journal* reporters in 1986 (Hymowitz and Schellhardt, 1986) coined this term to refer specifically to the invisible barricade blocking women's ascension into top corporate leadership positions. Not long after this metaphor gained wide appeal, researchers sought to better understand the glass ceiling. This barrier is even found within female-dominated occupations, professions where men ride a "glass escalator" up to the top roles (Maume, 1999).

The image of a glass ceiling played an important role in inserting this topic into both popular discourse and researchers' agendas; however, this metaphor has limitations and was replaced with the image of a "leadership labyrinth" (Eagly and Carli, 2007; a deeper discussion of women and leadership metaphors can be found in Chapter 3 of this *Handbook*). The image of a labyrinth conveys the impression of a journey riddled with challenges all along the way, not just a single indiscernible barrier, which can be successfully navigated by some women. Women encounter many hurdles within this maze, including those stemming from contemporary organizational structures and cultures, and the often inequitable divisions of domestic labor (Eagly and Carli, 2007). For example, although women's participation in the paid labor force has increased dramatically over the past few decades, women continue to do the majority, but not all, of the unpaid labor (Khazan, 2016). Thus, after returning from their first shift of paid labor, many women are burdened with a second shift of unpaid domestic work (Hochschild and Machung, 1989; Milkie et al., 2009). The hurdles that social psychologists focus on the most are those stemming from stereotype-based expectations.

Women and Lack of Fit: Stereotype-Based Expectations

Some of the largest hurdles women face in leadership arise from leadership beginning with "the process of being perceived by others as a leader" (Lord and Maher, 1991, p. 11). People hold beliefs of what it means to be a leader, termed implicit leadership theories, and they evaluate actual and potential leaders against these standards (Forsyth and Nye, 2008; Lord and Maher, 1991; Kenney et al., 1996). In addition to revolving around both task-oriented and people-oriented traits and behaviors, these implicit leadership theories are culturally masculine and reflect the dominant race (Koenig et al., 2011; Rosette et al., 2008). A prominent theoretical focus for social psychologists interested in gender and leadership concerns understanding the nature and impact of gender-based biases that stem from implicit leadership theories which create a stereotype-based lack of fit between women's characteristics, skills, and aspirations and those deemed necessary for leadership effectiveness. Whereas explicit biases against women in leadership have decreased over the last half-decade, there are powerful and pernicious subtle biases that work to undermine women's access to power (Hoyt, 2015; see also Chapter 20).

The notion that women do not fit the image of a leader has been articulated by various theorists including Heilman (1983, 2001) in her "lack of fit" model and Eagly and Karau (2002) in their role congruity theory of prejudice toward female leaders. According to these perspectives, the bias against female leaders stems from the mismatch between gender stereotypes and the leadership role. It is the deeply ingrained stereotypic beliefs that women take care and men take charge that give rise to crafty biases against female leaders (Eagly and Carli, 2007; Koenig et al., 2011). In the original research to investigate the mismatch between women and leadership, Schein (1973) employed the well-replicated "think manager, think male" paradigm where she asked participants to rate women, men, and successful middle managers on a list of gendered traits. Not surprisingly, successful middle managers were seen to require traits that were more commonly ascribed to men than to women.

Research into stereotypes within the field of social psychology began nearly a century ago and remains a prominent area of inquiry (Jussim and Rubinstein, 2012). Stereotypes refer to beliefs, or cognitive shortcuts, people have about groups or members of groups that influence the way people process information about them (Hamilton et al., 1994). According to social role theory (Eagly, 1987; Eagly et al., 2000), gender stereotypes are derived from traditional gendered division of labor; by viewing women and men in particular roles which require particular behaviors, people begin to associate traits commonly linked to those behaviors to specific genders. Historically, men have served as the primary economic providers and women have done the majority of the unpaid domestic work. Thus, men's greater participation in the paid labor force has promoted the stereotype of men possessing agentic characteristics that emphasize confidence, self-reliance, and dominance. Likewise, greater involvement in domestic responsibilities and care-related employment has fostered the stereotype that women possess communal characteristics that highlight a concern for others (Deaux and Kite, 1993; Eagly et al., 2000; Williams and Best, 1990). Importantly, these stereotypes both describe beliefs about the attributes of women and men and prescribe how women and men ought to be (Burgess and Borgida, 1999; Glick and Fiske, 1999). In working to better understand the impact of these stereotype-based expectations on female leaders, social psychologists generally take one of two theoretical approaches: they focus on how these expectations impact perceptions of leaders, or they focus on how they impact the women themselves.

Stereotypes Shape Perceivers' Expectations

Prejudice and discrimination
Social psychological research has provided ample evidence that the prejudice and discrimination results from women's perceived "lack of fit." Furthermore, this prejudice and discrimination contributes to women experiencing greater difficulty in attaining, and being perceived as effective in, leadership roles (Eagly and Karau, 2002). However, the stereotype-based prejudice and discrimination that women confront in the domain of leadership is subtle and often hard to detect. Social psychologists have devised clever approaches to illuminate these often inconspicuous biases. In one innovative experimental approach, termed the "Goldberg paradigm" (Goldberg, 1968), people are asked to evaluate identical information for a job application, such as resumes, with one catch: half the people are told it is a man's resume, the other half, a woman's. Using this paradigm, research has demonstrated clear and blatant discrimination against women in leadership selection, in that men with identical qualifications to women are more likely to be selected (Davison and Burke, 2000). Thus, identical qualifications are deemed "better" or "more meritorious" when a male name is attached.

Gendered expectations can also drive people to reconstruct the very criteria used to define merit. For example, when hiring for a masculine leadership position, such as police chief, people advantageously define meritorious qualifications to align with the strength of male, versus female, candidates (Uhlmann and Cohen, 2005). Moreover, these gendered expectations can result in women being given less credit or more blame when working on collective projects with men (Heilman and Haynes, 2005). These unconscious and unintentional gender biases flourish in unstructured settings rife with ambiguous information (Caleo and Heilman, 2014; Powell and Graves, 2003).

Not only do women experience discrimination based on descriptive gender stereotypes that influence how women are perceived, but the prescriptive nature of gender stereotypes places women in a double bind in leadership. That is, highly feminine women are criticized for being deficient leaders, and highly masculine women experience backlash for not being female enough (Eagly et al., 2014; Heilman, 2001; Heilman and Okimoto, 2007; Heilman et al., 2004). The contradictory expectations associated with being both a proper woman and an effective leader complicate many things, from deciding what to wear in an interview to navigating the proper emotional expression in an important meeting. Women are often disliked and vilified for violating the prescription for feminine niceness; they are penalized for expressing anger, talking more than others, and negotiating for their salary (Bowles et al., 2007; Brescoll, 2011; Brescoll and Uhlmann, 2008).

Beyond identifying barriers, much social psychological work has focused on pinpointing boundary conditions that either bolster or undermine gender bias in leadership. Taking a role congruity perspective, researchers often focus on factors associated with the leadership role or the perceived gender stereotypicality of the woman that might exacerbate or attenuate the "think leader, think male" bias. For example, women experience greater bias in contexts dominated by men, when evaluations are made by men, and when they are in line, rather than staff, positions (Eagly et al., 1992; Kanter, 1977; Lyness and Heilman, 2006; Pazy and Oron, 2001). Critically, it is the line positions that are the more likely route to higher leadership positions (Catalyst, 2004; Galinsky et al., 2003). Moreover, factors that increase reliance on female gender stereotypes, such as pregnancy, parenthood, or attractiveness, exacerbate gender bias against women (Fuegen and Biernat, 2013; Hebl et al., 2007; Heilman and Okimoto, 2008; Heilman and Stopeck, 1985).

Factors associated with perceivers also influence role incongruity-based biases. Not surprisingly, people's gender role attitudes strongly predict their evaluations of women in non-traditional roles (Ridgeway and Correll, 2004; Rudman and Kilianski, 2000; Simon and Hoyt, 2008). However, how and to what extent gender role beliefs reinforce or undermine gender bias in leadership depends upon other important belief systems. For example, political ideology predicts the extent to which people support more or less traditional gender roles, and in turn predicts bias against or in favor of female leaders (Hoyt, 2012). Additionally, whether people use their gender role attitudes to make judgments about leaders depends upon their beliefs about the very nature of people, whether people can change their personal attributes or whether they are fixed (Hoyt and Burnette, 2013). Extending this research, we recently examined how the extent to which people endorse hierarchical group relationships (that is, desire a hierarchy among groups in society) influences preference for female as well as racial and ethnic minority leaders (Hoyt and Simon, 2016). We found that the less people endorsed hierarchical group relationships, the more they favored female as well as black and Latino/Latina leaders. Research taking the perspective of understanding how the attributes of the perceivers impacts their evaluations of leaders reveals that while female and other non-traditional leaders, such as racial minorities, are often perceived negatively, this is not always the case. Indeed, at times they may be viewed more favorably than white males.

The glass cliff

Gender stereotypes also contribute to the type of leadership positions women tend to reach. Specifically, women are more likely than men to be placed on a "glass cliff," or appointed to precarious leadership situations associated with greater risk and criticism (Ryan and Haslam, 2005; Chapter 3 of this *Handbook* also discusses the glass cliff). Although some people originally argued that companies with women on their boards were performing worse than companies with all men on their boards (Judge, 2003), upon further analysis researchers uncovered that women were particularly likely to be placed in leadership positions in situations of financial downturn and decline in company performance, not that women cause poor performance (Brady et al., 2011; Cook and Glass, 2014; Ryan and Haslam, 2005).

A number of experimental studies help shed light on the theoretical underpinnings of the glass cliff. Specifically, researchers have examined whether women are preferentially appointed to leadership positions in times of crisis. These studies have demonstrated that when companies are declining (versus improving), women are seen as being more suitable for the leadership position and having greater leadership ability than men (Haslam and Ryan, 2008). Furthermore, the reason women seem to be preferred to men as leaders in times of crisis may be due to activation of a "think crisis, think female" association (Ryan et al., 2011; Ryan et al., 2016). While leadership roles are often thought of in stereotypically agentic traits associated with men, in times of crisis leadership is thought of as requiring more communal traits (for example, being caring and understanding) associated with women (Ryan et al., 2011). Thus, women may be selected for leadership positions in crisis situations because they are perceived to be better suited for these leadership roles than men are. Similarly, Brown et al. (2011) demonstrate in a series of studies that in times of threat that signal the need for organizational change, female leaders are preferred to male leaders because men are associated with stability and women with change.

While the glass cliff phenomenon may appear to demonstrate an example of gender parity in leadership, women do not necessarily desire these risky positions over more stable leadership positions. For example, women perceive leadership positions that are risky as less attractive than men do (Rink et al., 2012). Furthermore, as Ryan et al. (2016) astutely note, the glass cliff is partially driven by the fact that men are given preferential access to more desirable, stable leadership positions. Thus, equal opportunity in leadership extends beyond numerical parity. In order to pull woman back from the glass cliff, we must also consider the nature of the leadership positions and men's privileged access to the "glass cushion" (Ryan et al., 2016).

Intersectional theoretical perspectives

Because white men are viewed as prototypical leaders (Rosette et al., 2008), most past research has focused on comparisons between white men and white women when considering gender bias in leadership. However, recent research has taken an intersectionality approach (Purdie-Vaughns and Eibach, 2008), which investigates the experiences of people with multiple subordinate identities (for example, women of color). Researchers are starting to take seriously the importance of intersecting identities, and in doing so are discovering important new findings that may counter and expand established wisdom.

From an intersectionality approach, some argue that black women, for example, experience more prejudice and discrimination than white women or black men. In other words, black women experience "double jeopardy" in that they suffer the effects of both gender and racial prejudice (Beale, 1979; Hancock, 2007). In contrast to the double jeopardy hypothesis, others argue that people with intersectional identities experience distinctive forms of oppression known as "intersectional invisibility" (Purdie-Vaughns and Eibach, 2008). According to this perspective, black women are often marginalized or ignored

In P.G. Devine, D.L. Hamilton, and T.M. Ostrom (Eds), *Social Cognition: Impact on Social Psychology* (pp. 291–321). New York: Academic Press.

Hancock, A.M. (2007). When multiplication doesn't equal quick addition: Examining intersectionality as a research paradigm. *Perspectives on Politics*, *5*(1), 63–79. doi: 10.1017/S1537592707070065.

Haslam, S.A., and Ryan, M.K. (2008). The road to the glass cliff: Differences in the perceived suitability of men and women for leadership positions in succeeding and failing organizations. *Leadership Quarterly*, *19*(5), 530–546. doi:10.1016/j.leaqua.2008.07.011.

Hebl, M.R., King, E.B., Glick, P., Singletary, S.L., and Kazama, S. (2007). Hostile and benevolent reactions toward pregnant women: Complementary interpersonal punishments and rewards that maintain traditional roles. *Journal of Applied Psychology*, *92*(6), 1499–1511. doi: 10.1037/0021-9010.92.6.1499.

Heilman, M.E. (1983). Sex bias in work settings: The Lack of Fit model. *Research in Organizational Behavior*, *5*, 269–298.

Heilman, M. (2001). Description and prescription: How gender stereotypes prevent women's ascent up the organizational ladder. *Journal of Social Issues*, *57*(4), 657–674. doi: 10.1111/0022-4537.00234.

Heilman, M.E. and Haynes, M.C. (2005). No credit where credit is due: Attributional rationalization of women's success in male–female teams. *Journal of Applied Psychology*, *90*(5), 905–916. doi: 10.1037/0021-9010.90.5.905.

Heilman, M.E. and Okimoto. T.G. (2007). Why are women penalized for success at male tasks?: The implied communality deficit. *Journal of Applied Psychology*, *92*(1), 81–92. doi: 10.1037/0021-9010.92.1.81.

Heilman, M. E., and Okimoto, T.G. (2008). Motherhood: A potential source of bias in employment decisions. *Journal of Applied Psychology*, *93*(1), 189–198. doi:10.1037/0021-9010.93.1.189.

Heilman, M.E., and Stopeck, M.H. (1985). Attractiveness and corporate success: Different causal attributions for males and females. *Journal of Applied Psychology*, *70*(2), 379–388. doi:10.1037/0021-9010.70.2.379.

Heilman, M.E., Wallen, A.S., Fuchs, D., and Tamkins, M.M. (2004). Penalties for success: Reactions to women who succeed at male gender-typed tasks. *Journal of Applied Psychology*, *89*(3), 416–427. doi: 10.1037/0021-9010.89.3.416.

Hochschild, A.R., and Machung, A. (1989). *The Second Shift: Working Parents and the Revolution at Home.* New York, NY: Viking.

Hoyt, C.L. (2012). Gender bias in employment contexts: A closer examination of the role incongruity principle. *Journal of Experimental Social Psychology*, *48*(1), 86–96. doi: 10.1016/j.jesp.2011.08.004.

Hoyt, C. (2015). *Social identities and leadership: The case of gender.* In G. Goethals, S. Alison, R. Kramer, and D. Messick (Eds), *Conceptions of Leadership: Enduring Ideas and Emerging Insights* (pp. 71–91). New York, NY: Palgrave Macmillan.

Hoyt, C.L., and Blascovich, J. (2007). Leadership efficacy and women leaders' responses to stereotype activation. *Group Processes and Intergroup Relations*, *10*(4), 595–616. doi: 10.1177/1368430207084718.

Hoyt, C.L., and Blascovich, J. (2010). The role of leadership self-efficacy and stereotype activation on cardio-vascular, behavioral and self-report responses in the leadership domain. *Leadership Quarterly*, *21*(1), 89–103. doi: 10.1016/j.leaqua.2009.10.007.

Hoyt, C.L., and Burnette, J. (2013). Gender bias in leader evaluations: Merging implicit theories and role congruity perspectives. *Personality and Social Psychology Bulletin*, *39*(10), 1306–1319. doi: 10.1177/0146167213493643.

Hoyt, C.L., Johnson, S.K., Murphy, S.E., and Skinnell, K.H. (2010). The impact of blatant stereotype activation and group sex-composition on female leaders. *Leadership Quarterly*, *21*(5), 716–732. doi:10.1016/j.leaqua.2010.07.003.

Hoyt, C.L., and Murphy, S.E. (2016). Managing to clear the air: Stereotype threat, women, and leadership. *Leadership Quarterly*, *27*(3), 387–399. doi:10.1016/j.leaqua.2015.11.002.

Hoyt, C.L., and Simon, S. (2011). Female leaders: Injurious or inspiring role models for women? *Psychology of Women Quarterly*, *35*(1), 143–157. doi:10.1177/0361684310385216.

Hoyt, C., and Simon, S. (2016). The role of social dominance orientation and patriotism in the evaluation of racial minority and female leaders. *Journal of Applied Social Psychology*. doi:10.1016/j.leaqua.2015.11.002.

Hymowitz, C., and Schellhardt, T.D. (1986). The glass ceiling: Why women can't seem to break the invisible barrier that blocks them from the top jobs. *Wall Street Journal*, March 24, pp. D1, D4–D5.

Judge, E. (2003). 'Women on board: Help or hindrance?'. *The Times*, November 11, p. 21. Retrieved from http://www.thetimes.co.uk/tto/business/article2102633.ece.

Judge, T.A., and Piccolo, R.F. (2004). Transformational and transactional leadership: A meta-analytic test of their relative validity. *Journal of Applied Psychology*, *89*(5), 755–768. doi:10.1037/0021-9010.89.5.755.

Jussim, L, and Rubinstein, R. (2012) *Stereotypes*. Oxford Bibliographies Online. http://www.oxfordbibliographies.com/view/document/obo-9780199828340/obo-9780199828340-0086.xml?rskey=282D9Uandresult=1andq=jussim#firstMatch.

Kanter, R. (1977). *Men and Women of the Corporation.* New York, NY: Basic Books.

Kenney, R.A., Schwartz-Kenney, B.M., and Blascovich, J. (1996). Implicit leadership theories: Defining leaders described as worthy of influence. *Personality and Social Psychology Bulletin*, *22*(11), 1128–1143. doi:10.1177/01461672962211004.

Khazan, O. (2016). The scourge of the female chore burden. *Atlantic*, February 23. Retrieved from http://www.theatlantic.com/business/archive/2016/02/the-scourge-of-the-female-time-crunch/470379/.

Koenig, A., Eagly, A., Mitchell, A., and Ristikari, T. (2011). Are leader stereotypes masculine? A meta-analysis of three research paradigms. *Psychological Bulletin*, 137(4), 616–642. doi:10.1037/a0023557.

Kray, L.J., Galinsky, A.D., and Thompson, L. (2002). Reversing the gender gap in negotiations: An exploration of stereotype regeneration. *Organizational Behavior and Human Decision Processes*, 87(2), 386–410. doi:10.1006/obhd.2001.2979.

Kray, L.J., Reb, J., Galinsky, A.D., and Thompson, L. (2004). Stereotype reactance at the bargaining table: The effect of stereotype activation and power on claiming and creating value. *Personality and Social Psychology Bulletin*, 30(4), 399–411. doi:10.1177/0146167203261884.

Kray, L.J., Thompson, L., and Galinsky, A. (2001). Battle of the sexes: gender stereotype confirmation and reactance in negotiations. *Journal of Personality and Social Psychology*, 80(6), 942–958. doi:10.1037//0022-3514.80.6.942.

Latu, I.M., Schmid Mast, M., Lammers, J., and Bombari, D. (2013). Successful female leaders empower women's behavior in leadership tasks. *Journal of Experimental Social Psychology*, 49(3), 444–448. doi:10.1016/j.jesp.2013.01.003.

Lawless, J., and Fox, R. (2012). *Men Rule: The Continued Under-representation of Women in US Politics.* Washington, DC: Women and Politics Institute. Retrieved from https://www.american.edu/spa/wpi/upload/2012-Men-Rule-Report-web.pdf.

Leslie, S.J., Cimpian, A., Meyer, M., and Freeland, E. (2015). Expectations of brilliance underlie gender distributions across academic disciplines. *Science*, 347(6219), 262–265. doi:10.1126/science.1261375.

Livingston, R.W., and Pearce, N.A. (2009). The teddy-bear effect: Does having a baby face benefit Black chief executive officers?. *Psychological Science*, 20(10), 1229–1236. doi:10.1111/j.1467-9280.2009.02431.x.

Livingston, R.W., Rosette, A.S., and Washington, E.F. (2012). Can an agentic Black woman get ahead? The impact of race and interpersonal dominance on perceptions of female leaders. *Psychological Science*, 23(4), 354–358. doi:10.1177/0956797611428079.

Lord, R.G., and Maher, K.J. (1991). *Leadership and Information Processing: Linking Perceptions and Performance.* Cambridge, MA: Unwin Hyman.

Lyness, K.S., and Heilman, M.E. (2006). When fit is fundamental: Performance evaluations and promotions of upper-level female and male managers. *Journal of Applied Psychology*, 91(4), 777–785. doi:10.1037/0021-9010.91.4.777.

Marx, D.M., Ko, S.J., and Friedman, R.A. (2009). The "Obama Effect": How a salient role model reduces race-based performance differences. *Journal of Experimental Social Psychology*, 45(4), 953–956. doi:10.1016/j.jesp.2009.03.012.

Maume, D.J., Jr. (1999). Glass ceilings and glass escalators. *Work and Occupations*, 26(4), 483–509. doi:10.1177/0730888499026004005.

Milkie, M., Raley, S., and Bianchi, S. (2009). Taking on the second shift: Time allocations and time pressures of US parents with preschoolers. *Social Forces*, 88(2), 487–517. doi:10.1353/sof.0.0268.

Murphy, M.C., Steele, C.M., and Gross, J.J. (2007). Signaling threat: How situational cues affect women in math, science, and engineering settings. *Psychological Science*, 18(10), 879–885. doi:10.1111/j.1467-9280.2007.01995.x.

Niederle, M., and Vesterlund, L. (2008). Gender differences in competition. *Negotiation Journal*, 24(4), 447–463. doi:10.1111/j.1571-9979.2008.00197.x.

Parks-Stamm, E.J., Heilman, M.E., and Hearns, K.A. (2008). Motivated to penalize: Women's strategic rejection of successful women. *Personality and Social Psychology Bulletin*, 34(2), 237–247. doi:10.1177/0146167207310027.

Pazy, A., and Oron, I. (2001). Sex proportion and performance evaluation among high-ranking military officers. *Journal of Organizational Behavior*, 22(6), 689–702. doi: 10.1002/job.109.

Pew Research Center Social and Demographic Trends (2015). Women and leadership. Retrieved from http://www.pewsocialtrends.org/2015/01/14/chapter-1-women-in-leadership/.

Pollack, J.M., Burnette, J., and Hoyt, C. (2012). Self-efficacy in the face of threats to entrepreneurial success: mind-sets matter. *Basic and Applied Social Psychology*, 34(3), 287–294. doi:10.1080/01973533.2012.674452.

Powell, G.N., and Graves, L.M. (2003). *Women and Men in Management*, 3rd edn. Thousand Oaks, CA: Sage.

Purdie-Vaughns, V., and Eibach, R. (2008). Intersectional invisibility: The distinctive advantages and disadvantages of multiple subordinate-group identities. *Sex Roles*, 59(5–6), 377–391. doi:10.1007/s11199-008-9424-4.

Ridgeway, C.L., and Correll, S.J. (2004). Unpacking the gender system: A theoretical perspective on cultural beliefs in social relations. *Gender and Society*, 18(4), 510–531. doi: 10.1177/0891243204265269.

Rink, F., Ryan, M.K., and Stoker, J.I. (2012). Influence in times of crisis: How social and financial resources affect men's and women's evaluations of glass-cliff positions. *Psychological Science*, 23(11), 1306–1313. doi:10.1177/0956797612453115.

Rosette, A.S., Leonardelli, G.J., and Phillips, K.W. (2008). The White standard: Racial bias in leader categorization. *Journal of Applied Psychology*, 93(4), 758–777. doi:10.1037/0021-9010.93.4.758.

Rosette, A.S., and Livingston, R.W. (2012). Failure is not an option for Black women: Effects of organizational performance on leaders with single versus dual-subordinate identities. *Journal of Experimental Social Psychology*, *48*(5), 1162–1167. doi:10.1016/j.jesp.2012.05.002.

Rudman, L.A., and Kilianski, S.E. (2000). Implicit and explicit attitudes toward female authority. *Personality and Social Psychology Bulletin*, *26*(11), 1315–1328. doi: 10.1177/0146167200263001.

Rudman, L.A., and Phelan, J.E. (2010). The effect of priming gender roles on women's implicit gender beliefs and career aspirations. *Social Psychology*, *41*(3), 192–202. doi:10.1027/1864-9335/a000027.

Ryan, M.K., and Haslam, S.A. (2005). The Glass Cliff: Evidence that women are over-represented in precarious leadership positions. *British Journal of Management*, *16*(2), 81–90. doi:10.1111/j.1467-8551.2005.00433.x.

Ryan, M.K., Haslam, S.A., Hersby, M.D., and Bongiorno, R. (2011). Think crisis – think female: The glass cliff and contextual variation in the think manager – think male stereotype. *Journal of Applied Psychology*, *96*(3), 470–484. doi:10.1037/a0022133.

Ryan, M.K., Haslam, S.A., Morgenroth, T., Rink, F., Stoker, J., and Peters, K. (2016). Getting on top of the glass cliff: Reviewing a decade of evidence, explanations, and impact. *Leadership Quarterly*, doi:10.1016/j.leaqua.2015.10.008.

Schein, V.E. (1973). The relationship between sex role stereotypes and requisite management characteristics. *Journal of Applied Psychology*, *57*(2), 95–100. doi:10.1037/h0037128.

Schwartz, S.H., and Rubel, T. (2005). Sex differences in value priorities: Cross-cultural and multimethod studies. *Journal of Personality and Social Psychology*, *89*(6), 1010–1028. doi:10.1037/0022-3514.89.6.1010.

Simon, S., and Hoyt, C.L. (2008). Exploring the gender gap in support for a woman for president. *Analyses of Social Issues and Public Policy (ASAP)*, *8*(1), 157–181. doi:10.1111/j.1530-2415.2008.00167.x.

Simon, S., and Hoyt, C.L. (2012). Exploring the effect of media images on women's leadership self-perceptions and aspirations. *Group Processes and Intergroup Relations*, *16*(2), 232–245. doi:10.1177/1368430212451176.

Small, D., Gelfand, M., Babcock, L., and Gettman, H. (2007). Who goes to the bargaining table? The influence of gender and framing on the initiation of negotiation. *Journal of Personality and Social Psychology*, *93*(4), 600–613. doi:10.1037/0022-3514.93.4.600.

Stangor, C., Carr, C., and Kiang, L. (1998). Activating stereotypes undermines task performance expectations. *Journal of Personality and Social Psychology*, *75*(5), 1191–1197. doi:10.1037/0022-3514.75.5.1191.

Steele, C.M. (1997). A threat in the air: How stereotypes shape intellectual identity and performance. *American Psychologist*, *52*(6), 613–629. doi:10.1037/0003-066X.52.6.613.

Steele, C.M., and Aronson, J. (1995). Stereotype threat and the intellectual test performance of African Americans. *Journal of Personality and Social Psychology*, *69*(5), 797–811. doi:10.1037/0022-3514.69.5.797.

Steele, C.M., Spencer, S.J., and Aronson, J. (2002). Contending with group image: The psychology of stereotype and social identity threat. In M. Zanna (Ed.), *Advances in Experimental Social Psychology*, Vol. 34 (pp. 379–440). New York, NY: Academic Press.

Uhlmann, E.L., and Cohen, G. (2005). Constructed criteria: Redefining merit to justify discrimination. *Psychological Science*, *16*(6), 474–480.

von Hippel, C., Kalokerinos, E., and Henry, J. (2013). Stereotype threat among older employees: relationship with job attitudes and turnover intentions. *Psychology and Aging*, *28*(1), 17–27. doi:10.1037/a0029825.

von Hippel, C., Walsh, A.M., and Zouroudis, A. (2011). Identity separation in response to stereotype threat. *Social Psychological and Personality Science*, *2*(3), 317–324. doi:10.1177/1948550610390391.

Williams, J.E., and Best, D.L. (1990). *Sex and Psyche: Gender and Self Viewed Cross-Culturally.* Thousand Oaks, CA: Sage Publications.

Williams, R.J. (2003). Women on corporate boards of directors and their influence on corporate philanthropy. *Journal of Business Ethics*, *42*(1), 1–10. doi:10.1023/A:1021626024014.

World Economic Forum. (2014). The global gender gap report 2014. Retrieved from http://reports.weforum.org/global-gender-gap-report-2014/.

6. Sociological approaches to women and leadership theory
Christy Glass and Alicia Ingersoll

As a discipline, sociology is characterized by a relative absence of a strong theoretical tradition related to the complexities of organizational leadership. Indeed, in contrast to other related fields where leadership studies have thrived, including economics, management, and psychology, there is no clear subfield related to the sociology of leadership particularly in the context of work organizations (Whiteford and Ganem, 2015).

The relative absence of a scholarly focus on organizational leadership can be explained by two key features unique to the discipline, one theoretical and one empirical. Theoretically, sociological traditions from conflict theory to functionalism to more interpretive theoretical perspectives have largely centered on broad social forces, such as the division of labor, class relations, institutional structures, and cultural norms. This theoretical focus on large social structures and processes has set limits on the degree to which sociological research has engaged questions related to individual agency, including questions related to leadership. Indeed, sociologists' focus on structural challenges to individual agency (such as that exercised by individual leaders within an organization) has inspired skepticism (Guillén, 2010).

The empirical limitations to an engaged study of leadership relate to sociologists' focus on social structures as well. Because much of the discipline's theoretical tradition concerns social forces that produce inequality, there is a long tradition of "studying down." That is to say, a great deal of the empirical research of sociology is focused on marginalized populations, sources and forms of oppression, and the range of limits to institutional influence and power. Much less empirical attention has focused on elites, including top leaders. This omission is due as much to the focus of the discipline's theoretical traditions as to existing methodological limitations. Quite simply, access to elites by sociological scholars is and has historically been limited (see Khan, 2011 for an important exception). In the words of sociologist Sudhir Venkatesh, "elites don't grant us interviews. They don't let us hang out at their country clubs" (Sullivan, 2010, p. B6).

Two areas of the discipline where the study of leadership has thrived are the fields of political and economic sociology. The study of leadership within these overlapping fields has historically focused more on inequality, power, and conflict rather than the experiences or opportunities that individual leaders face. This is not to suggest an absence of theory and research on leaders; however, much of the classical sociological tradition regarding leadership concerned larger structural patterns of inequality and the unequal distribution of power, prestige, and status. And classical formulations of power, authority, and inequality rarely considered the role of gender or gender norms in shaping social outcomes. The extension of classical theory to the understanding of gender and leadership came later with gender and feminist scholars attempting to understand the ways in which gender shapes access to leadership and the experience of leaders. Before turning

of these studies). Therefore, according to Reskin's theory, women's lack of access to and mobility within leadership roles may be less attributed to overt discrimination or the exercise of hegemonic masculinity and better explained through unconscious bias.

Unconscious bias is commonly associated with race as well as gender. In their field experiment on labor market discrimination, Bertrand and Mullainathan (2004) highlighted the unconscious bias present in hiring by sending out identical resumes differentiated only by traditional white- or black-sounding names. Their findings show an overwhelming preference for white job candidates on the part of employers, and validate assumptions of unconscious bias in the hiring process. Within the context of organizational leadership, unconscious bias manifests not only as a barrier to entry, but also as an obstacle one must continuously grapple with once in a position of authority. The intersectionality between race and gender biases also serves to add complexity to the barriers women of color face during their ascent to leadership roles (Bell and Nkomo, 2001).

Status characteristics theory

To understand how difference manifests and is reproduced by individuals and groups in the form of inequality, sociologists have considered the role of social status. Social status serves as both an input into social organization practices and an outcome of the organizing process (Ridgeway, 1993). At the micro level, status seeking can be a strong motivator for individual performance and attainment goals. At the macro level, however, status acts in conjunction with power and resources in order to reproduce inequality (Weber, 1946).

Status characteristics theory grew out of studies conducted in the 1950s analyzing interpersonal behavior within small groups (Bales, 1950). Berger and colleagues (Berger et al., 1974; Berger et al., 1977) extended the findings of these early studies to formulate expectation states theory, which accounts for and explains how status structures form within groups. Specifically, the theory seeks to explain how status hierarchies emerge within groups with a collective goal or task (Correll and Ridgeway, 2003). Expectation states theory originated with group observations where the participation and influence of group members varied based upon their status characteristics.

A status characteristic can be defined as an attribute possessed by individuals that provides differing amounts of worthiness, confidence, and esteem (Ridgeway, 1993). The amount of status, esteem, and worthiness attributed to various characteristics is based upon cultural norms and attitudes. Ridgeway (2011) expands upon expectation states theory with the inclusion of status construction to explain that over time, as groups interact, status hierarchies will often develop to cause one group to be seen as more competent and worthy than another. Ridgeway (2014) theorizes social status as an independent force in producing inequality based upon individual characteristics, such as gender, race, and social class.

Ridgeway's (2014) formulation of status contrasts with Weber's (1946) classic theory by identifying social status as equivalent to power and material resources in the ability to produce social inequality. Shared cultural beliefs form the basis of status, and status beliefs are reproduced so as to advantage one group over another based upon key characteristics. When power and resources are equal, status provides the advantage. Once status beliefs develop to stabilize inequality, the beliefs then advantage people in the high-status groups not due to power or resources, but due to the related status category they occupy (Ridgeway, 2014). For example, men in general hold a higher status position not necessarily because they have access to greater material resources but because they hold a status (that is, men/manhood) that is culturally valued more than the alternative status (that is, women/womanhood). As a result, men receive an added advantage in situations where men and women have equal access to power and resources, because a man is perceived to be more competent and worthy. Therefore, status creates a new form of inequality and becomes an independent force for creating inequality between people and among groups (Ridgeway, 2014).

Status biases and biased expectations for different status groups have a broader effect than unconscious bias in that they not only affect how others perceive and react, but also influence how individuals present themselves within a situation (Ridgeway, 2014). The impact of status biases on women can lead them to hesitate in situations where they perceive others as more confident based upon status characteristics. For example, Sheryl Sandberg's (2013) discussion of the need for women to "lean in" incorporates elements of both dominant group assimilation and overcoming personal status bias in order to gain opportunities for career mobility and advancement. Unfortunately, the hesitancy associated with the personal effect of status bias can create a negative impression due to lack of confidence, and it can further entrench the status hierarchies between groups (Ridgeway, 2014). This means that, in order to emerge and be successful as a leader, women must navigate societal expectations for their gender and for their leadership position. Status beliefs can bias not only others' expectations, but also one's own beliefs about competence and suitability for leadership roles (Ridgeway, 2014). Importantly, research on status expectations finds that race and ethnicity interact with gender in important ways to produce social expectations related to leadership in work organizations (Livingston et al., 2012; Wingfield, 2013).

Kanter's token theory

In 1977, sociologist Rosabeth Moss Kanter published her book *Men and Women of the Corporation*, which represented a multi-year organizational ethnography of a large corporation. Through her groundbreaking research, Kanter introduced mechanisms that entrench inequality within corporate settings related to the numerical representation of different groups. According to Kanter's work, both token status and homosocial reproduction work to maintain status differences based upon ascribed characteristics, such as gender.

Token theory suggests that an individual's status within the organization is determined by his or her numerical representation within a given rank or position (Kanter, 1977). "Tokens" are defined as members of a group who represent 15 percent or fewer of the individuals within a rank, position or organization; "solos" are defined as individuals who are the sole members of their group within the rank, position, or organization. Compared to members of the numerical majority, tokens and solos have lower status, prestige, and influence within the organization. Tokens experience a variety of challenges as a result of their under-representation such as heightened visibility, performance pressures, and negative evaluation bias.

Kanter (1977) identified three main areas where tokens were more likely to experience negative outcomes consisting of increased visibility, polarization, and stereotyping. First, tokens experience heightened visibility as a result of being more easily noticed due to their minority status. The increased visibility leads to performance pressure for tokens

7. Sociolinguistic approaches to gender and leadership theory

Judith Baxter

This chapter is about the extraordinary role of language in both enabling and constraining women to be effective leaders in the business world and elsewhere. It explores the range of sociolinguistic theories that account for the crucial role of language used in women's performance of leadership, as well as the ways women are represented as leaders in the public domain. While there are numerous studies investigating women's leadership from organization, management, political, psychological, and sociological perspectives, there is relatively little scholarship from a sociolinguistic ("language in society") perspective. Yet, many women leaders say that understanding the language of leadership helps to bring their own experiences to life and makes sense of them in ways they had not previously realized (Baxter, 2014; Baxter and Al A'ali, 2016). This is because the ways in which we use language in our everyday interactions with colleagues are fundamental to constructing effective leadership identities, roles, relationships, practices, and corporate cultures (Clifton, 2012; Holmes, 2006).

Language (both verbal and non-verbal) is a key constructive and iterative aspect of our professional identities, rather than just a channel or medium by which messages are encoded and decoded. The sociolinguistic approach moves the locus of interest away from being a leader to doing leadership (Clifton, 2012), which involves the judicious selection of linguistic resources for accomplishing particular leadership goals effectively. Stated simply, every time senior people speak, they are creating and managing an impression of their profile as leaders (e.g., Clifton, 2012; Holmes and Stubbe, 2003). Language does not simply reflect states of mind but is actually responsible for constructing attitudes, impressions, and behavior that ultimately constitute leadership practices and identities. This links to a larger corporate role for language. Bargiela-Chiappini and Harris (1997) claim that "organizations are talked into being and maintained by means of the talk of the people within and around them. Among the 'competing discourses' that shape daily organizational life, some become dominant" (p. 4).

If leadership language and the discourses that circulate within organizations are so influential, they could provide a key reason to explain why women are under-represented at senior levels, and a means to investigate potential explanations and solutions to this issue. Conversely, language also provides women with a powerful set of resources for accomplishing leadership successfully (Holmes and Vine, in press). Language is so much more than simple communication as this chapter will explore.

There are two central approaches to current sociolinguistic research on women's leadership. The first is primarily descriptive, comprising research that observes and assesses the types of language women use to accomplish leadership "effectively" with their colleagues (e.g., Holmes, 2006; Holmes and Vine, in press; Schnurr, 2009). This vein of research is often "appreciative," noting the skillfulness with which women conduct their interactional practices with colleagues, for example in leading team meetings or negotiating with clients. Such descriptive research can also be practitioner-based, working with business leaders to improve their professional practice through observation and feedback. The second approach is more explicitly critical, comprising (usually feminist) theories that interrogate the linguistic reasons why women encounter barriers to their career progress in workplaces that continue to be male-dominated at senior levels (e.g., Angouri, 2011; Baxter, 2010; Litosseliti and Leadbeater, 2013; Mullany, 2007). Studies associated with this approach tend to be written for the academy or for policy makers, providing scholarly insights but little obvious strategic guidance for the practitioner worlds to which they refer.

The descriptive and critical approaches intersect with three gender and language theories explaining women's use of leadership language, all of which have a strong influence on research in the field. First, dominance theory is primarily critical and proposes that, historically, the reason why women have found access to leadership roles so challenging is because of the social nature of language. This historically constructs men as natural-born leaders and women as followers or outsiders to the role. Second, difference theory tends to be descriptive and suggests that men and women use language to perform leadership in contrasting yet complementary ways. Third, discourse theory is described variously as discursive, social constructionist, or performative, and it mostly takes a critical stance to propose that leadership is constructed through the linguistic choices people make. However, leadership language is also circumscribed by "discourses": that is, gendered norms and expectations about how women and men should use language to perform leadership (Sunderland, 2004). Because discourses tend to be hegemonic, they impose constraints upon the ways women in particular are permitted to conduct leadership.

In this chapter, I review these three major theories that all share the view that language is the principal medium through which women's leadership identities are performed, as well as the means of constructing barriers for women who aspire to leadership in the workplace. I also present examples from gender, language, and leadership studies to reveal insights that are transforming the ways both scholars and practitioners view the challenges facing women in leadership roles. Throughout this chapter, a distinction is made between individuals who self-identify as "women" and "men" (usually, but not always, because of biological characteristics), and the notion that gender is a cultural construct that assigns conventional and stereotyped meanings to the performance of "masculinity" and "femininity."

SOCIOLINGUISTIC THEORIES OF GENDER AND LEADERSHIP

The sociolinguistic field of gender and leadership focuses on the relationship between a leader's use of language and her assigned or acquired gender/sexual identity. This field has theorized the relationship between language and gender from three perspectives: dominance, difference, and discursive. I now consider how each theory seeks to describe, appreciate, and/or critique women's leadership.

Dominance Theory

According to theorists (e.g., Schulz, 1990; Spender, 1980; Still, 2006), men have historically dominated most professions and have taken the majority of leadership roles, and thus leadership has evolved as a masculine construct. Within many traditional models of leadership, the necessary and desirable qualities of toughness, decisiveness, and competitiveness have long been assumed to be masculine (Still, 2006). In terms of career development and progression, "corporate masculinity" operates as a norm that all managers aspiring to the top must adopt, whether they are male or female. Following the "male as norm" rule (Spender, 1980, p. 158), women in leadership positions are marked as "the other," the exception to the male norm, and are therefore judged to be less fit or competent for the role. Dominance theory takes the argument about the predominance of "corporate masculinity" and suggests that it may have profound implications for the ways women and men use language to perform leadership, as well as the ways language is used to represent them in the workplace, the media, and other public settings. Generally, research conducted from a dominance perspective has now been superseded by discursive perspectives (Litosseliti, 2006; see below), but many of the arguments and findings from dominance studies remain pertinent to women's experiences of leadership.

In terms of how women perform leadership, dominance theorists are primarily interested in the notion of "conversational dominance," which refers to the phenomenon of a male speaker dominating women in interaction (Coates, 2004). Research focusing on mixed gender talk in a variety of work contexts has revealed asymmetrical patterns, with men's usage of certain strategies being associated with demonstrating power over others, and women's usage of other strategies being associated with acceptance, resignation, and submission to male power. Dominance research studied interactional features such as interruptions, which were indexical of either exercising power over others or yielding power to others. For example, a classic study by Zimmerman and West (1975) comparing discussions within mixed- and same-gender pairs found that the majority of interruptions (where the intention was to "grab the floor") were cases of a man interrupting a woman. There were far fewer cases of men interrupting other men, or women interrupting each other, and virtually no cases of women interrupting men. Other studies, such as that by Holmes (1995), confirmed these findings. In the following example from a meeting of colleagues in a government department, a man's use of interruption makes it far more difficult for a female colleague to get her point across in this professional arena:

Peter:	what has your section done in this area for instance?
Judith:	well we have begun thinking about it; we've been holding regular review sessions [on
Peter:	[it'll take a lot more than that I can tell you; this is a serious matter

(Holmes, 1995, p. 51.)

Key: [= exact moment in speech where interruption occurs.

This tendency for men to interrupt women in work settings appeared to occur regardless of status. Woods (1988) discovered that a woman leader was more likely to be interrupted by a male subordinate than to interrupt him. The author showed that men use interruptions as a way of getting access to the floor, and they succeed in 85 percent of their attempts. Interruptions appear to be a way of controlling topics which normally might be shared equally by participants in a conversation. Another conversational feature where equal rights to talk might be expected is the amount of talking time available to participants. Studies such as that by Edelsky and Adams (1990) found that men do most of the talking in high-status, public settings where competing for turns is expected, such as meetings, debates, conferences, seminars, and presentations.

Recent studies have challenged the binary assumptions of dominance theory that most men (as an all-encompassing social category) seek to demonstrate power over most women, and that women, regardless of status or expertise, capitulate to men in workplace settings. For example, Muhr (2011) uses the metaphor of the "cyborg" to explore the way in which a top female manager tries to fight for gender equality by employing powerful masculine linguistic strategies (such as interruption) in a female body. However, contrary to the usual argument that women become masculinized leaders, Muhr (2011) proposes that female leadership becomes both excessively masculine and excessively feminine, challenging simplified readings of asymmetrical gendered leadership. In her case study, the high-performance language and behavior from a senior female leader in effect ends up reinforcing gender inequality because it suggests that women have to work twice as hard as men to achieve comparable effects as leaders. More typically, women leaders are trapped by the masculinized attitudes of the "double bind." That is, if they speak and sound overly "masculine," they are characterized by colleagues as aggressive, and if they speak and sound overly "feminine," they are characterized as tentative, hesitant, or weak (Holmes, 2006).

In terms of the ways language is used to represent women leaders, dominance theory argues that women are often depicted by others in negative, reductive, and sexualized ways. In a classic study, Kanter (1993) proposed that women leaders are targeted because they are highly visible as people who are different, and yet they are not permitted the individuality of "their own unique, non-stereotypical characteristics" (p. 217). They are often women in a masculine domain, who are perceived to aspire inappropriately to the privileges of the dominant order. Kanter (1993) suggested that because women leaders are viewed by corporates as outsiders, there are a limited range of leadership roles that women are permitted to perform, which she named the seductress, the iron maiden, the pet, and the mother (see Chapters 20, 21, and 22 of this *Handbook* for more details on labels given to women). She contends that these roles restrict the range of behavior available to women leaders by inappropriately reducing and sexualizing them. I have since argued (Baxter, 2012) that women leaders can challenge these stereotyped roles by appropriating them as resources to demonstrate a wider variety of leadership practices. Thus, a woman might utilize some aspects of the mother role, but also exploit other aspects of the iron maiden role to achieve specific outcomes according to context. However, overall, such stereotypes do little in the longer term to enable women leaders to be taken seriously and to achieve equal footing with men.

Dominance theorists have critiqued language as a means of perpetuating the strong association between normative masculinity and leadership. Mills (2014) argues that the way female leaders are spoken about by others in the workplace can be prejudicial to women as they go about their daily business. She cites examples such as referring to grown women as "girls" in work contexts, or calling a female leader "scary" because she speaks

whether they work in a masculine or feminine "community of practice" or "CofP": that is, "an aggregate of people who come together around mutual engagement in endeavor" (Eckert and McConnell-Ginet, 1998, p. 464). Marra et al. (2006) explain what they mean by the gendered nature of CofPs:

> New Zealanders readily describe workplaces as more or less "feminine" and more or less "masculine" in orientation. Rather than simply referring to the gender composition of the group, however, the gendered labels refer to the practices, including communicative practices, consistent with the CofP framework. (p. 243)

So, if a male leader is working in a "feminine" CofP, he is more likely to use interactional practices that are relational – that is, indirect, collaborative, and supportive in style – rather than the conventional skill set associated with men. Whereas if a female leader is working in a "masculine" CofP, she is more likely to use practices that are transactional – that is, direct, competitive, and confrontational in style – than the normative practices associated with women. This is illustrated in the following extract, where Clara, a managing director and chair of the meeting, is using language consistent with a "masculine" community of practice:

1	**Har:**	looks like there's been actually a request for screendumps
2		I know it was outside of the scope
3		but people will be pretty worried about it
4	**Cla:**	no screendumps
5	**Matt:**	we-
6	**Cla:**	no screendumps
7	**Peg:**	(*sarcastically*) thank you Clara
8	**Cla:**	[no screendumps
9	**Matt:**	[we know] we know you didn't want them and we um er [we've
10	**Cla:**	[that does not] meet the criteria

(Holmes, 2006, p. 57.)

Key: Har = Harold; Cla = Clara; Peg = Peggy; [= overlapping speech.

Here Clara gives a very clear directive to her team that under no circumstances will people be allowed to print material from their screens. She states her position clearly and explicitly on no fewer than three occasions without any qualification, thus conveying her message in very strong terms indeed. She is "doing power" over her colleagues quite explicitly by using repeated, staccato commands and apparently disregarding conventional politeness. Holmes (2006) suggests that the extract shows Clara exercising leadership "in an authoritative and conventionally masculine way" (p. 58). This reflects a CofP in which "authoritative decision-making" and "formality" were part of routine daily practices (p. 58).

Holmes and her colleagues claim that they use an "appreciative" approach to their leader subjects (Holmes and Vine, in press), which is intentionally descriptive and non-critical. In so doing, they demonstrate that while the most effective leaders are strongly influenced by the gendered character of their CofP, they are not restricted by this. Both female and male leaders can "skillfully" deploy linguistic strategies that range along the feminine–masculine continuum according to topic, purpose, the degree of "publicness" of the meeting, and the norms of the professional community to which they belong (p. 256). The authors do not attempt to critique the gendered ideologies or discourses that might penalize and prohibit women leaders from speaking and interacting in overly masculine ways. Rather, a CofP is conceptualized as an ideology-free haven within which women are permitted to transgress normative gender boundaries and to speak and interact in a gender-neutral space.

Adopting a more critical stance toward the view that language is a set of strategies upon which women can draw to accomplish participation and leadership, Ford (2008) uses the method of conversation analysis (CA) to "document ways that women enact local power in workplaces where, in the aggregate, women continue to be undercompensated and also underrepresented in the higher ranks" (p. 168). She recorded meetings in a range of United States (US) workplace settings in science, medicine, and engineering and found, unexpectedly, that "women are already contributing to workplace talk even in domains and events in which they are relatively new" (p. 168). Her observations are based on the ways in which women use language in order to participate influentially in senior management meetings, and these contributions include the use of quite technical linguistic strategies such as "turn-launching, turn-building, turn extension, action formulation and sequence expansion," all of which enable these women to "have a voice" (p. 168). Rather than finding that women are denied a voice in these senior settings, Ford was delighted to discover that women not only support each other in creating opportunities to speak, but are able to "command diverse, skillful, and adaptable repertoires for contributing to, and affecting the flow of actions and ideas in meetings" (Ford, 2008, p. 168).

Other discourse theorists aim to bring together the micro-analysis of exactly how women leaders utilize different linguistic strategies to achieve their goals, with a macro-analysis of institutional and gendered discourses that they have identified in the broader workplace setting. Mullany (2007) uses discourse analysis of meeting transcripts to identify exactly how both women and men leaders perform their professional roles with their teams. While Mullany reaches similar conclusions to the LWP team mentioned above in observing that both male and female managers use "masculine" and "feminine" linguistic strategies to achieve leadership goals, she also uses these data to identify various gendered discourses (p. 35). She argues that potentially "damaging" gendered discourses filtering through the United Kingdom (UK) business organization she studied (which she has labeled as emotionality/irrationality, image and sexuality, and career progression and motherhood), work against middle management and senior women in highly negative ways. These discourses served to construct corporate assumptions by which women leaders were judged more harshly than men, regardless of women's apparently skillful use of a broad repertoire of linguistic strategies to manage their teams.

In order to understand how gendered discourses affect women leaders in different cultural settings, a colleague and I conducted a study of the language of senior business women in the UK and the Middle East (Baxter and Al A'ali, 2016). While I observed and analyzed the linguistic experiences of women leaders in seven different UK companies, Al A'ali conducted a related study of women leaders within one Bahraini multinational company. Our studies were conducted independently of each other, but our research aims, methods, and tools of analysis to interrogate the data were carried out in collaboration with each other. We both applied the method of feminist poststructuralist discourse analysis (FPDA) to the data, which examines transcripts in close detail and helps to identify discourses from spoken interactions. The method is also used to analyze how discourses "position" speakers as subjects, which influences how powerful or powerless they are within a conversation (Baxter, 2003, p. 32). Across both Western and Bahraini contexts, we discovered that there were a number of corporate and/or gendered discourses in common that we defined as the following:

- *Hierarchy and status:* a leader's status in her organization and the degree to which this helps to support and empower her.
- *Historical legacy:* the length of service a leader has given the organization and how instrumental this is to the powerfulness of her position.
- *Relational practices:* a relational style expected of women leaders, which distinguishes them from men; in different contexts this can either empower or disempower women.
- *Masculinization:* leadership as a masculine activity with women viewed as outsiders.

Additionally, we identified several culturally distinct, corporate discourses. Within the UK context, we identified discourses such as change and uncertainty (leaders required to manage the pressure of chronic organizational change). Within the Bahraini context, we identified the gendered discourse of family (organizations mythologized as families with the head of the company seen as the "father" and women middle managers seen as "mothers") and loyalty (all employees, regardless of gender, expected to remain loyal, dutiful, and respectful to the company throughout their time there).

Without doubt, one of the most surprising findings of our study was that the Bahraini women leaders seemed more empowered by the prevailing, institutional discourses than the UK leaders. In the following extract, we gain insights about Fatima, a Bahraini leader with over 20 years of service, who is able to negotiate a consistently powerful subject position for herself across several competing discourses. Here, she informs her team that the executive committee (the level above her) is making job cuts across the company, which could be "bad news" for members of her own section:

```
 1 F:    your situation is critical; also your section is in a critical
 2       position; your section is one of those that Multico has a
 3       strong view about
 4       (some people laugh)
 5 S:    heheheheh
 6 F:    so: I can't tell you anything now because the
 7       management might not agree with their view of the section; I
 8       mean even before and this happened a few times that
 9       suggestions come up that why don't you give this section to
10       for example instead of you doing it; give it to another
11       company to handle it
12 S:    what about us?
13 F:    and you; we will have you rotate
14       (everyone laughs)
15 F:    we can't let you off (smiley voice)
16 S:    rotation how?
17 F:    no no; this is just me
```

(Baxter and Al A'ali, 2016, p. 62.)

Key: F = Fatima, Head of Section and Chair; S = Salem, male team member; Multico = a consultancy company with the responsibility of "restructuring" the company.

Here, Fatima uses a series of bald, unqualified statements in lines 1 to 3 to express the news, consistent with a direct, masculinized leadership style. This is undercut by her use of a euphemism that raises a laugh: "your section is one of those that Multico has a strong view about." These statements index a discourse of hierarchy and status: Fatima is a leader who is endowed with the authority to deliver bad news directly and to deal with her team's reactions. The fact that people laugh indicates her positioning within a discourse of relational practices: Fatima has established an underlying good relationship with her team through her use of humor, despite her blunt delivery of the bad news. From lines 6 to10, Fatima distances herself somewhat from the force of the message by giving a series of qualifications about how she is not directly party to senior management's thoughts on the subject, but it is clear that she has been involved in its deliberations, once again indexing a powerful subject position within the discourses of both hierarchy and status and loyalty to her bosses. From line 12, she engages in a bantering dialogue with her subordinate, Salem, although he seems distressed and uneasy, using rather querulous, child-like language: "what about us?" (line 12); "rotation how?" (line 16). Arguably, Fatima positions herself within a discourse of family as the consoling mother to the petulant child, but this is done ironically and knowingly, as indexed by the laughter from other team members. In order to deal with the testy response from her subordinate, Fatima shows herself to be thoroughly in control over her team while delivering bad news by using a range of leadership linguistic strategies ranging from direct statements to gentle, teasing humor.

A discourse analysis of this extract indicates that one reason why Bahraini women may find themselves more empowered as leaders than their UK women counterparts is that they are strongly positioned within the dual discourses of loyalty and family, discourses not found in the UK context. Alongside hierarchy and status, loyalty affirms Fatima's position as a leader in the corporate pecking order. Just as her loyalty to senior management ensures that she will receive her bosses' unconditional support as a leader, her team's loyalty to her guarantees that any individual resistance to her leadership is never more than superficial or transient. The embedding of authority structures within this Bahraini organization by means of the gendered discourse of family is of course a "double-edged sword" for Bahraini women leaders. As a "mother," she is unlikely to progress to be the head of her organization as her UK counterpart might conceivably do. While such a corporate context might be perceived as paternalistic and gender-divided from a Western perspective, it does protect women leaders with long service from the insecurities that we observed in the UK context. There, women leaders had to manage random executive decisions, ever-shifting job roles, and peremptory job losses (Baxter and Al A'ali, 2016). Women were also powerlessly positioned within the discourse of relational practices simply because they rarely had time to get to know their team members before people were moved on to different roles.

Discourse theory shows that gendered discourses intersect with other corporate discourses to enable as well as constrain women's experiences of leadership. Women leaders were at times empowered, but at other times disempowered by the dominant discourses within their leadership context.

SUMMING UP: THE VALUE OF LINGUISTIC THEORIES

The three major theories reviewed in this chapter all have value in explaining the crucial role of language in women's performance of leadership, as well as the ways women are represented as leaders in the public domain. Each theory also helps to explain why women remain under-represented at senior level and indicates possible linguistic solutions to this issue. However, of the three theories, it is discourse theory which claims that women and men are not ultimately constrained by their gender. Rather, gender is viewed as just one, if significant, facet of our diverse, multiple, and fluid identities that often comes into play when power relations are salient. Discourse theory argues that our professional identities emerge primarily through spoken interactions; people can prove themselves to be effective leaders through their speech, actions, and performance. The influences and interplay of multiple identity categories alongside gender, such as age, status, experience, and expertise, all play a part in determining who is influential and who leads people effectively in today's world. We saw that interacting corporate discourses (such as change and uncertainty, loyalty, hierarchy and status, and family) exert discursive prohibitions upon the free play of these multiple identity categories. Leaders are positioned and repositioned by these powerful corporate discourses, some of which are gendered and serve to constrain the potential of women leaders according to circumstance and context. Gendered discourses such as image and sexuality and masculinization remain deeply ingrained across wider society, and they continue to have damaging effects upon the career progress of women regardless of how diverse and progressive a team, community of practice, or company may seek to be. One way forward for aspiring women leaders is to learn that language can be a versatile, creative, and context-rich set of strategies for achieving the transactional, relational, and transformational goals of effective leadership. If women leaders were also to gain some knowledge of the sociolinguistic theories of gender and leadership, this would provide them with a vital toolkit to challenge hegemonic language and discourses, wherever these appear.

REFERENCES

Angouri, J. (2011). "We are in a masculine profession. . .": Constructing gender identities in a consortium of two multinational engineering companies. *Gender and Language*, 5(2), 343–371.

Bargiela-Chiappini, F., and Harris, S. (1997). *Managing Language: The Discourse of Corporate Meetings*. Amsterdam, The Netherlands: John Benjamins.

Baxter, J. (2003). *Positioning Gender in Discourse: A Feminist Methodology*. Basingstoke, UK: Palgrave.

Baxter, J. (2010). *The Language of Female Leadership*. Basingstoke, UK: Palgrave.

Baxter, J. (2012). Women of the corporation: A sociolinguistic perspective of senior women's leadership language in the UK. *Journal of Sociolinguistics*, 16(1), 81–107.

Baxter, J. (2014). *Double-Voicing at Work: Power, Gender and Linguistic Expertise*. Basingstoke, UK: Palgrave.

Baxter, J., and Al A'ali, H. (2016). *Speaking as Women Leaders: Meetings in Middle Eastern and Western Contexts*. Basingstoke, UK: Palgrave.

Bucholtz, M., and Hall, K. (1995). *Gender Articulated: Language and the Socially Constructed Self*. New York, NY: Routledge.

Butler, J. (1990). *Gender Trouble and the Subversion of Identity*. New York, NY: Routledge.

Clifton, J. (2012). A discursive approach to leadership: Doing assessments and managing organizational meanings. *International Journal of Business Communication*, 49(2), 148–168.

Coates, J. (2004). *Women, Men and Language*. London, UK: Longman.

Crawford, M. (1995). *Talking Difference: On Gender and Language*. London: Sage Publications.

Eagly, A., and Carli, L. (2007). *Through the Labyrinth: The Truth about how Women Become Leaders*. Boston, MA: Harvard Business School Press.

Eckert, P., and McConnell-Ginet, S. (1998). Communities of practice: Where language, gender and power all live. In J. Coates (Ed.) *Language and Gender: A Reader* (pp. 484–494). Oxford, UK: Blackwell.

Edelsky, C., and Adams, A. (1990). Creating inequality: Breaking the rules in debates. *Journal of Language and Social Equality*, *9*(3), 171–90.

Fletcher, J.K. (1999). *Disappearing Acts: Gender, Power and Relational Practice*. Cambridge, MA: MIT Press.

Ford, C. (2008). *Women Speaking Up*. Basingstoke, UK: Palgrave.

Foucault, M. (1972). *The Archaeology of Knowledge and the Discourse on Language*. New York, NY: Pantheon.

Gray, J. (1992). *Men are from Mars, Women are from Venus*. London, UK: Harper Collins.

Helgesen, S. (1990). *The Female Advantage: Women's Ways of Leadership*. New York, NY: Doubleday/Currency.

Holmes, J. (1995). *Women, Men and Politeness*. London, UK: Longman.

Holmes, J. (2006). *Gendered Talk at Work*. Oxford, UK: Blackwell.

Holmes, J., and Stubbe, M. (2003). *Power and Politeness in the Workplace*. London, UK: Longman.

Holmes, J., and Vine, B. (in press). "That's just how we do things round here": Researching workplace discourse for the benefit of employees. In V. Vander and J. Rahilly (Eds), *Crossing Boundaries: Interdisciplinarity in Language Studies* (pp. 00–00). Amsterdam, The Netherlands: John Benjamins.

Kanter, R.M. (1993). *Men and Women of the Corporation*. New York, NY: Basic Books.

Koller, V. (2004). *Metaphor and Gender in Business Media Discourse*. Basingstoke, UK: Palgrave.

Litosseliti, L. (2006). *Gender and Language: Theory and Practice*. London, UK: Hodder Arnold.

Litosseliti, L., and Leadbeater, C. (2013). Gendered discourses in speech and language therapy. *Journal of Applied Linguistics and Professional Practice*, *8*(3), 295–314.

Maltz, D., and Borker, R. (1982). A cultural approach to male–female miscommunication. In J. Gumperz (ed.), *Language and Social Identity* (pp. 196–216). Cambridge, UK: Cambridge University Press.

Marra, M., Schnurr, S., and Holmes, J. (2006). Effective leadership in New Zealand workplaces. In J. Baxter (Ed.), *Speaking Out: The Female Voice in Public Contexts* (pp. 240–260). Basingstoke, UK: Palgrave.

Mills, E. (2014). Bossy boots are made for walkin' – right to the top. Retrieved from http://www.thesundaytimes.co.uk/sto/comment/columns/eleanormills/article1387534.ece.

Muhr, S.L. (2011). Caught in the gendered machine: On the masculine and feminine in cyborg leadership. *Gender, Work and Organization*, *18*(3), 337–357.

Mullany, L. (2007). *Gendered Discourse in the Professional Workplace*. Basingstoke, UK: Palgrave.

Olsson, S. (2006). We don't need another hero!: Organizational storytelling as a vehicle for communicating a female archetype of workplace leadership. In M. Barrett and M. J. Davidson (Eds), *Gender and Communication at Work* (pp. 195–210). Aldershot, UK: Ashgate.

Pease, A., and Pease, B. (2001). *Why Men Don't Listen and Women Can't Read Maps*. London, UK: Orion.

Rosener, J.B. (1990). Ways women lead. *Harvard Business Review*, *68*(6), 119–125.

Schnurr, S. (2009). *Leadership Discourse at Work. Interactions of Humor, Gender and Workplace Culture*. Basingstoke, UK: Palgrave.

Schulz, M. (1990). The semantic derogation of women. In D. Cameron (ed.), *The Feminist Critique of Language* (pp. 134–147). London, UK: Routledge.

Spender, D. (1980). *Man-Made Language*. London, UK: Pandora Press.

Still, L.V. (2006). Gender, leadership and communication. In M. Barrett and M. J. Davidson (Eds), *Gender and Communication at Work* (pp. 183–194). Aldershot, UK: Ashgate.

Sunderland, J. (2004). *Gendered Discourses*. Basingstoke, UK: Palgrave.

Tannen, D. (1995). *Talking from 9 to 5: Women and Men in the Workplace*. New York, NY: Avon.

UN Women (2015). *Women's Participation: Facts and Figures*. Retrieved from http://www.unwomen.org/en/what-we-do/leadership-and-political-participation.

Vinnicombe, S., Doldor, E., Sealy, R., Pryce, P., and Turner, C. (2015). *The Female FTSE Board Report*. Cranfield University, UK: Cranfield Centre for Women Leaders.

Vinnicombe, S., and Singh, V. (2002). Sex role stereotyping and requisites of successful top managers. *Women in Management Review*, *17*(3/4), 120–130.

Walker, R., and Aritz, J. (2015). Women doing leadership: Leadership styles and organizational culture. *International Journal of Business Communication*, *52*(4), 452–478.

Woods, N. (1988). Talking shop: Sex and status as determinants of floor apportionment in a work setting. In J. Coates and D. Cameron (Eds), *Women in their Speech Communities* (pp. 141–157). London, UK: Longman.

Zimmerman, D., and West, C. (1975). Sex roles, interruptions and silences in conversation. In B. Thorne and N. Henley (Eds), *Language and Sex: Difference and Dominance* (pp. 105–129). Rowley, MA: Newbury House.

8. Using organizational and management science theories to understand women and leadership

Chantal van Esch, Karlygash Assylkhan, and Diana Bilimoria

This chapter provides researchers with an overview of a number of organizational science theories that inform women and leadership research. Women and leadership can be understood at the most micro levels (that is, how an individual's competencies or personality deter or facilitate leadership actions) to the most macro levels (that is, how societal structures hinder or help women achieve and enact leadership). We start by offering a broad overview of general theories in the organizational and management sciences at the individual, interpersonal, and organizational levels of analysis that are relevant for women and leadership research. We provide a sampling of these theories by level, offering a brief description of each as well as potential research questions that may advance extant understanding of women and leadership from the perspective of each theory.

Since there are few theories in the organizational and management sciences that directly address women and leadership, our goal is first to introduce a broad array of theories which impact women in leadership; and then, to illustrate how a gender conversation within these theories could be important and helpful for future women and leadership research, we will take a deeper dive into a few general theories in these disciplines. We follow the introduction of each selected theory with an overview of research findings specific to women and leadership based on that theory, and then we provide guidance for future research in this direction. Finally, we summarize the implications for further exploration of women and leadership in the organizational sciences.

At the outset we recognize that few theories relating specifically to women and leadership have been developed in the organizational and management sciences. While some theories relating to women's career development have emerged in these disciplines (e.g., Betz and Fitzgerald, 1987; Mainiero and Sullivan, 2005; O'Neil et al., 2008) – encouraging a women-specific research focus in career development, selection, and advancement – theories focusing specifically on women's leadership are not as common. Frameworks of leadership in the organizational and management sciences remain largely male-centric (see Ibarra et al., 2013; Woolley et al., 2011), often relying on conceptions and standards derived primarily, if not exclusively, from men's experiences. Even when general leadership models incorporate conventionally feminine preferences, such as attention to values and purpose, relationship building, inclusiveness, and process sensitivity, the implications and outcomes of their implementation differ substantially for women and men leaders. Men leaders benefit more from their implementation than do women leaders (O'Neil and Hopkins, 2015), potentially because the application of such communal leadership approaches deviates positively from gender role expectations for men but is expected for women.

In addition, we recognize that gender is only one aspect of a person's social identity influencing leadership and that the intersectionality of other social identities needs to be considered in understanding women and leadership. While in this chapter we primarily discuss gender-related effects, intersectional effects on women and leadership (for example, race/ethnicity, age, sexual orientation, nationality, citizenship, and physical appearance) must also be considered to fully understand the topic. Next, we discuss general theories in organizational and management science relevant to women and leadership.

GENERAL THEORIES OF ORGANIZATIONAL AND MANAGEMENT SCIENCES

Table 8.1 provides a sampling of general theories from the organizational and management sciences that are relevant for advancing extant knowledge about women and leadership. We provide in this table a brief description of each theory and some potential research questions aimed to catalyze future research and advance current knowledge about women and leadership.

Below we take a deeper dive into selected theories at different levels, describing extant research addressing women and leadership within each framework and drawing implications for future research. Our purpose here is to illustrate how a few general theories from the organizational and management sciences listed in Table 8.1 may be employed to advance current knowledge about women and leadership. The particular theories selected for further examination are sampled from each level – individual, interpersonal, and organizational – to give a flavor of the kinds of women-specific research that has been conducted to date and to offer suggestions for future research. We picked these particular theories for deeper exploration because of previous work done within these frameworks to make the linkage with women and leadership.

INDIVIDUAL (MICRO) LEVEL

At the micro (individual) level of analysis we highlight below how the theory of emotional intelligence can advance extant understanding of women and leadership. Although emotional intelligence has its roots in psychology, as do many other individual-level theories, its application and development largely has occurred in the organizational and management sciences, and so we include it for discussion in this chapter.

Emotional Intelligence

Emotional intelligence is the "capacity for recognizing our own emotions and those of others, for motivating ourselves and others, and for managing emotions well in ourselves and in our relationships" (Goleman, 1998, p. 317). Although debate exists around the distinction between emotional intelligence and personality traits (for more information, see Zeidner et al., 2004), a growing body of evidence suggests that emotional intelligence is distinct from personality traits and cognitive intelligence (Cote and Miners, 2006; Law et al., 2004; Rosete and Ciarrochi, 2005; Van Rooy et al., 2005). Higher levels of emotional competence are linked to better performance in managers (Cavallo and Brienza, 2006).

Table 8.1 Application of select organizational/management theories to women and leadership

Theory	Description	Potential research questions advancing women and leadership research
Individual-level theories		
Emotional intelligence theory	Discussed in main text	
Equity theory	Equity theory suggests that people are motivated by fairness and equity and will act to achieve perceived equity within their referent groups. In the face of perceived inequity, employees may change their inputs or outcomes, distort perceptions of self or of others, pick a different referent group, or leave the field (Langton et al., 2015).	How do women and men leaders respond to perceived inequities? What can organizations do to address perceived inequities in women's advancement to leadership?
Expectancy theory	Expectancy theory suggests that employee behaviors depend on the degree to which they want to achieve certain outcomes. Motivation occurs when employees perceive that their acts will lead to better performance appraisal (effort–performance relationship), extrinsic and intrinsic rewards (performance–reward relationship), and ultimately, achievement of their personal goals (rewards–personal goals relationship) (Donovan, 2001; Porter and Lawler, 1968).	Do women and men have different expectations of the effort–performance relationship, performance–reward relationship, and rewards–personal goals relationship for themselves and others? Are women leaders rewarded differently than men leaders for equivalent effort and performance results?
Goal setting theory	This theory, sometimes referred to as management by objectives, suggests the importance of setting goals to increase performance. Generally, the more specific the goals, the higher the likely performance. The difficulty level of goals also leads to improved achievements, as does feedback (Locke and Latham, 2006; Tubbs, 1986).	Are there differences in the goals or goal setting processes used by women and men leaders? Do women leaders seek feedback differently than men?

Table 8.1 (continued)

Theory	Description	Potential research questions advancing women and leadership research
Individual-level theories		
Self-efficacy theory	Self-efficacy theory, also known as social learning theory or social cognitive theory, asserts that managers can motivate employees to complete tasks by helping employees become more confident in their ability to accomplish the work (Bandura, 1994; Locke and Latham, 2002).	Are women leaders motivated in different ways than men? How can managers help increase women's confidence for leadership positions? What roles do the organizational/team environment and workplace equity play in facilitating women's self-efficacy?
Interpersonal-level theories		
Authentic leadership	Discussed in the main text	
Contingency theories of leadership	These theories assert that it is important to match leadership styles to organizational situations. For example, Fiedler's theory of contingent leadership identifies different leadership styles (e.g., task-oriented versus relationship-oriented) and different situational characteristics (identified by the level of trust in the leader, whether the task is structured or unstructured, and the strength of the leader's position power). Effectiveness is predicted to occur when a leader's style matches the demands of the situation (Fiedler et al., 1976).	Under what organizational circumstances are women leaders more likely to engage in task-oriented versus relationship-oriented styles? How are these styles rewarded when displayed by women and men leaders?
Relational leadership theory	Relational leadership theory is framework developed by Uhl-Bien (2006) for the study of relational dynamics between leaders and followers that evolve and construct organizational coordination and change. Relational leadership is described as a social influence process involving ethics, inclusiveness, purpose, and empowerment.	Are women leaders expected to engage in relational leadership and how are they treated when they do or do not?

Servant leadership theory	Discussed in the main text	
Social exchange theory	Discussed in the main text	
Social network theory	Discussed in the main text	
Team effectiveness theory	McGrath (1964) developed an input–process–outcome (IPO) framework of team effectiveness. Inputs are pre-existing factors that affect performance, either positively or negatively, such as competencies, personalities, task structure, and organizational design features. Team processes comprise how team members interact and communicate, and how they contribute toward completing a task. Outcomes are measured by performance and members' affective states such as commitment and satisfaction.	How does gender diversity contribute to team performance? How can women leaders use their distinctive perspectives to contribute to overall team effectiveness?
Transformational leadership theory	Discussed in the main text	
Organizational-level theories		
Institutional theories	Discussed in the main text	
Organizational culture theory	This theory suggests that corporate culture, consisting of shared values, meaning, and assumptions, govern employee behavior (O'Donnell-Trujillo and Pacanowsky, 1983). The unique culture of an organization, shaped and shared by its formal and informal leaders, drives organizational behavior.	How do women leaders shape corporate culture differently than men leaders? How and when do women leaders experience organizational meaningfulness?

131

Table 8.1 (continued)

Theory	Description	Potential research questions advancing women and leadership research
Organizational-level theories		
Resource dependence theory	Resource dependence theory states that because each organization depends on resources that are obtained from its environment for its survival strategies are limited by environmental constraints (Salancik and Pfeffer, 1978).	Under what environmental conditions are organizations more likely to have greater gender diversity in their top management teams and boards of directors? Are women directors more likely to hold multiple directorships than men directors?
Upper echelons theory	Upper echelons theory asserts that organizations are a reflection of their top executives and that organizational outcomes and strategic decisions may be understood by examining the personal characteristics of those in top management (Hambrick and Mason, 1984). Differences in executives' experiences, values, and other characteristics result in different construals of corporate situations and strategies, and ultimately engender varying organizational outcomes (see also Finkelstein et al., 2009).	What are the characteristics of female and male leaders at the top of organizations? What organizational outcomes emanate from top leadership teams that have higher proportions of women?

Interestingly, previous research consistently has found gender differences in emotional intelligence, specifically that women score higher on particular competencies of emotional intelligence than men (e.g., Bar-On, 2000; Fernández-Berrocal et al., 2012; Goldenberg et al., 2006; Korn Ferry, 2016; Mayer et al., 1999; Naghavi and Redzuan, 2011; Petrides and Furnham, 2006; Van Rooy et al., 2005).

Further research is needed to clarify the relationship between the demonstration of emotional intelligence competencies and the leadership effectiveness of women and men. In addition, we recommend that future research focus on how high levels of emotional intelligence can foster women's leadership development. Especially since we know of the double-bind that women face in being perceived as either competent or likeable (Eagly and Carli, 2007), understanding the moderating role of gender in the relationship between emotional intelligence and leadership will be important moving forward. Future research should also assess the rewards and outcomes of displaying emotional intelligence by women and men leaders. For example, do men leaders who engage their followers with emotional intelligence gain greater rewards and better work, career, and organizational outcomes than women leaders? An understanding of emotional intelligence theory thus offers new avenues for examining the selection, performance, advancement, and outcomes of women leaders.

INTERPERSONAL (MESO) LEVEL

At the interpersonal (meso) level of analysis, we delve more deeply into three mainstream theories of leadership (servant leadership, transformational leadership, and authentic leadership), as well as into two theories explaining interpersonal interactions (social exchange theory and social network theory) in order to understand their usefulness for women and leadership research. We selected the three leadership theories because they explicitly include communality (versus agentic) principles conventionally associated with feminine leadership approaches (Eagly et al., 2003; Heilman, 2001), including a focus on values and purpose, other-centeredness, relational dynamics, process sensitivity, inclusiveness, and service. Below, we first discuss leadership theories in general, then describe the three leadership theories selected for further exploration, and finally draw out the implications for women and leadership from these three theories. Following this discussion, we describe the usefulness of the two theories of interpersonal interactions for women and leadership research.

Leadership Theories

Leadership is a theoretically dense area in the management and organizational science literatures (Dinh et al., 2014). An understanding of women and leadership issues will, of course, pull heavily from these theories, which explain varying aspects through different foci and lenses (Hernandez et al., 2011). Leadership is a complex subject with many theoretical implications since it involves complex interactions between leader, follower, and situation at multiple levels of the organization, and has a direct link to practice (see Day et al., 2014). Leadership theory has been approached in a number of ways, including trait, skills, behavior, situation, process, relationship, and psychodynamic based approaches (see Northouse, 2015; Yukl, 2010). This has resulted in a number of different leadership theories, including, but not limited to, path–goal theory, contingency theory, leader–member exchange theory, relational leadership theory, servant leadership theory, transformational leadership theory, and authentic leadership theory. In this chapter we focus on the latter three leadership theories since these are well-studied, communal theories. After brief descriptions of each of these three theories below, we draw out their collective implications for understanding women and leadership.

Servant Leadership

Servant leadership was introduced by Greenleaf (1970) almost 50 years ago to represent a leadership theory that was paradoxically focused on service to the follower, rather than the specific concerns of the organization or leader. Some have viewed servant leadership as controversial and detrimental to organizational goals (e.g., Andersen, 2009). For Greenleaf, leadership as service was not controversial, but rather the fundamental starting point. Indeed, Greenleaf wrote that (servant) leadership "begins with the natural feeling that one wants to serve, to serve first" (Greenleaf, 1970, p. 15). The style of leadership that Greenleaf (1970) postulated suggested focusing first on the followers and their needs, urged communication and collective support, and had a strong social justice orientation. While researchers struggle to crystallize the definition and measurement of servant leadership theory, empirical work has shown conceptualizations of it to help organizations and followers (Parris and Peachey, 2013). Current research is focused on addressing these issues by clarifying the construct (Liden et al., 2015; Van Dierendonck, 2011) as well as understanding the impact of servant leadership. For example, servant leadership has been linked not only to increased service by followers (Liden et al., 2014) but also to individual (Chiniara and Bentein, 2016), team (Hu and Liden, 2011), and organizational (Peterson et al., 2012) performance. Other research suggests that self-efficacy (Walumbwa et al., 2010), creativity (Liden et al., 2014; Neubert et al., 2008), promotion focus (Neubert et al., 2008), and just work climates (Ehrhart, 2004; Walumbwa et al., 2010) are encouraged by servant leaders. Servant leaders enjoy increased trust (Schaubroeck et al., 2011) and commitment from followers (Walumbwa et al., 2010).

Transformational Leadership

Introduced around the same time as servant leadership, transformational leadership looked to the leader's ability to inspire their followers (Burns, 1978). Specifically, Burns presented transformational leadership in opposition to transactional leadership, so rather than focusing on what a follower does for a leader, a transformational leader focuses on how they can build "a collective purpose in ways that transform, motivate, and enhance the actions and ethical aspirations of followers" (Burns, 1978, p. 804). Subsequent scholars clarified that transformational and transactional leadership are not opposite but, rather, complementary styles (Bass, 1985), and both are needed for organizational effectiveness (Bass et al., 2003). Transformational leadership theory suggests that by bridging employees' self-interests to organizational goals, leaders can use intellectual stimulation, inspirational motivation, individualized consideration, and charisma to enhance employee job performance (Avolio et al., 1999). Extant research has shown transformational leadership styles lead to higher levels of leadership effectiveness, employee satisfaction, and job performance (Bass, 1985), as well as employee empowerment (Özaralli, 2003), organizational citizenship behaviors (Koh et al., 1995), and commitment (Barling et al., 2000).

Authentic Leadership

Building on the idea of transformational leadership theory, authentic leadership theory was more recently introduced to deal with the complexities of contemporary leadership issues (Avolio et al., 2004). Authentic leadership theory focuses on aspirations, values, leadership style, and integration (O'Neil and Hopkins, 2015). This theory focuses on the importance of leaders being authentic to themselves and their values. Authentic leaders have high moral character, embody psychological capital (for example, confidence, hope, optimism, and resiliency), and are deeply aware of themselves and others (Avolio et al., 2004); characteristics that are particularly important for leadership in today's complex and global environment (Avolio and Gardner, 2005). The understanding of one's own and others' values, or authenticity, is crucial in dealing with multifarious global ethical business decisions. Authentic leadership has been shown to restore followers' confidence and sense of security (Eagly, 2005) and to build followers' confidence, optimism, hope, and resiliency (Luthans et al., 2007). Additionally, authenticity has been found to be positively correlated with career success, as authentic leaders' actions are more aligned with their own values and beliefs (Mainiero and Sullivan, 2005; Ruderman and Ohlott, 2002, 2005).

Application of Servant, Transformational, and Authentic Leadership Theories to Women and Leadership

Previous research has indicated that women and men use and embody different leadership approaches (Javidan et al., 2016). Women are more likely to enact "person-centered leadership approaches" (Duff, 2013, p. 215) and therefore they stereotypically fit the servant style of leadership (Liden et al., 2014). Additionally, women are generally more communal then men (Heilman, 2001), having higher levels of intellectual stimulation, individualized consideration, and inspirational motivation (Eagly et al., 2003), and thus are more likely to participate in transformational rather than transactional leadership (Eagly et al., 2003). However, research has also shown a discrepancy between stereotypically masculine views of leadership and feminine traits (Schein, 1973, 1975), making it harder for women to act authentically and be perceived as leaders.

Critiques of leadership theories, such as authentic leadership, point to the gendered organizational norms and circumstances uniquely faced by women leaders, which pose challenges for them to assert authentic leadership (e.g., O'Neil and Hopkins, 2015). Additionally, the authentic leadership construct may itself be gendered in that it is based on individualistic (agentic and stereotypically masculine) versus collective (communal and stereotypically feminine) principles (Ibarra, 2015; Woolley et al., 2011), disadvantaging women leaders who may engage authentically. In this context, more research needs to be undertaken on how contemporary and popular leadership theories, such as authentic leadership, translate to the enactment and perception of women's leadership. Additionally, much of the previous research has been conducted in countries valuing individualism; application of these theories in countries with different norms and values for communal traits may yield different understandings of women and leadership.

Future research on women and leadership should make use of servant, transformational, and authentic leadership theories in developing more nuanced understandings of leadership, inclusive of how women and men across the world who engage in specific leadership approaches may be perceived. Understanding which style(s) of leadership women are more likely to enact (Eagly et al., 2003; Fridell et al., 2009), and their impact on individuals and organizations, will help us to understand the unique characteristics and advantages of women's leadership. We recommend that future research add to extant knowledge by examining not only how women may benefit from enacting servant, transformational, and authentic styles of leadership, but also what the impact of men's use of these leadership approaches may be.

These leadership theories can also help to develop further understanding of how leadership development education and training should be implemented for women. In light of the unique barriers and challenges faced by women leaders, such as double binds, gendered career paths, few role models, and barriers to accessing networks and sponsors (Ibarra et al., 2013), scholars have called for organizations to implement developmental programs specifically for women in leadership (Debebe et al., 2016; Ely et al., 2011). A recent global comparison of general and women-only leadership development programs found that different theoretical frameworks underlie the design of these programs: general leadership development programs were driven more exclusively by individualized, agentic, and stereotypically male leadership theories; while women-only leadership development programs incorporated more communal and stereotypically female leadership theories (Sugiyama et al., 2016). Chapters 25 and 27 of this *Handbook* offer more detail on women-only leadership programs.

Social Exchange Theory

Continuing at the interpersonal level, social exchange theory provides organizational scholars with an understanding of how interactions between individuals are maintained. Social exchange theory states that individuals operate under particular rules of exchange in interacting with others (for a review, see Cropanzano and Mitchell, 2005). Relationships are built when people engage in continuous interactions within these rules (Emerson, 1976), specifically the rule of reciprocity, which indicates that when one person makes an exchange the other is expected to reciprocate (Gouldner, 1960). According to social exchange theory, when exchanges are reciprocal the relationship will continue; however, when they are not, the relationship will end (Blau, 1964).

In the organizational and management sciences, organizational citizenship behavior (OCB) is one of the most well-studied forms of social exchange (Smith et al., 1983). OCBs are optional behaviors outside of an employee's job description (Organ, 1997). Also known as "good soldier" behavior (Bateman and Organ, 1983) or "contextual performance" (Borman and Motowidlo, 1993), OCBs are defined as "contributions to the maintenance and enhancement of the social and psychological context that supports task performance" (Organ, 1997, p.91). OCBs have been shown to help organizations function effectively as employees exchange favors and help others and the organization (for a further review, see Podsakoff et al., 2009).

Hence, as social exchanges, OCBs are expected to be reciprocal and therefore help to form relationships for the betterment not only of those involved (Blau, 1964), but also of the organization (Podsakoff et al., 2009). A number of studies have started to look into gender differences in the impact of these exchanges. Kidder and Parks (2001) argued that what is considered to be optional OCB and what is considered required in-role behavior fluctuates. A meta-analysis of original OCB work showed no gender differences (Organ and Ryan, 1995), but more recent work indicates that this might be due to the type of OCB (Lin, 2008).

Understanding the implications of social exchanges in general, and OCB specifically, will be important in advancing women and leadership research, especially as the negative consequences of OCB are explored (Bergeron, 2007). This area could help to develop understanding around the differing expectations held about exchanges from women and men leaders. These dissimilar expectations may well be one of the missing variables in understanding the gender leadership gap. Future research should also use social exchange theory to develop hypotheses about inequitable exchanges across genders and leadership levels, as the interactions of women and leadership may lead to inequitable returns on investment from similar exchanges (Bergeron et al., 2012). In this regard, we encourage research around the outcomes of the time invested in OCB by women and men leaders in organizations. The moderating effects of leadership power and privilege should also be explored in terms of gender-based outcomes of social exchanges.

Social Network Theory

While social exchange theory helps to explain how relationships between leaders and others are maintained, social network theory looks at how the structure of these relationships affects leaders and leadership outcomes. Social network theory helps to develop an understanding of how women's and men's relational ties impact their leadership. This theory has focused on understanding the relationships that exist and how ties connect and divide (Freeman, 2004). Social network theory posits that an individual's network structure – measured by variables such as breadth, number and type of ties, centrality, and influence within a network – influences selection for and effectiveness in leadership (e.g., Hodigere and Bilimoria, 2015).

Understanding how different network structures affect women and men as leaders is important in understanding not only their professional and social networks, but also their personal career success (McGuire, 2000) and organizational effectiveness as leaders (Burt, 1992). These structural differences are imperative in understanding issues around gender equity in leadership. One important tenet of social network theory for women and leadership research is that of homophily, or an individual's preference to interact with others who are similar to them (McPherson and Smith-Lovin, 1987). Homophily suggests that there will be fewer relationships and less communication between people who are dissimilar for any reason including, but not limited to, gender, race, class, and position (McPherson and Smith-Lovin, 1987). This directly impacts women leaders as it has been shown that this lack of connection leads to decreased individual performance (e.g., Ibarra, 1992; Krackhardt and Stern, 1988; Reagans and Zuckerman, 2001). For example, in male-dominated organizations, men's networks are more likely than women's networks to contain powerful individuals (Brass, 1985; Ibarra, 1992). Being excluded from powerful networks inhibits female leaders due to a lack of mentoring (Noe, 1988), information access (McDonald and Westphal, 2013), and human capital development (Hollenbeck and Jamieson, 2015).

We encourage organizational scholars to employ social network theory to do future research, not only on the structural implications of networks, but also to understand how social network theory can inform women leaders to advance in their careers and successfully access the necessary information and human capital to be effective in their leadership roles. Future research should use a longitudinal social network theory lens not only to understand which network structures benefit individuals and organizations, but also to understand how they are built and how issues such as the preference for homophily may be overcome.

ORGANIZATIONAL (MACRO) LEVEL

At the organizational level, we look at the usefulness of institutionalization theory for advancing extant understanding of women and leadership. We selected this theory because it holds clear and well-studied implications for women and leadership, and it offers good potential for further examination in this regard.

Institutionalization Theory

Institutionalization theory explains how norms or socially constructed expectations and patterns shape organizations and outcomes. Thornton and Ocasio (1999) defined institutional logic as "the socially constructed, historical patterns of material practices, assumptions, values, beliefs, and rules by which individuals produce and reproduce their material subsistence, organize time and space, and provide meaning to their social reality" (p. 804). At this most macro level, women and leadership scholars look to institutionalization theory to understand how societal norms and structures create and sustain gendered patterns of leadership.

An oft-studied implication of institutionalization theory is the development of the masculine norm in organizations and society. Organizations are often based around historical patterns that came about in a time when most incumbents were men with stay-at-home wives (Pateman, 1988). This impacted the formation of organizational and societal norms that now shape not only the way that people behave, but also how they are expected to behave in organizations (Heilman, 2001). The discrepancy between egalitarian expectations and gender-typed expectations causes a double-bind for women where they are considered either competent or agreeable, but not both (Heilman et al., 2004). Since female leaders are judged on contradictory stereotypes of women and leaders and constitute very small proportions of organizational leadership, they are scrutinized more than majority members and are often subject to token dynamics (Biernat and Kobrynowicz, 1997; Foschi, 2000; Kanter, 1977; Miller et al., 1991). A better understanding of how stereotypes differ in cross-cultural contexts will also allow us to grasp how institutional logics differentially affect women and leadership in various countries.

Another way in which institutionalization theory sheds light on women and leadership issues is through the understanding of differential institutional barriers in career progression. Researchers have employed institutionalism to understand women and leadership because it explains how institutions continue to reinforce gender norms and therefore hinder women's progress toward equality (Ely, 1995). While women's career development may no longer be blocked across the board by glass ceilings, in contemporary times women's careers may look more like a labyrinth with many obstacles and false pathways that they must effectively navigate to advance to and succeed in leadership (Eagly and Carli, 2007).

Institutional theory is paramount in understanding why the progression toward gender equality in leadership has been so slow across the board (Valian, 1998). For example, women remain scarce in boardrooms and other leadership contexts due to systematic gender bias (e.g., Bilimoria and Piderit, 1994). Previous research indicates that the proportion of women in leadership can change with intentional effort; for example, the proportion of women directors in the boardroom is associated with greater numbers of women in top management teams (Bilimoria, 2006; Joy, 2008). An increased knowledge of how institutionalism impacts organizations is necessary for understanding gender in leadership, because this theory underlies the continuing structures that women have to manage when rising into leadership.

Future research should clarify how institutional pressures on female leaders combined with social norms and expectations stretch the tension between diverse leadership and the rituals of the business world. We encourage the cross-cultural study of the differing role and effects of power and privilege from the long-standing preference toward the masculine norm which is still embedded in societies and institutions. Researchers should work to understand how and when organizational changes occur, as the institutional barriers that women and organizations face hinder faster progress toward equality in leadership (Valian, 1998). Such research must inform women leaders about how to combat stereotypes or prejudice in institutional contexts where they do not traditionally hold positions of power.

CONCLUSION

The theories presented in Table 8.1 and described in this chapter provide an introduction to the framing lenses through which researchers in the organizational and management sciences examine women and leadership. While they provide an important basis for conducting rigorous research, the theories mentioned in this chapter are by no means exhaustive in understanding women and leadership. Nevertheless, empirical investigation based on these theories has contributed greatly in developing knowledge of how gender impacts leadership and its outcomes to date.

We encourage future researchers working on women and leadership topics to continue to draw extensively on the organizational and management science theories discussed in this chapter. This will advance current understanding of the dynamics and dimensions of women and leadership, recognizing that this is a multidisciplinary topic and that theories from other fields found in various chapters of this book must be incorporated to get a full picture. Future research still has fertile ground to cover to advance the goal of gender parity in organizational and societal leadership, and theories in the organizational and management sciences have much to offer.

The strong theoretical basis of these frameworks will assist in developing future insights about women and leadership, and in this regard we see three distinctive advantages to utilizing the organizational and management science theories presented in this chapter. First, there is a strong popular press and management practice call for a more comprehensive understanding of women and leadership, and these theories can help ground recommendations in rigorous and systematic ways. Second, organizational and management science theories can allow us to understand the dimensions and dynamics of women in leadership in more nuanced and context-sensitive ways, including by addressing important issues of cross-cultural differences. And finally, because these theories span from the micro to the macro, they can be used in understanding the transformation of individuals as well as of organizations, institutions, and societies. The multilevel approach offered by organizational and management science theories can help to address barriers to and opportunities for women and leadership at all levels, potentially advancing knowledge and practice leading to lasting change.

REFERENCES

Andersen, J.A. (2009). When a servant-leader comes knocking. *Leadership and Organization Development Journal*, 30(1), 4–15.
Avolio, B.J., Bass, B.M., and Jung, D.I. (1999). Re-examining the components of transformational and transactional leadership using the Multifactor Leadership Questionnaire. *Journal of Occupational and Organizational Psychology*, 72(4), 441–462.
Avolio, B.J., and Gardner, W.L. (2005). Authentic leadership development: Getting to the root of positive forms of leadership. *Leadership Quarterly*, 16(3), 315–338.
Avolio, B.J., Luthans, F., and Walumbwa, F.O. (2004). *Authentic Leadership: Theory Building for Veritable Sustained Performance*. Lincoln, NE: Gallup Leadership Institute.
Bandura, A. (1994). Self-efficacy. In V.S. Ramachaudran (Ed.), *Encyclopedia of Human Behavior*, Vol. 4 (pp. 71–81). New York, NY: Academic Press.
Barling, J., Slater, F., and Kelloway, K.E. (2000). Transformational leadership and emotional intelligence: An exploratory study. *Leadership and Organization Development Journal*, 21(3), 157–161.
Bar-On, R. (2000). Emotional and social intelligence: Insights from the emotional quotient inventory (EQ-i). In R. Bar-On and J.D.A. Parker (Eds), *The Handbook of Emotional Intelligence* (pp. 363–388). San Francisco, CA: Jossey-Bass.
Bass, B.M. (1985). *Leadership and Performance beyond Expectations*. New York, NY: Free Press.
Bass, B.M., Avolio, B.J., Jung, D.I., and Berson, Y. (2003). Predicting unit performance by assessing transformational and transactional leadership. *Journal of Applied Psychology*, 88(2), 207–218.
Bateman, T.S., and Organ, D.W. (1983). Job satisfaction and the good soldier: The relationship between affect and employee "citizenship." *Academy of Management Journal*, 26(4), 587–595.
Bergeron, D.M. (2007). The potential paradox of organizational citizenship behavior: Good citizens at what cost?. *Academy of Management Review*, 32(4), 1078–1095.
Bergeron, D.M., Schroeder, T.D., Martinez, H.M., Amdurer, E.E., and van Esch, C. (2012). The stability of organizational citizenship behavior over time: Women as good citizens. Paper presented at Academy of Management Conference, Boston, MA.
Betz, N.E., and Fitzgerald, L.F. (1987). *The Career Psychology of Women*. New York, NY: Academic Press.
Biernat, M., and Kobrynowicz, D. (1997). Gender- and race-based standards of competence: Lower minimum standards but higher ability standards for devalued groups. *Journal of Personality and Social Psychology*, 72(3), 544–557.
Bilimoria, D. (2006). The relationship between women corporate directors and women corporate officers. *Journal of Managerial Issues*, 18(1), 47–61.
Bilimoria, D., and Piderit, S.K. (1994). Board committee membership: Effects of sex-based bias. *Academy of Management Journal*, 37(6), 1453–1477.
Blau, P. (1964). *Exchange and Power in Social Life*. New York, NY: Wiley.
Borman, W.C., and Motowidlo, S.J. (1993). Expanding the criterion domain to include elements of contextual performance. In N. Schmitt and W.C. Borman (Eds), *Personnel Selection in Organizations* (pp. 71–98). San Francisco, CA: Jossey-Bass.

Brass, D.J. (1985). Men's and women's networks: A study of interaction patterns and influence in an organization. *Academy of Management Journal*, *28*(2), 327–343.

Burns, J.M. (1978). *Leadership*. New York, NY: Harper & Row.

Burt, R.S. (1992) *Structural Holes: The Social Structure of Competition*. Cambridge, MA: Harvard University Press.

Cavallo, K., and Brienza, D. (2006). Emotional competence and leadership excellence at Johnson & Johnson. *Europe's Journal of Psychology*, *2*(1). Retrieved from http://ejop.psychopen.eu/article/view/313/html.

Chiniara, M., and Bentein, K. (2016). Linking servant leadership to individual performance: Differentiating the mediating role of autonomy, competence and relatedness need satisfaction. *Leadership Quarterly*, *27*(1), 124–141.

Cote, S., and Miners, C.T. (2006). Emotional intelligence, cognitive intelligence, and job performance. *Administrative Science Quarterly*, *51*(1), 1–28.

Cropanzano, R., and Mitchell, M.S. (2005). Social exchange theory: An interdisciplinary review. *Journal of Management*, *31*(6), 874–900.

Day, D.V., Fleenor, J.W., Atwater, L.E., Sturm, R.E., and McKee, R.A. (2014). Advances in leader and leadership development: A review of 25 years of research and theory. *Leadership Quarterly*, *25*(1), 63–82.

Debebe, G., Anderson, D., Bilimoria, D., and Vinnicombe, S.M. (2016). Women's leadership development programs: Lessons learned and new frontiers. *Journal of Management Education*, *40*(3), 231–252.

Dinh, J.E., Lord, R.G., Gardner, W., Meuser, J.D., Liden, R.C., and Hu, J. (2014). Leadership theory and research in the new millennium: Current theoretical trends and changing perspectives. *Leadership Quarterly*, *25*(1), 36–62.

Donovan, J.J. (2001). Work motivation. In N. Anderson, D.S. Ones, H.K. Sinangil, and C. Viswesvaran (Eds), *Handbook of Industrial, Work and Organizational Psychology: Volume 2: Organizational Psychology* (pp. 56–59). Thousand Oaks, CA: Sage Publications.

Duff, A.J. (2013). Performance management coaching: Servant leadership and gender implications. *Leadership and Organization Development Journal*, *34*(3), 204–221.

Eagly, A.H. (2005). Achieving relational authenticity in leadership: Does gender matter?. *Leadership Quarterly*, *16*(3), 459–474.

Eagly, A.H., and Carli, L.L. (2007). *Through the Labyrinth: The Truth about how Women become Leaders*. Boston, MA: Harvard Business School Press.

Eagly, A.H., Johannesen-Schmidt, M.C., and Van Engen, M.L. (2003). Transformational, transactional, and laissez-faire leadership styles: A meta-analysis comparing women and men. *Psychological Bulletin*, *129*(4), 569–591.

Ehrhart, M.G. (2004). Leadership and procedural justice climate as antecedents of unit-level organizational citizenship behavior. *Personnel Psychology*, *57*(1), 61–94.

Ely, R.J. (1995). The power in demography: Women's social constructions of gender identity at work. *Academy of Management Journal*, *38*(3), 589–634.

Ely, R.J., Ibarra, H., and Kolb, D.M. (2011). Taking gender into account: Theory and design for women's leadership development programs. *Academy of Management Learning and Education*, *10*(3), 474–493.

Emerson, R.M. (1976). Social exchange theory. *Annual Review of Sociology*, *2*, 335–362.

Fernández-Berrocal, P., Cabello, R., Castillo, R., and Extremera, N. (2012). Gender differences in emotional intelligence: The mediating effect of age. *Behavioral Psychology*, *20*(1), 77–89.

Fiedler, F.E., Chemers, M.M., and Mahar, L. (1976). *Improving Leadership Effectiveness: The Leader Match Concept*. New York, NY: John Wiley & Sons.

Finkelstein, S., Hambrick, D.C., and Cannella, A.A. (2009). *Strategic Leadership: Theory and Research on Executives, Top Management Teams, and Boards*. New York, NY: Oxford University Press.

Foschi, M. (2000). Double standards for competence: Theory and research. *Annual Review of Sociology*, *26*, 21–42.

Freeman, L. (2004). *The Development of Social Network Analysis: A Study in the Sociology of Science*. North Charleston, SC: Book Surge, LLC.

Fridell, M., Newcom Belcher, R., and Messner, P.E. (2009). Discriminate analysis gender public school principal servant leadership differences. *Leadership and Organization Development Journal*, *30*(8), 722–736.

Goldenberg, I., Matheson, K., and Mantler, J. (2006). The assessment of emotional intelligence: A comparison of performance-used and self-report methodologies. *Journal of Personality Assessment*, *86*(1), 33–45.

Goleman, D. (1998). *Working with Emotional Intelligence*. New York, NY: Bantam Dell.

Gouldner, A.W. (1960). The norm of reciprocity: A preliminary statement. *American Sociological Review*, *25*(2), 161–178.

Greenleaf, R. (1970). *The Servant as Leader*. New York, NY: Paulist Press.

Hambrick, D.C., and Mason, P.A. (1984). Upper echelons: The organization as a reflection of its top managers. *Academy of Management Review*, *9*(2), 193–206.

Heilman, M.E. (2001). Description and prescription: How gender stereotypes prevent women's ascent up the organizational ladder. *Journal of Social Issues*, *57*(4), 657–674.

Heilman, M.E., Wallen, A.S., Fuchs, D., and Tamkins, M.M. (2004). Penalties for success: Reactions to women who succeed at male gender-typed tasks. *Journal of Applied Psychology*, *89*(3), 416–427.

Hernandez, M., Eberly, M.B., Avolio, B.J., and Johnson, M.D. (2011). The loci and mechanisms of leadership: Exploring a more comprehensive view of leadership theory. *Leadership Quarterly*, *22*(6), 1165–1185.

Hodigere, R., and Bilimoria, D. (2015). Human capital and professional network effects on women's odds of corporate board directorships. *Gender in Management: An International Journal*, *30*(7), 523–550.

Hollenbeck, J.R., and Jamieson, B.B. (2015). Human capital, social capital, and social network analysis: Implications for strategic human resource management. *Academy of Management Perspectives*, *29*(3), 370–385.

Hu, J., and Liden, R.C. (2011). Antecedents of team potency and team effectiveness: An examination of goal and process clarity and servant leadership. *Journal of Applied Psychology*, *96*(4), 851–862.

Ibarra, H. (1992). Homophily and differential returns: Sex differences in network structure and access in an advertising firm. *Administrative Science Quarterly*, *37*(3), 422–447.

Ibarra, H. (2015). The authenticity paradox: Why feeling like a fake can be a sign of growth. *Harvard Business Review*, *93*(1/2), 53–59.

Ibarra, H., Ely, R., and Kolb, D. (2013). Women rising: The unseen barriers. *Harvard Business Review*, *91*(9), 60–66.

Javidan, M., Bullough, A., and Dibble, R. (2016). Mind the gap: Gender differences in global leadership self-efficacies. *Academy of Management Perspectives*, *30*(1), 59–73.

Joy, L. (2008). Advancing women leaders: The connection between women board directors and women corporate officers. Retrieved on July 20, 2016 from http://www.catalyst.org/knowledge/advancing-women-leaders-connection-between-women-board-directors-and-women-corporate.

Kanter, R.M. (1977). *Work and Family in the United States: A Critical Review and Agenda for Research and Policy.* New York, NY: Russell Sage Foundation.

Kidder, D.L., and Parks, J.M. (2001). The good soldier: who is s(he)?. *Journal of Organizational Behavior*, *22*(8), 939–959.

Koh, W.L., Steers, R.M., and Terborg, J.R. (1995). The effects of transformational leadership on teacher attitudes and student performance in Singapore. *Journal of Organizational Behavior*, *16*(4), 319–333.

Korn Ferry. (2016). New research shows women are better at using soft skills crucial for effective leadership and superior business performance, finds Korn Ferry Hay Group. March 4. Retrieved on July 20, 2016 from http://www.kornferry.com/press/new-research-shows-women-are-better-at-using-soft-skills-crucial-for-effective-leadership/.

Krackhardt, D., and Stern, R.N. (1988). Informal networks and organizational crises: An experimental simulation. *Social Psychology Quarterly*, *51*(2), 123–140.

Langton, N., Robbins, S.P., and Judge, T.A. (2015). *Fundamentals of Organizational Behavior*. Toronto, Canada: Pearson Education Canada.

Law, K.S., Wong, C.S., and Song, L.J. (2004). The construct and criterion validity of emotional intelligence and its potential utility for management studies. *Journal of Applied Psychology*, *89*(3), 483–496.

Liden, R.C., Wayne, S.J., Liao, C., and Meuser, J.D. (2014). Servant leadership and serving culture: Influence on individual and unit performance. *Academy of Management Journal*, *57*(5), 1434–1452.

Liden, R.C., Wayne, S.J., Meuser, J.D., Hu, J., Wu, J., and Liao, C. (2015). Servant leadership: Validation of a short form of the SL-28. *Leadership Quarterly*, *26*(2), 254–269.

Lin, C. (2008). Clarifying the relationship between organizational citizenship behaviors, gender, and knowledge sharing in workplace organizations in Taiwan. *Journal of Business and Psychology*, *22*(3), 241–250.

Locke, E.A., and Latham, G.P. (2002). Building a practically useful theory of goal setting and task motivation: A 35-year odyssey. *American Psychologist*, *57*(9), 705–717.

Locke, E.A., and Latham, G.P. (2006). New directions in goal-setting theory. *Current Directions in Psychological Science*, *15*(5), 265–268.

Luthans, F., Youssef, C.M., and Avolio, B.J. (2007). *Psychological Capital*. New York, NY: Oxford University Press.

Mainiero, L.A., and Sullivan, S.E. (2005). Kaleidoscope careers: An alternate explanation for the opt-out revolution. *Academy of Management Executive*, *19*(1), 106–123.

Mayer, J.D., Caruso, D.R., and Salovey, P. (1999). Emotional intelligence meets traditional standards for an intelligence. *Intelligence*, *27*(4), 267–298.

McDonald, M.L., and Westphal, J.D. (2013). Access denied: Low mentoring of women and minority first-time directors and its negative effects on appointments to additional boards. *Academy of Management Journal*, *56*(4), 1169–1198.

McGrath, J.E. (1964). *Social Psychology: A Brief Introduction*. New York, NY: Holt, Rinehart & Winston.

McGuire, G.M. (2000). Gender, race, ethnicity, and networks. The factors affecting the status of employees' network members. *Work and Occupations*, 27(4), 501–524.

McPherson, J.M., and Smith-Lovin, L. (1987). Homophily in voluntary organizations: Status distance and the composition of face-to-face groups. *American Sociological Review*, 52(3), 370–379.

Miller, D.T., Taylor, B., and Buck, M.L. (1991). Gender gaps: Who needs to be explained?. *Journal of Personality and Social Psychology*, 61(1), 5–12.

Naghavi, F., and Redzuan, M. (2011). The relationship between gender and emotional intelligence. *World Applied Sciences Journal*, 15(4), 555–561.

Neubert, M.J., Kacmar, K.M., Carlson, D.S., Chonko, L.B., and Roberts, J.A. (2008). Regulatory focus as a mediator of the influence of initiating structure and servant leadership on employee behavior. *Journal of Applied Psychology*, 93(6), 1220–1233.

Noe, R.A. (1988). Women and mentoring: A review and research agenda. *Academy of Management Review*, 13(1), 65–78.

Northouse, P.G. (2015). *Leadership: Theory and Practice*. Thousand Oaks, CA: Sage Publications.

O'Donnell-Trujillo, N., and Pacanowsky, M.E. (1983). The interpretation of organizational cultures. *Communication in Transition: Issues and Debates in Current Research*, 50(2), 225–241.

O'Neil, D.A., and Hopkins, M.M. (2015). Authentic leadership: Application to women leaders. *Frontiers in Psychology*, 6. doi: http://dx.doi.org/10.3389/fpsyg.2015.00959.

O'Neil, D.A., Hopkins, M.M., and Bilimoria, D. (2008). Women's careers at the start of the 21st century: Patterns and paradoxes. *Journal of Business Ethics*, 80(4), 727–743.

Organ, D.W. (1997). Organizational citizenship behavior: It's construct clean-up time. *Human Performance*, 10(2), 85–97.

Organ, D.W., and Ryan, K. (1995). A meta-analytic review of attitudinal and dispositional predictors of organizational citizenship behavior. *Personnel Psychology*, 48(4), 775–802.

Özaralli, N. (2003). Effects of transformational leadership on empowerment and team effectiveness. *Leadership and Organization Development Journal*, 24(6), 335–344.

Parris, D.L., and Peachey, J.W. (2013). A systematic literature review of servant leadership theory in organizational contexts. *Journal of Business Ethics*, 113(3), 377–393.

Pateman, C. (1988). *The Sexual Contract*. Stanford, CA: Stanford University Press.

Peterson, S., Galvin, B.M., and Lange, D. (2012). CEO servant leadership: Exploring executive characteristics and firm performance. *Personnel Psychology*, 65(3), 565–596.

Petrides, J.V., and Furnham, A. (2006). The role of trait emotional intelligence in a gender-specific model of organizational variables. *Journal of Applied Social Psychology*, 36(2), 552–569.

Podsakoff, N.P., Whiting, S.W., Podsakoff, P.M., and Blume, B.D. (2009). Individual- and organizational-level consequences of organizational citizenship behaviors: A meta-analysis. *Journal of Applied Psychology*, 94(1), 122–141.

Porter, L.W., and Lawler, E.E. (1968). *Managerial Attitudes and Performance*. Homewood, IL: Irwin.

Reagans, R., and Zuckerman, E.W. (2001). Networks, diversity, and productivity: The social capital of corporate R&D teams. *Organization Science*, 12(4), 502–517.

Rosete, D., and Ciarrochi, J. (2005). Emotional intelligence and its relationship to workplace performance outcomes of leadership effectiveness. *Leadership and Organization Development Journal*, 26(5), 388–399.

Ruderman, M.N., and Ohlott, P.J. (2002). *Standing at the Crossroads*. San Francisco, CA: Jossey-Bass.

Ruderman, M.N., and Ohlott, P.J. (2005). Leading roles: What coaches of women need to know. *Leadership in Action*, 25(3), 3–9.

Salancik, G.R., and Pfeffer, J. (1978). A social information processing approach to job attitudes and task design. *Administrative Science Quarterly*, 23(2), 224–253.

Schaubroeck, J., Lam, S.S.K., and Peng, A.C. (2011). Cognition-based and affect-based trust as mediators of leader behavior influences on team performance. *Journal of Applied Psychology*, 96(4), 863–871.

Schein, V.E. (1973). The relationship between sex role stereotypes and requisite management characteristics. *Journal of Applied Psychology*, 57(2), 95–100.

Schein, V.E. (1975). Relationships between sex role stereotypes and requisite management characteristics among female managers. *Journal of Applied Psychology*, 60(3), 340–344.

Smith, C.A., Organ, D.W., and Near, J.P. (1983). Organizational citizenship behavior: Its nature and antecedents. *Journal of Applied Psychology*, 68(4), 653–663.

Sugiyama, K., Cavanagh, K.V., van Esch, C., Bilimoria, D., and Brown, C. (2016). Inclusive leadership development: Drawing from pedagogies of women's and general leadership development programs. *Journal of Management Education*, 40(3), 253–292.

Thornton, P.H., and Ocasio, W. (1999). Institutional logics and the historical contingency of power in organizations: Executive succession in the higher education publishing industry, 1958–1990. *American Journal of Sociology*, 105(3), 801–843.

Tubbs, M.E. (1986). Goal setting: A meta-analytic examination of the empirical evidence. *Journal of Applied Psychology*, *71*(3), 474–483.

Uhl-Bien, M. (2006). Relational leadership theory: Exploring the social processes of leadership and organizing. *Leadership Quarterly*, *17*(6), 654–676.

Valian, V. (1998). *Why so Slow? The Advancement of Women*. Cambridge, MA: MIT Press.

Van Dierendonck, D. (2011). Servant leadership: A review and synthesis. *Journal of Management*, *37*(4), 1228–1261.

Van Rooy, D.L., Alonso, A., and Viswesvaran, C. (2005). Group differences in emotional intelligence scores: Theoretical and practical implications. *Personality and Individual Differences*, *38*(3), 689–700.

Walumbwa, F.O., Hartnell, C.A., and Oke, A. (2010). Servant leadership, procedural justice climate, service climate, employee attitudes, and organizational citizenship behavior: A cross-level investigation. *Journal of Applied Psychology*, *95*(3), 517–529.

Woolley, L., Caza, A., and Levy, L. (2011). Authentic leadership and follower development: Psychological capital, positive work climate, and gender. *Journal of Leadership and Organizational Studies*, 18(4), 438–448.

Yukl, G. (2010). *Leadership in Organizations*. New Jersey, NY: Prentice Hall.

Zeidner, M., Matthews, G., and Roberts, R.D. (2004). Emotional intelligence in the workplace: a critical review. *Applied Psychology*, *53*(3), 371–399.

9. No woman left behind: critical leadership development to build gender consciousness and transform organizations
Laura L. Bierema

Mary Parker Follett (*The Creative Experience*, 1924, quoted in Hamel and Breen, 2007) once said, "Leadership is not defined by the exercise of power but by the capacity to increase the sense of power among those led. The most essential work of the leader is to create more leaders" (Hamel and Breen, 2007, p. 186). Considered by some to be the "Mother of Modern Management," Follett was a social worker, management consultant, philosopher, and pioneer in the fields of organizational theory and organizational behavior. Her groundbreaking leadership beliefs are more relevant today than ever because they challenge us to do the important work of creating more leaders. This chapter takes up Follett's commitment to developing leaders that benefit the organization, the led, and the broader community, in its examination of leadership, women leaders, and their development. Ever mindful that most organizations have undertaken these efforts only to benefit the leadership careers of men, I contend that cultivating mostly male leaders is not what Follett meant by "creating more leaders."

The authors in this book have established that organization structure marginalizes women. The playing field is not level for women, no matter how chief executive officers (CEOs) spin evidence of equality or claim that organizations are gender-blind. Women are sidelined by less access to opportunities for experience, development, and advancement; a playbook that has not changed in decades. When will we stop applying the same instrumental, technical solutions that have not worked to solve this problem? It is time to shift our perceptions and habits around developing and promoting women leaders so that no woman is left behind in her quest to advance:

> Simply placing more women in senior positions without working to combat gendered leadership beliefs or reducing organizational gender bias is suboptimal. In fact, such a strategy is likely to backfire as it may decrease, rather than increase, career opportunities for individual women as well as for women as a group. (Ellemers et al., 2012, p. 170)

Women are being left behind when they continually get pushed into the same oppressive organization structures that have not worked, are not working, and will not work. If organization leaders are to meet their goal of creating strong, sustainable, and successful businesses, they must fully embrace diversity and discover new ways of thinking and structuring that eradicate gender bias. This challenge is daunting and threatening, perhaps causing a collective shying away from finding lasting solutions by both leaders and leadership development professionals. Follett (in Metcalf and Urwick, 2013) argued, "what people often mean by getting rid of conflict is getting rid of diversity, and it is of the utmost importance that these should not be considered the same" (Graham, 2003,

145

p. 86). Applying new thinking to this old problem requires opening minds and changing behaviors, and truly valuing diversity.

The goal of this chapter is to interrogate prevailing understandings and practices of leadership development using a critical, feminist lens to chart a new path for developing women leaders. Critical feminism offers an unvarnished look at the realities of sexist, patriarchal organizations and analyzes how they perpetuate implicit bias that blocks women from full access to development experiences and advancement opportunities. Follett was a novel, revolutionary thinker who addressed leadership issues with alacrity and invention, years before her ideas gained traction. Sadly, like the experience of many women leaders, her contributions are largely overlooked or forgotten. Follett often pointed out that the best leaders were learning continually. This chapter embraces Follett's primacy of learning and the process of leadership development to draw on the fields of adult learning and human resource development to offer alternative conceptualizations and pedagogies for leadership development.

LEADERSHIP DEVELOPMENT IS VALUED, COSTLY, AND FLAWED

Creating new leaders is a learning and development (L&D) process. Countless hours and dollars are spent annually developing leaders and other workers. For example, the 2015 Training Industry Report (*Training*, 2014) has been surveying United States (US)-based organizations for 34 years. The total US training expenditures were $70.6 billion (including payroll and external spending on products and services). Organizations spent an average of $702 per employee on L&D activities, with employees receiving an average of 53.8 hours of training per year.

More funding than ever was allocated in the decade to 2014 to train executives – over $15 billion in 2013 (Bersin by Deloitte, 2014) – yet a 2012 poll by the Center for Public Leadership at Harvard University showed that as many as 70 percent of Americans blame a crisis in leadership as a factor in the national economic decline (Williams, 2014). The confidence levels of US citizens in governments, corporations, and Wall Street plummeted from 90 percent in 1996 to 60 percent in 2013 (Harris Poll, 2013). A survey of over 14,000 human resource (HR) professionals and line leaders (LL) rated the quality of leadership across their organizations as "excellent" or "very good" only 26 percent (HR) or 38 percent (LL) of the time. Survey respondents rated their capacity to meet future leadership needs as "very strong" or "strong" at a rate of only 18 percent among HR and 32 percent among LL (Boatman and Wellins, 2011). The bottom line is that spending on leadership development keeps rising, even though there is less and less satisfaction with the results (Kaiser and Curphy, 2013).

Organizations claim that leadership development is a priority, yet a 2015 *State of Leadership Development* study (Loew, 2015) rated leadership development as below average or poor in 36 percent of organizations, although 83 percent of those surveyed rated leadership development at all levels as "important" or "very important." The study found that requirements for good leadership are infrequently defined, with only 8 percent of organizations articulating leadership requirements and 77 percent indicating that leadership strategy was only somewhat or not at all aligned with business strategy. There is a global deficit of leaders possessing high-quality skills with over half of organizations indicating that their leadership is not at all ready or only somewhat ready to lead their organization today. The study noted that key areas where necessary mastery was lacking included coaching, communication, resiliency, critical thinking, collaboration, and data analysis.

If leadership development is so important and costly, why is it done so poorly? Blame is leveled at failing to do appropriate succession planning (Bersin by Deloitte, 2014), focusing on training at the expense of development (Myatt, 2012), overlooking evaluation, defining leadership as a competency or position (Kaiser and Curphy, 2013), and failing to emphasize emotional intelligence (Doe et al., 2015). Although these certainly may be flaws of leadership development, they seem too instrumental, too technical, and too shortsighted to guide reform. A fundamental problem with leadership development is that it ignores the political, social, economic, and gendered context where leaders work. The meta-context of the world has been described as volatile, uncertain, complex, and ambiguous (VUCA) (Conference Board, 2014), and there are new approaches to develop leaders more effectively to deal with this environment. Nicolaides (2015) proposed the term "liquid modernity" (p. 1) to capture the essence of modern times. Liquid modernity is the fluidity of life where highly interconnected and interdependent professionals struggle to keep pace with relentless change and unpredictable outcomes. Embedded in this phenomenon is the challenge of also learning about gendered power relations and negotiating gender within organization context. This fluidity creates ambiguity where there are no clear or easy answers. Learning is one solution to this state of liquid ambiguity and a constructive response is to practice a more adaptive leadership style.

We know that organizations value leadership development and spend exorbitant amounts of money on it, with low returns on investment. There is also limited research showing that leadership development even works. For example, Sashkin's (2014) chapter on "Management and leadership in HRD" in the *Handbook of Human Resource Development* offered a historical scan of leadership studies and found little evidence of leadership theories' effectiveness or whether leadership development itself is even effective. An exception in Sashkin's research was Smith et al.'s (1984) 20-year study of Methodist ministers' congregational performance outcomes. This research pointed to a causal relationship between leaders and performance results. In contrast to previous inconclusive evidence for effective leadership development measures, Burke and Day's (1986) review of management and leadership development programs between 1951 and 1982 concluded that such programs have positive results, although their sample had more examples of management development than leadership development. Collins and Holton (2004) found similar results in a meta-analysis of studies from 1982 to 2001 on the effects of leadership training. It is important to realize that these large studies have only looked at instrumental variables such as the impact of training on performance, not issues such as changing organizational culture or promoting women. It is clear that more research is needed as well.

What is wrong with leadership development? Leadership development is often being done by the wrong people (Vaughn, 2013) and focusing on the wrong issues (for example, training instead of development) (Myatt, 2012). First, it is an erroneous assumption to believe that just because someone knows something about leadership that they will be good at teaching it. If people designing and implementing leadership development know little or nothing about facilitating adult learning or implementing organization change, it is unlikely that their efforts will have immediate impact or enduring effect. Second, the focus of leadership development is often off-target. Organizations are gendered (Acker, 1990, 2006; Bierema, 2003, 2005; Dembe and Yao, 2016). Navigating asymmetrical power relations is real for all leaders, particularly women who are regarded by the culture as out-of-place and underqualified, and suffer multiple inequities as a consequence. Effective development programs appreciate the volatile, uncertain, complex, and ambiguous (VUCA) context of gendered organizations and meld that insight with pedagogy that resonates with adult learners and helps them understand how to effectively function in this context. Leadership development for both women and men should acknowledge these gendered disparities and give leaders the tools to engage with, question, and change their organization cultures.

WOMEN LEADERS: MIND THE GAP

To contextualize the charge that leadership development is not working, let us consider the gaps in the playing field regarding women's leadership, women's leadership theory, and women's leadership development.

The Women's Leadership Gap

Women are a dominant presence in the worldwide workforce where they pursue careers in corporations, communities, governments, and countries that are suffused in patriarchal culture that has been wrought by geography, traditions, politics, and history. Patriarchal culture propagates biases that stereotype women. Often these biases are unconscious, unquestioned, and tacit. Women's total worldwide employment is 47.1 percent (International Labour Organization, 2014), although the wage gap is persistent globally with women earning on average only 60–75 percent of men's wages (World Bank, 2012). Further, working women lack equitable treatment, equal pay, access to mentors, participation in key development experiences, and equivalent advancement as compared to men, and have life roles complicated by social expectations that they bear the bulk of household and family responsibilities (International Labour Organization, 2014; World Bank, 2012). According to the Organisation for Economic Co-operation and Development (OECD), women have been outpacing men in higher education across the world population since approximately the 1990s (OECD Gender Data, n.d.; ICEF Monitor, 2014). Yet, unfortunately, women's global gains in education are not translating into equitable pay or positions as compared with men.

The "women's leadership gap" in the US has been illustrated by several researchers and agencies (e.g., Catalyst, 2014; Warner, 2014), noting the following statistics. Women are 50.8 percent of the US population, 47 percent of the labor force, and 59 percent of the college-educated, entry-level workforce. Women earn nearly 60 percent of undergraduate degrees, 60 percent of all master's degrees, 47 percent of all law degrees, 48 percent of all medical degrees, and more than 44 percent of master's degrees in business and management, including 37 percent of MBAs. Although they hold almost 52 percent of all professional-level jobs, there is a leadership gap when it comes to women's representation in the higher echelons of management. Women are only 14.6 percent of executive officers, 8.1 percent of top earners, and 4.6 percent of Fortune 500 CEOs. They hold just 16.9 percent of Fortune 500 board seats (see Chapter 1 of this *Handbook* for more details). This leadership gap between women and men holds across the professions in financial services, health care, law, medicine, information technology, advertising and other fields. The statistics worsen for women of color, who are 36.3 percent of the US's female population, making up about one-third of the female workforce. Yet, women of color in the US occupy only 11.9 percent of managerial and professional positions, with the composition being 5.3 percent African American, 2.7 percent Asian American, and 3.9 percent Latina. Women of color hold only 3.2 percent of the board seats of Fortune 500 companies and over two-thirds of these companies have no women of color as board directors at all.

Notwithstanding all the important contributions women are prepared to make, most organizations today are still not woman-friendly. Further, the US trails other countries according to the World Economic Forum's (2014) Global Gender Gap Index. This index measures gender-based disparities based on countries' longitudinal eradication of the gender gap according to economic participation and opportunity, educational attainment, health and survival, and political empowerment. The highest possible score on the index is 1, indicating that the country has entirely eradicated the gender gap in all four categories. No country has achieved this score since the index's 2006 launch. Iceland tops the index with a score of 0.859. The US score is 0.746, ranking lower than some countries with considerably less economic development, such as Rwanda and Nicaragua. The US ranked lowest across the four categories in health and survival, and was also penalized by the shortage of women in political power. According to the report, the global gender gap is not predicted to close until 2095. Chapter 1 of this *Handbook* highlights these results in more depth, specifically for political representation.

Women's health and unpaid work is sometimes overlooked in our laments over unequal pay, gender segregation, sexual harassment, and lack of access to advancement. Yet, women must put in long hours at both work and home while climbing the career ladder, and also contend with inhospitable work cultures. Long working weeks and stress often result in bad consequences for health, particularly women who work 40+ hours each week (Dembe and Yao, 2016). Dembe and Yao conducted a longitudinal study to determine how full-time jobs affect health from 1978 to 2009 and whether gender played a role. They used data from the National Longitudinal Survey of Youth to track the work and health histories of 7,492 men and women over the course of 32 years. The researchers looked specifically at eight conditions: heart disease, failure, or other heart problems; cancer of any kind (except skin); arthritis; diabetes; chronic lung disease; asthma; depression; and high blood pressure. They concluded that working long hours was significantly associated with elevated risks for four types of the chronic conditions:

- Heart disease risk was elevated for people working 51 or more hours per week.
- Cancer risk (not including skin cancer) was elevated for people working 51 or more hours per week.
- Arthritis risk was elevated for people working 40 or more hours per week.
- Diabetes was more likely to be reported by people who worked more than 40 hours per week.

Although Dembe and Yao's (2016) findings are concerning, they were even more star-tling when broken out by gender: women are at a much greater health risk than men for these conditions. The only risk to men was increased risk of developing arthritis, without adverse risk for other conditions. In fact, the men had less associated risks for heart disease, chronic lung disease, or depression even when working moderately long hours (41–50 per week). The risks are more pronounced for women, who had triple the risk of diabetes, cancer, heart trouble, and arthritis when working 60+ hours per week. The researchers also found an association between hypertension and asthma among women working 51 to 60 hours per week. What is behind the gender differences in health outcomes? Dembe and Yao hypothesized that women's "second shift" of shouldering the majority of housework and dependent care in addition to working full-time increases their total work time, time pressures, and stress. Further, women encounter "negative psychosocial work characteristics" at work, where sexism manifests into a lack of control, a paucity of learning opportunities, less satisfying work, and a deprivation of upward mobility. Dembe and Yao (2016) advocated for more equal treatment of women in the workplace and urged employers to implement social policies (for example, flexible schedules, child care programs, increased paid maternity leave, telecommuting, and more paid sick leave) to help alleviate the double duty women face by juggling life and work.

Women's Leadership Theory Gap

So far, this chapter has illustrated that there is a serious women's leadership gap and inequity when it comes to how women are developed to move into leadership roles. Although women are outpacing men in education, they are left behind in the workforce with diminished access to positions, pay and promotions, and potentially damaged health as a result of trying to juggle life and work. In addition, we still do not understand enough about women leaders or how they learn. Classic leadership studies included few women in their samples and, when they did, women were often excluded from the analysis to avoid skewing the results (Stogdill, 1974). Consequently, early leadership theory described men's leadership. Stead and Elliott (2009) critiqued the lack of empirical research about women leaders, noting that existing studies tend to focus on men leading traditional, hier-archical organizations such as the military. The problem with existing leadership theory is captured by Fletcher's (2004) analysis:

> While the rhetoric about leadership has changed at the macro level, the everyday narrative about leadership and leadership practices – the stories that people tell about leadership, the mythical legends that get passed on as exemplars of leadership behaviour – remain stuck in old images of heroic individualism. (p. 652)

"Heroic leadership" has dominated management theory and practice and is charac-terized by masculine behaviors such as individualism, command and control, aggres-siveness, advocacy, and domination. Follett critiqued heroic-type leadership as seeking "power-over," and was instead an advocate for what she called "power-with" (Metcalf and Urwick, 2013), noting:

> It seems to me that whereas power usually means power-over, the power of some person or group over some other person or group, it is possible to develop the conception of power-with, a jointly developed power, a co-active, not a coercive power. (p. 101)

Leadership has been theorized as a gender-neutral activity (that is, leadership theories such as transactional, transformational, authentic, and servant leadership do not include gender as a meaningful concept), which functions to mask gendered power relations (Acker, 1990, 2006). These male-centric theoretical perspectives perpetuate our tacit understanding of leadership as men's work. As such, leadership theories should be read with a critical eye, considering what, if anything, they tell us about women leaders. Further, the failure of any existing leadership theory to adequately explain women's leadership creates a significant need for developing new theory (see Chapter 4 of this *Handbook* for more detail on the need for new theory).

The Women's Leadership Development Gap

The gap in women's leadership is widely discussed. Although it is important to understand women's standing in the world, it takes more than knowing the statistics to change it. The gap requires further examination to understand what other gaps might be creating it, such as gaps in our thinking about gender in organizations, gaps in how leaders are developed, and particularly gaps in how women leaders are developed. Disparities between women's and men's development have persisted for decades, creating a women leaders' development chasm. Previous studies have shown that women and men receive different developmental experiences in their careers (Federal Glass Ceiling Commission, 1995; Knoke and Ishio, 1998; Kolb, 1999; Ohlott et al., 1994) that may be caused by the primarily male managerial hierarchical structure that systematically excludes women from opportunities for career encouragement and training (Tharenou et al., 1994). According to Ruderman et al. (1995), women are also expected to demonstrate higher levels of personal strength and professional accomplishment than men before being awarded promotions.

Fast-forward to the present and consider the 2015 National Institute of Adult and Continuing Education (NIACE) survey of women and men to examine their experiences with employer training (Aldridge and Egglestone, 2015). This chapter has already demonstrated that leadership development in general gets a vote of no confidence when it comes to current research. Aldridge and Egglestone's study, which consisted of face-to-face interviews with a total of 6,217 United Kingdom adults, found disparities between women and men when it comes to workplace training. Thirty-one percent of women reported receiving no employer-sponsored training during the previous 12 months, as compared to 26 percent of men. Further, not only are women significantly less likely to receive any employer training compared to men, but when they do, the type of training differs. In this study, men were more likely to be given training leading to pay raises and promotions. For example, women were significantly more likely than men to have received equality and diversity training (39 percent of women; 24 percent of men) and health and safety training (61 percent of women; 52 percent of men), whereas men were more likely to have received supervisory training (17 percent of men; 12 percent of women).

The outcomes of workplace training for men and women also differ. Financially, 16 percent of men received a pay raise as a result of training as compared to 11 percent of the women. The study (Aldridge and Egglestone, 2015) also reported that part-time workers were at a disadvantage, with only 19 percent of them having access to employer-provided training, as compared to 32 percent of full-time staff. The research also found that a part-time penalty existed, with those working full-time being significantly more likely than their part-time colleagues to have access to employer-provided training. Thirty-two percent of full-time staff had accessed both on-the-job and off-the-job training in the previous 12 months, whereas only 19 percent of part-time staff had done so. Further, more women work part-time to balance family responsibilities, and suffer a 25 percent hourly pay penalty. Finally, the study also found that young men earn 21 percent more than young women on an apprenticeship.

FACILITATING CRITICAL LEADERSHIP DEVELOPMENT

Given that multiple gaps exist in our theoretical understanding of women leaders' experience and development, not to mention other gaps in terms of pay and access to advancement, it is time to reassess how we develop leaders and who does this work. The case has been made, in this chapter and by others in this *Handbook*, that neither leadership development theory nor practice have served women well. They are biased toward men and masculine images of leadership. This chapter has underscored the problems with leadership development and how it breeds inequity. It is time for a more critical approach to theorizing leadership development, as well as a process to help women be more discerning about their career decisions, learning, development, and advancement. Historically, women's career development has been uncritical, recommending women follow instrumental, masculine models and assimilate to inhospitable cultures (Bierema, 2003). It is time to shift the conversation to recast and reclaim how we think about and do leadership development, using a critical, feminist lens that is grounded in adult learning, human resource, and organization development theories.

The field of leadership development appears to be suffering from a lack of know-how: just because its practitioners know something about leadership theory and practice does not mean that they know anything about designing robust leadership development programs that eradicate workplace inequity. Further, even leadership acumen on the behalf of leadership developers is not enough to help their learners (current and future leaders) excel in gendered organizations. Women's leadership development would benefit significantly by the integration of theories from human resource development, organization development, and adult learning. These fields provoke powerful learning, interrogate power and positionality, consider how organizations affect learning and work, and innovate to transform workplaces for equity and inclusion. Chapters 25 and 27 of this *Handbook* also discuss the design of leadership development programs for women.

The book *Adult Learning: Bridging Theory and Practice* (Merriam and Bierema, 2014) discusses theoretical and practical approaches to facilitating learning for both learners and educators. The ability to think critically and transform knowledge about how one views the self and the world are hallmarks of adult education and should be built into leadership development; effective leadership development requires deep, introspective work to build self-knowledge and understand the "self" within the organization and social context. Merriam and Bierema (2014) presented a framework for integrating criticality into education. The framework is built around three aspects of being critical: critical theory, critical thinking, and critical action. I will use this framework (summarized in Table 9.1) to discuss how it might be applied as a model for rethinking leadership development that

Table 9.1 Aspects of being critical

Critical theory: a philosophy	Critical thinking: a thought process	Critical action: a mindful and timely intervention
Critiques social conditions and how they create unequal power relations based on attributes such as race, gender, class, age, sexual orientation, physical ability, and so on. Challenges "truth" that is advanced by dominant groups such as "women won't relocate" or "women are emotional." Seeks emancipation and elimination of oppression in society.	Reflects on assumptions and beliefs. Critiques self-thought and action. Hunts assumptions. Checks assumptions. Sees things from different viewpoints. Connects individual experience to broader social conditions.	Takes informed action. Monitors and corrects actions of self/group. Clarifies or changes thought. Changes behavior. Makes timely interventions. Justifies actions.

Source: Adapted from Merriam and Bierema (2014, p. 214). Copyright 2014 by Jossey-Bass. Adapted with permission.

brings gender into the conversation and helps both learners and organizations to think and act in ways that promote change.

Aspect 1: Critical Theory

The first aspect of critical education, critical theory, is a philosophical perspective that critiques unequal power relations in society with the goal of seeking change and creating equity. It helps learners see how they can get co-opted into participating in behaviors that oppress them or maintain the status quo; such as people ignoring women's ideas in meetings and only paying attention to them when men repeat them. Developers of women leaders and their organizations should be willing and able to assess organization perspectives, policies, and practices that prevent women from advancing. Unfortunately, this analysis is nearly always conspicuously absent from leadership development programs, perhaps because it is an uncomfortable subject and many leadership developers do not know how to engage the topic. Skilled educators and organization developers know how to facilitate these conversations. Understanding critical theory is important because organizations need more critical analysis and calling-out of problems that have persisted for decades. This perspective can be used to analyze individual, group, or organization phenomena.

Although I would not recommend that leadership development programs spend time discussing the philosophical tenets of critical theory, which can be quite obtuse, leadership developers interested in changing thought and practice should become familiar with it and use it as an operating philosophy in their design and facilitation. Brookfield's 2005 book, *The Power of Critical Theory: Liberating Adult Learning and Teaching*, is a great source written for educators, and Bierema's 2010 book, *Implementing a Critical Approach to Organization Development*, explains how to put critical human resource development theory into practice.

Critical theory is useful for developing justification for a more gender-sensitive leadership development process, because some leaders abdicate responsibility for cultures, claiming that they are broken and turning a blind eye to benevolent sexism. This allows leaders to do little or nothing to eradicate gender bias, because they either do not know how to address the problem, or they simply do not want to. Heifetz et al. (2009) disregarded the idea of a broken organizational system, observing, "The reality is that any social system (including an organization or a country or a family) is the way it is because the people in that system (at least those individuals and factions with the most leverage) want it that way" (p. 17). Hence, the system works fine even if it appears to be dysfunctional. The lack of women leaders and corresponding women's leadership theory fits neatly into such an idea: it is working fine for the white males who have the most leverage in the system. Further, it works fine with our current theoretical conceptions of leadership. Heifetz et al. emphasized that the dynamic pointing out of organization dysfunction is no way to win a popularity contest, noting that those who expose gaps between espoused theory (for example, "we value diversity and inclusion") and theory-in-use (for example, few women are appointed leadership roles and many more leave the organization) will not likely be recognized or rewarded by the system. These authors stated that "clearly the system as a whole has decided to live with the gap between the espoused value and the current reality, the value-in-practice. Closing that gap would be more painful to the dominant coalition than living with it" (p. 18). Critical theory provides a framework for understanding and discussing women's leadership gaps that is useful for women, men, and organizations – if leadership developers are brave and skilled enough to use it – because it acknowledges and challenges power differentials.

Aspect 2: Critical Thinking

The second aspect of being critical, critical thinking (Brookfield, 2012), is a learning process that reflects on assumptions and beliefs that guide thought and action. This method helps leaders and organizations to engage in careful assessment of assumptions driving thought and action to ensure that implicit bias is not seeping into their leadership development programs and workplace practices. A powerful concept to engage leaders in critical thinking that puts women's issues front and center is "gender consciousness."

Gender consciousness has been defined in political terms as experiencing an awakening that results in a sense of shared interdependence and fate between women. It recognizes women's relatively low status and power as compared to men, attributing power differentials to illegitimate sources such as institutionalized sexism, and is oriented toward taking collective action to improve women's organizational and social status (Gurin, 1985; Gurin et al., 1980; Reid and Purcell, 2004). My own research projects on how women developed an understanding of gendered power relations resulted in a definition and model of gender consciousness development: the process whereby individuals and organizations develop awareness of asymmetrical, gendered power relations and the extent to which they are willing to take action to change them (Bierema, 2003, 2005).

Gender consciousness is an important learning process for leaders because it impacts levels of confidence and ambition. Herring and Marken (2008) studied the effects of gender consciousness among information technology students at five US universities. They found that students with high gender consciousness were disproportionately women graduate students, whereas the disproportionately low gender consciousness students were men. Median consciousness was observed in equal proportions among women and men and functioned to maintain the status quo, making the findings seem plausible as students at those levels would not question gender inequity. Low consciousness students were those least affected by gender disparity: males in computer science, and both women and men in fields that were relatively gender-equitable such as instructional science and library and information studies.

Herring and Marken (2008) also reported that women were most ambitious and self-confident when they possessed high gender awareness, while men appeared most ambitious and self-confident when they were moderately gender-aware. The least self-confident and ambitious were those in the low gender consciousness category. They also found that highly gender-conscious individuals are more likely to recognize that gender issues require collective, political solutions and cannot be addressed through individual efforts. They concluded that gender consciousness raising might be beneficial at both the individual and societal levels. Given these results, it seems that helping leaders to develop moderate to high levels of gender awareness would help to bolster self-confidence, ambition, and concern for organization equity.

Aspect 3: Critical Action

Finally, the third aspect of being critical, critical action, is the process of taking mindful steps to correct the self or group when slipping back into implicit bias or behaviors that marginalize women and other underrepresented groups. Leadership development programs should focus on the VUCA context and teach leaders to adapt. Adaptive leadership is "the practice of mobilizing people to tackle tough challenges and thrive" (Heifetz et al., 2009, p. 14). It requires leaders to move beyond their current know-how and form improvisational expertise, or ways of experimenting with untried relationships, communication methods, and interactions in ways that transcend the current wisdom.

This aspect of the model of integrating criticality into pedagogy advocates that learners engage with their environment to learn and take risks. We often think of organized, formal training classes as a way to facilitate leadership development, but most of the learning that leaders engage in to learn their craft is experiential: informal knowledge acquisition through observation, conversation, mistakes, reflection, and experimentation. Experiential learning of this type is the hallmark of effective adult learning and human resource development. Providing real-life leadership development depends on regular, ongoing feedback that allows the leader to learn from experience and make adjustments in future leadership behaviors. The Center for Creative Leadership (CCL), a premier US-based provider of leadership development, concluded after 30 years of study of its own programs that leadership development is most effective when 70 percent of it is challenging assignments, 20 percent is developmental relationships (for example, mentoring, sponsorship, coaching), and 10 percent formal training (Wilson et al., 2011) (see Chapter 24 of this *Handbook* for more details on the CCL model). Yet, women are already at a disadvantage when it comes to receiving any of these interventions. Sashkin (2014) concludes his survey of leadership development by noting that the modernist approaches of the twentieth century no longer work:

> No longer is there a clear "equation" that, in effect says to a leader, "if you do X, the result will be Y." This uncertainty results partly from the fact that an organization is a "complex adaptive system" in which individual actors or "agents" behave in ways that are, to a degree, unpredictable. Moreover, an agent – and every member of an organization is an agent – may engage in actions that are clearly leadership, whether or not that agent is in a position of "formal" leadership. (pp. 73–74)

Although taking action may be the first reaction that leaders and organizations choose to begin diminishing gaps in women's leadership, not all interventions are created equal. Action alone is not enough, as it must be critiqued and evaluated as to whether or not it will bring about real and lasting change. Most change strategies will not foster greater gender equity, as a brief assessment will now show.

Assessing active change strategies for pertinence
When gender is acknowledged as a basic organizing feature of organizations, we are better able to analyze the practices and processes that comprise women's leadership experiences and how gender operates in women leaders' relationships, social practices, processes, activities, and interactions (Stead and Elliott, 2009). Assuming that women's leadership is not a neutral activity allows the process of leadership development to be approached more critically, appreciating the complexity and dynamism of organization environments as spaces where women work and learn, and where gender is actively constructed and reconstructed through women's daily leadership activities (Stead and Elliott, 2009).

There is a range of approaches that organizations can take on issues related to developing and advancing woman leaders according to theories of change from a feminist perspective (Coleman and Rippin, 2000; Ely and Meyerson, 2000a, 2000b; Martin, 2003; Meyerson and Kolb, 2000). These each have pros and cons as ways in which organizations can respond to developing more women leaders, and they are summarized in Table 9.2.

Fostering gender conscious leadership development
Returning to the idea of gender consciousness and my research in this area, Table 9.3 depicts the intersection of awareness of and action on gendered power relations based on prior studies (Bierema, 2003, 2005). When individuals or organizations lack awareness of gendered power relations, they operate in a state of "gender unconsciousness" whereby there is no awareness of these dynamics and therefore no corresponding action. There may be little or no leadership development in this case, except for what is already required by law or general education that may or may not address issues like diversity. When there is low awareness, but high action, an "unconscious bustle" results where there may be a lot of activities that lack strategy or focus on structural inequity that result in ineffective leadership development that focuses on fixing individuals, not the organization. My research has shown that many women leaders have high levels of awareness about gendered power relations, but are unable or unwilling to act on them. This is a state of "conscious unconsciousness" where there is tentative activity that is usually not strategic, structural, or effective at eradicating gendered organization practices. Finally, when awareness and willingness to take action are high, "conscious advocacy" is present. This is the only state where leadership development can have the leverage and power to address inequity and

Aldridge, F., and Egglestone, C. (2015). Learning, skills and progression at work: Analysis from the 2015 Adult Participation in Learning Survey. Leicester, UK: National Institute of Adult Continuing Education. Retrieved from http://www.learningandwork.org.uk/sites/niace_en/files/resources/Learning skills and progression at work_0.pdf.

Bersin by Deloitte. (2014). Bersin by Deloitte research shows US leadership development spending up again 14 percent to more than $15 billion in 2013. Bersin by Deloitte. May 14. Retrieved from http://www.bersin.com/News/Content.aspx?id=17488.

Bierema, L.L. (2003). The role of gender consciousness in challenging patriarchy. *International Journal of Lifelong Education, 22*(1), 3–12.

Bierema, L.L. (2005). Women executives' concerns related to implementing and sustaining a women's network in a corporate context. *Organization Development Journal, 23*(2), 8–20.

Bierema, L.L. (2010). *Implementing a Critical Approach to Organization Development.* Malabar, FL: Krieger Publishing Company.

Boatman, J., and Wellins, R.S. (2011). *Global Leadership Forecast.* Pittsburg, PA: Development Dimensions International.

Brookfield, S.D. (2005). *The Power of Critical Theory: Liberating Adult Learning and Teaching.* San Francisco, CA: Jossey-Bass.

Brookfield, S.D. (2012). *Teaching for Critical Thinking: Tools and Techniques to Help Students Question their Assumptions.* San Francisco, CA: Jossey-Bass.

Burke, M.J., and Day, R.R. (1986). A cumulative study of the effectiveness of managerial training. *Journal of Applied Psychology, 71*(2), 232–245.

Catalyst. (2014). Quick take: Statistical overview of women in the workplace. March 3. New York, NY: Catalyst. Retrieved from http://www.catalyst.org/knowledge/statistical-overview-women-workplace.

Coleman, G., and Rippin, A. (2000). Putting feminist theory to work: Collaboration as a means toward organizational change. *Organization, 7*(4), 573–587.

Collins, D.B., and Holton III, E.F. (2004). The effectiveness of managerial leadership development programs: A meta-analysis of studies from 1982–2001. *Human Resource Development Quarterly, 15*(2), 217–248.

Conference Board. (2014). *Ready-Now Leaders: 25 Findings to meet Tomorrow's Business Challenges.* Pittsburgh, PA: Conference Board. Retrieved from https://www.ddiworld.com/DDI/media/trend-research/global-leadership-forecast-2014-2015_tr_ddi.pdf?ext=.pdf.

Dembe, A.E., and Yao, X. (2016). Chronic disease risks from exposure to long-hour work schedules over a 32-year period. *Journal of Occupational and Environmental Medicine.* Advance online publication. doi: 10.1097/JOM.0000000000000810.

Doe, R., Ndinguri, E., and Phillips, S.T.A. (2015). Emotional intelligence: The link to success and failure of leadership. *Academy of Educational Leadership Journal, 19*(3), 105–114.

Ellemers, N., Rink, F., Derks, B., and Ryan, M.K. (2012). Women in high places: When and why promoting women into top positions can harm them individually or as a group (and how to prevent this). *Research in Organization Behavior, 32*, 163–187.

Ely, R.J., and Meyerson, D. (2000a). Theories of gender in organization: A new approach to organizational analysis and change. In B. Staw and R. Sutton (Eds), *Research in Organizational Behaviour* (pp. 105–153). Greenwich, CN: JAI Press.

Ely, R.J., and Meyerson, D. (2000b). Advancing gender equality in organizations: The challenge and importance of maintaining a gender narrative. *Organization, 7*(4), 589–608.

Federal Glass Ceiling Commission. (1995). Good for business: Making full use of the nation's human capital. Retrieved from https://www.dol.gov/dol/aboutdol/history/reich/reports/ceiling.pdf.

Fletcher, J. (2004). The paradox of post-heroic leadership: An essay on gender, power, and transformational change. *Leadership Quarterly, 15*(5), 647–661.

Graham, P. (2003). *Mary Parker Follett Prophet of Management.* Frederick, MA: Beard Books.

Gurin, P. (1985). Women's gender consciousness. *Public Opinion Quarterly, 49*(2), 143–163.

Gurin, P., Miller, A.H., and Gurin, G. (1980). Stratum identification and consciousness. *Social Psychology Quarterly, 43*(1), 30–47.

Hamel, G., and Breen, B. (2007). *The Future of Management.* Boston, MA: Harvard Business Review Press.

Harris Poll. (2013). Archival data. Retrieved from http://harrisinteractive.com/Insights/HarrisVault.apx.

Heifetz, R., Grashow, A., and Linsky, M. (2009). *The Practice of Adaptive Leadership: Tools and Tactics for Changing your Organization and the World.* Boston, MA: Harvard Business Press.

Herring, S.C., and Marken, J.A. (2008). Implications of gender consciousness for students in information technology. *Women's Studies, 37*(3), 299–256.

ICEF Monitor. (2014). Women increasingly outpacing men's higher education participation in many world markets. October 22. Retrieved from http://monitor.icef.com/2014/10/women-increasingly-outpacing-mens-higher-education-participation-many-world-markets/.

International Labour Organization (2014). Global employment trends 2014: Risk of a jobless recovery?

Retrieved from http://www.ilo.org/wcmsp5/groups/public/---dgreports/---dcomm/---publ/documents/publication/wcms_233953.pdf.

Kaiser, R.B., and Curphy, G. (2013). Leadership development: The failure of an industry and the opportunity for consulting psychologists. *Consulting Psychology Journal, 65*(4), 294–302.

Knoke, D., and Ishio, Y. (1998). The gender gap in company training. *Work and Occupations, 25*(2), 141–167.

Kolb, J. (1999). The effect of gender role, attitude toward leadership, and self-confidence on leader emergence: Implications for leadership development. *Human Resource Development Quarterly, 10*(4), 305–320.

Loew, L. (2015). *State of Leadership Development 2015: The Time to Act is Now.* Bridgeville, PA: Brandon Hall Group, DDI. Retrieved from http://www.ddiworld.com/DDI/media/trend-research/state-of-leadership-development_tr_brandon-hall.pdf?ext=.pdf.

Martin, J. (2003). Feminist theory and critical theory: Unexplored synergies. In M. Alvesson and S. Deetz (Eds.), *Studying Management Critically* (pp. 66–91). London, UK: Sage.

Merriam, S.B., and Bierema, L.L. (2014). *Adult Learning: Bridging Theory and Practice.* San Francisco, CA: Jossey-Bass.

Metcalf, H.C., and Urwick, L. (2013). *Dynamic Administration: The Collected Papers of Mary Parker Follett.* Mansfield Centre, CT: Martino Publishing.

Meyerson, D., and Kolb, D. (2000). Moving out of the armchair: Developing a framework to bridge the gap between feminist theory and practice. *Organization, 7*(4), 553–571.

Myatt, M. (2012, December 19). The #1 reason leadership development fails. *Forbes.* Retrieved from http://www.forbes.com/sites/mikemyatt/2012/12/19/the-1-reason-leadership-development-fails/ – 4abc7fac34ce.

Nicolaides, A. (2015). Generative learning: Adults learning within ambiguity. *Adult Education Quarterly, 65*(3), 179–195.

OECD Gender Data (n.d.). Balancing paid work, unpaid work and leisure. Retrieved from http://www.oecd.org/gender/data/balancingpaidworkunpaidworkandleisure.htm.

Ohlott, P.J., Ruderman, M.N., and McCauley, C.D. (1994). Gender differences in managers' developmental job experiences. *Academy of Management Journal (37)*1, 46–68.

Reid, A., and Purcell, N. (2004). Pathways to feminist identification. *Sex Roles, 50*(11/12), 759–769.

Ruderman, M.N., Ohlott, P.J., and Kram, K.E. (1995). Promotional decisions as a diversity practice. *Journal of Management Development 14*(2), 6–23.

Sandberg, S. (2013). *Lean In: Women, Work, and the Will to Lead.* New York, NY: Alfred A. Knopf.

Sashkin, M. (2014). Management and leadership in HRD. In N.E. Chalofsky, T.S. Rocco, and M.L. Morris (Eds), *Handbook of Human Resource Development* (pp. 62–79). Hoboken, NJ: Wiley.

Smith, J.E., Carson, K.P., and Alexander, R.A. (1984). Leadership: It can make a difference. *Academy of Management Journal, 27*(4), 765–776.

Stead, V., and Elliott, C. (2009). *Women's Leadership.* London, UK: Palgrave Macmillan.

Stogdill, R.M. (1974). *Handbook of Leadership.* New York, NY: Free Press.

Training. (2014). The 2015 training industry report. Retrieved from https://trainingmag.com/trgmag-article/2o15-training-industry-report.

Tharenou, P., Latimer, S., and Conroy, D. (1994). How do you make it to the top? An examination of influences on women's and men's managerial advancement. *Academy of Management Journal, 37*(4), 899–931.

Vaughn, A. (2013). 10 reasons leadership development programs fail. *Chief Learning Officer,* July 31. Retrieved from http://www.clomedia.com/2013/07/31/10-reasons-leadership-development-programs-fail/.

Warner, J. (2014, March 7). Fact sheet: The women's leadership gap. Women's leadership by the numbers. Center for American Progress. Retrieved from https://www.americanprogress.org/issues/women/report/2014/03/07/85457/fact-sheet-the-womens-leadership-gap/.

Williams, I. (2014). 6 leadership trends for 2015. *The Switch and Shift Change Playbook.* December 5. Retrieved from http://switchandshift.com/6-leadership-development-trends-for-2015.

Wilson, M.S., Van Velsor, E., Chandrasekar, A., and Criswell, C. (2011). Grooming top leaders: Cultural perspectives from China, India, Singapore, and the United States. Retrieved from http://insights.ccl.org/wp-content/uploads/2011/04/GroomingTopLeaders.pdf.

World Bank (2012). *World Development Report: Gender Equality and Development.* Retrieved from http://siteresources.worldbank.org/INTWDR2012/Resources/7778105-1299699968583/7786210-1315936222006/Complete-Report.pdf.

World Economic Forum. (2014). *The Global Gender Gap Index 2014.* Retrieved from http://reports.weforum.org/global-gender-gap-report-2014/.

PART III

INDIVIDUAL MOTIVATORS TO LEAD

10. Women's leadership aspirations
Lynne E. Devnew, Ann M. Berghout Austin, Marlene Janzen Le Ber, and Mary Shapiro

Although it is quite easy to identify women leaders, men continue to occupy the vast majority of leadership roles in the world. It has been argued that one of the reasons for this differential is that women's aspirations for leadership are less than men's. Women's leadership aspirations are defined in this chapter as girls' and women's longing for and intentional seeking after a future that catalyzes their visions, goals, or calling for themselves into reality, whether or not they use the term "leadership" to describe their aspirations.

There is ample support for this hypothesis. While studying women managers in Australia, Ross-Smith and Chesterman (2009) found something they labeled "girl disease"; among its symptoms is the reticence of women managers to pursue or accept advancement. Ramakrishnan et al. (2014) observed that women often limit their options within medicine by the choices they make even before entering their careers. Shapiro et al. (2009) found that women's goals for success are not limited to those associated with career advancement, but also include work–life balance goals, being passionate about their work, and doing work that makes a difference. Even those who seek to be leaders sometimes eschew being identified as a leader (Arminio et al., 2000), preferring to be seen as addressing social or community issues (Stead and Elliott, 2009) rather than to "be in charge" per se. Not surprisingly, then, women often struggle with seeing themselves and being seen by others as leaders (Ibarra et al., 2013).

Studies have demonstrated that young girls and teens may have lofty goals for adulthood, but their career aspirations remain largely gendered, that is, linked to professions considered more "typical" for women, such as nursing and teaching (Shapiro et al., 2012). In the United States and elsewhere in the Western world, there are equal or higher numbers of girls compared to boys pursuing post-secondary educational training and degrees. Yet leadership in elected office, in the most senior jobs in corporations, and in the upper ranks of higher education administration, remains largely a male province (see Shapiro et al., 2012).

To understand women's leadership aspirations, we have organized this chapter as follows. In the section below we describe two models that provide the foundation for the organizing framework we have created to provide a more comprehensive understanding of women's leadership aspirations. We then describe the components of our framework to provide deeper insight into how it might be useful to both scholars and practitioners. Finally, we conclude with implications for moving forward.

ORGANIZING FRAMEWORK

To explore women's aspirations for leadership we began with Singer's (1989) leadership aspiration model and Stead and Elliott's (2009) "leadership web."

Singer's Leadership Aspiration Model

In a comprehensive study of college seniors' leadership aspirations and leadership self-efficacy, Singer (1989) found that men in comparison to women had significantly higher aspirations to become leaders, as measured by their response to the question, "How much would you like to be in a leadership position?" (p. 28). When asked why a leadership position seemed attractive, men were more likely than women to say that leadership would put them "in a position of power and authority" (p. 29). Women said that leadership positions were attractive because they offered opportunities to "develop contacts with high status people" and "with subordinates" (p. 29). Thus, from the initial research question, participants in Singer's study reinforced the pervasive stereotype that men are drawn to agentic tasks while women like tasks that involve developing relationships with others. Regarding leadership self-efficacy – that is, how well the participants thought they possessed the skills and attitudes of true leaders – men were significantly more likely than women to believe that they had leadership abilities, that they would be effective as a leader, and that they would be successful.

Singer (1989) found that women had a significantly more complex view of leadership than men, believing that it required the internal characteristics of specific personality traits, intelligence, and competence; external support from subordinates; and a positive climate in which to lead. Women's leadership aspirations were best predicted by the relational aspects they anticipated would be part of leadership (that is, opportunities to work with others), along with their beliefs about how well their abilities matched those necessary for leadership. Men's leadership aspirations were best predicted by the opportunities they thought leadership offered to preside, hold power, and influence outcomes.

Singer (1989) has thus described a woman's aspirations to lead as a function of three important perceptions: (1) how she perceives leaders to behave (implicit leadership theory); (2) her self-efficacy related to perceptions of these expected leadership behaviors; and (3) her evaluation of the benefits and costs of being in a leadership position. However, aspirations are dynamic (Brown and Segrist, 2016; Coffman and Neuenfeld, 2014). Each of these perceptions is based on a woman's answers to a variety of questions she might ask herself at different times throughout her lifetime. Her answers might well change, given changing circumstances and experiences; and as they change, her leadership aspirations also change.

Stead and Elliott's Leadership Web

Singer's work relates well to Stead and Elliott's (2009) "leadership web," a comprehensive description of the personal and environmental factors that shape a woman's approach to leadership and her aspirations for leadership. The leadership web is shaped by: (1) work, or the often unconscious biases and gendered dynamics of work (that is, "male" jobs and "female" jobs) and other features within a workplace; (2) relationships with others in

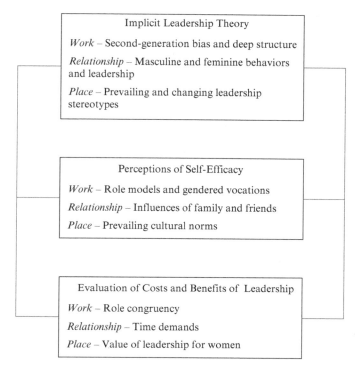

Figure 10.1   Organizing framework to understand women's leadership aspirations

all aspects of life; and (3) place, or "the physical and geographical location in which the women leaders were brought up and in which they live" (p. 75). All three elements of the leadership web are shaped, modified, and informed by the social environment.

To deepen our understanding of women's leadership aspirations in this chapter, we continue our discussion using the three components of Singer's leadership aspirations framework (that is, implicit leadership theory, perceptions of self-efficacy, and evaluation of costs and benefits of leadership) with elements of Stead's and Elliott's (2009) leadership web (work, relationship, and place) used within each of these Singer components (see Figure 10.1).

IMPLICIT LEADERSHIP THEORY

Implicit leadership theory asserts that individuals have an understanding of what it means to be a leader (Eden and Leviatan, 1975). However, relative to Stead and Elliott (2009), it is a theory that needs to be seen through the lens of work, relationships, and place. Not surprisingly the ideal model of a leader is of one who implicitly or explicitly exemplifies the norms within a specific culture (Schein, 2001). Singer (1989) observed, "An individual's implicit leadership theory refers to the theory or beliefs held by the individual about how leaders behave in general and what is expected of leaders" (p. 27). We would expect women and girls in different time periods and in different cultures to have diverse answers to the first question they might ask: "How do leaders behave?" or perhaps even "How do women leaders behave?" We suggest that these questions are supplemented by another set of questions not included in the original Singer model: "Is this behavior consistent with the way I view myself?" and "Do I want to behave this way?"

Relative to work in the leadership web, cultural notions often prescribe "masculine" fields such as construction jobs or the science, technology, engineering, and math (STEM) disciplines for men, who should also, more often than women, assume the role of leader. Women, on the other hand, should be in "feminine" jobs, such as nursing and teaching (Diekman and Goodfried, 2006; Eagly et al., 2000; Evans and Diekman, 2009; Prentice and Carranza, 2002) and assume feminine roles of nurturing and supporting. So inculcated are these roles that Ibarra et al. (2013) asserted that systemic changes must take place in organizational cultures in order for them to be suitable environments for women not only to learn to be leaders, but also to be seen as legitimate and credible leaders. These implicit leadership theory-related systemic changes include, but are not limited to, issues related to second-generation bias and deep structure (work), masculine and feminine behaviors and leadership (relationship), and prevailing and changing leadership stereotypes (place) (see Figure 10.1).

Second-Generation Bias and Deep Structure

In developing leadership aspirations, women must acknowledge and work through invisible though persistent second-generation bias, including cultural traditions, assumptions, and implicit prohibitions that often discourage women as leaders. A manifestation of second-generation bias is found in the "deep structure" of organizations (Batliwala, 2011) consisting of unspoken, unwritten rules for male and female roles (relationships), behavior, presentation of self, and utilization of skills, including leadership skills (place). In this way, deep structures in the workplace can challenge women's leadership aspirations in all three realms of the leadership web. Even more pernicious, the influence of the deep structure, and thereby many forms of second-generational bias, can be so subtle that few women are aware of its presence, assuming instead that they are deficient in some way when they encounter workplace resistance.

Masculine and Feminine Behaviors and Leadership

With leadership seen as masculine behavior, it is not surprising that Boatwright and Egidio (2003) found that women whose self-image included stereotypical feminine characteristics had lower leadership aspirations. In fact, in their study, the largest significant beta predicting leadership aspirations was for feminine characteristics, and although a need for connectedness had a significant positive beta in predicting leadership aspirations, it was a very small one. Regarding leadership aspirations, the implicit message is that an individual cannot be too feminine if she wants to be a leader, and although a desire for connectedness will reinforce leadership aspirations, the reinforcement will be weak at best.

Koenig et al.'s (2011) comprehensive meta-analysis of studies about leadership stereotypes reinforced the leadership web by demonstrating that in the spheres of work, relationships, and place, stereotypes clearly uphold the conflation of masculine traits with leadership traits. Relative to the work aspect of the leadership web, Koenig et al.

found that across 40 studies, descriptors for generic leadership positions upheld the Schein (2001) paradigm, "think manager, think male" (p. 631). Regarding relationships, they also found that agentic or stereotypically masculine characteristics were more often used across 22 studies to describe typical leadership behaviors. The internal dynamics and intersections of place were well represented by seven studies in which participants were asked to consider the suitability of men and women for specific leadership roles such as bank president, university president, and government leader. Typical of other findings in this meta-analysis, men were perceived as more suitable than women for holding most medium- and high-status leadership positions.

Clearly, all three aspects of the leadership web – work, relationships with others, and place – appear to be skewed by gendered stereotypes. If the web influences personal aspirations as we believe it does, a woman likely feels significant dissonance between what she observes as what it takes to be acknowledged as a leader and who she aspires to be.

Prevailing and Changing Leadership Stereotypes

The place where leadership is practiced has long conflated masculinity with leadership. Changing that conflation is an evolving process given that cultural stereotypes are very slow to change (Schein, 2001). Organizational models of leadership evolve slowly, as they are repeatedly replicated by those who have gained the most power in the organization and who would have the most to lose if the assumptions of how a leader should behave were to change (Eagly and Carli, 2007). On the positive side, as women increasingly populate leadership roles at work, the list of expected leadership traits will expand to include more feminine traits (Cabrera et al., 2009; Diekman and Eagly, 2000).

Other researchers agree that leadership stereotypes might be slowly changing, as highlighted in a number of chapters within this *Handbook*. Schein's (2001) international studies not only demonstrate that both men and women continue to associate men's traits with leadership, but also indicate that women in the United States (US) are beginning to associate women's traits with transformational leadership, servant leadership, and authentic leadership styles. Hints of this shift were suggested by Singer (1989), who found that women aspired to leadership for the opportunities to develop relationships with others; while more recently, Boatwright and Egidio (2003) found a positive relationship between students' stated needs for connectedness and their leadership aspirations. Hopefully these changes will broaden women's personal leadership theories and thereby provide greater support for their leadership aspirations.

While there are signs of progress as noted above, researchers continue to find an implicit association of leadership with gendered (male) descriptors. A study done by Johanson (2008) helped to explain why many people still think "male" when they think leader. In Johanson's study, participants were asked to sort a lengthy list of leader characteristics between structural (task-related) and consideration (people-related) behaviors. Not surprisingly, participants associated structural tasks with men and consideration tasks with women. Moreover, Johanson's research found that both men and women prioritized structural over consideration behaviors in their characterizations of leaders.

More recently, Ingols et al. (2015) queried a sample of 471 business women about professional workplace behaviors and the desirability of each behavior in a business environment. They found that six traits classified 50 years ago as masculine (that is, decisive, rational, disciplined, athletic, self-esteem, and self-reliant) and six classified as feminine (that is loyal, sensitive, spiritual, wholesome, excitable, and flirtatious) were now labeled as androgynous. Traits that remained masculine and professionally desirable for men included aggressive, ambitious, assertive, competitive, forceful, intense, strong personality, and risk taking. Traits that remained feminine and professionally desirable for women were attention to appearance, cheerful, clean, cooperative, patient, polite, warm, kind, and friendly.

These results have implications for a woman's leadership aspirations. Characteristics previously seen as male-only can now be "claimed" by women; however, women's professional presence in the workplace is still linked to appearance, self-presentation, and degree of nurturance. Stereotypes are both changing and remaining the same, creating considerable confusion in the formation of women's and girls' leadership aspirations.

PERCEPTIONS OF SELF-EFFICACY

The second aspect of Singer's leadership aspiration model, leader self-efficacy, refers to the specific belief that one has the requisite skills and knowledge to be an effective leader. The development of leadership self-efficacy implies a growing understanding of one's ability to plan, to build, and to nurture, influence, guide, motivate, and rally others; skills that may not be as widely recognized, nurtured, or even legitimized as part of leadership development. Bandura (1982) emphasized that to be effective, self-efficacy must be a belief focused on a specific action, role, or talent, such as self-efficacy as a musician or writer or, in this case, a leader. Although self-efficacy is not an actual predictor of success, it is a powerful mediator of action. Low self-efficacy can hinder performance and even prevent an individual from experimenting with or practicing a skill.

Self-efficacy is also best understood using the lenses of work, relationships, and place. Yet for a woman, developing leadership self-efficacy is further complicated because leadership stereotypes are still largely masculine for every aspect of the leadership web, and often rigidly reinforced by organizational deep structures. Whether at work as a girl in school or church, or as an adult in an organization, she must first decide whether she has sufficient self-efficacy to be a leader, and second, whether her leadership self-efficacy is strong enough to allow her to go against gendered stereotypes. Role models in the workplace can provide evidence that women can lead and are actually rewarded for leading; key relationships, such as family and friends, can support or discourage her earlier aspirations; and finally, the culture of her birthplace and growth-place is fundamental in legitimizing and validating her aspirations for leadership.

Role Models and Gendered Vocations

Work, from the leadership web, exerts a powerful influence on leadership self-efficacy. Seeing women leaders is a crucial step in the complex process of building one's leadership identity, and it is not as simple as "see it, be it." Rudman and Phelan (2010) found that exposure to examples of women in typically female jobs increased college-aged women's interest in choosing stereotypical female professions, but exposure to examples of women who excelled in typically male professions decreased students' perceptions about their own leadership abilities. Hoyt and Simon (2011) found that teenaged girls are not necessarily empowered by seeing prominent women senators, chief executive officers (CEOs), and Pulitzer Prize winners because they consider these exceptional individuals to be too far "above them." Apparently exposure to examples of outstanding women leaders can evoke strong feelings of not "measuring up."

However, in another study, Beaman et al. (2012) found that leadership aspirations were higher after observing the leadership of similar individuals, that is, individuals in one's own contextual place. Their study was carried out in India soon after the implementation of a new regulation that required the leadership position in one-third of the villages be reserved for a woman. Leadership aspirations of girls and boys living in villages which had not experienced a woman leader were compared to girls' and boys' aspirations in villages which had experienced one term with a woman leader, and with another group who experienced two terms with a woman leader. Boys' leadership aspirations were unaffected by the presence of women leaders, but girls' aspirations were significantly higher after only two terms of women's leadership.

In addition to similarity, sharing real-life experiences about overcoming biases at work (leadership web) or "telling it like it is" may be a strategy for increasing the impact of role models on leadership self-efficacy and aspirations. Weisgram and Bigler (2007) studied the change in interest and aspirations of adolescent girls who listened to one of two types of talks by women leaders in STEM disciplines. In one version, the women leaders spoke about the variety of interesting careers in STEM. In the other version, the leaders discussed the gendered barriers they faced in their work and how they overcame them. Girls' interest in pursuing STEM careers was heightened only in the second condition. The authors noted that it is possible that hearing about gender-related difficulties helped the young women to think through and understand their own experiences in STEM classes. Perhaps the girls replaced their thoughts about perceived personal inadequacies in STEM subjects with the speculation that they may have disliked the classes because they encountered invisible barriers in them. It is also possible that by specifically discussing workplace discrimination, the speakers were not only addressing and allaying concerns the girls had about bias and discrimination, but also effectively conveying the message that women with strong self-efficacy can move through these barriers successfully.

Self-efficacy does not remain stagnant; it strengthens or weakens over time (Bandura, 1997). It is abundantly clear from other work (e.g., Batliwala, 2011; Hoyt and Murphy, 2016) that self-efficacy can be limited or erased entirely by events or barriers outside the woman's control; these events or barriers might be located within the deep structure of an organization. Bandura (1982) wrote that to be effective, self-efficacy beliefs must be strong enough to promote resiliency in the face of adversity and challenge. Setbacks happen to everyone, but a person with strong self-efficacy will persist and even work harder (Bandura, 1997).

Influences of Family and Friends

Relationships (leadership web) include the influence a woman's family and friends have on her perceptions of leadership and her personal leadership aspirations (Stead and Elliott, 2009). Family and friends provide or promote certain role models, discount others, and give commentary on girls' and women's choices and practices, thereby influencing, either directly or indirectly, the woman's leadership self-efficacy.

In an unpublished study, Austin (2016) assigned undergraduate university students to discuss with parents, spouses, and friends the reasons why there were not more women leaders in the United States and, more specifically, in the state in which their university was located. (As background, this state typically ranks in the bottom ten states for women's political participation and executive-level leadership; Hess et al., 2015.) Austin found that, for these students, women's lives were seen as strictly bifurcated. They saw leadership and motherhood as polar opposites and could not imagine a "good" mother combining the two. They focused on the observable main effects of traditional mothering roles, biology (monthly mood swings), and personality without consideration for the intersectionalities that might constrain leadership aspirations and expression of talent. None of the students said that women's self-efficacy or self-esteem might be a hindrance to leadership; rather, the hindrance had to do with the demands of the mothering role.

Given that the roots of self-efficacy begin early in life, usually in the family of orientation, but reinforced shortly thereafter by friends, an important way to encourage women's leadership aspirations is to encourage the development during childhood and adolescence of the notion that even as young girls and teens they can influence and work with others to purposeful ends, and that they – not anyone else – can determine their own path in life. Clearly, "gender begins at home" (Valian, 1999, p. 23), starting with parents' need to know the sex of the neonate so that they can launch the gendered socialization of their child beginning with the baby's first cries. A family's and later friends' views of "a woman's place" and "a woman's role" shape self-expectations, self-awareness, and thereby self-efficacy from the very earliest days of childhood and onwards.

The constraints of place, so damaging to self-efficacy and often conveyed through work and relationships aspects of the leadership web as well, are listed by Reis (1999) as internal barriers that young women face during adolescence and beyond. These include the social expectation that women should take care of others before themselves, a fear of success, doubting and hiding their own abilities, the "imposter syndrome" (that is, attributing success to external factors including luck, rather than attributing success to their own capabilities), a crushing demand for perfectionism coupled with feelings of criticism, and feeling inferior when compared to others. Each of these expectations alone can significantly truncate leadership self-efficacy, and when taken together the influence can be crushing. More recently, Hinshaw and Kranz (2009) and Simmons (2009) added the "triple bind" to the list of barriers to describe the societal expectation that young women should be good at traditional female roles, traditional male roles, and perfect besides (that is, both a star athlete and an all "A" student).

Prevailing Cultural Norms

Place, at its most fundamental level, may be one's culture, in a sense one's birthplace, as it represents "the collective programming of the mind distinguishing the members of one group ... from others" (Hofstede et al., 2010, p. 6). That "collective programming" is synonymous with the messages one receives from one's relationships, starting with one's family and expanding outwardly to one's community, including the spheres of work and society at large. This messaging or programming defines social roles (what men and women are supposed to do), and leadership roles (who can be leaders and how leadership is to be enacted). It would follow that women's leadership aspirations would be shaped by their national culture and, specifically relevant to our discussion, how differentially cultures value femininity or collectivism or are infused with religion.

Hofstede (1980) began his work identifying dimensions of national culture to explain different values in the workplace. His six dimensions included the degree to which a culture values masculinity versus femininity. High-masculine cultures, such as Japan, German-speaking countries, and some Latin countries such as Italy and Mexico, value "achievement, heroism, assertiveness and material rewards for success"; high-feminine cultures, such as France, Spain, Korea, and Thailand, value "cooperation, modesty, caring for the weak and quality of life" (Hofstede et al., 2010). The implicit ideal of leadership is one that exemplifies the norms of the culture (Schein, 2001); in this case, masculine or feminine. Indeed, Ayman and Korabik (2015) determined that women are more likely to be accepted as a leader in cultures where femininity is valued than in cultures where masculinity is valued, and thus more likely to aspire to and achieve a leadership position. This dimension links place with work.

A second Hofstede cultural dimension, namely individualism versus collectivism, links place with relationships. Individualist cultures, such as those of most Western countries, value autonomy, independence, and self-reliance; collectivist cultures, present in many Eastern countries, value tight group cohesion, which offers support and protection in exchange for loyalty (Hofstede, 2011). Leong et al. (2010) argued that while collectivism "usually involves the subordination of personal goals to be able to attain the goals of the group/community" (p. 466), individuals from collectivist cultures do not necessarily reject their own personal goals. Instead, collective goals have often been so deeply internalized as to conflate with personal goals.

Leong et al. (2010) did not articulate a differential impact of collectivism on men and women. However, when integrated with trait expectations of women being caring and nurturing, the authors argue that women from collectivist cultures could experience greater pressure to consider any aspiration for leadership in the context of its impact on their in-groups, whether families, communities, or organizations. Aspirations to lead may be dampened if the cost to relationships is high; or it may be invigorated if a woman's leadership contributes to the welfare of the group.

Religion adds to the "collective programming" in many world cultures. Hunter and Sargeant (1993) focused on the changes in the leadership and philosophies within Protestantism and Reformed Judaism in the United States. They observed:

> what is really at stake is the cultural meaning of womanhood, and this, as we have seen, is related to still larger philosophical questions about the nature of moral authority, the meaning of tradition, the ontology of sacredness, and the relation of human experience to the sacred. (pp. 569–570)

In her studies of European countries, Leyenaar (2008) observed that the more religious the country (specifically, Catholicism and forms of fundamentalism including Islam and evangelicalism), the fewer women there are in leadership. Another study by Yun (2013) focused on the influence of Confucianism on the subordinate positions of Asian women both within the family and within society, and speculated on how the expectations associated with subordinate roles would change with more exposure to Western cultures.

Religious influences, while slowly evolving, predominantly define women's roles as subservient to men.

EVALUATION OF THE COSTS AND BENEFITS OF LEADERSHIP

While an implicit understanding of leadership behavior consistent with her self-image and strong self-efficacy are important to women's and girls' leadership aspirations, Singer (1989) found that a woman must also believe that the benefits of being a leader will be worth the costs. This is consistent with the motivational metatheory developed by Leonard et al. (1999), which identified the ideal self (the implicit leader), the perceived self which includes perceived self-efficacy, and value-based goal internalization as combining to motivate action. Thus, she also considers, "What would I have to give up or sacrifice to be a leader, and am I willing to do that?" and "What would be gained if I were a leader?" Research indicates that the list of what she might expect to give up or sacrifice is long; at work she may incur the penalties associated with role incongruency; the time demands associated with leading may negatively impact critical relationships in her life; and finally, the place where leadership sits in a woman's list of priorities may be sufficiently low so as not to be worth the costs incurred.

Role Congruency

Even if a woman believes that her personal self-image is congruent with leadership behaviors, she is likely to face challenges in all aspects of the leadership web (that is, work, relationship, and place). Role congruency, for example, challenges each of the three aspects simultaneously and separately. Relative to place and work, the expectations others have of how leaders will behave are inconsistent with the gender traits they associate with women. This role incongruence comes with a steep price. Eagly and Karau (2002) named two forms of prejudice toward female leaders embodied in their role congruity theory. One is that there are less favorable evaluations of women's potential for leadership (because leadership ability is more stereotypical of men than women). The second is a less favorable evaluation of the actual leadership behavior of women in comparison to men, because leadership behavior is perceived as less desirable in women than men (Silverman, 2015).

This prejudice becomes more pronounced the more masculine the context (for example, male-dominated leadership and/or greater number of male subordinates). The classic "double bind" occurs when women must choose between the (masculine) traits associated with leadership or feminine traits; enact the masculine leadership traits and be castigated as unfeminine, or enact feminine traits and not be seen as a leader. By enacting feminine traits, women also run the risk of their motives being misinterpreted and finding that the value of bringing compassion and collaboration into the workplace is invisible and "gets disappeared" (Fletcher, 1999).

By enacting masculine traits, women might earn the title of leader but will still be "punished." Diekman and Goodfried (2006) identified two other responses: (1) women behaving as leaders being perceived as less likeable or hostile; and (2) women being penalized for self-promotion (Rudman, 1998), speaking directly, or enacting an autocratic leadership style. Prentice and Carranza (2002) found that the harshest punishments resulting from enacting gender-intensified proscriptive traits are meted against women in masculine (leadership) roles.

This high price helps to explain why women, when presented with an opportunity for leadership, may not step up as they correctly anticipate the problems of role incongruence. This hesitation starts well before a woman enters the workforce. As young children, girls get labeled "bossy" when taking up leadership (Girl Scout Research Institute, 2008; Valian, 1999). Lips (2000) found that college women were less optimistic about holding powerful leadership positions, not because they did not have self-confidence, but because they had reservations about how they would be perceived and treated in those positions of power. Relative to the section on self-efficacy, they ask themselves if they have sufficient self-efficacy to move past the negativity they know they will encounter.

Role congruency challenges are exacerbated by intersectionality, including race, age, and class. Intersectionality captures the complexities of an individual's life experiences and challenges model and theory development to move away from not only binary conceptions of identities (male or female, black or white), but also from homogeneous (all women) and even from additive categories of identities (women, plus race, plus class). By exploring race, gender, social class (and other identities) together, one can more accurately understand an individual's multidimensional lived experiences, including the complexities of often simultaneously conflicting expectations for and feedback on their leadership (Davis and Maldonado, 2015; Debebe and Reinert, 2014; Holvino, 2010).

As noted earlier in the discussion of implicit leadership, changes are occurring in society's implicit leadership model. As this change is occurring simultaneously with an evolution in the gendered perceptions of appropriate male and female behavior, the combination is slowly enabling greater congruity between female and leader roles. If so, taking on what were previously perceived as masculine traits associated with leadership may come with fewer penalties. Bem (1974) predicted that as more women move into conventionally masculine roles, the traits associated with those roles will become androgynous; women, as well as men, will be able to enact those traits. Many scholars have now called for a more androgynous concept of leadership (Ayman and Korabik, 2015; Gartzia and van Engen, 2012; Watson and Newby, 2005).

The intersectionality of racial and ethnic identities significantly adds complexity to women's leadership aspirations and decision making. Arminio et al. (2000) identified how college students of color responded to leadership opportunities, including the personal costs of holding positions (that is, facing unattainable expectations, "being watched 24/7"), having to prioritize group or team loyalty over individual needs, and a lack of campus staff and faculty role models. Many of the college students in their study rejected even being labeled a leader, as that label marked them as someone who had "sold out" to the "system that oppressed their racial group"; and leadership was generally regarded as a "burden" (Arminio et al., 2000, pp. 500–501).

Time Demands

Coffman and Neuenfeld (2014) found that the time commitment of being "always on" deterred women from wanting to proceed into leadership. Many leadership roles require 24/7 availability which defines an evolving category of jobs labeled "extreme jobs" (Hewlett and Luce, 2006) with required hours up 9 percent since 1979. In general, the average number of hours worked by women in the United States has increased by 181 hours annually since 1979, representing a 10.7 percent increase or another 4.5 weeks of work per year (Mishel, 2013). While women have increased their hours at work, they have simultaneously increased the amount of time they spend with their children (Bianchi, 2000), moving from an average of ten hours per week to 14, or a 40 percent increase (Parker and Wang, 2013). Similar to how a women's self-image might conflict with her implicit leadership theory, her understanding of the time required to achieve her personal relationship goals to be a good partner, daughter, friend, and mother are often inconsistent with her understanding of the time demands associated with being a good leader. Time demands of both roles influence women's aspirations for leadership.

Value of Leadership for Women

While leadership has conventionally been regarded as the ultimate endpoint for career planning and advancement, Eccles (2009) recognized that a key component of taking up leadership is "subjective task value" (p. 82). A woman may ask: "Is leadership important to me? Does it have 'interest' value or 'attainment' value?" The answer for many women may be no: taking up leadership may have low subjective task value. O'Neil and Bilimoria (2005) observed that women are motivated primarily by "personal fulfillment/happiness" (p. 181), which is often tied to satisfying relationships, and are motivated least by "winning or competing" over their entire arc of career. O'Neill et al. (2013) found that out of 16 possible goals, the goals of "do work I am passionate about" and "do work that makes a positive impact on people and communities" were ranked as the top two across white, black, and Latina women. In contrast, the goal of "progress to top leadership positions" factored in third for Asian American women, eighth for white women, eleventh for black women, and twelfth for Latina women. If this study were conducted in places other than the United States, leadership ranking would be expected to reflect the cultural values of the participants.

CONCLUSION

Seeking to develop an understanding of the influences on women's leadership aspirations, Singer's leadership aspiration model was supplemented by Elliot and Stead's leadership web to create a framework for the review and discussion of relevant literature. Work, relationships, and place were addressed within a discussion of women's implicit understanding of leadership behavior, women's self-efficacy related to their understanding of leadership behavior, and women's evaluation of the costs and benefits of leadership behavior. The literature cited in this chapter has identified influences, often conflicting ones, from every aspect of the leadership web that impact women's leadership aspirations.

It became apparent that increasing women's leadership aspirations is likely to require changes throughout our societal systems, and strong communications in all media to reinforce changing societal norms toward equality. One area of change needed is the inclusion of and greater respect for relationships and better alignment with feminine or androgynous characteristics within society's implicit leadership model. While it appears that this evolution in implicit understandings of leadership is occurring, due in part to changes in technology and increasing globalization, change is slow. Moving to new understandings of leadership will require greater changes in some places than in others, as the cultures of countries', industries', and organizations' work environments vary. Each of these entities can begin to institute changes in leadership expectations and scholars can lend research support for these changes.

The barriers inhibiting women's confidence in their self-efficacy for leadership must also be reduced, with an increase in the congruity between leaders' roles and women's roles. Organizations, individuals, and researchers can work to understand and reduce the current incongruity challenges. Increasing women's leadership aspirations is also expected to require an evolution in the expectations of what is considered an appropriate allocation of home and family-related work responsibilities between men and women. These changes would be expected to decrease the costs of leadership behavior for women, such that when women consider the costs and benefits of leadership, benefits will outweigh the costs.

As noted throughout the chapter, aspirations are developmental and dynamic (Brown and Segrist, 2016; Coffman and Neuenfeld, 2014); as her environment and self-efficacy continue to shift, so may a girl's or woman's aspirations. Thus, when women see leadership behaviors as desirable behaviors, when they see those behaviors as consistent with their own self-images, when they believe they are prepared and have the capability to be leaders, and when they see the value of the impact they can make as leaders to be more important than the personal losses they believe they would suffer if they chose to be leaders, only then will women's aspirations for leadership increase.

REFERENCES

Arminio, J.L., Carter, S., Jones, S.E., Kruger, K., Lucas, N., Washington, J., . . . Scott, A. (2000). Leadership experiences of students of color. *NASPA Journal*, *37(*3*)*, 496–510.

Austin, A.M.B. (2016). Perceptions of, and reactions to, women's leadership. Working paper, Center for Women and Gender, Utah State University, Logan, Utah.

Ayman, R., and Korabik, K. (2015). Women and global leadership: Three theoretical perspectives. In F.W. Ngunjiri and S.R. Madsen (Eds), *Women as Global Leaders* (pp. 53–72). Charlotte, NC: Information Age Publishing.

Bandura, A. (1982). Self-efficacy mechanism in human agency. *American Psychologist*, *37*(2), 122–147.

Bandura, A. (1997). *Self-Efficacy: The Exercise of Control*. New York, NY: W.H. Freeman & Company.

Batliwala, S. (2011). *Feminist leadership for social transformation: Clearing the conceptual cloud*. New York, NY: CREA.

Beaman, L., Duflo, E., Pande, R., and Topalova, P. (2012). Female leadership raises aspirations and educational attainment for girls: A policy experiment in India. *Science*, *335*(6068), 582–586. doi: 10.1126/science.1212382.

Bem, S.L. (1974). Bem sex role inventory. American Psychological Association, APA PsycNET. doi: 10.1037/t00748-000.

Bianchi, S.M. (2000). Maternal employment and time with children: Dramatic change or surprising continuity? *Demography*, *37*(4), 401–414.

Boatwright, K.J., and Egidio, R.K. (2003). Psychological predictors of college women's leadership aspirations. *Journal of College Student Development*, *44*(5), 653–669.

Brown, D.L., and Segrist, D.L. (2016). African American career aspirations: Examining the relative influence of internalized racism. *Journal of Career Development*, *43*(2), 177–189.

Cabrera, S.F., Sauer, S.J., and Hunt, M.C. (2009). The evolving manager stereotype: The effects of industry gender typing on performance expectations for leaders and their teams. *Psychology of Women Quarterly*, *33*(4), 419–428.

Coffman, J., and Neuenfeld, B. (2014). Everyday moments of truth: Frontline managers are key to women's career aspirations. Boston, MA: Bain & Company. Retrieved from http://www.bain.com/publications/articles/everyday-moments-of-truth.aspx.

Davis, D.R., and Maldonado, C. (2015). Shattering the glass ceiling: The leadership development of African American women in higher education. *Advancing Women in Leadership*, *35*, 48–64.

Debebe, G., and Reinert, K. (2014). Leading with our whole selves: A multiple identity approach to leadership development. In M. Miville and A. Ferguson (Eds), *Handbook on Race-Ethnicity and Gender in Psychology* (pp. 271–293). New York, NY: Springer.

Diekman, A.B., and Eagly, A.H. (2000). Stereotypes as dynamic constructs: Women and men of the past, present and future. *Personality and Social Psychology Bulletin*, *26*(10), 1171–1188.

Diekman, A.B., and Goodfried, W. (2006). Rolling with the changes: A role congruity perspective on gender norms. *Psychology of Women Quarterly*, *30*(4), 369–383.

Eagly, A.H., and Carli, L.L. (2007). *Through the Labyrinth: The Truth about how Women become Leaders*. Boston, MA: Harvard Business School Press.

Eagly, A.H., and Karau, S. (2002). Role congruity theory of prejudice toward female leaders. *Psychological Review*, *109*(3), 573–598.

Eagly, A.H., Wood, W., and Diekman, A.B. (2000). Social role theory of sex differences and similarities: A current appraisal. In T. Eckes, and H.M. Trautner (Eds), *The Developmental Social Psychology of Gender* (pp. 123–174). Mahwah, NJ: Erlbaum.

Eccles, J. (2009). Who am I and what am I going to do with my life? Personal and collective identities as motivators of action. *Educational Psychologist*, *44*(2), 78–89.

Eden, D., and Leviatan, U. (1975). Implicit leadership theory as the determinant of the factor structure underlying supervisory behavioral scales. *Journal of Applied Psychology*, *60*(6), 736–741.

Evans, C., and Diekman, A. (2009). On motivated role selection: Gender beliefs, distant goals, and career interest. *Psychology of Women Quarterly*, *33*(2), 235–249.

Fletcher, J.K. (1999). *Disappearing Acts: Gender, Power and Relational Practice at Work*. Boston, MA: MIT Press.

Gartzia, L., and van Engen, M. (2012). Are (male) leaders "feminine" enough? *Gender in Management*, *27*(5), 296–314.

Girl Scout Research Institute. (2008). Change it up: What girls say about redefining leadership. Retrieved from http://www.girlscouts.org/content/dam/girlscouts-gsusa/forms-and-documents/about-girl-scouts/research/change_it_up_executive_summary_english.pdf.

Hess, C., Milli, J., Hayes, J., and Hegewisch, A. (2015). The status of women in the states: 2015. Washington, DC: Institute for Women's Policy Research. Retrieved from http://statusofwomendata.org/app/uploads/2015/02/Status-of-Women-in-the-States-2015-Full-National-Report.pdf.

Hewlett, S.A., and Luce, C.B. (2006). Extreme jobs: The dangerous allure of the 70-hour workweek. *Harvard Business Review*, *84*(12), 49–59.

Hinshaw, S., and Kranz, R. (2009). *The Triple Bind: Saving our Teenage Girls from Today's Pressures*. New York, NY: Ballantine Books.

Hofstede, G. (1980). *Culture's Consequences: International Differences in Work-Related Values*. London, UK: Sage Publications.

Hofstede, G. (2011). Dimensionalizing cultures: The Hofstede model in context. *Online Readings in Psychology and Culture*, *2*(1), 1–26. http://dx.doi.org/10.9707/2307-0919.1014.

Hofstede, G., Hofstede, G.J., and Minkov, M. (2010). *Cultures and Organizations: Software of the Mind*, 3rd edn. New York, NY: McGraw-Hill.

Holvino, E. (2010). Intersections: The simultaneity of race, gender and class in organization studies. *Gender, Work and Organization*, *17*(3), 248–277.

Hoyt, C.L., and Murphy, S.E. (2016). Managing to clear the air: Stereotype threat, women, and leadership. *Leadership Quarterly*, *27*(3), 387–399.

Hoyt, C.L., and Simon, S. (2011). Female leaders: Injurious or inspiring role models for women? *Psychology of Women Quarterly*, *35*(1), 143–157.

Hunter, J.D., and Sargeant, K.H. (1993). Religion, women, and the transformation of public culture. *Social Research*, *60*(3), 545–570.

Ibarra, H., Ely, R., and Kolb, D. (2013). Persistent gender bias too often disrupts the learning process at the heart of becoming a leader. Here's how to correct the problem. *Harvard Business Review*, *91*(9), 60–67.

Ingols, C., Shapiro, M., and Tyson, J. (2015). Throwing like a girl: How traits for women business leaders are shifting in 2015. GCO Insights No. 41, Boston, MA: Center of Gender in Organizations. Retrieved from https://www.simmons.edu/~/media/Simmons/About/CGO/Documents/INsights/Insights-41.ashx?la=en.

Johanson, J.C. (2008). Perceptions of femininity in leadership: Modern trend or classic component? *Sex Roles*, *58*(11/12), 784–789. doi: 10.1007/s11199-008-9398-2.

Koenig, A.M., Eagly, A.E., Mitchell, A.A., and Ristikari, T. (2011). Are leader stereotypes masculine? A meta-analysis of three research paradigms. *Psychological Bulletin*, *137*(4), 616–642.

Leonard, N.H., Beauvais, L.L., and Scholl, R.W. (1999). Work motivation: The incorporation of self-concept-based processes. *Human Relations, 52*(8), 969–998.

Leong, F.T., Hardin, E.E., and Gupta, A. (2010). A cultural formulation approach to career assessment and career counseling with Asian American clients. *Journal of Career Development, 37*(1), 465–486.

Leyenaar, M. (2008). Challenges to women's political representation in Europe. *Signs: Journal of Women in Culture and Society, 34*(1), 1–7.

Lips, H.M. (2000). College students' visions of power and possibility as moderated by gender. *Psychology of Women Quarterly, 24(*1), 39–43.

Mishel, L. (2013). Trends in US work hours and wages over 1979–2007. *Economic Policy Institute.* January 30. Retrieved from http://www.epi.org/publication/ib348-trends-us-work-hours-wages-1979-2007/.

O'Neil, D., and Bilimoria, D. (2005). Women's career development phases: Idealism, endurance, and reinvention. *Career Development International, 10*(3), 168–189.

O'Neill, R.M., Shapiro, M., Ingols, C., and Blake-Beard, S. (2013). Understanding women's career goals across ethnic identities. *Advancing Women in Leadership, 33*, 214–226.

Parker, K., and Wang, W. (2013). Modern parenthood roles: Roles of Moms and Dads converge as they balance work and family. Washington, DC: Pew Research Center. http://www.pewsocialtrends.org/2013/03/14/modern-parenthood-roles-of-moms-and-dads-converge-as-they-balance-work-and-family/.

Prentice, D.A., and Carranza, E. (2002). What women and men should be, shouldn't be, are allowed to be and don't have to be: The contents of prescriptive gender stereotypes. *Psychology of Women Quarterly, 26*(4), 269–281.

Ramakrishnan, A., Sambuco, D., and Jagsi, R. (2014). Women's participation in the medical profession: Insights from experiences in Japan, Scandinavia, Russia, and Eastern Europe. *Journal of Women's Health, 23*(11), 927–934. doi: 10.1089/jwh.2014.4736.

Reis, S.M. (1999). Internal barriers, personal issues, and decisions faced by gifted and talented females. NEAG Center for Creativity, Gifted Education and Talent Development, University of Connecticut. Retrieved from http://gifted.uconn.edu/schoolwide-enrichment-model/internal_barriers_gifted_females/.

Ross-Smith, A., and Chesterman, C. (2009). "Girl disease": Women managers' reticence and ambivalence towards organizational advancement. *Journal of Management and Organization, 15*(5), 582–595.

Rudman, L.A. (1998). Self promotion as a risk factor for women: The costs and benefits of counter stereotypical impression management. *Journal of Personality and Social Psychology, 74*(3), 629–645.

Rudman, L.A., and Phelan, J.E. (2010). The effects of priming gender roles on women's implicit gender beliefs and career aspirations. *Social Psychology, 4*(3), 192–202. doi: 10.1027/1864-9335/a000027.

Schein, V.E. (2001). A global look at psychological barriers to women's progress in management. *Journal of Social Issues, 57*(4), 675–688.

Shapiro, M.I., Deyton, P., Martin, K.L., Carter, S., Grossman, D., and Hammer, D. (2012). Dreaming big: What's gender got to do with it? CGO Insights, 35. Boston, MA: Center for Gender in Organizations. Retrieved from https://www.simmons.edu/~/media/Simmons/About/CGO/Documents/INsights/Insights-35.ashx?la=en.

Shapiro, M., Ingols, C., O'Neill, R., and Blake-Beard, S. (2009). Making sense of women as career self-agents: Implications for human resource development. *Human Resource Development Quarterly, 20*(4), 477–501. doi: 10.1002/hrdq.

Silverman, R.E. (2015). Gender bias at work turns up in feedback. *Wall Street Journal*, September 30. Retrieved from http://www.wsj.com/articles/gender-bias-at-work-turns-up-in-feedback-1443600759.

Simmons, R. (2009). *The Curse of the Good Girl: Raising Authentic Girls with Courage and Confidence.* New York, NY: Penguin Books.

Singer, M. (1989). Gender differences in leadership aspirations. *New Zealand Journal of Psychology, 18*, 25–35.

Stead, V. and Elliott, C. (2009). *Women's Leadership.* London, UK: Palgrave Macmillan.

Valian, V. (1999). *Why So Slow? The Advancement of Women.* Boston, MA: MIT Press.

Watson, J., and Newby, R. (2005). Biological sex, stereotypical sex-roles, and SME owner characteristics. *International Journal of Entrepreneurial Behavior and Research, 11*(2), 129–143.

Weisgram, E.S., and Bigler, R.S. (2007). Effects of learning about gender discrimination on adolescent girls' attitudes toward and interest in science. *Psychology of Women Quarterly, 31*(3), 262–269.

Yun, S.H. (2013). An analysis of Confucianism's *yin–yang* harmony with nature and the traditional oppression of women: Implications for social work practice. *Journal of Social Work, 13*(6), 582–598.

11. Women's leadership ambition in early careers
Ruth Sealy and Charlotte Harman

The "opt-out revolution" was coined by Belkin (2003) to describe the phenomenon of women leaving organizations in their thirties and forties, just as leadership positions appeared to be within their reach. Assumptions were made that women were choosing to become stay-at-home mothers, implying that women have inherently lower career ambition than men. This, despite the fact that young women in the United Kingdom (UK) have been "overachieving" at university level, receiving more and better-graded degrees than young men for several years (Higher Education Statistics Agency, 2014).

Research has thus started to cast a more critical eye over women's career exit, especially given drives to increase the number of women at senior levels of organizations. It has focused on alternative explanations for women's exit, such as the lack of flexibility (Anderson et al., 2010); the lack of appropriate role models (Sealy and Singh, 2010); diminishing perceptions of organizational meritocracy (Sealy, 2010); a lack of identity fit (Peters et al., 2012); and the composite challenges of career and life stage (O'Neil and Bilimoria, 2005), all of which affect career ambition for the senior most organizational roles.

Anecdotal evidence from practitioners in professional service firms in the UK and Ireland reported a recent deterioration in stated ambition levels of young female lawyers, based on the perceived lack of success in the generation of women ahead of them. Extant research has tended to focus either on student perceptions of careers and aspirations (Lent et al., 1994; Lent et al., 2003; Lips, 2000; Nauta and Epperson, 2003) or on the older age-group struggling to stay in organizational life (Antecol, 2010; Elfenbein and O'Reilly, 2007; Hewlett and Luce, 2005; Liff and Ward, 2001; Mallon and Cohen, 2001). Therefore, this chapter will explore perceptions of women's ambition in early career stages in professional services.

The remainder of the chapter is organized as follows. First, we give a review of existing literature looking at career motivation and ambition in women. Following a brief outline of our empirical qualitative study with early career professional women, the findings of the study are then discussed in the context of the literature.

BACKGROUND

A significant outcome of Belkin's "opt-out revolution" article was the perpetuation of the view that women have inherently lower ambition than men and simply do not desire senior organizational positions. While this may appear controversial or even offensive, there are several studies that seemingly support this claim (Powell, 1999; Terjesen and Singh, 2008). Van Vianen and Fischer (2002), for example, examined 350 Dutch government employees from both middle management and general staff positions and found that males at both levels had significantly stronger ambitions to pursue higher managerial positions than females. In a qualitative study, Fels (2004) found that women refused to identify with the word "ambition," associating it with negative qualities such as selfishness, manipulation, and egotism; whereas males asserted that it was an integral part of their working lives. Such results could suggest that women neither desire senior positions nor wish to be seen as ambitious, which Fels attributes to early socialization.

In contrast, more recent research has challenged the argument that women lack ambition, especially when they enter the workplace. Watts et al. (2015), for example, found female students in the US to express significantly higher career aspirations than male students. Project 28–40, a survey of 23,000 working women across the UK and Ireland in 2014, affirmed that women rated themselves as ambitious and actively sought opportunities for career progression, with 70 percent stating that they desired leadership positions (Opportunity Now, 2014). Furthermore, several studies have found that when women left, many did not opt-out of the workplace altogether but instead moved to roles in which they could better achieve work–life balance (Anderson et al., 2010; Hewlett and Luce, 2005; Mallon and Cohen, 2001; Marshall, 2000). These results suggest that women are ambitious, but they leave organizations where they feel their ambitions cannot be fulfilled. This then calls into question how we define "ambition" or "career motivation," and whether they are the same thing.

Recent qualitative research has the potential to explain women's reluctance to position themselves as ambitious, seen in prior research. Based on social role theory (Eagly and Karau, 2002), Sools et al.'s (2007) qualitative study found explicit associations between women's ambition and role incongruity. Both male and female participants tried to disassociate themselves from a negative side of ambition, which referred to a desire for quick progression at the expense of others. Instead, they associated themselves with a drive and keenness that must be implicitly portrayed and not explicitly stated in order to be socially acceptable. However, it was clear that this drive and keenness were associated with long working hours, incongruent with motherhood (as opposed to fatherhood), and women's social role in society. Therefore, participants reported a common assumption that ambition disappears after women have children. Women thus face a double bind: it is very difficult both to convey ambition implicitly and to counter the stereotype against them. This finding suggests that the women in Fels's (2004) study may have refused to identify as ambitious due to the negative connotations associated with explicitly confirming their ambition and its incongruence with their feminine role in society. These stereotypes therefore conceal gender discrimination and ensure that men have a better chance of being, and wanting to be, promoted (Sools et al., 2007; Lewis and Simpson, 2012), perpetuating demographic imbalances at managerial levels.

In the early 1990s, Ely (1994, 1995) compared women's attitudes to their careers in professional service firms (PSFs) with gender balanced and imbalanced leadership to identify social influences. Based on Kanter's (1977) work on tokenism, Ely showed how, when there was fewer than 15 percent female leadership, women became socially constructed as "other." Social identity theory explains clear status differences that exist between social groups (for example, male and female, white and ethnic minority). When individuals belong to a lower-status group, their group identification is less attractive and they may engage in strategies to enhance their self-concept. In applying this theory to women in the workplace, Ely suggested that women may either lower their career goals in order to preserve their self-concept or de-feminize by distancing themselves from other women and taking on male attributes in order to progress. Women in male-dominated organizations were less likely to respect the few women in senior positions and did not perceive them as legitimate role models. They were also less likely to identify positively with their female peers and did not find support in same-sex relationships, evidencing de-feminization. The reverse was true in the gender balanced organizations. Subsequently, junior female managers found it hard to identify with leaders in a male-dominated environment and, as Lewis and Simpson (2012) advocated, it seems that continuing gendered processes reinforced women's lower social status. But these studies are over 20 years old, so one has to wonder whether the world of work is different for junior- or middle-manager women today. Over the subsequent two and a half decades, there has been a spate of studies at mid-managerial levels endeavoring to explain why women were not reaching the most senior roles, often with a focus on demographic dissimilarity (e.g., Kirchmeyer, 2002; Liff and Ward, 2001; Polzer et al., 2002).

Whereas management literature has focused significantly on the barriers to women's careers, often organizational and structural, literature from psychology has focused more on turnover theory. Such literature often highlights the cost of turnover to organizations (see Allen et al., 2010 for a review) and tends to be dominated by cross-sectional survey designs, attempting to correlate particular variables and implying causality. However, despite decades of research, the literature can only explain a very limited variance in turnover decisions (Griffiths et al., 2000), and as Russell (2013) suggested, it does not substantially "help managers deal with real voluntary turnover problems" (p. 161). Allen et al. (2014) suggested that this reluctance to move away from such a dominant analytical mindset (that is, single measureable variables causing turnover) "may slow theoretical progress by constraining the conceptualization of research questions" (pp. S61–62), and called for consideration of more varied perspectives.

Recent qualitative research has considered the interaction of both organizational and psychological factors on women's career designs, affected by the lack of appropriate role models (Sealy and Singh, 2010) and the impact of a changing view of meritocracy leading to a declining sense of belief of possibility (Sealy, 2010). Building on this, a theoretical model has also challenged the lower ambition assumption, articulating that women's ambition erodes over time due to organizational factors. Peters et al. (2012) suggested that, at middle levels, women's perceived lack of similarity with male-dominated leadership positions (for example, in consultant surgery) leads to disidentification, and this is associated with increased psychological exit and female surgeons leaving. Similarly, men's perceived lack of fit with more macho marine commandos was found to be associated with reduced identification and motivation (Peters et al., 2015). Based on questionnaire data across a range of sectors and samples, these authors have proposed their identity fit model of career motivation (IFMCM). They defined career ambition and motivation as the extent to which individuals desired promotion and recognition, prioritized their career goals, and were willing to make sacrifices for their career (Peters et al., 2013). Individuals' diminishing belief in the possibility of their success caused them to recalibrate their ambition and ultimately leave.

An alternative theory applied to women's ambition is social cognitive career theory (SCCT), implicating further internal factors important for career choices and persistence (Day and Allen, 2004; Lent et al., 1994; Lent et al., 2003). Based on Bandura's social learning theory (Bandura, 1986), SCCT explains the key roles of belief in one's ability to be successful at a task (self-efficacy) and the cost–benefit analysis of expected outcomes (outcome expectations), which takes into account perceived barriers and supports. SCCT was initially proposed to explain student subject choice and persistence, and it has more recently looked at women's "non-traditional" subject choice (e.g., see Nauta and Epperson, 2003, looking at science, math, and engineering), subsequent career choice, and interest shown in elite leadership positions (Dickerson and Taylor, 2000; Yeagley et al., 2010). In all cases, self-efficacy was a key predictor.

However, research has also shown that, even if women have self-efficacy about their leadership capability, if they believe there to be significant barriers, they may either be discouraged from pursuing such roles (Lips, 2000) or this may lead to intentions to leave (Singh et al., 2013). Women's leadership interest and aspiration is affected first and foremost by their belief in their competence and ability to perform, but then also by the likelihood of their success. As Yeagley et al. (2010) pointed out, these internal beliefs of self-efficacy "do not develop in a social vacuum," but rather "are formed in the context of other background experiences, culture, and contextual affordances" (p. 37). Recent work in the UK considered how gendered cultures are prevalent in senior schools, thus affecting subject choice and careers advice for girls (Institute of Physics, 2013). As Lewis and Simpson (2012) state, male-dominated organizations, discriminatory stereotypes, and gendered processes are associated with a disconnect between women and leadership and a diminished possibility of women fulfilling both their gender role and the role of the successful businesswoman. This leads to a recalibration of career goals to preserve the self-concept. The broader background of these women's careers, including the sex roles into which men and women have been socialized, and the contextual influences that affect women's willingness to translate interest into goals for leadership, cannot be ignored and require further investigation (Fitzsimmons et al., 2014; Yeagley et al., 2010).

The SCCT empirical studies have focused predominantly on college students, and managerial studies have focused on more senior levels, or non-business settings. Unfortunately, 20 years since Ely's (1994, 1995) seminal work, we still do not know how young female professionals view their careers and ambition levels. Therefore, for this project, we asked the question: "How do women construe their ambition at early career stages in a professional services organization?"

THE STUDY

This research focused on eliciting women's subjective experience and perceptions of ambition in order to address the gap in the literature and extend theoretical frameworks. Therefore, we followed an interpretivist approach and adopted an abductive strategy through a qualitative design (Denzin and Lincoln, 2005; Willig, 2013). The study focused on 20 women in their twenties and early thirties, from the London-based advisory function of a professional services organization (PSORG). The industry was chosen due to its traditionally masculine culture, but more recent increase in feminization and sustained efforts to increase diversity. To capture their experiences at the start of the prime opt-out period, the women in the sample had all been with PSORG for a minimum of two years; they had been sufficiently immersed into the organizational culture but had not yet made managerial level.

We conducted semi-structured interviews face-to-face. There were 18 questions to explore how these women defined and experienced ambition; the extent of their ambition and how this had changed during their time at their organization; and the importance of prototype similarity, self-efficacy, outcome expectations, and barriers to them for their ambition. The data were analyzed using template analysis (King, 1998), as it is not bound to a particular epistemological position and permits the use of a priori themes that relate to the existing literature. These a priori themes were based on the IFMCM and SCCT, and through the analysis were revised and expanded upon to create a comprehensive thematic map. These themes are discussed in the following sections.

Defining and Declaring Ambition

The young professional women in this study were very clear that they identified as ambitious and were motivated to be successful in their careers. However, they were also clear that their definition of "success" included work and non-work domains and, even at this early stage (that is, before parenthood), they were taking a more holistic approach to their working lives. There were many different goals or areas toward which their ambition was directed, including achieving work–life balance and happiness. This leads us to question whether our academic definition of career ambition is still too biased toward a narrow masculine-stereotyped version of success.

Characteristic of their life stage (O'Neil and Bilimoria, 2005), their in-work ambition was directed toward learning, being challenged, making a difference, and adding value. When talking about success in the work environment, their desire for reaching seniority defined the strength of their ambition. However, there was also near unanimity in declaring their futures at PSORG were uncertain, with an unwillingness to commit to a role at PSORG or long-term goals. These women wanted to keep their options open, not limit themselves, and be able to adapt to the changeable working environment. They distinguished between a long-term, stable "drive to succeed" and a short-term motivation to carry out those ambitions within a role at PSORG, which they acknowledged was affected by external and organizational factors. In doing so, they implied that the determination to pursue their goals, despite some reduced motivation, demonstrated high ambition. Some acknowledged that this reluctance to commit solely to PSORG may hinder their progress, but they felt that by doing so, they were protecting their ambition.

This was because their ambition was seen as a state rather than a specified end-goal, as something that was theirs alone and formed part of their identity. They wanted to be seen as ambitious, albeit to varying extents. There was a strong theme that ambition was synonymous with being driven, proactive, and pursuing success; not only having goals, but also knowing how to achieve them. Only a few participants acknowledged a negative side to ambition in their definition, which was more associated with negative "cut-throat" style behaviors of certain individuals. These participants still had a clear view that they could be, and indeed were, ambitious without needing to engage in such behaviors.

Fit and Their Future

The young women in this study had left the university environment with high ambitions and what a few described as "unrealistic enthusiasm." Having always achieved in education, these women were unprepared for the requirements of workplace success. Gender differences became apparent for the first time, and they spoke of being confronted by a new reality and having to adjust their ambitions.

Considering the demographics of the organization and the IFMCM, many of the women spoke of looking up and seeing three issues of "fit": only one type of individual succeeding, only one approach to work, and only "defeminized" women. While the demographics at peer level were reasonably diverse, the participants saw the partners as very male-dominated – all from a similar, privileged background – to which they found hard to relate; hence, they struggled to envisage themselves reaching senior positions. Gender was not the sole reason participants lacked similarity with leaders; they also contrasted their skill set and approach to work, which made senior positions appear less attractive or unobtainable. The young women reported that, of the few female senior leaders, most were defeminized, labeled as "fierce," and (to their knowledge) did not have children. They believed that the female leaders neither had the work–life balance they themselves desired, nor had to overcome the additional challenges of motherhood, which was particularly problematic for those young women who wanted a family. Therefore, many reported feeling frustrated and unsure whether they could reach, or would enjoy, senior positions, while also being true to themselves. Together, in line with the IFMCM, these issues of "fit" caused the young women to lower their expectations of career success, or they considered leaving. Interestingly, the perspectives of one subgroup, with participants from a specific, gender-diverse department, actually contrasted starkly. These individuals felt that they could relate to those around them at all levels, felt unrestricted, and believed they could reach senior levels while remaining authentic. Echoing Sealy and Singh (2010), some participants identified with "close role models" at a more senior level to them (not necessarily at partner or director level), who they felt were exceptional male or female leaders and signaled hope of progression. They also experienced a collaborative and supportive environment within which they felt they "fit." This fit was associated with feelings of belonging, enjoyment, and a desire to fulfill their ambitions at PSORG.

However, for most, there were several references to a "boys' club," to which they did not belong. They inferred that only men reap the benefits of in-group membership, such as more natural relationships with senior employees. Relatedly, they felt that the ways in which they could add value by being different were not recognized; they reported that they were "stagnating," not fulfilling their ambitions, and gaining insufficient enjoyment from their work. This lack of fit permeated their long-term outlook of PSORG, questioning the likelihood of their success and therefore their PSORG ambitions, leading to exit thoughts and desires to pursue ambition elsewhere.

A Violation of Trust

What was clear from these interviews, but is perhaps lacking in the IFMCM, is the strength of the affective reaction of the participants. IFMCM can be considered as a rational, cognitive process – a logical deduction from what appears to have gone before – that success is unlikely and therefore exit is the sensible option. However, extant literature is lacking in explaining the emotional side of such decision-making. One possible explanation is that participants experienced a violation of trust over time, a gradual erosion of the psychological contract of expectations with the organization (Searle and Ball,

2004). When things go wrong for individuals in organizations, a bank of trust built up over time can be drawn upon to cushion negative impacts (Dietz and Den Hartog, 2006). Also over time, however, individuals can use observations of behavioral evidence (Weick, 2001) to create a mental model of the intent of the organization, which may not include their personal career success. This breakdown of trust can affect employees' workplace well-being, motivation, and intentions to remain (Chartered Institute of Personnel and Development, 2012).

Many of the young women in this study felt undervalued, with their efforts unrecognized, triggering the desire to leave and pursue their ambitions in an environment where women would be more respected and would face less hindrance. The perceived intent of the organization is often conveyed through human resource practices (Searle and Ball, 2004), and the participants expressed frustration at the strict grading system imposed on them (that is, time served was valued more than quality of output). They reported a lack of recognition for high performers, making it difficult to progress quickly or exceed expectations. Furthermore, hierarchical pressures often encouraged presenteeism (that is, long working hours and pressure to be in the office), which they resented for being unnecessary and impeding their work–life balance.

Many participants reported that the current promotion process was vague and subjective, with little focus on skills or merit and more emphasis on partner sponsorship. They therefore did not understand requirements for promotion, voiced frustration over the lack of honesty and openness of communication, and questioned the fairness of the process. Other participants reported a need to "learn to play the corporate game" in order to progress. Specifically, it was important to self-promote, network, and develop relationships with partners who were responsible for sponsoring their progress. This was more challenging for young women, excluded from "the boys' club," who struggled to find common ground upon which to build such relationships. Echoing Kumra and Vinnicombe's (2008) professional service firm study, most of these young women reported feeling uncomfortable and "fake" when trying to achieve this visibility, and thus they felt disadvantaged in the promotion process.

Social Role Conflicts

The promotion process, as reported by the participants, reflected very masculine gendered notions of how to get on in PSORG, which conflicted with their values and placed them in the "double-bind" of social role theory by needing them to be both "communal" and "agentic." Participants reported the need to overcome the stereotypes that label them as unambitious and ineffective in their roles, and they faced negative reactions induced by acting inconsistently with these labels. Most of these women also reported a perception that they would inevitably face increased resentment and sexism from peers and wider society if they tried to be both a successful businesswoman and a mother, due to the incongruence between the two. Given their belief that few senior women had children or achieved work–life balance, they did not appear to register the irony of facing such sexism from female peers, assuming that others would be in the same situation. In addition, negative media influences and stereotypes of success that they reported as incongruent with their real-life experiences appeared to perpetuate the intransigence of the normative social roles. Resultantly, some reported a reduction in ambition due to the belief that stereotypes were unbreakable, and that achieving workplace ambitions would no longer be satisfying or enjoyable due to the resentment they would face.

Disappointingly, the majority of participants believed that it would be impossible to be "a responsible parent" or to achieve work–life balance alongside career progression and success. This belief caused severe frustration, exasperation, and the need to make sacrifices and adapt their ambitions accordingly. They implied that the pressure to make this sacrifice was exclusively women's and that men did not face the same challenges. Also disappointing was that they did not mention that they would challenge these normative social roles in the future. PSORG's promotion structure and diversity and inclusion programs were reported to exacerbate this pressure, expecting women to progress at the same rate as men but not expecting men to have parenting responsibilities. Therefore, many participants reported adapting their ambitions in the face of this impossibility, for example by increasing their effort in order to reach a level of sufficient seniority before having children, or by abandoning their career ambitions altogether.

Due to the stereotypes against them, increased pressure, and the need to take time out to have children, these young women reported that they would need to try harder, take longer, and outperform men in order to achieve the same level of success. Consequently, some expressed the need to adapt their ambitions to be more realistic and reflect these challenges. Implicit in most participants' responses was the need to be robust and resilient in order to face the role incongruity, resentment, and the pressure associated with being a female in the workplace, and maintain their ambition.

Self-Efficacy, Upbringing, and Support as Enablers of Ambition

Despite the challenges mentioned above, most of the women were positive about their ambitions and aspirations. Throughout the interviews, many participants reported that their socio-economic status, schooling, and parental influences had been particularly important instillers of ambition; whether schools encouraged competition and expected professional jobs was cited as a justification for the women's self-efficacy and drive. In addition, the extent to which parents had role-modeled working in professional arenas shaped participants' efficacy beliefs and determined how much help they had received in preparation for the work environment. So, to misquote Alexandre Dumas (1984 [1854], Chapter 7): "Nothing succeeds like (expectations of) success" (original quote: "Rien ne réussit comme le succès").

While the majority of the women reported very strong ambition when they graduated from universities, they now varied in the degree to which they believed their ambition to be stable, which could be linked to their levels of self-efficacy (that is, belief in their ability to succeed at higher organizational levels). Some emphasized that self-efficacy was integral to having the persistence to conquer adversity, maintain levels of ambition, and also be able to progress within the male-dominated culture and achieve success in the organization. And, if they had a strong belief in their own abilities and their chances of success, gender similarity for them was less important; they emphasized meritocracy and similarity of skills, convinced that they could reach senior positions by being good at their job.

However, women who expressed lower levels of self-belief also experienced fluctuations or a decline in ambition, and were more strongly influenced by external factors affecting their outcome expectations. These women were only confident if they had proof that they could perform the required behaviors and that their goals were entirely realistic; while they were also aware that this lack of self-belief would hinder their progression. This need for proof relates to the seminal work of Ibarra (1999) on the (contextual) need and (gendered) ability to form "provisional selves." Ibarra found that, in gender-imbalanced environments, women in professional service firms searched (often in vain) for "global" role models rather than cherry-picking positive attributes from various leaders, as their male colleagues did, and thus found it much harder to envision themselves in leadership roles.

For some participants, the self-doubt grew during their time at PSORG as they recognized the barriers and concluded that the potential costs (lack of work–life balance, and dual-role conflict in trying to reach higher levels) did not appear to be justified by potential benefits. From this, they adjusted their outcome expectations and questioned their ability and ambition.

For these women who struggled with low self-efficacy and fluctuating ambition, three forms of support from others were cited as particularly integral to enabling their ambition. The first, as suggested by SCCT, was having organizational support which helped them to progress and "play the corporate game" (that is, having managers or mentors who held open and honest conversations with them, supported them in the promotion process, and helped to push them to overcome their development areas and barriers). Recognition of achievements was also cited as a form of support, increasing participants' self-efficacy and affirming their ambitions. Those who reported receiving little support and little recognition, therefore, felt more alone in the process. The third form was having a supportive partner at home who shared similar career perspectives, valued not resented women's high ambition, and supported and shared family responsibilities. Participants reported this home support as enabling them to fulfill their ambitions, dedicate sufficient time to work to progress, and maintain work–life balance. Otherwise, participants reported the need to sacrifice their ambitions.

CONCLUDING THOUGHTS

It was encouraging to see that the definitions of ambition given by these early career women were positive and, in particular, that negative attributes of behaviors associated with overly ambitious individuals did not sully the whole concept. In this way, ambition and career motivation appeared much more acceptable to these young women than their predecessors. However, as academics, we have work to do on the definition of these terms, in understanding that ambition is not confined to particular elite leadership roles. While understanding that there are varied definitions of success, researchers need to consider whether future work should give credence to definitions of "ambition" that include non-work domains rather than dismissing them as irrelevant, as is often the case.

It was disappointing that, for the most part, these young women perceived there to be a lack of leaders to whom they felt similar (for example, personality, work approach, or challenges faced), and a male-dominated culture created feelings that they did not belong and that, therefore, success was unrealistic. In that respect, very little progress appears to have been made since Ely's work in the 1990s. This had the effect of a decrease in level of ambition, and/or a decrease in desire to fulfill their ambition at PSORG, and/or a change in their definition of success. These barriers to their career progression meant that the women experienced a violation of trust, conveyed through poor human resources processes and practices around promotion and recognition. The frustration at slow career progress and an abhorrence of presenteeism are issues cited in other research on the Millennial Generation. Therefore, future research might examine whether young men at PSORG feel the same.

The intransigence of normative social roles still leads many to assume that women leave organizational life only due to caring commitments and the challenges of not being able to maintain an acceptable level of work–life balance. However, this study shows that the ambition and motivation levels of many young women (in this case aged 24–32) were, even before they encountered parenthood, already in decline or directed toward other definitions of success.

The findings from this study revealed a complex interplay of internal and external factors. While the temporal precedence of self-efficacy is shown in longitudinal work by Lent et al. (2008), this must not be used as an excuse for a lack of responsibility within the organization. Self-efficacy is likely to have developed over time with long-term influences, but outcome expectations will have been formed during the period at PSORG and, as the findings from this study suggest, those expectations can be addressed and managed. Therefore, some practical suggestions from this study are that mentors, coaches, and managers should help women to consider their future, acknowledge inevitable future barriers, and create strategies for the organization to help overcome them. Improving clarity and objectivity of the promotion process would be welcomed by these young women and perhaps most other workers too, with a shift in value from hours worked to quality of output. While some would advocate "learning the rules to play the game," we would question why women and others should need to self-promote to such an extent in order to get recognized. Strong organizational human resource talent management systems should be better at recognizing talent and, rather than relying on those best at self-promotion "pushing" themselves through, talent managers should encourage and support their talented workers by "pulling" them through.

Very few participants said that their gender positively impacted their ambition, by driving them to succeed more and prove others wrong. This drive is associated with a desire to make a difference, be a role model, and ensure that organizational life will be easier for women in the future, demonstrating awareness of gender at some level. However, when questioned at the end of the interview, the majority of the women declared that they had never consciously considered gender to affect their ambition, and that the interview had been illuminating. This may just have brought to the fore issues that, at some level, had become apparent. One of the challenges of claiming ambition to be highly intrinsic is that it plays into Western society's individualized and increasingly psychologized approach to problems that individuals encounter within the workplace. The concept of "self-confidence" has become prevalent in recent years in explaining women's lack of career progress. Gill and Orgad (2016) explained how the "cult(ure) of confidence" (p. 324) is used to identify, diagnose, and propose solutions particularly to women's issues. This neoliberal postfeminist approach individualizes problems of career self-confidence, turning the spotlight away from structural inequalities and reifying "self-work and self-regulation" (p. 324), pathologizing the problem (and therefore the solution) to what we know are organizational and societal issues.

In conclusion, this chapter gave a detailed account of women's early career identification with ambition and their struggle to maintain it in the current working environment. Findings from the study partially supported existing models and research, implicating self-efficacy, organizational barriers, and a lack of similar leaders as key influences on ambition. Yet, they also revealed how issues that organizations are currently trying to tackle at senior levels are already influencing how women identify with ambition early on. Women's ambition is affected by the workplace context from the early stages of their career. Our advice: if organizations want to stem the outflow of women leaving in their thirties and forties, they should address the issues identified above a decade earlier.

REFERENCES

Allen, D.G., Bryant, P.C., and Vardaman, J.M. (2010). Retaining talent: Replacing misconceptions with evidence-based strategies. *Academy of Management Perspectives*, 24(2), 48–64.
Allen, D.G., Hancock, J.I., Vardaman, J.M., and Mckee, D.N. (2014). Analytical mindsets in turnover research. *Journal of Organizational Behavior*, 35(1), S61–S86. doi: 10.1002/job.1912.
Anderson, D., Vinnicombe, S., and Singh, V. (2010). Women partners leaving the firm: Choice, what choice?. *Gender in Management: An International Journal*, 25(3), 170–183.
Antecol, H. (2010). The opt-out revolution: A descriptive analysis. IZA Discussion Paper No. 5089. Retrieved from http://ftp.iza.org/dp5089.pdf.
Bandura, A. (1986). *Social Foundations of Thought and Action: A Social Cognitive Theory*. Englewood Cliffs, NJ: Prentice Hall.
Belkin, L. (2003, October 26). Q: Why don't more women choose to get to the top? A: They choose not to. *New York Times Magazine*, 58, 42–47.
Chartered Institute of Personnel and Development. (2012). *Where has all the Trust Gone: Stewardship, Leadership and Governance*. London, UK: Chartered Institute of Personnel and Development.
Day, R., and Allen, T.D. (2004). The relationship between career motivation and self-efficacy with protégé success. *Journal of Vocational Behavior*, 64(1), 72–91.
Denzin, N.K., and Lincoln, Y.S. (2005). *The SAGE Handbook of Qualitative Research*. London, UK: Sage Publications.
Dickerson, A., and Taylor, A. (2000). Self-limiting behavior in women: Self-esteem and self-efficacy as predictors. *Group and Organization Management*, 25(2), 191–210.
Dietz, G., and Den Hartog, D.N. (2006). Measuring trust inside organizations. *Personnel Review*, 35(5), 557–588.
Dumas, A. (1984 [1854]). *Ange Pitou*, Vol. 1, London, UK: Forgotten Books.
Eagly, A.H., and Karau, J. (2002). Role congruity theory of prejudice toward female leaders. *Psychological Review*, 109(3), 573–598.
Elfenbein, H.A., and O'Reilly, C.A. (2007). Fitting in: The effects of relational demography and person–culture fit on group process and performance. *Group and Organisation Management*, 32(1), 109–142.
Ely, R.J. (1994). The effects of organisational demographics and social identity on relationships among professional women. *Administrative Science Quarterly*, 39(2), 203–238.
Ely, R.J. (1995). The power of demography: women's social constructions of gender identity at work. *Academy of Management Journal*, 38(3), 589–634.
Fels, A. (2004). Do women lack ambition?. *Harvard Business Review*, 82(4), 50–60.
Fitzsimmons, T.W., Callan, V.J., and Paulsen, N. (2014). Gender disparity in the C-suite: Do male and female CEOs differ in how they reached the top? *Leadership Quarterly*, 25(2), 245–266.
Gill, R., and Orgad, S. (2016). The confidence cult(ure). *Australian Feminist Studies*, 30(86), 324–344. doi:10.1080/08164649.2016.1148001.
Griffiths, R.W., Hom, P.W., and Gaertner, S. (2000). A meta-analysis of antecedents and correlates of employee turnover: Update, moderator tests, and research implications for the next millennium. *Journal of Management*, 26(3), 463–488.
Hewlett, S.A., and Luce, C.B. (2005). Off-ramps and on-ramps: keeping talented women on the road to success. *Harvard Business Review*, 83(3), 43–54.
Higher Education Statistics Agency. (2014). First degree qualifiers by sex, mode of study and class of first degree 2010/11 to 2014/15. Retrieved from https://www.hesa.ac.uk/news/11-02-2016/higher-education-qualifications (accessed 3 January, 2016).
Ibarra, H. (1999). Provisional selves: Experimenting with image and identity in professional adaptation. *Administrative Science Quarterly*, 44(4), 764–791. doi: 10.2307/2667055.

Institute of Physics. (2013). Closing doors: Exploring gender and subject choice in schools. Report by Institute of Physics, London, UK. Retrieved from http://www.iop.org/education/teacher/support/girls_physics/closing-doors/page_62076.html.

Kanter, R.M. (1977). *Men and Women of the Corporation*. New York, NY: Basic Books.

King, N. (1998). Template analysis. In G. Symon and C. Cassell (Eds), *Qualitative Methods and Analysis in Organizational Research*. London, UK: Sage.

Kirchmeyer, C. (2002). Change and stability in managers' gender roles. *Journal of Applied Psychology*, *87*(5), 929–940.

Kumra, S., and Vinnicombe, S. (2008). A study of the promotion to partner process in a professional services firm: How women are disadvantaged. *British Journal of Management*, *19*(s1), S65–S74.

Lent, R.W., Brown, S.D., and Hackett, G. (1994). Toward a unifying social cognitive theory of career and academic interest, choice, and performance. *Journal of Vocational Behavior*, *45*(1), 79–122. doi: 10.1006/jvbe.1994.1027.

Lent, R.W., Brown, S.D., Schmidt, J., Brenner, B., Lyons, H., and Treistman, D. (2003). Relation of contextual supports and barriers to choice behavior in engineering majors: Test of alternative social cognitive models. *Journal of Counseling Psychology*, *50*(4), 458–465.

Lent, R.W., Sheu, H., Singley, D., Schmidt, J.A., Schmidt, L.C., and Gloster, C.S. (2008). Longitudinal relations of self-efficacy to outcome expectations, interests, and major choice goals in engineering students. *Journal of Vocational Behavior*, *73*(2), 328–335.

Lewis, P., and Simpson, R. (2012). Kanter revisited: Gender, power and (in)visibility. *International Journal of Management Reviews*, *14*(2), 141–158.

Liff, S., and Ward, K. (2001). Distorted views through the glass ceiling: the construction of women's understandings of promotion and senior management positions. *Gender, Work and Organisation*, *8*(1), 19–36.

Lips, H.M. (2000). College students' visions of power and possibility as moderated by gender. *Psychology of Women Quarterly*, *24*(1), 37–41.

Mallon, M., and Cohen, L. (2001). Time for change? Women's accounts of the move from organisational careers to self-employment. *British Journal of Management*, *12*(3), 217–230.

Marshall, J. (2000). Living lives of change: Examining facets of women managers' career stories. In M. Peiperl, M. Arthur, R. Goffee, and T. Morris (Eds), *Career Frontiers: New Conceptions of Working Lives* (pp. 202–227). Oxford, UK: Oxford University Press.

Nauta, M.M., and Epperson, D.L. (2003). A longitudinal examination of the social-cognitive model applied to high school girls' choices of nontraditional college majors and aspirations. *Journal of Counseling Psychology*, *50*(4), 448–457.

O'Neil, D.A., and Bilimoria, D. (2005). Women's career development phases: Idealism, endurance, and reinvention, *Career Development International*, *10*(3), 168–189.

Opportunity Now. (2014). Project 28–40 report. Retrieved from http://www.bitc.org.uk/system/files/project_28-40_the_report.pdf.

Peters, K., Ryan, M., and Haslam, S.A. (2013) Women's occupational motivation: the impact of being a woman in a man's world. In S.M. Vinnicombe, R. Burke, S. Blake-Beard, and L. Moore (Eds), *Handbook of Research on Promoting Women's Careers* (pp. 162–177). Cheltenham, UK and Northampton, MA, USA: Edward Elgar Publishing.

Peters, K., Ryan, M.K., and Haslam, S.A. (2015). Marines, medics and machismo: Lack of fit with masculine occupational stereotypes discourages men's participation. *British Journal of Psychology*, *106*(4), 635–655. doi:10.1111/bjop.12106.

Peters, K., Ryan, M., Haslam, S.A., and Fernandes, H. (2012). To belong or not to belong: Evidence that women's occupational disidentification is promoted by lack of fit with masculine occupational prototypes. *Journal of Personnel Psychology*, *11*(3), 148–158.

Polzer, J., Milton, L., and Swann, W. (2002). Capitalising on diversity: Interpersonal congruence in small groups. *Administrative Science Quarterly*, *47*(2), 296–324.

Powell, G.N. (1999). *Handbook of Gender in Organisations*. Thousand Oaks, CA: Sage.

Russell, C.J. (2013). Is it time to voluntarily turn over theories of voluntary turnover? *Industrial and Organizational Psychology*, *6*(2), 156–173. doi: 10.1111/iops.12028.

Sealy, R. (2010). Changing perceptions of meritocracy in senior women's careers. *Gender in Management: An International Journal*, *25*(3), 184–197.

Sealy, R.H.V., and Singh, V. (2010). The importance of role models and demographic context for senior women's work identity development. *International Journal of Management Reviews*, *12*(3), 284–300.

Searle, R.H., and Ball, K.S. (2004). The development of trust and distrust in a merger. *Journal of Managerial Psychology*, *19*(7), 708–721.

Singh, R., Fouad, N.A., Fitzpatrick, M.E., Liu, J.P., Cappaert, K.J., and Figuereido, C. (2013). Stemming the tide: Predicting women engineers' intentions to leave. *Journal of Vocational Behavior*, *83*(3), 281–294.

Sools, A.M., Van Engen, M.L., and Baerveldt, C. (2007). Gendered career-making practices: On "doing ambition" or how managers discursively position themselves in a multinational corporation. *Journal of Occupational and Organizational Psychology*, *80*(3), 413–435.

Terjesen, S., and Singh, V. (2008). Female presence on corporate boards: A multi-country study of environmental context. *Journal of Business Ethics*, *83*(1), 55–63.

van Vianen, A.E.M., and Fischer, A.H. (2002). Illuminating the glass ceiling: The role of organisational culture preferences. *Journal of Occupational and Organizational Psychology*, *75*(3), 315–337.

Watts, L.L., Frame, M.C., Moffett, R.G., Van Hein, J.L., and Hein, M. (2015). The relationship between gender, perceived career barriers, and occupational aspirations. *Journal of Applied Social Psychology*, *45*(1), 10–22.

Weick, K. (2001). *Making Sense of the Organisation*. Oxford, UK: Blackwell Publishers.

Willig, C. (2013). *Introducing Qualitative Research in Psychology*. New York, NY: Open University Press.

Yeagley, E.E., Subich, L.M., and Tokar, D.M. (2010). Modelling college women's perceptions of elite leadership positions with social cognitive career theory. *Journal of Vocational Behavior*, *77*(1), 30–38.

12. Women's leadership identity: exploring person and context in theory
Wendy Fox-Kirk, Constance Campbell, and Chrys Egan

This chapter presents a critical review of the concepts of person (intra-individual factors) and context (extra-individual factors) as presented in extant views of the relationship between gender and leadership identity or identities. Our work is grounded in the assumption that both gender and identity are socially constructed (Alsop et al., 2002) through a process that involves the interaction of intra- and extra-individual forces; thus, we view the inclusion of the nature of person–context interactions to be an essential component of theories about both leadership and leader identity development programs targeting women's leadership identities.

Although the general populace may not invoke formal theories when forming an identity, people use implicit identity theories as a framework to make sense of their own and others' identities (Engle and Lord, 1997; Weick et al., 2005). Our implicit theories may be consciously or unconsciously driving our thoughts and actions; hence, it is important to recognize the way we think about identity, not only as individuals but also in our communities. Society's dominant theory of identity is likely to be a key component of the contextual factors that most of us internalize; consequently, societal norms are likely to be considered to reflect "true" theory (Yuval-Davis, 2006).

The chapter addresses three separate but related concerns. Firstly, we begin with a brief historical review of the variety of existing definitions of identity. Secondly, as we narrow our focus more specifically to leader identity, we outline the value of understanding the relationships between leadership identity and gender. Thirdly, throughout the discussion, we assess theories in relation to their position regarding the role of person and context in leadership identities. We also observe implications for the development of women leaders and the value of diversity in leadership throughout the chapter.

WHAT IS IDENTITY?

Identity theories span time and scholarly disciplines, including psychology, sociology, philosophy, and communication studies, yet identity has proven to be difficult to define (Knights and Willmott, 1999; Lemert, 2011). Early work focused on the exploration of identity in terms of the self-concept. William James (1950 [1890]), often considered to be the founder of modern psychology, foresaw the challenges of understanding person–context interactions in his discussions on the riddle of self-identity. James (1950) proposed the existence of several selves – material, social, spiritual, and pure ego – which, considered together, span both person and context. The material self is a precursor of intra-individual factors in current identity theories, whereas the social self, "the recognition [one] gets from his [*sic*] mates" (James, 1950 [1890], p. 293), is a contextual element of identity, as is further illustrated in James's statement that, "properly speaking, a man [*sic*] has as many social selves as there are individuals who recognize him and carry an image of him in their mind" (1950 [1890], p. 294). Thus, James's work, although its primary focus is on the individual and the internal life, also recognizes the key role of the perceptions of others.

Freud's (1997 [1899]) seminal work, *The Interpretation of Dreams*, introduced the tripartite self, comprised of the id, ego, and superego. The latter concept is the only part of the self that is contextual, or linked to the external world. Although the validity of Freud's theory has been seriously questioned for its lack of empirical support (Crews, 1996; Kihlstrom et al., 2003; Westen, 1998), Freud's work was instrumental in shaping the perspective on identity presented by his student Erik Erikson, who discussed individuals' task of constructing an ego identity out of the building blocks of comparisons of self with relevant others and of others' perceptions of self (Goethals and Strauss, 2012). Once again, even though internal factors are a greater focus in Erikson's work, he noted that person and context interact in the formation of identity.

In the mid-twentieth century, Carl Rogers advanced the psychological narrative on identity, proposing the self-concept as an internal, organized, and stable construct that comprises the individual's thoughts, perceptions, and beliefs about themself. Rogers's two main constructs are the ideal-self and the self-image. The ideal-self refers to the individual's idea of how they should be, while the self-image is the individual's actual behavior. Rogers (1959) stated that psychological health is dependent on a high degree of congruence between the ideal-self and the self-image. As with James's (1950 [1890]) theory of self-identity, Rogers's (1959) theory stresses the internal and person-centered nature of identity. Although both James and Rogers recognized that the individual engages with other people and objects, their focus was on the individual's internal world, a focus shared with most psychological theories of identity, in which identity is viewed as a stable, internal construct.

In contrast to the idea of self-identity as largely internal and stable, sociologists Charles Horton Cooley and George Herbert Mead stressed the importance of social interaction. In 1902, Cooley coined the phrase "looking glass self" (1992 [1902], p. 152) and described self-identity as a process in which the "I" sees itself as others see it. Mead, publishing in 1934, agreed with Cooley's notion and added the role of dialogue. Using constructs similar to those used by William James in the 1890s, Mead (2015 [1934]) viewed the self as emergent from an ongoing, dynamic interior dialogue between a personal self (me) and a social self (I). Both Cooley and Mead move toward a greater focus on the role of the social context in constructing identity.

The increased focus on social context and the role of language and communication in shaping identities continues with theorists such as Butler (2011), Foucault (1997), and Ricoeur (1991), who consider identity as a function of language and communication and view "self-identity" as a verb rather than as a noun. Thus, identity is a process – a form of action – rather than something that one is. In agreement with James (1950 [1890]), this view of identity prefers to talk about identities, as in multiple identities, but here self-identity is fragmented rather than united. Ricoeur's (1991) concept of the narrative self, in common with Mead's theory formulated in the 1930s (Mead, 2015 [1934]), presented the identity construction process as driven by internal dialogue with the self and external dialogue in communications with the outside world. Ricoeur argues that we are constantly shifting and negotiating identities in response to our social context as we engage in the creation of meaningful narratives of self. Foucault (1997) and Butler (2011) agree with the central role of language and communication in identity, but they go further, saying that identity work is shaped through power processes. These theorists introduce the idea of socially acceptable and socially deviant identities, which are key concepts relevant to women's leader identity challenges.

Ricoeur (1991) talked about the concept of self and identity in a way that foregrounds the role of context in identity construction, a view that is perpetuated in some current work in leader identity research and leader development practice (see Ely et al., 2011; Ibarra, 1999; Ibarra and Barbulescu, 2010; Ibarra et al., 2010). Ricoeur (1991) presented a very different view of self and identity than that described earlier from the psychological literature: that identity is primarily contained within the individual and that there is a true self, inner self, or self-essence. Rather, much like the symbolic interactionists Erving Goffman (1959) and George Herbert Mead (2015 [1934]), Ricoeur (1991) suggested that self-identity is in constant flux, being created and re-created through the narrative process. He said that humans are constantly inventing and reinventing themselves to fit with the social situations in which they engage. Thus, identity construction is not divorced from the historical, social, and political. In the 1930s, Mead (2015 [1934]) described this narrative process as one that occurs through both internal and external dialogues. Individuals, through interaction with others, develop a sense of who they are and who they can be; for women, they also discover who they are allowed to be. This identity negotiation process creates a two-way interaction between person and context, in which the person is in reaction to the context.

Ricoeur (1992) introduced the concept of the "self as other" (p. 3) to explain how the individual engages in metacognitive acts to assess a sense of self through the eyes of others. Further, he suggested that individuals make adjustments to self to fit in with the social context. Ricoeur's (1991) narrative self provides a link with social identity theory, which is discussed below. Leader identity is one of the social identities we enact; if leader identity is considered normatively male, then women are immediately perceived as "other" or "deviant" when they take on a leader identity. This dilemma results in a need to engage in complex identity work to maintain a sense of coherence between the incongruity of playing two conflicting roles, such as the respectable female and the credible leader. This complex and nuanced struggle is necessary because the nature of being human is fully intertwined with and shaped by context, according to Ricoeur (1991). Further explanation of this central concept follows.

Ricoeur (1991) built on Heidegger's *Dasein* concept (Heidegger, 1996). *Dasein* literally translates as "being there" (German: *da*, there; *sein*, being); "being" represents human beings, and "there" represents location or place and time (p. 9). By deliberately combining "being" and "there" into one word, Heidegger (1996) asserted that being cannot be separated from context. This distinction encapsulates an existential duality of humanity (that people are simultaneously both individual human beings and social entities shaped by context) rather than viewing human beings with an essentialist dualism ontology (that people inherently are defined by a fundamental, predictable nature of what it means to be). An individual's being is fully located in place and time, highlighting the importance of what Hans-Georg Gadamer called "historically effected consciousness" (Risser, 1997, p. 7), which posits that an individual is never separate from their context but rather can only be viewed as in relationship with all the elements that comprise the context (for example, history, culture, current setting, and other people). Based on Gadamer's view, the study of the individual's thoughts, emotions, intentions, and behaviors as if they were divorced from their context results in a false deduction; the meanings surrounding the individual's behavior are essential to understanding behavior.

This contextual perspective on identity illustrates the significant impact of one's theoretical views regarding an individual's agency and social determinism. The theories discussed raise and propose answers to questions such as: Do individuals have full control over their own identity construction? Are individuals merely puppets controlled by the strings of social forces? Is there an interaction between person and context? The theoretical perspective we ascribe to regarding identity has a great impact upon our ideas about whether and how identities can be developed, changed, or effectively performed. For example, if we think about identity as a fairly stable internal entity, then the notion of changing one's identity or having a range of different – and sometimes competing – identities is problematic. Specifically, this more permanent conceptualization leads to an essentialist view of identity as immutable. This tendency toward essentialism encourages the acceptance of fixed rather than fluid and dynamic identities.

Another important reason for surfacing one's theoretical perspective with respect to these questions is that it is a driving force for whether leader identity development is directed toward person, context, or both. The construction of a leader identity viewed through the lens of internal identity theory may create leader development programs focused on helping the individual to identify his or her "hidden" leader strengths. The same approach, when applied to leader selection processes, is likely to focus on individuals whose identities demonstrate "leader potential." However, given the normative masculine nature of the "ideal leader" as outlined earlier, "potential" is likely to be defined in terms of stereotypical masculine behaviors resulting in an adverse impact for women. In the following section, we turn our attention to the importance of considering identity theory, especially when addressing leader identity in relation to women.

THE IMPORTANCE OF DISCUSSING LEADERSHIP IDENTITY IN RELATION TO GENDER

Amidst the burgeoning interest in leadership in the last 20 years (Grint, 2009; Western, 2013), there has been a prominent focus on the "heroic" leader (Meindl, 1995; Tourish, 2008; Tourish and Pinnington, 2002), a leader who is considered to be pivotal to an organization's success. Researchers have referred to the heroic perspective on leaders as "leaderism," or "the leaderist turn" (Morley, 2013; O'Reilly and Reed, 2010), or even "Messiah leadership discourse" (Western, 2013, p. iii) because "as social despair and help-lessness deepen, the search and wish for a messiah (leader) or magical rescue (leadership) also begins to accelerate" (Gemmill and Oakley, 1992, p. 115). From the heroic leader perspective, the correct selection of the "right" leader with the "right" qualities is all that is required to save the organization.

This heroic perspective of leaders, however, is likely to eliminate women from the category of "right" leader. Due to gendered socialization, the terms "hero" and "messiah" invoke images of masculine identities (Bagilhole and White, 2011; Connell, 1987).

group will emerge as the group leader because of a good fit between their enacted leader identity and the leader prototype. Note that this leader selection occurs through social cognitive processes and not through a defined set of behaviors that can be labeled as leadership ability or competences. This is important to stress because it has an impact on the idea that organizations can train leadership competencies. If leader emergence is due to social processes and not a defined set of abilities or competencies, then leadership cannot, in this sense, be trained (Bolden and Gosling, 2006; Fisher and Robbins, 2014). Through social attraction, the individual will get compliance for their ideas and suggestions. Over time, in a stable group, this process will be attributed to some internal leadership disposition. Thus, because of the process of human cognition and a desire to reduce uncertainty, social identity processes of leadership take on the guise of an internal, individual ability. Hogg points to some empirical support for this theory (Conger and Kanungo, 1987, 1988; Fiske, 1993; Fiske and Dépret, 1996).

These concepts address some of the key concerns related to leader-centric, highly person-focused approaches to leadership that disadvantage women by shifting the focus from the individual to the social, or from person to context, through group processes. This view introduces a different understanding of leader identity formation resulting in a need to observe and understand social and sense-making processes. It provides an explanation for the overemphasis on the individual in the leadership process and, more importantly, it is a leadership identity theory that provides an explanation for why women are not present in many senior leadership positions. Hogg (2001) points out that the desire for the most prototypical of the group results in a greater difficulty for "social minorities" (p. 195) to gain access to leadership positions; and if they achieve formal positions they are likely to find it harder to gain acceptance. Being female is technically not a social minority, but those identified as female are likely to experience the workplace in the same way that social minorities do because they are a numerical minority, particularly at managerial levels. The major criticism of this approach is that supporting research comes mainly from laboratory experiments.

Nonetheless, in their recent review of leadership research, Dinh et al. (2014) note that leadership identity perspectives, based on Hogg's (2001) social identity theory, are growing at an impressive rate. One particularly interesting model from this field is that of DeRue and Ashford (2010). In agreement with Hogg (2001), they propose a social process of leadership that hinges on the role of identity or identities. Their main difference with Hogg (2001) is that leadership identities are more dynamic and shifting, and occur through the key processes of claiming and granting. Rather than aligning entirely with a social cognitive view, DeRue and Ashford draw on symbolic interactionism to understand identity processes or identity work (Goffman, 1959; Mead, 2015 [1934]), suggesting that the identities of leader and follower are available to anyone. Although these identities may be available to anyone, they are not equally available to everyone. As we explore this theory further, it will become apparent that certain individuals, due to additional significant identities such as gender and ethnicity, have greater difficulty than others in claiming and being granted a leadership identity. DeRue and Ashford (2010) identified a tri-level model of identity – individual, relational, and collective – in which each level has the same three components: individual internalization, relational recognition, and collective endorsement.

DeRue and Ashford (2010) proposed that individual identity refers to the internalized leader identity construct, but that the internalized leader identity is constructed through a social process. In other words, a person is shaped by the context. Relational identity refers to the notion that an individual does not possess a leader identity; rather, that the identity is mutually recognized and validated among leaders and followers. Collective endorsement refers to the process whereby an individual's leader identity is recognized by the wider community. Thus, leadership is about the construction of a relationship or relationships. The relative roles within this relationship are delineated through the claiming and granting of behaviors.

In DeRue and Ashford's (2010) model, an individual projects a leadership identity through claiming behaviors, actions they take to claim leadership. These acts can be verbal or non-verbal, and direct or indirect. Other people can then choose to reflect the individual's claim by engaging in granting behaviors that acknowledge the leadership that has been claimed. Alternatively, others can reject this claim by not engaging in granting behaviors. DeRue and Ashford (2010) further stated that if the initial claim is not supported, then there is a failure in the internalization of the leader identity at the individual level; therefore, the individual is not recognized as a leader at the relational level and will not be endorsed by the collective. With this view, unlike the prototype and social cognitive view, even those who are not well matched with the group's norms for leader identity may make leadership claiming acts. Kempster (2006) and Ibarra (1999) describe this claiming process as experimenting or trying out a possible self or selves that may be valued by the organization. In this way, people can take small steps to assess whether the leader identity fits with them and whether others engage in granting acts. When their claiming acts are granted, the individual is further motivated to engage in more leader identity claiming acts.

Leadership roles represent not only reward but also risk and responsibilities. Gemmill and Oakley (1992) suggested that taking on the follower identity may be a defense mechanism used to mitigate against perceived risks associated with the leader identity. These authors also point out that leader identity claims are less likely to be granted if an individual is new to the situation, has no track record of leading, or uses a new or different style from the one expected by the collective. We would suggest that there is another condition on which claims are less likely to be granted, and that is when the individual has an identity, or is perceived to have an identity, that conflicts with the leader identity prototype. This conflict could be the individual's gender or ethnicity, but it could also be related to their organizational role, such as moving from subordinate to superior or from industry to academia.

Finally, DeRue and Ashford (2010) also discussed the importance of organizational structures that act to facilitate granting acts more quickly to those who make claims from authority-based role positions. Thus, their model can provide an explanation for leadership emergence and leadership as a given position. It also helps to understand how some individuals have difficulty enacting a leader identity despite holding an organizationally mandated leadership position, and also why some individuals gain the leader identity without a perceived mandate. Problems with this approach lie in the lack of consideration for the historical and cultural to impede on, shape, and constrain these reciprocal relations. Individuals' relations within organizations are not free from the role identity norms that operate outside the organization. Also, claiming and granting behaviors are ill-defined and, as such, any observational research to validate or test this theory could, at present, be problematic. However, this approach introduces the importance of leader identity as a social process, not just as an issue of individual traits, preferred styles, or even simply internal cognitions. Importantly, this view presents leader identity as a negotiated construct as dynamic and shifting. Applied to organizational processes such as leadership selection and development, the theory recognizes that, for those who do not represent the dominant prototype, the organization will need to create structures of support to enable these individuals to make valid leader identity claims and to encourage followers to engage in granting behaviors. In other words, to achieve diversity in leadership, it is not enough to run diversity leader training programs; there is a need for a shift in organizational practices. Considering identity as relational and dynamic is also central to theories that focus on the role of dialogue and language in which self-identity is viewed as a narrative process (Ricoeur, 1991).

CONCLUSION

The key points from this historically grounded review of identity, gender, and leader identity are that identity work, including the development of leader identities, is ongoing, dynamic, and contextual. Thus, leader development practices should extend beyond helping individuals to strengthen general identity management skills so that leader development becomes highly context-relevant and should take place within the context. As DeRue and Ashford (2010) explain, the role of context is not just an added feature; it is integral to the ability to develop accepted leader identities. If, as a society, we are genuinely concerned with improving diversity in the leadership of our organizations, we need to work on the context as well as the person. By moving the lens toward our social practices and how they act to constrain some whilst enabling others, we will begin to illuminate new ways of developing a genuinely diverse leadership.

REFERENCES

Alsop, R., Fitzsimons, A., and Lennon, K. (2002). *Theorizing Gender: An Introduction.* Cambridge, UK: Polity.

Alvesson, M., and Billing, Y.D. (2009). *Understanding Gender and Organizations.* Los Angeles, CA: Sage.

Avolio, B.J., and Gardner, W.L. (2005). Authentic leadership development: Getting to the root of positive forms of leadership. *Leadership Quarterly, 16*(3), 315–338. doi:10.1016/j.leaqua.2005.03.001.

Ayman, R., Korabik, K., and Morris, S. (2009). Is transformational leadership always perceived as effective? Male subordinates' devaluation of female transformational leaders. *Journal of Applied Social Psychology, 39*(4), 852–879. doi:10.1111/j.159-1816.2009.00463.x.

Bagilhole, B., and White, K. (2011). Introduction: Building a feminist research network. In B. Bagilhole and K. White (Eds), *Gender, Power and Management: A Cross-Cultural Analysis of Higher Education* (pp. 1–19). Chippenham, UK: Palgrave Macmillan.

Billing, Y.D., and Alvesson, M. (2014). Leadership: A matter of gender?. In S. Kumra, R. Simpson, and R.J. Burke (Eds), *Oxford Handbook of Gender in Organizations* (pp. 200–222). New York, NY: Oxford University Press.

Bolden, R., and Gosling, J. (2006). Leadership competencies: Time to change the tune?. *Leadership, 2*(2), 147–163.

Butler, J. (2011). *Gender Trouble: Feminism and the Subversion of Identity.* New York, NY: Routledge.

Carli, L.L., and Eagly, A.H. (1999). Gender effects on social influence and emergent leadership. In G.N. Powell (Ed.), *Handbook of Gender and Work* (pp. 203–222). Thousand Oaks, CA: Sage Publications.

Conger, J.A., and Kanungo, R.N. (1987). Toward a behavioral theory of charismatic leadership in organizational settings. *Academy of Management Review, 12*(4), 637–647. doi:10.5465/AMR.1987.4306715.

Conger, J.A., and Kanungo, R.N. (1988). The empowerment process: Integrating theory and practice. *Academy of Management Review, 13*(3), 471–482. doi:10.5465/AMR.1988.4306983.

Connell, R.W. (1987). *Gender and Power: Society, the Person, and Sexual Politics*. Cambridge, UK: Polity Press.

Cooley, C.H. (1992 [1902]). *Human Nature and the Social Order*. New Brunswick, NJ: Transaction Publishers.

Crews, F. (1996). The verdict on Freud. *Psychological Science, 7*(2),63–68.

de la Rey, C. (2005). Gender, women and leadership. *Women and Leadership, 19*(65) 4–11. doi:10.1080/101309 50.2005.9674614.

DeRue, D.S., and Ashford, S.J. (2010). Who will lead and who will follow? A social process of leadership identity construction in organizations. *Academy of Management Review, 35*(4), 627–647.

Desvaux, G., Devillard-Hoellinger, S., and Meaney, M.C. (2008). A business case for women. *McKinsey Quarterly, 4*, 26–33.

Dinh, J.E., Lord, R.G., Gardner, W.L., Meuser, J.D., Liden, R.C., and Hu, J. (2014). Leadership theory and research in the new millennium: Current theoretical trends and changing perspectives. *Leadership Quarterly, 25*(1), 36–62. doi:10.1016/j.leaqua.2013.11.005.

Ely, R.J., Ibarra, H., and Kolb, D.M. (2011). Taking gender into account: Theory and design for women's leadership development programs. *Academy of Management Learning and Education, 10*(3), 473–493. doi:10.5465/ amle.2010.0046.

Engle, E.M., and Lord, R.G. (1997). Implicit theories, self-schemas, and leader-member exchange. *Academy of Management Journal, 40*(4), 988–1010. doi:10.2307/256956.

Epitropaki, O., and Martin, R. (2004). Implicit leadership theories in applied settings: Factor structure, generalizability, and stability over time. *Journal of Applied Psychology, 89*(2), 293–310. doi:10.1037/0021-9010.89.2.293.

Fisher, K., and Robbins, C.R. (2014). Embodied leadership: Moving from leadership competencies to leaderful practices. *Leadership, 11*(3), 281–299. doi:10.1177/1742715014522680.

Fiske, S.T. (1993). Controlling other people: The impact of power on stereotyping. *American Psychologist, 48*(6), 621–628.

Fiske, S.T., and Dépret, E. (1996). Control, interdependence and power: Understanding social cognition in its social context. *European Review of Social Psychology, 7*(1), 31–61. doi:10.1080/14792779443000094.

Foucault, M. (1997). Sex, power and the politics of identity. In P. Rabinow (Ed.), *Ethics: Subjectivity and Truth (Essential Works of Foucault, 1954–1984, Vol. I)*, R. Hurley (Trans.), (pp. 163–173). New York, NY: New Press.

Freud, S. (1997 [1899]). *The Interpretation of Dreams*, A.A. Brill (Trans.). Ware, UK: Wordsworth Editions.

Galbreath, J. (2011). Are there gender-related influences on corporate sustainability? A study of women on boards of directors. *Journal of Management and Organization, 17*(1), 17–38.

Gardiner, R.A. (2011). Critique of the discourse of authentic leadership. *International Journal of Business and Social Science, 2*(15), 99–104.

Gardner, W.L., and Avolio, B.J. (1998). The charismatic relationship: A dramaturgical perspective. *Academy of Management Review, 23*(1), 32–58. doi:10.5465/AMR.1998.192958.

Gemmill, G., and Oakley, J. (1992). Leadership: An alienating social myth?. *Human Relations, 45*(2), 113–129. doi:10.1177/00187269204500201.

Goethals, G.R., and Strauss, J. (2012). The study of self: Historical perspectives and contemporary issues. In J. Strauss and G.R. Goethals (Eds), *The Self: Interdisciplinary Approaches* (pp. 1–17). New York, NY: Springer Science & Business Media.

Goffman, E. (1959). *The Presentation of Self in Everyday Life*. New York, NY: Doubleday.

Grint, K. (2009). Reading Tolstoy's wave. In J. Billsberry (Ed.), *Discovering Leadership* (pp. 15–23). Basingstoke, UK: Palgrave Macmillan.

Hall, S., and du Gay, P. (1996). *Questions of Cultural Identity*. Los Angeles, CA: Sage Publishers.

Haslett, B., Geis, F.L., and Carter, M.R. (1992). *The Organizational Woman: Power and Paradox*. Norwood, NJ: Ablex Publishing Corporation.

Heidegger, M. (1996). *Being and Time: A Translation of Seit und Zeit*, J. Stambaugh (Trans.). SUNY Series in Contemporary Continental Philosophy. Albany, NY: State University of New York Press.

Hogg, M.A. (2001). A social identity theory of leadership. *Personality and Social Psychology Review, 5*(3), 184–200. doi:10.1207/S15327957PSPR0503_1.

Hogg, M.A. (2006). Social identity theory. In P.J. Burke (Ed.), *Contemporary Social Psychological Theories* (pp. 111–136). Stanford, CA: Stanford University Press.

Hogg, M.A., Hains, S.C., and Mason, I. (1998). Identification and leadership in small groups: Salience, frame of reference, and leader stereotypicality effects on leader evaluations. *Journal of Personality and Social Psychology, 75*(5), 1248–1263.

Hogg, M.A., and Hardie, E.A. (1991). Social attraction, personal attraction, and self-categorization: A field study. *Personality and Social Psychology Bulletin, 17*(2), 175–180. doi:10.1177/014616729101700209.

Hogg, M.A., and Mullin, B.A. (1999). Joining groups to reduce uncertainty: Subjective uncertainty reduction and group identification. In D. Abrams and M.A. Hogg (Eds), *Social Identity and Social Cognition* (pp. 249–279). Malden, MA: Blackwell Publishers.

Hogue, M., and Lord, R.G. (2007). A multilevel, complexity theory approach to understanding gender bias in leadership. *Leadership Quarterly, 18*(4), 370–390. doi:10.1016/j.leaqua.2007.04.006.

Ibarra, H. (1999). Provisional selves: Experimenting with image and identity in professional adaptation. *Administrative Science Quarterly*, *44*(4), 764–791. doi:10.2307/2667055.

Ibarra, H., and Barbulescu, R. (2010). Identity as narrative: Prevalence, effectiveness, and consequences of narrative identity work in macro work role transitions. *Academy of Management Review*, *35*(1), 135–154.

Ibarra, H., Carter, N.M., and Silva, C. (2010). Why men still get more promotions than women. *Harvard Business Review*, *88*(9), 80–85.

James, W. (1950 [1890]). *The Principles of Psychology: Volume I*. Dove books on Biology, Psychology, and Medicine. New York: Dover Publications.

Karp, T., and Helgø, T.I.T. (2009). Leadership as identity construction: The act of leading people in organizations: A perspective from the complexity sciences. *Journal of Management Development*, *28*(10), 880–896. doi:10.1108/02621710911000659.

Kempster, S. (2006). Leadership learning through lived experience: A process of apprenticeship. *Journal of Management and Organization*, *12*(1), 4–22. doi:10.1017/S1833367200004132.

Kihlstrom, J.F., Beer, J.S., and Klein, S.B. (2003). Self and identity as memory. In M.R. Leary and J.P. Tangney (Eds), *Handbook of Self and Identity* (pp. 68–90). New York, NY: Guilford.

Knights, D., and Willmott, H. (1999). *Management Lives: Power and Identity in Work Organizations*. London, UK: Sage Publications.

Lemert, C. (2011). A history of identity: the riddle at the heart of the mystery of life. In A. Elliott (Ed.), *Routledge Handbook of Identity Studies* (pp. 3–29). Routledge International Handbooks. New York, NY: Routledge.

Liu, H., Cutcher, L., and Grant, D. (2015). Doing authenticity: The gendered construction of authentic leadership. *Gender, Work and Organization*, *22*(3), 237–255.

Lord, R.G., Brown, D.J., and Freiberg, S.J. (1999). Understanding the dynamics of leadership: The role of follower self-concepts in the leader/follower relationship. *Organizational Behavior and Human Decision Processes*, *78*(3), 167–203. doi:10.1006/obhd.1999.2832.

Lord, R.G., Brown, D.J., Harvey, J.L., and Hall, R. (2001). Contextual constraints on prototype generation and their multilevel consequences for leadership perceptions. *Leadership Quarterly*, *12*(3), 311–338. doi:10.1016/S1048-9843(01)00081-9.

Lord, R.G., De Vader, C.L., and Alliger, G.M. (1986). A meta-analysis of the relations between personality traits and leadership perceptions: An application of validity generalization procedures. *Journal of Applied Psychology*, *71*(3), 402–410. doi:10.1037/0021-9010.71.3.402.

Lord, R.G., Foti, R.J., and De Vader, C.L. (1984). A test of leadership categorization theory: Internal structure, information processing, and leadership perceptions. *Organizational Behavior and Human Performance*, *34*(3), 343–378. doi:10.1016/0030-5073(84)90043-6.

Lord, R.G., and Hall, R.J. (2005). Identity, deep structure and the development of leadership skill. *Leadership Quarterly*, *16*(4), 591–615. doi:10.1016/j.leaqua.2005.06.003.

Mead, G.H. (2015 [1934]). *Mind, Self and Society: The Definitive Edition*. Chicago, IL: University of Chicago Press.

Meindl, J.R. (1995). The romance of leadership as a follower-centric theory: A social constructioninst approach, *Leadership Quarterly*, *6*(3), 329–341. doi:10.1016/1048-9843(95)90012-8.

Morley, L. (2013). The rules of the game: Women and the leaderist turn in higher education. *Gender and Education*, *25*(1), 116–131.

Mumby, D.K. (2004). Discourse, power, and ideology: Unpacking the critical approach. In D. Grant, C. Hardy, C. Oswick, and L. Putnam (Eds), *The SAGE Handbook of Organizational Discourse* (pp. 237–258). London, UK: Sage Publications.

O'Reilly, D., and Reed, M. (2010). "Leaderism": An evolution of managerialism in UK public service reform. *Public Administration*, *88*(4), 960–978. doi:10.1111/j.1467-9299.2010.01864.x.

Powell, G.N. (2011). The gender and leadership wars. *Organizational Dynamics*, *40*(1), 1–9.

Ricoeur, P. (1991). Narrative identity. *Philosophy Today*, *35*(1), 73–81. doi:10.5840/philtoday199135136.

Ricoeur, P. (1992). *Oneself as another*. Chicago, IL: University of Chicago Press.

Risser, J. (1997). *Hermeneutics and the Voice of the Other: Re-reading Gadamer's Philosophical Hermeneutics*. Albany, NY: SUNY Press.

Rogers, C. (1959). A theory of therapy, personality, and interpersonal relationships, as developed in the client-centered framework. In S. Koch (Ed.), *Psychology: A Study of Science, Vol. 3, Study 1: Conceptual and Systematic* (pp. 184–256). New York, NY: McGraw-Hill.

Ross, L., and Nisbett, R.E. (1991). *The Person and the Situation: Perspectives of Social Psychology*. New York, NY: McGraw-Hill.

Scott, K.A., and Brown, D.J. (2006). Female first, leader second? Gender bias in the encoding of leadership behavior. *Organziational Behavior and Human Decision Processes*, *101*(2), 230–242.

Sinclair, A. (2007). *Leadership for the Disillusioned: Moving beyond Myths and Heroes to Leading that Liberates*. Crows Nest, AU: Allen & Unwin.

Tajfel, H.T., and Turner, J.C. (1986). The social identity theory of intergroup behavior. In S. Worchel, and
   G. Austin (Eds), *Psychology of Intergroup Relations* (pp. 7–24). The Nelson Hall Series in Psychology.
   Chicago, IL: Nelson-Hall.
Tourish, D. (2008). Challenging the transformational agenda: Leadership theory in transition?. *Management
   Communication Quarterly 21*(4), 522–528.
Tourish, D., and Pinnington, A. (2002). Transformational leadership, corporate cultism and the spirituality
   paradigm: An unholy trinity in the workplace?. *Human Relations*, *55*(2), 147–172.
Turner, J.C. (1985). Social categorization and the self-concept: A social cognitive theory of group behavior.
   Advances in Group Processes, *2*, 77–122.
Van Knippenberg, D. and Hogg, M.A. (2003). A social identity model of leadership effectiveness in organiza-
   tions, *Research in Organizational Behavior*, *25*, 243–295. doi:10.1016/S0191-3085(03)25006-1.
Wajcman, J. (2013). *Managing like a Man: Women and Men in Corporate Management*. Cambridge, UK:
   Blackwell Publishers.
Weick, K.E., Sutcliffe, K.M., and Obstfeld, D. (2005). Organizing and the process of sensemaking. *Organization
   Science*, 16(4), 409–421. doi:10.1287/orsc.1050.0133.
Westen, D. (1998). The scientific legacy of Sigmund Freud: Toward a psychodynamically informed psychological
   science. *Psychological Bulletin 124*(3), 333–371. doi:10.1037/0033-2909.124.3.333.
Western, S. (2013). *Leadership: A Critical Text*, 2nd edn. London, UK: Sage.
Woetzel, J., Madgavkar, A., Ellingrud, K., Labaye, E., Devillard, S., Kutcher, E., Manyika, J., Dobbs, R., and
   Krishnan, M. (2015). The power of parity: How advancing women's equality can add $12 trillion to global
   growth. McKinsey Global Institute Report, September. Retrieved from http://ma.mckinsey.com/practicecrm/
   MGI_Power_of_parity.pdf.
Yukl, G. (1999). An evaluative essay on current conceptions of effective leadership. *European Journal of Work
   and Organizational Psychology*, *8*(1), 33–48. doi:10.1080/135943299398429.
Yuval-Davis, N. (2006). Intersectionality and feminist politics. *European Journal of Women's Studies*, *13*(3),
   193–209. doi:10.1177/1350506806065752.

13. The role of purpose and calling in women's leadership experiences
Karen A. Longman and Debbie Lamm Bray

The challenges that hinder the advancement of women into senior-level leadership roles have been documented in various chapters of this *Handbook* and by scholars elsewhere. Apart from scattered glimmers of hope, these challenges persist almost universally (Madsen et al., 2015) as the result of a complex array of both external and internal influences (see, for example, the summary compiled by Ely and Rhode, 2010). This chapter briefly reviews some of these key influences, then explores the potential of increasing the number of women entering senior-level leadership by placing greater emphasis on the role of purpose and calling as motivational factors to women's leadership aspirations, rather than relying primarily upon the highly touted "pipeline" approach to reach that goal.

Simply stated, the existing strategy has advocated filling the pipeline by expanding the percentage of women in lower-level positions with the expectation that they will then aspire to (and advance into) senior-level roles. Within the context of higher education, for example, White (2005) argued that greater attention to filling the pipeline would result in "many women flowing out of the 'pipeline' to swell the most senior ranks of the faculty and administrative leadership positions" (p. 22). Yet concerns have been raised due to evidence that the pipeline strategy simply is not working. Writing from the perspective of the corporate world, Ibarra et al. (2013) observed that "companies spend time, money, and good intentions on efforts to build a more robust pipeline of upwardly mobile women, and then not much happens" (p. 62). Similarly, Kellerman and Rhode (2014) described the pipeline theory actually to be a "pipe dream" (p. 24), noting: "Since the theory achieved currency more than 30 years ago, the number of women at the top of their professions, the number of women in high positions of leadership and management, has remained, dauntingly, depressingly low" (p. 24). In part, the leakages – even blockages – in the pipeline may relate to the fact that male-normed assumptions about leadership motivations appear to be largely inconsistent with women's priorities and lived experiences.

Following a brief summary of the external and internal barriers that prevent women from moving into leadership, this chapter presents a discussion of: (1) how having a sense of purpose can motivate women to step into leadership; (2) the literature that relates to purpose and calling; and (3) the interconnectedness of these constructs in relationship to women's leadership aspirations and experiences. Because the pipeline metaphor has proven to be less effective than assumed in terms of expanding the percentage of women in leadership roles, the proposed focused attentiveness to purpose, calling, and leader identity development may prove to be a more effective strategy, or at least a contributor, toward achieving that goal.

EXTERNAL BARRIERS TO WOMEN'S ADVANCEMENT

Foundational to an array of external barriers that impede the advancement of women into leadership is the reality of worldwide systemic discrimination against women. Former President Jimmy Carter, in his 2014 book titled *A Call to Action: Women, Religion, Violence, and Power*, describes the deep-seated belief – often rooted in distortions of the teaching of many sacred texts – that "men and boys are superior to women and girls [and the] claim that females are, in some basic ways, inferior to them" (Carter, 2014, p. 2). This belief is played out in the psyche of both men and women, reflected in overt or subtle assumptions that leadership roles are typecast for men, with women expected to follow; this worldview framework has been described by Gallagher (2004) as a "hierarchically ordered universe" (p. 219).

The implications of this belief system are lived out daily in various ways. For example, the numerical dominance of men in organizational leadership contributes to workplace cultures that are off-putting to women (Helgesen and Johnson, 2010; Kezar, 2014). Early research by Yoder (2001) found male-normed contexts to be oriented toward goal achievement, hierarchy, and use of power; in contrast, female-normed contexts were typically characterized as egalitarian, collaborative, and valuing influence over power. As a result of this disconnect, women often feel "out of sync" with what the workplace expects. Helgesen and Johnson (2010), based on research in the corporate sector, have observed: "[It is] difficult to feel fully engaged when your vision, your fundamental way of seeing things, is not understood, recognized, or valued" (p. 4). Additionally, Helgesen and Johnson documented that the competitive mindset that characterizes male-normed cultures, as well as the expectation of maintaining a 24/7 schedule, are unattractive to many women.

On a similar note, Ely and Rhode (2010) described the challenge of women who hold traditionally male roles feeling that they cannot be true to themselves, often facing trade-offs between being perceived as competent (that is, successful) and being likeable. Other external barriers to women's advancement into leadership include the relative paucity of role models, mentors, and professional networks (Kellerman and Rhode, 2014; Keohane, 2014); the price of carrying greater responsibility for household and elder care (Kellerman and Rhode, 2014); the negative influences of tokenism (Kanter, 1977); and the impact of what has been termed "second-generation gender bias" (Ibarra et al., 2013). Such bias, according to Ibarra et al., produces "subtle and often invisible barriers for women that arise from cultural assumptions and organizational structures, practices, and patterns of interaction that inadvertently benefit men while putting women at a disadvantage" (p. 64). Although second-generation gender bias – also known as "unconscious bias" – may not be evident in overt discriminatory actions, women often feel unsupported in reaching their full potential. A more comprehensive discussion of external barriers can be found in Chapter 17 ("An overview of gender-based leadership barriers"), Chapter 18 ("Organizational processes and systems that affect women in leadership"), and other chapters in Part IV ("Gender-Based Leadership Challenges and Barriers") of this *Handbook*.

Although most of the research related to the under-representation of women in leadership has focused on these external barriers, a growing body of literature has begun to explore an equally powerful set of internal constraining forces that must be considered, as described in Sandberg's (2013) bestseller *Lean In*.

INTERNAL BARRIERS TO WOMEN'S ADVANCEMENT

Assumptions about ambition, competition, and hierarchy are critical to the pipeline theory, which may explain the theory's apparent relative ineffectiveness in advancing women into leadership in contrast to men. According to Turner (2012), the "masculine view of self in the world is of competing for position in a hierarchy" (p. 53), yet women's orientation is typically understood to be geared toward collaboration and a desire to empower others (Kezar, 2014; Yoder, 2001). In fact, for many women the concept of building one's career around power, competition, and ambition is regarded as foreign and uncomfortable. *Harvard Business Review* reported research findings by Fels (2004) that documented women's dislike for the concept of ambition, viewing it as being egotistical and self-aggrandizing. Hewlett (2013) reinforced the current relevance of that view, stating that "female ambition is laced with ambivalence" (p. 55), creating hesitation to chase "every fluttering flag . . . on the horizon" (p. 55). More recently, van Ogtrop (2015) reviewed numerous studies in seeking to understand why the concept of ambition did not resonate with women. According to van Ogtrop, being very ambitious was viewed as "code for so many other things, nearly all of them bad" (p. 53). See Chapter 11 of this *Handbook* for a deeper discussion of ambition in women's early careers.

Other internal barriers that challenge the effectiveness of the pipeline theory include the "imposter syndrome" (Sandberg, 2013, p. 29), which occurs more frequently in women than men. A lack of confidence can hamper the leadership trajectory of women. Kay and Shipman (2014), for example, reported that women tend to avoid making decisions that might displease others, and they are reticent to take risks – a requisite to leading change and leadership in general. Kay and Shipman also observed that men tend to carry themselves with confidence, regardless of their competence level, and accordingly are viewed as having leadership capacity. In contrast, women often do not signal the visible confidence that conveys leadership potential, even when they are fully competent.

Thus, a variety of external and internal barriers hold women back from embracing their leadership potential, even as research is clear that advancing more women into leadership benefits the well-being of individuals and organizations. Research by Woolley et al. (2010) has documented the advantage of a "collective intelligence" (p. 686) that pools many perspectives, and Page (2007) has summarized the ways in which diversity contributes to better functioning within groups and organizations.

Specifically, the skills and perspectives that characterize women's leadership include consultation, participation, team-building, harnessing multiple perspectives, integrity, and empowerment (Kezar, 2014). Research in corporate settings by Helgesen and Johnson (2010) affirmed women's contributions in terms of attending to the social fabric of the organizational culture and creating an environment that provides satisfaction for employees "day-by-day" (p. 57).

And an international study involving surveys of 26,000 participants by Gerzema and D'Antonio (2013) concluded that "many of the qualities of an ideal modern leader are considered feminine" (p. 11). In a helpful synthesis of the literature, Madsen (2015) highlighted five areas in which organizational culture and effectiveness were enhanced when greater numbers of women served on boards and held leadership roles: (1) higher levels of financial performance; (2) a more cohesive organizational climate; (3) increased corporate social responsibility and reputation; (4) leveraging talent; and (5) enhanced organizational innovation and collective intelligence.

Given that the pipeline theory appears to be faulty as a strategy for advancing more women into leadership (Ibarra et al., 2013; Kellerman and Rhode, 2014), it is time to step back and ask deeper questions regarding what motivates women to consider, aspire to, and/or advance into leadership. The sections that follow examine the literature related to the role of purpose and perceptions of calling as potentially significant motivating factors in both women's aspirations for leadership and their experiences while in leadership that can trump both external and internal barriers.

THE MOTIVATING POWER OF PURPOSE

Within the recent leadership literature, questions about the efficacy of the pipeline theory point to different sources of motivation as women consider the possibility of moving into leadership. For example, the allure of the higher status and salaries appears to hold less sway for women, who are more concerned with honoring relational commitments than "winning" in a competitive one-upmanship race to the top (Helgesen and Johnson, 2010; Turner, 2012). In contrast, having a sense of purpose around a worthy cause, and making a difference in the lives of others, do appear to play a role in motivation, work engagement, and leadership aspirations (Keohane, 2014; Kezar, 2014). At a foundational level, some scholars have identified having a sense of purpose as being a prerequisite for motivation in the workplace (Duchon and Plowman, 2005). Milliman et al. (2016) have observed an increasing interest in the topic of purpose in work, given that purpose provides a sense of connection to a cause larger than the self. In short, purpose gives meaning to work, which increases an individual's motivation to work (Rosso et al., 2010). Thus, leaders who are able to articulate an organization's mission in ways that allow team members to determine whether their personal values and goals are congruent with those of the organization are regarded as effective leaders (Ibarra et al., 2013), facilitating higher levels of motivation.

Purpose and Motivation to Work

Fulfilling a sense of purpose through one's work is beneficial to an individual in several ways. Many studies have established that personal well-being is increased when individuals' values are aligned with their professional work (Dik and Duffy, 2009; Hunter et al., 2010; Steger et al., 2010). In addition, Milliman et al. (2016) proposed that individuals who share a sense of purpose with their work teams increase their person–group fit, which contributes to job satisfaction and a sense of meaningfulness in work. A sense of purpose – the greater good to which individuals can make a contribution by using their unique skills, passions, and experiences, and a sense of obligation or compulsion to do so – is an important aspect of finding meaning in work. Having a sense of purpose also appears to be an important contributor to women's motivation to lead.

THE INTERSECTION OF WOMEN'S CALLING AND WOMEN IN LEADERSHIP

Although research suggests that women and men are equally likely to search for and/ or perceive a calling (Duffy and Sedlacek, 2010), gender-specific aspects of calling have emerged in the findings of various studies. Some scholars have focused their research specifically on the ways in which women discern, develop, and/or live out their sense of calling (French, 2006; French and Domene, 2010; Lamm Bray, 2016; Moore, 2008), and a few studies have specifically referenced the role of calling on the motivation and experiences of women leaders (Boatwright et al., 2003; Longman et al., 2011). Several findings from these studies suggest potentially beneficial implications for practice in the leadership development of women. Specifically, women's discernment of calling appears to develop primarily in the context of relationships, is influenced by perspectives on gender roles, interacts with identity development, and is related to purpose. Additionally, women leaders have described how finding a sense of calling has been an invaluable motivational aspect of their work engagement and leadership.

Two significant studies that suggest the potential impact of awareness of calling on women's leadership aspirations and experiences have emerged within the context of higher education. The findings of both studies, which drew participants from faith-based higher education, hint that women are motivated and even eager to step forward if they feel called to lead, whether or not that calling is affirmed in male-normed cultures. Longman et al. (2011) studied women who had been identified as emerging leaders within the context of Christian colleges and universities. Key findings included that having a sense of calling to lead, and in some cases a calling to lead in a particular institution, was one of the core motivators for the study's participants to take on leadership roles. Tunheim and Goldschmidt (2013) interviewed 15 women presidents of post-secondary institutions, five of whom served in church-related settings. Tunheim and Goldschmidt similarly found that a sense of calling was an important motivator to lead for most of the participants in their study, both those in church-related colleges and those in institutions that were not. Although these studies demonstrate a potentially formative connection between women discerning a sense of calling and their leadership aspirations and experiences, additional research is needed to explore this relationship in other organizational settings.

The Importance of Relationships

Another piece of the equation that merits exploration as a potential motivator for women's leadership is that of interpersonal relationships, which play an important role in calling development for women. Using a quantitative research methodology known as structural equation modeling, Phillips (2009) developed a path theory that identified the factors that contributed to the development of calling awareness in undergraduate college students. Among the key findings was the critical role of relationships in the discernment of calling for women, to a much greater extent than for male students. Phillips's findings corroborated those of other researchers that relationships influence women's calling development (French and Domene, 2010; Thompson and Miller-Perrin, 2008) and various other aspects of women's development (Boatwright et al., 2003; Boatwright and Forrest, 2000; Forrest and Mikolaitis, 1986; Gersick et al., 2000; Gibson, 2008; Hirschi and Herrmann,

2013; Killeen et al., 2006; O'Neil and Bilimoria, 2005). Therefore, encouraging participation in supportive networks and formal or informal mentoring could help to facilitate women's professional and leadership development, as related to heightened awareness of personal calling. When women discover a sense of calling and find that their calling can be at least partially fulfilled in their work, job and organizational commitment typically increase, along with general quality of life and the level of satisfaction found in their work.

The Impact of Gender Role Perspectives

The influence of a woman's perceptions of gender role on her leadership aspirations or her interest in various types of work has also been noted in the literature. Boatwright and Forrest (2000) found a negative correlation between commitment to traditional gender role ideology and leadership. Colaner and Warner (2005) studied undergraduate women students enrolled in a theologically conservative Christian college and found that commitment to traditional gender roles was correlated with lower career aspirations. Although not specifically measuring leadership aspiration, Colaner and Warner's findings suggest a relationship between women's leadership journeys and identification with traditional gender roles. Thus, the likelihood of a woman recognizing her own capacity for leadership – let alone pursuing leadership opportunities – may well be inversely correlated to her assent to traditional male and female roles.

Historically, women had far fewer options for fulfilling a calling than are available today (Placher, 2005), almost inevitably influencing the ways in which women have interpreted and envisioned their calling. In a recent qualitative study of females who were ending their college careers, Lamm Bray (2016) found that graduates whose views of gender roles had been challenged and transformed during college became more open and committed to callings that have traditionally been largely male-dominated, such as Christian ministry and leadership. The influence of a change in worldview – in terms of the roles of women – upon an individual's interpretation of her calling is consistent with Helms's womanist identity theory (see Ossana et al., 1992). Helms proposed that when women who held traditional, socially compliant views of gender norms faced an alternative perspective, the new perspective provided the opportunity for those women to adopt a broader self-constructed view of gender roles. Helms's theory and Lamm Bray's findings therefore suggest that when traditional views of women's roles are challenged with other optional views, broader opportunities are opened for women to explore and embrace their passions and calling, utilizing their gifts to their fullest capacity, including possibilities for leadership roles.

A sense of calling is related to several influences in a woman's professional development. In addition, researchers have found that awareness of calling typically develops in tandem with identity (see Chapter 12 of this *Handbook* for an in-depth discussion of women's leadership identity). This relationship between calling and identity development is examined in the subsection that follows.

The Inter-relatedness of Calling Development and Identity Development

Many who have written about calling from a theological and reflective perspective have considered calling to be interwoven with one's sense of identity. Smith (2014) and

Witherington (2011) both viewed awareness of calling as being connected to a person's strengths, passions, and opportunities to meet the needs of other individuals, groups, or societies. This understanding of calling is evident in the frequently cited description of vocation offered by Buechner (1973) as "the place where your deep gladness and the world's deep hunger meet" (p. 95). Obviously, self-awareness in terms of the unique strengths and passions of an individual plays a critical role in the development of that individual's identity and in the discernment of calling.

Whereas Duffy and Sedlacek (2007) described calling and identity as related constructs, Elangovan et al. (2010) went further when they defined calling in terms of identity. These scholars asserted that their review of the calling literature led them to define calling as "the convergence of the ideal, ought, and actual selves" (p. 434). Elangovan et al. noted that the awareness of calling requires individuals to have already developed a sense of identity to some extent, and that maturing awareness of calling over time will contribute to the ongoing progression of identity formation and awareness. Thus, for Elangovan et al. it seems that calling both is reliant upon and contributes to identity development, an observation that seems particularly important given the research emphasis of Ibarra et al. (2013) on the process of developing the self-perception of being a leader.

Researchers have also observed that young adulthood typically includes reflection on meaning in life (Astin et al., 2011), which has been found to be closely related to a sense of calling (Dik and Duffy, 2009; Hunter et al., 2010). Other researchers have observed that identity development and various related developmental constructs contribute to the discernment of calling (Dik and Duffy, 2012; Duffy and Sedlacek, 2007, 2010). However, recent research has provided evidence of a much deeper connection between identity and calling development. In a qualitative study of women undergraduate students, for example, Lamm Bray (2016) observed that participants often used "calling" and "identity" as interchangeable terms, both representing a congruence of self that joined all aspects of life, including work or career, under an overarching purpose or toward contributing to a greater good. For the participants in Lamm Bray's study, the development of calling and identity were so tightly intertwined as to be inseparable; calling and identity relied upon the development of one another for their mutual growth.

The inextricability of calling development from identity development, as found by Lamm Bray (2016), suggests that the individual components of identity deserve attention from scholars who seek to understand women's awareness of calling. This conclusion is consistent with and highlights the importance of Longman et al.'s (2011) findings that developing a leadership identity was crucial to the women leaders who participated in their study. Another study specifically explored the relationship between two particular segments of women leaders' identities and calling (Karalaia and Guille'n, 2014): whether gender identity or leader identity had a more salient influence on women's motivation to lead. Karalaia and Guille'n found that gender identity was significantly more influential on the participants' motivation to lead than was leader identity. This finding suggests that achieving a healthy leader identity without finding a level of comfort in being a woman may not produce the motivation to lead that one may desire.

The relationship between women's aspirations and experiences in leadership and calling is crystallizing as we near the conclusion of this chapter. A sense of calling can motivate women to lead in organizations and roles aligned with that calling. Developing an awareness of calling could therefore be an important aspect of professional growth for women as one means of addressing the under-representation of women in senior-level leadership roles. Calling development and identity development may be inseparable processes, thus making the components of identity development crucial to an individual's progress in recognizing, understanding, and living out a calling. It logically follows that a fully developed sense of calling may therefore contribute to gender identity and leader identity, which synergistically influence the development of calling. For a woman who has matured in her sense of calling, leader identity, and gender identity, leadership opportunities that align with her sense of self and purpose, as well as her values, represent open doors for broader positive influence on individuals and organizations.

The Influence of a Calling to Lead

Scholars have sought to explain why some women pursue and achieve top leadership, whereas the majority do not. At least within the context of faith-based higher education, a common theme discerned in the research involving those who do choose to lead relates to their sense of calling. Women who lead have often been found to believe that they are called to lead, called either via summons by a divine being or by personal awareness of their own gifts and the needs those gifts could meet. Living out of a sense of calling therefore is a powerful motivator to lead.

Beyond the context of faith-based higher education, a construct that is similar to calling is meaning or meaningfulness. In a study of more than 5,000 first-year students at a large public university, Duffy and Sedlacek (2010) found that students who self-reported a perception of a calling were moderately more likely than others to report that they also perceived that their life had meaning. Those who were searching for calling were moderately more likely than those who were not to indicate that they were also searching for meaning. Further, some researchers have found that meaning or fulfillment of meaning is a component of calling. In their study, Hunter et al. (2010) noted that participants described the scope of calling as influencing the meaning of relationships as well as activities such as sports and using other talents. Although meaning and meaningfulness were important concepts in the authors' findings, Hunter et al. did not offer a definition of either. After reviewing the literature on calling, Dik and Duffy (2012) noted that calling research is often housed within the research on meaningful work. Dik and Duffy also identified making work meaningful as one of three main dimensions of calling. Additional research into the interconnectedness of these constructs might provide further insights into how women's leadership aspirations and capacities can more effectively be developed.

CONCLUSION

Having a sense of calling, which is similar to and includes an understanding of one's purpose in life and work, is a powerful motivator for women to lead. Viewing leadership as the opportunity to fulfill one's purpose in broader spheres of influence, or for the benefit of those serving in the workplace, can engender tenacity and motivation for women to navigate or even counter the effects of a challenging male-normed organizational environment. Beyond its connection to purpose, awareness of calling is also inextricably aligned with identity development, both of which contribute to confidence. For women, a sense of calling can be discovered and then nurtured by engaging in networks and developing relationships that facilitate personal and professional growth. Women's callings are influenced by the individual's commitment to gender-role ideologies and through the stages of identity development. Calling to lead and a personal sense of purpose that is congruent with organizational values and work can motivate women to pursue and accept senior-level leadership positions. The inter-relatedness of calling and identity development underscores the importance of calling awareness to the process of forming a leader identity.

What implications for practice might flow from the body of literature examined in this chapter? For too long, assumptions about what motivates leadership aspirations have been male-normed and largely ineffective (Kellerman and Rhode, 2014) in addressing the under-representation of women in the senior-level roles. Given the power of purpose and calling as motivators for women to step into leadership, assisting women to discern their gifts, passions, and sense of calling could be a powerful additional component in the curriculum of leadership development programming. Within and beyond organizations and institutions, strengthening the confidence and resolve of women by facilitating personal awareness of areas of giftedness and calling could be enhanced through providing networking opportunities both within and beyond organizations. Drawing from Boatwright and Forrest's (2000) research findings, even women who were committed to traditional gender roles, and were therefore less likely to be interested in leadership roles, could be influenced through relationship-based mentoring, education, and coaching.

A multifaceted array of cultural, historical, sociological, relational, and even theological issues and perspectives has created barriers for women to aspire to – and enter – leadership roles. As questions have been raised about the effectiveness of the pipeline strategy to advance more women into leadership, new approaches are needed. Attentiveness to the values prioritized by women and the motivators for women to step into leadership, including a more full-orbed understanding and application of the role of purpose and calling, may be one key to changing the status quo.

REFERENCES

Astin, A.W., Astin, H.S., and Lindholm, J.A. (2011). *Cultivating the Spirit: How College can Enhance Students' Lives.* San Francisco, CA: Jossey-Bass.

Boatwright, K.J., Egidio, R.K., and Associates (2003). Psychological predictors of college women's leadership aspirations. *Journal of College Student Development,* 44(5), 653–669.

Boatwright, K.J., and Forrest, L.K. (2000). The influence of gender and needs for connection on workers' ideal preferences for leadership behaviors. *Journal of Leadership Studies,* 7(2), 18–34.

Buechner, F. (1973). *Wishful Thinking: A Theological ABC.* New York, NY: Harper & Row.

Carter, J. (2014). *A Call to Action: Women, Religion, Violence, and Power.* New York, NY: Simon & Schuster.

Chickering, A.W., and Reisser, L. (1993). *Education and Identity,* 2nd ed. San Francisco, CA: Jossey-Bass.

Colaner, C., and Warner, S.C. (2005). The effect of egalitarian and complementarian gender role attitudes on career aspirations in Evangelical female undergraduate college students. *Journal of Psychology and Theology,* 33(3), 224–229.

Constantine, M.G., Miville, M.L., Warren, A.K., Gainor, K.A., and Lewis-Coles, M.E.L. (2006). Religion, spirituality, and career development in African American college students: A qualitative inquiry. *Career Development Quarterly,* 54(3), 227–241.

Dehler, G.E., and Welsh, M.A. (2003). The experience of work: Spirituality and the new workplace. In R.A. Giacalone and C.L. Jurkiewicz (Eds), *Handbook of Workplace Spirituality and Organizational Performance* (pp. 108–122). Armonk, NY: M.E. Sharp.

Dik, B.J., and Duffy, R.D. (2009). Calling and vocation at work: Definitions and prospects for research and practice. *Counseling Psychologist, 37*(3), 424–250.

Dik, B.J., and Duffy, R.D. (2012). *Make your Job a Calling: How the Psychology of Vocation can Change your Life at Work*. West Conshohocken, PA: Templeton Press.

Duchon, D., and Plowman, D. (2005). Nurturing the spirit at work: Impact on work unit performance. *Leadership Quarterly, 16*(5), 807–833.

Duffy, R.D., and Dik, B.J. (2013). Research on calling: What have we learned and where are we going?. *Journal of Vocational Behavior, 83*(3), 428–436.

Duffy, R.D., Dik, B.J., and Steger, M.F. (2011). Calling and work-related outcomes: Career commitment as a mediator. *Journal of Vocational Behavior, 78*(2), 210–218.

Duffy, R.D., Foley, P.F., Raque-Bodgan, T.L., Reid-Marks, L., Dik, B.J., Castano, M.C., and Adams, C.M. (2012). Counseling psychologists who view their careers as a calling: A qualitative study. *Journal of Career Assessment, 20*(3), 293–308. doi: 10.1177/1069072711436145.

Duffy, R.D., and Sedlacek, W.E. (2007). The presence of and search for a calling: Connections to career development. *Journal of Vocational Behavior, 70*(3), 590–601.

Duffy, R.D., and Sedlacek, W.E. (2010). The salience of a career calling among college students: Exploring group differences and links to religiousness, life meaning, and life satisfaction. *Career Development Quarterly, 59*(1), 27–41.

Elangovan, A.R., Pinder, C.C., and McLean, M. (2010). Callings and organizational behavior. *Journal of Vocational Behavior, 76*(3), 428–440.

Ely, R., and Rhode, D. (2010). Women and leadership: Defining the challenges. In N. Nohria and R. Khurana (Eds.), *Handbook of Leadership Theory and Practice* (pp. 377–410). Boston, MA: Harvard Business Publishing.

Fels, A. (2004). Do women lack ambition?. *Harvard Business Review, 82*(4), 50–60.

Forrest, L., and Mikolaitis, N. (1986). The relational component of identity: An expansion of career development theory. *Career Development Quarterly, 35*(2), 76–88.

French, J.R. (2006). Life calling and vocation: An exploratory qualitative analytical examination among university students. Doctoral dissertation, Trinity Western University. Retrieved from http://0-search.proquest.com. patris.apu.edu/pqdtft/ docview/304913705/fulltextPDF/B10F609DE59E4985PQ/1?accountid=8459.

French, J.R., and Domene, J.F. (2010). Sense of "calling": An organizing principle for the lives and values of young women in university. *Canadian Journal of Counselling, 44*(1), 1–14.

Gallagher, S.K. (2004). The marginalization of evangelical feminism. *Sociology of Religion, 65*(3), 215–237.

Gersick, C.J., Dutton, J.E., and Bartunek, J.M. (2000). Learning from academia: The importance of relationships in professional life. *Academy of Management Journal, 43*(6), 1026–1044.

Gerzema, J., and D'Antonio, M. (2013). *The Athena Doctrine: How Women (and the Men Who Think Like Them) Will Rule the Future*. San Francisco, CA: Jossey-Bass.

Gibson, S.K. (2008). The developmental relationships of women leaders in career transitions: Implications for leader development. *Advances in Developing Human Resources, 10*(5), 651–670. doi: 10.1177/1523422308323935.

Hahnenberg, E.P. (2010). *Awakening Vocation: A Theology of Christian Call*. Collegeville, MN: Liturgical Press.

Hall, D.T., and Chandler, D.E. (2005). Psychological success: When the career is a calling. *Journal of Organizational Behavior, 26*(2), 155–176.

Helgesen, S., and Johnson, J. (2010). *The Female Vision: Women's Real Power at Work*. San Francisco, CA: Berrett-Koehler Publishers.

Hewlett, S.A. (2013). *(Forget a Mentor) Find a Sponsor*. Boston, MA: Harvard Business School Publishing.

Hirschi, A., and Herrmann, A. (2013). Calling and career preparation: Investigating developmental patterns and temporal precedence. *Journal of Vocational Behavior, 83*(1), 51–60.

Hunter, I., Dik, B.J., and Banning, J.H. (2010). College students' perceptions of calling in work and life: A qualitative analysis. *Journal of Vocational Behavior, 76*(2), 178–186.

Ibarra, H., Ely, R., and Kolb, D. (2013). Women rising: The unseen barriers. *Harvard Business Review, 91*(9), 60–66.

Kanter, R.M. (1977). Some effects of proportions on group life: Skewed sex ratios and responses from token women. *American Journal of Sociology, 82*(5), 965–990.

Karalaia, N., and Guille'n, L. (2014). Me, a woman and a leader: Positive social identity and identity conflict. *Organizational Behavior and Human Decision Processes, 125*(2), 204–219.

Kay, K., and Shipman, C. (2014). *The Confidence Code: The Science and Art of Self-Assurance – What Women Should Know*. New York, NY: Harper Business.

Kellerman, B., and Rhode, D.L. (2014). Women at the top: The pipeline reconsidered. In K.A. Longman and S.R. Madsen (Eds.), *Women and Leadership in Higher Education* (pp. 24–39). Charlotte, NC: Information Age Publishing.

Keohane, N.O. (2014). Leadership out front and behind the scenes: Young women's ambitions for leadership today. In K.A. Longman and S.R. Madsen (Eds.), *Women and Leadership in Higher Education* (pp. 41–55). Charlotte, NC: Information Age Publishing.

Kezar, A. (2014). Women's contributions to higher education leadership and the road ahead. In K.A. Longman and S.R. Madsen (Eds.), *Women and Leadership in Higher Education* (pp. 117–134). Charlotte, NC: Information Age Publishing.

Killeen, L.A., Lopez-Zafra, E., and Eagly, A.H. (2006). Envisioning oneself as a leader: Comparisons of women and men in Spain and the United States. *Psychology of Women Quarterly*, 30(3), 312–322.

Lamm Bray, D. (2016). Women undergraduates' experiences in developing a sense of calling. Doctoral dissertation, Azusa Pacific University.

Longman, K.A., Dahlvig, J., Wikkerink, R.J., Cunningham, D., and O'Connor, C.M. (2011). Conceptualization of calling: A grounded theory exploration of CCCU women leaders. *Christian Higher Education*, 10(3–4), 254–275.

Madsen, S.R. (2015). Why do we need more women leaders in higher education? HERS Research Brief, No. 1. Retrieved from http://hersnet.org/wp-content/uploads/ 2015/07/HERS-Research-Brief-No.-1-Susan-Madsen-.pdf.

Madsen, S.R., Ngunjiri, F.W., Longman, K.A., and Cherrey, C. (Eds.). (2015). *Women and Leadership around the World*. Charlotte, NC: Information Age Publishing.

Miller-Perrin, C., and Thompson, D. (2010). The development of vocational calling, identity, and faith in college students: A preliminary study of the impact of study abroad. *Frontiers: The Interdisciplinary Journal of Study Abroad*, 19(Fall/Winter), 87–103.

Milliman, J., Gatlin, A., and Bradley-Geist, J.C. (2016). The implications of workplace spirituality for person–environment fit theory. *Psychology of Religion and Spirituality*, March 17. http://dx.doi.org/10.1037/rel0000068.

Moore, M.E.M. (2008). Stories of vocation: Education for vocational discernment. *Religious Education*, 103(2), 218–239. doi: 10.1080/00344080801910024.

O'Neil, D.A., and Bilimoria, D. (2005). Women's career development phases: Idealism, endurance, and reinvention. *Career Development International*, 10(3), 168–189. doi: 10/1108.13620430510598300.

Ossana, S.M., Helms, J.E., and Leonard, M.M. (1992). Do "womanist" identity attitudes influence college women's self esteem and perceptions of environmental bias?. *Journal of Counseling and Development*, 70(3), 402–408.

Page, S.E. (2007). *The Difference: How the Power of Diversity Creates Better Groups, Firms, Schools, and Societies*. Princeton, NJ: Princeton University Press.

Palmer, P. (2000). *Let Your Life Speak: Listening for the Voice of Vocation*. San Francisco, CA: Jossey-Bass.

Parks, S.D. (1986). *The Critical Years: Young Adults and the Search for Meaning, Faith, and Commitment*. San Francisco, CA: Harper San Francisco.

Parks, S.D. (2000). *Big Questions, Worthy Dreams: Mentoring Young Adults in their Search for Meaning, Purpose, and Faith*. San Francisco, CA: Jossey-Bass.

Phillips, S.L. (2009). Predictors of vocational calling in Christian college students: A structural equation model. Doctoral dissertation, Azusa Pacific University. Retrieved from http://0-search.proquest.com.patris.apu.edu/pqdtft/ docview/305159001/fulltextPDF/ 140419A2D0964C764E6/1?accountid=8459.

Placher, W.C. (Ed.). (2005). *Callings: Twenty Centuries of Christian Wisdom on Vocation*. Grand Rapids, MI: Eerdmans.

Rosso, B.D., Dekas, K.H., and Wrzesniewski, A. (2010). On the meaning of work: A theoretical integration and review. *Research in Organizational Behavior*, 30, 91–127.

Royce-Davis, J., and Stewart, M. (2000). Addressing the relationship between career development and spirituality when working with college students. Unpublished manuscript. University of the Pacific. Retrieved from ERIC, document 452,444.

Sandberg, C. (2013). *Lean In: Women, Work, and the Will to Lead*. New York, NY: Alfred A. Knopf.

Sherman, A.L. (2011). *Kingdom Calling: Vocational Stewardship for the Common Good*. Downers Grove, IL: InterVarsity Press.

Smith, G.T. (2011). *Courage and Calling: Embracing Your God-Given Potential*. Downers Grove, IL: InterVarsity Press.

Smith, G.T. (2014). *Called to be Saints: An Invitation to Christian Maturity*. Downers Grove, IL: IVP Academic.

Steger, M.F., Pickering, N.K., Shin, J.Y., and Dik, B.J. (2010). Calling in work: Secular or sacred?. *Journal of Career Assessment*, 18(82), 82–96.

Taylor, J.S. (2012). The relationship between college student success and the student's degree of perceived self-efficacy, career focus, and sense of life calling or purpose. Doctoral dissertation, Union University. Retrieved from http://0-search.proquest.com.patris.apu.edu/pqdtft/docview/1288021665/fulltextPDF/ A055B97B718F49E2PQ/1? accountid=8459.

Thompson, D., and Miller-Perrin, C. (2008). Vocational discernment and action: An exploratory study of male and female university professors. *Review of Religious Research*, 50(1), 97–119.

Tunheim, K.A., and Goldschmidt, A.N. (2013). Exploring the role of calling in the professional journeys of college presidents. *Journal of Leadership, Accountability, and Ethics*, 10(4), 30–40.

Turner, C. (2012). *Difference Works: Improving Retention, Productivity, and Profitability through Inclusion.* Austin, TX: Live Oak Publishing.

Van Ogtrop, K. (2015). Why ambition isn't working for women. *Time*, September 28, *186*(12), 53–56.

Volf, M. (1991). *Work in the Spirit: Toward a Theology of Work.* Eugene, OR: Wipf & Stock Publishers.

White, J. (2005). Pipelines to pathways: New directions for improving the status of women on campus. *Liberal Education*, *91*(1), 22–27.

Witherington, B., III. (2011). *Work: A Kingdom Perspective on Labor.* Grand Rapids, MI: W.B. Eerdmans.

Woolley, A.W., Chabris, C.F., Pentland, A., Hashmi, N., and Malone, T. (2010). Evidence for a collective intelligence factor in the performance of human groups. *Science*, October 29, *330*(6004), 686–688.

Yakushko, O. (2007). Do feminist women feel better about their lives? Examining patterns of feminist identity development and women's subjective well-being. *Sex Roles*, *57*(3), 223–234. doi: 10.1007/s11199-007-9249-6.

Yoder, J.D. (2001). Making leadership work more effectively for women. *Journal of Social Issues*, *57*(4), 815–828.

14. Women, leadership, and power
Katharina Pick

A discussion of gender and leadership is not complete without an exploration of power. After all, it is difficult to articulate any definition of leadership that does not involve the ability to influence others: in other words, using power (French and Raven, 1959; Ragins and Sundstrom, 1989). Researchers have suggested for decades that considering the complex relationship between gender and power may illuminate why women, despite progress in other areas, continue to be under-represented in leadership positions in almost all sectors (Hoobler et al., 2014).

This chapter examines the power-related dynamics that are most relevant to women rising to leadership. Some are observed at the individual behavioral level, where gender appears to place certain constraints on the exercise of power. Others are explored at the organizational level, where structural factors and organizational processes impede women's ability to gain and use power. Finally, at the conceptual level, it is important to consider how evolving conceptions of leadership and gender may enable women to assume leadership roles in greater numbers. Certainly, the mechanisms operating at each level are interconnected and reinforce each other. They are separated here only for the purpose of discussion.

Power has been defined in many ways across different disciplines and across time. Various definitions have presumed power to exist as an individual trait (McClelland, 1975), as a feature of an interpersonal relationship or interaction (Pfeffer, 1981), or as something more structural, related to authority and control over resources and outcomes, as in an organization (Mintzberg, 1983; Pfeffer, 1981). This chapter uses a working definition that assumes power can stem from a variety of sources including position, access to valued resources, personal skill, and interpersonal relationships, but ultimately requires the ability to influence the behaviors or beliefs of others (Ragins and Sundstrom, 1989).

INDIVIDUAL BEHAVIORAL FACTORS

Research reveals several power-related gender differences that pertain to leadership. First, women and men appear to have differential results when exercising power, particularly direct power that is commonly associated with management and leadership (Aguinis and Adams, 1998). Second, women and men may appear to engage in power practices differently, with men somewhat more likely to exhibit agentic behavior associated with having power (Bowles et al., 2007). Third, women express a more conflicted relationship with power, which may relate to observed behavioral differences (Lips, 2000). Stereotypes, gender roles, and structural constraints help to explain why these differences emerge.

Scholars have long hypothesized that women use power differently from men. Social role theory posits that gender role expectations call for women to be communal, kind, and nurturing, while men are expected to be assertive, dominant, and competitive (Deaux and Lewis, 1984; Eagly and Steffen, 1984). The male gender role is congruent with direct, agentic displays of power, while the female gender role is not. This suggests that women would struggle to use this type of power, while men would not. Stereotypes play an important role here, since they both impose expectations and are typically internalized by actors.

Structural theory, in contrast, argues that it is women's low-power status that predominantly prevents them from exhibiting the same power behaviors as men. Because low-power people are expected to act in a way that is congruent with their position, they cannot effectively use high-power behaviors (for example, agentic, direct) (Aguinis and Adams, 1998). Since women are almost universally seen as having lower status and less power, they are constrained in what is acceptable and likely to be effective (Rudman et al., 2012). These two theoretical models provide important context for examining the research on gender differences in using power.

Gender Differences in Outcomes

Consistent with both structural and social role perspectives, research has supported the idea that women are better off not using power in ways that reflect agency or assertiveness. Studies have found that women were rated more negatively than men when initiating negotiation (Amanatullah and Tinsley, 2013), using assertive language in negotiation (Bowles et al., 2007), or engaging in self-promotion (Giacalone and Riordan, 1990; Rudman, 1998). In another study, undergraduate men rated women who acted confident and assertive as less trustworthy and likeable than those who acted tentative (Carli, 1991). A study of chief executive officer (CEO) leaders showed that female CEOs who spoke disproportionately more than other group members were rated as significantly less competent and significantly less suitable for leadership than male CEOs who spoke the same amount (Brescoll, 2011). Another study showed that women who exhibited intellectual assertiveness in group work received more visible negative non-verbal cues from group members and fewer positive cues than men who exhibited the same behavior. These women were also rated lower on ability, skill, and intelligence (Butler and Geis, 1990). Finally, a meta-analysis of 61 leadership studies revealed that women were rated more negatively than men when enacting a directive leadership style (Eagly et al., 1992).

Both gender congruency and the structural model may explain these differential results, as primarily driven by role violations (either gender or power). However, some studies have shown that women and men did not necessarily experience different outcomes when using the same power strategies (Amanatullah and Tinsley, 2013; Johnson, 1994; Ragins, 1989). These studies suggest that individuating information can help to overcome the gender effects (Ragins, 1989). For example, when women had formal legitimate authority in one study (Johnson, 1994) or externally conferred high status (for example, job title) in another (Amanatullah and Tinsley, 2013), perceptions of their use of power was equivalent to men. These findings highlight the importance of setting and contextual factors that make powerful behavior more or less accessible to women.

Gender Differences in Use of Power

If women are more reluctant to enact power directly, it could be costing them, particularly if they aspire to leadership roles. Effective use of power has been linked consistently to managerial success and organizational advancement (Pfeffer, 1981), as well as perceived suitability for leadership (Yukl, 1994). Although results are mixed (Kanter, 1977a; Sagrestano, 1992), some studies have found that women are less likely to engage in direct power than men. Specifically, women were less likely to initiate negotiation (Bowles et al., 2007), less likely to use verbal displays of power (Dovidio et al., 1988), less likely to use direct, power-based influence strategies (Ansari, 1989), and more likely to use buffering, qualifying language (Carli, 1990; Tannen, 1995). Women have also been found to enact their power in a more democratic and non-hierarchical fashion than men (Helgesen, 1995 [1990]) and to be less likely to take actions to acquire power (McClelland, 1975).

These findings of behavioral differences are significant in themselves, since they have direct implications for women's professional outcomes. What is additionally important, however, is to understand what causes the behavioral differences in the first place. The above studies are also informative in this regard, since they reveal some of the underlying drivers of the behaviors. The most prominent are fear of backlash, gender stereotypes, and status differences.

Fear of backlash

One explanation for the observed differences in behavior is that women's fear of backlash (that is, social and economic penalties) leads them to avoid stereotype-defying powerful behaviors (Rudman, 1998). Several recent studies support this idea. Amanatullah and Morris (2010) found that fear of backlash is the main driver of women's failure to engage in aggressive negotiations. Brescoll (2011) found that women who became leaders did not increase their speaking time to the same degree that men did, primarily in order to avoid backlash. Another study showed that women's failure to self-promote was also driven by a fear of backlash (Moss-Racusin and Rudman, 2010). In other words, women have learned, either through experience or through strongly internalized stereotypes, that they must avoid certain powerful behaviors.

Stereotypes

The effect of stereotypes figures strongly into many discussions of women's power behaviors. Social role theory posits that gender stereotypes emerge from the activities, behaviors, and traits called for in the social roles to which men and women are traditionally assigned (Eagly and Steffen, 1984). Women are viewed to be communal and nurturing because their domestic family role calls for this. Men, who are traditionally employed in the public sphere, are viewed as being more competitive, individualistic, and dominant (Deaux and Lewis, 1984; Eagly and Steffen, 1984).

Stereotypes affect women's actual use of power in two ways. First, they do so indirectly (as suggested above) because women are less effective when exhibiting behaviors that are incongruent with their gender role and stereotype (Eagly and Steffen, 1984). Second, they drive behavior more directly, as women unconsciously act in accordance with the stereotypes. Numerous studies have demonstrated that stereotype awareness leads people to perform in ways that confirm the stereotype (Hirnstein et al., 2014). This means that whatever actual differences there may be between the sexes on a particular behavior or skill, the differences are heightened when subjects are made aware of an associated negative or positive stereotype (Spencer et al., 1999). This occurs, for example, when women perform more poorly on a math test because they are afraid of confirming the inferior abilities associated with their gender (Steele and Aronson, 1995). The same effect holds for positive stereotypes (e.g., Walton and Cohen, 2003), and is one reason why stereotypes are so resilient.

This type of effect may be particularly problematic in the context of power. As one study showed, when women perceived others to have power over them (situational power), they were more likely to engage in behaviors confirming the others' expectations of them (Copeland, 1992). Both power imbalance and a high salience of gender stereotypes are likely to be present in settings where women are striving for leadership roles.

Status differences

Some studies, which have found no differences in how men and women use power, showed the importance of status and structural variables (Kipnis et al., 1980; Sagrestano, 1992). Kipnis et al. (1980), for example, found a significant relationship between a subject's choice of influence strategy and both their organizational status and power relative to an influence target; but they found no relationship between influence strategy and sex. These findings are consistent with the structural model (see Ely, 1995; Kanter, 1977a), which suggests that the primary driver of behavior is not any personal characteristic (like gender), but rather the power and status of one's role in a given situation (Aguinis and Adams, 1998; Rudman et al., 2012). People are expected to behave in a way that is congruent with their status. Because women are generally ascribed lower status and hold lower power positions than men, they encounter backlash and are less effective when they act in power-seeking ways (for example, initiating, asserting) (Rudman et al., 2012).

This alternate structural explanation for differences in power behaviors also highlights a key challenge in studying gender and power: the two variables are almost always confounded (Dovidio et al., 1988). Do observed behavioral differences in the use of power reflect a true gender difference, or are they an outcome of relative lower status that happens to coincide with gender? One recent study using field data from the US Senate convincingly disentangled power and gender (Brescoll, 2011). It examined the relationship between volubility and power, and found an interaction effect for gender and power but no main effect for gender. In other words, men and women did not differ in volubility. However, for men, higher power meant more speaking. For women there was no such effect, meaning that women did not increase their speaking time when they had higher power (Brescoll, 2011). More details on speaking time can be found in Chapter 7 of this *Handbook*. Future research on power differences between men and women will add great value to the extent that researchers can tease apart the distinct effects of gender and power.

Gender Differences in Attitudes about Power

A final difference between men and women that pertains to power and leadership is the varied beliefs and attitudes about power. A common conception is that women have ambivalent feelings about power (Pfeffer, 2010). Research indicates that women do express more negative attitudes toward holding power (Lips, 2000; Offermann and Schrier, 1985). Lips (2000) found that although women appear to aspire equally to imagined positions of power, college-aged women already had the perception that being in positions of power would be problematic for them and, specifically, that it would cause relationship challenges with others. Men did not have a similar concern. A more recent

women and power, Johnson (1976) hypothesized that the use of indirect (low) power strategies like helplessness could actually reinforce the user's self-concept of not being strong, damage self-esteem, and thus become self-perpetuating – further supporting both low power status and low self-esteem. Overall, this work suggests that structural realities and correspondent behavioral responses may become self-reinforcing and self-fulfilling.

In conclusion, historical and existing organizational power inequities impact women's ability to acquire both power and positions of leadership. This section has highlighted not only the visible structural challenges, but also the motivational and psychological aspects that may affect women's advancement given current organizational realities (Pfeffer, 2010). Of course, these dynamics are also influenced by the larger milieu – the discourse and evolution of ideas around power, gender, and leadership – which are discussed in the next section.

CONCEPTUAL FACTORS

Power, leadership, and gender are all fluid concepts. As they evolve, so too does the relationship among them. Research shows that both gender and leadership have changed in ways that may influence women's accessibility to power and leadership.

Gender Conceptions

Many have suggested, at least theoretically, that as more women enter the workplace, social roles assigned to men and women change and thus gender stereotypes should also shift (Duehr and Bono, 2006, p. 817). Diekman and Eagly (2000) further suggest that the directionality of change matters and that, as women's roles and stereotypes move toward those of men, beliefs about the ability to change will become a part of the actual gender stereotype.

Whether or not the stereotype changes in general are actually happening is somewhat unclear. Several older studies have indicated a shift in female stereotypes toward greater masculinity (Diekman and Eagly, 2000; Twenge, 1997), while other studies during the same time period suggested no shift (Lueptow et al., 2001). Extending previous research on gendered conceptions of managerial attributes, Duehr and Bono (2006) showed that views about women's suitability for management appeared to be changing. Managers rated women as less passive and submissive and more competent, analytical, assertive, and leader-like than did samples from 15 and 30 years earlier. Additionally, successful male and female managers were rated more similarly than in previous years (Duehr and Bono, 2006).

This study (Duehr and Bono, 2006) also revealed that, while experienced managers' views had shifted, those of male students had not. This difference may highlight one criticism levied at research on stereotypes, which is that most of it has been conducted in lab settings. Landy (2008) argued that stereotype effects may be overstated and would be mitigated in real organizations by individuating information (for example, task performance, job-related behavior, organizational position) that overrides group-level status characteristics. Nadler and Stockdale (2012) cautioned that, while this dynamic may affect descriptive stereotypes, it does not overcome the effect of prescriptive stereotypes.

Researchers have long known that stereotypes do not develop only in one direction (for example, gathering information in order to understand the world more accurately). Rather, stereotypes often reflect desired beliefs and an effort to justify the existing order (Kennedy and Kray, 2015). According to the "belief in a just world concept," stereotypes satisfy the need to believe that the world is fair (Furnham, 2003). This line of thought suggests that negative stereotypes about women's ability to be assertive are appealing, because they justify the fact that women are not allowed to be powerful in the current system (Kennedy and Kray, 2015). As we look toward changes in gender conceptions, this alternative view of why stereotypes emerge must be considered.

Conceptions of Leadership

Finally, both the theory and practice of leadership have evolved significantly over the last 30 years. Traditional leadership models have reflected mainly masculine characteristics and thus have served to exclude women from leadership positions (Eagly and Karau, 2002; Schein, 1973, 1975). However, conceptions of leadership have changed. They no longer emphasize execution of authority, individualism, and power over resources and people. Rather they highlight the mutuality that exists between leaders and followers and the relational behaviors that are necessary in such a reality (Lipman Blumen, 1996; Useem, 2001). This modern conception of leadership makes room for traditionally feminine behaviors and attributes, which initially led to optimism that women would finally begin to reach leadership positions in greater numbers (Eagly and Karau, 2002; Helgesen, 1995 [1990]; Rosener, 1995; Sharpe, 2000). Particularly relevant here, the shift from power over in leadership to less hierarchical uses of power (for example, power with and power through others) could help women to enact power more effectively. One recent study reflects the shift specifically with regard to management, though not leadership per se. It found that successful managers were perceived as more communal and less agentic in 2005 than they were in 1989 (Duehr and Bono, 2006). If new models of leadership enable the use of power in more gender-congruent (Eagly and Karau, 2002; Eagly and Steffen, 1984) and status-congruent (Rudman et al., 2012) ways, might this ease the path to leadership for women?

Research on transformational leadership supports the notion that women may "do leadership" in ways that both reflect a less hierarchical, more empowering style, and are effective. Transformational leadership, with its learning-oriented and empowering characteristics, has been linked to effectiveness on a variety of measures (Eagly and Carli, 2007; Judge and Piccolo, 2004). Research has also shown that women are slightly more likely to use transformational leadership than men (Eagly et al., 2003).

Together these findings suggest that what is termed as the "female advantage" (Helgesen, 1995 [1990]), in using effective leadership behaviors such as collaborating, relating, and empowering, may enable women to reach, and succeed in, leadership roles more easily. The fact that these changes have yet to materialize has been explored mainly in two ways. Some have challenged the stereotype-driven idea that there is any kind of gender advantage in leadership (Vecchio, 2002). Others have focused on identifying continued prejudice and institutionalized discrimination (Eagly and Carli, 2003).

There are some additional reasons for restraint and caution. First, the excitement about a "female advantage" in leadership may lead to a perpetuation of leadership as a gendered activity (Pittinsky et al., 2007). Second, the link to gender of any leadership behavior may be problematic. Some research suggests that women leaders who do this feminine relational work in organizations do not get credit for their contributions or their leadership ability (Fletcher, 1999). Third, even though these new forms of leadership are much touted and desired, they seem not to have replaced the old images of heroic individualism in accounts of leadership success (Beer, 1999; Khurana, 2003). Finally, some scholars point to the slow progress of women in leadership. While there are more women in political leadership, CEO positions, executive roles (Catalyst, 2013), and boards of directors (Catalyst, 2015), the numbers are nowhere near parity. Given that women have been earning more Bachelor's degrees and Master's degrees than men since 1984 (and more PhDs than men since 2006) (Catalyst, 2014), some ask why more women are not making it into leadership (Eagly and Carli, 2007; Fletcher, 2004; Ngunjira and Madsen, 2015).

Pittinsky et al. (2007) call attention to the dangers of associating any leadership behavior with gender, as it is limiting both to women and men and to leadership itself. Instead, they call for a de-gendered view of leadership that focuses on the functions that are required of leadership, functions that can be fulfilled through a variety of different behaviors. Focusing on function would allow for commonality across gendered styles, and it would make leadership as a whole neither masculine nor feminine (Pittinsky et al., 2007).

Fletcher (2004) also suggests that the link between gender and leadership behaviors is problematic. She argues that it may be precisely the link to gender that prevents the new leadership models from bringing about significant change. In her ethnographic study of female design engineers, she found that the relational behaviors they used (for example, supporting, empowering) were essentially invisible in the organization. Although ostensibly desired by the organization, the relational contributions were often entirely neglected in performance reviews, and in many cases were even coded as deficiencies (Fletcher, 1999). This dynamic, she argues, may be precisely why the new "post-heroic" model of leadership may not transform the current system of individualism and hierarchy, but rather be co-opted by it.

First, when leadership is enacted in a way that is relational, mutual, and interdependent, this behavior is linked to powerlessness, which leads to a resistance to explain leadership or present oneself in these terms (Fletcher, 2004). Others note the propensity to explain personal leadership success (Beer, 1999) and organizational performance (Khurana, 2003) almost exclusively in individual rather than relational terms. This encourages the maintenance of static, hierarchical, and masculine notions of power (Fletcher, 2004).

A second dynamic is more directly related to gender. When "post-heroic" leadership was enacted by women, Fletcher (1999) found that it was coded as something to be expected of a woman rather than as a leadership behavior. The conflation of relational behavior and female gender expectations set in motion a disempowering and disappearing dynamic. Because this conflation of relational behavior and gender role does not exist for men, they are likely simply to be viewed as trying a new (relational) leadership behavior. As Fletcher (1999) found, women's leadership behaviors that used a (relational) conception of power with, rather than power over, were essentially "disappeared" from the organization. This means that women do not get credit for the precise leadership behaviors that are supposed to be their "female advantage." This ultimately results in the continued invisibility of female power in organizations (Fletcher, 2004).

In summary, while conceptions of gender and leadership are evolving, what this means for women's advancement toward power and leadership remains unclear. Further qualitative work would be particularly useful in capturing shifting expectations.

CONCLUSION

The research on gender and leadership is vast and complex. Power is one lens through which we can understand differential behaviors and outcomes observed between men and women. This chapter has briefly reviewed basic themes of historical and ongoing research, specifically focusing on the role that power may play in women's leadership outcomes. It has concluded with a discussion of gender, leadership, and power as evolving concepts. As they change over time and in interaction with each other, gender and power will continue to be fruitful ground for research and also yield new ideas for practice.

In practice, a deeper understanding of the interaction between gender and power can inform how leadership is taught, as well as the content of organizational development programs, evaluation materials, mentoring, and advancement discussions. If organizations want their highest-potential employees to rise and contribute, considering how power is gained and used is an essential component. If organizations want to draw on diverse leadership capabilities throughout their ranks, they must consider the effects that organizational culture and structure have on women's access to power. Finally, as the world and organizations shift toward less hierarchically driven styles of leadership, bringing a more gender-informed understanding of power and leadership may be the path to effectiveness.

REFERENCES

Aguinis, H., and Adams, S.K.R. (1998). Social role versus structural models of gender and influence use in organizations: A strong inference approach. *Group and Organization Management, 23*(4), 414–446.

Amanatullah, E.T., and Morris, M.W. (2010). Negotiating gender roles: Gender differences in assertive negotiating are mediated by women's fear of backlash and are attenuated when negotiating on behalf of others. *Journal of Personality and Social Psychology, 98*(2), 256–267.

Amanatullah, E.T., and Tinsley, C.H. (2013). Ask and ye shall receive? How gender and status moderate negotiation success. *Negotiation and Conflict Management Research, 6*(4), 253–272.

Ansari, M.A. (1989). Effects of leader sex, subordinate sex, and subordinate performance on the use of influence strategies. *Sex Roles, 20*(5), 283–293.

Beer, M. (1999). Leading learning and learning to lead. In J. Conger, G. Spreitzer, and E. Lawler (Eds), *The Leader's Change Handbook* (pp. 127–161). San Francisco, CA: Jossey-Bass.

Belkin, L. (2003). The opt-out revolution. *New York Times Magazine*, October 26, pp. 42–47, 58, 85–86.

Bilimoria, D. (2006). The relationship between women corporate directors and women corporate officers. *Journal of Managerial Issues, 18*(1), 47–61.

Bowles, H.R., Babcock, L., and Lai, L. (2007). Social incentives for gender differences in the propensity to initiate negotiations: Sometimes it does hurt to ask. *Organizational Behavior and Human Decision Processes, 103*(1), 84–103.

Brass, D.J. (1985). Men's and women's networks: A study of interaction patterns and influence in an organization. *Academy of Management Journal, 28*(2), 327–343.

Brescoll, V.L. (2011). Who takes the floor and why: Gender, power, and volubility in organizations. *Administrative Science Quarterly, 56*(4), 622–641.

Butler, D., and Geis, F.L. (1990). Nonverbal affect responses to male and female leaders: Implications for leadership evaluations. *Journal of Personality and Social Psychology, 58*(1), 48–59.

Carli, L.L. (1990). Gender, language, and influence. *Journal of Personality and Social Psychology, 59*(5), 941–951.

Carli, L.L. (1991). Gender, status, and influence. In E.J. Lawler, B. Markowsky, C. Ridgeway, and H.A. Walker (Eds), *Advances in Group Processes: Theory and Research*, Vol. 8 (pp. 89–113). Greenwich, CT: JAI Press.

Catalyst. (2004). Women and men in US corporate leadership 2003. Retrieved from http://www.catalyst.org/system/files/Women%20and_Men_in_U.S._Corporate_Leadership_Same_Workplace_Different_Realities.pdf.

Catalyst. (2008). Mentoring: Necessary but insufficient for advancement. Retrieved from http://www.catalyst.org/system/files/Mentoring_Necessary_But_Insufficient_for_Advancement_Final_120610.pdf.

interpretations and observations. More importantly, neuro-methods allow us to ask more complex questions regarding gender phenomena, such as: how genetic is confidence, does a confidence gap really exist between men and women or even between women, and if so, how big is the gap? Even further, neuroscience may help us address other questions such as: how quickly does confidence rise and fall in people, and how malleable is it to being built or rebuilt once lost?

Current advances in neuroscience are equipped to answer such questions. It is now possible for researchers to measure and predict differences in leader confidence between women and men by viewing and measuring areas of the brain associated with courage, fear, pride, or dominance, or other physiological correlates (for example, testosterone is associated with confidence). It is also possible to borrow from improvements in the behavioral genetics field to compare female and male twin pairs with hopes of understanding the degree to which confidence differences between men and women is innate. Quite simply, neuroscience allows for a more ecologically valid approach to the study of gender and leadership in organizations.

The overarching purpose of this chapter is to inform researchers and practitioners interested in the fields of gender, leadership, and psychology on how neuroscience methods can complement and advance the study of gender and leadership. Our goal is not to provide a technical review of neuroscience research methods, as such an approach would be beyond the interest and expertise of the target audience of this chapter. Instead, we provide a fairly general and simplified picture to introduce the audience to the possibilities of neuro-research applied to leadership and gender. We begin by introducing the most commonly used, and increasingly accessible, neuroscience methods available. We pay particular attention to some of the current research in the area of leadership that has already benefited from the use of these methods. Next, we discuss three areas that we believe to be especially ripe to benefit from neuroscience methods: confidence, risk taking, and leadership style. We end by suggesting a way forward and a discussion of pragmatic concerns related to the use of neuro-methods.

NEUROSCIENCE METHODS AND LEADERSHIP

Neuroscience is typically considered an umbrella term that encompasses the study of virtually every aspect of the nervous system. The point of neuroscience research is to assess similarities and differences between people in areas such as brain activity and structure, physiology, and genetics. Such methods are becoming more user-friendly and affordable, making them a key complement to more traditional research methods (Waldman et al., 2016). That being said, it is well beyond the scope of this chapter to discuss all existing neuroscience areas and applications. Therefore, we will give a brief and high-level overview of the areas of neuroscience that we believe have the greatest potential to be relevant for the study of gender and leadership.

Brain Scanning and Neuroimaging

Brain scanning is an assessment of individual differences in neural activity and forms the foundation of neuroscience assessment methods. The two most popular scanning techniques to date in the study of leadership are: (1) functional magnetic resonance imaging or fMRI; and (2) quantitative electroencephalogram or qEEG. fMRI emphasizes changing blood flow in the brain associated with neural activity (Waldman et al., 2011b). The most common metric produced by fMRI is known as blood oxygen level dependence (BOLD), which can easily be integrated into statistical analyses and matched with other types of data, such as those created by surveys. This is important in part because it provides a way to validate survey findings. For example, a follower may rate a leader as having high confidence on a survey, but based on fMRI data, the area of the brain most associated with confidence (that is, orbitofrontal cortex) does not "light up" or correspond to this assessment, indicating a disconnect between the follower's perceptions and the neurological evidence as to the leader's "true" level of confidence (Lak et al., 2014). These inconsistent results may lead us to question the validity of survey data and may provoke questions pertaining to theoretical accuracy. Does a mismatch between survey data and neural data mean that confidence is being faked (for example, imposter syndrome) or being mistaken for something else (for example, self-awareness, self-esteem, risk aversion)? Neuroscience data would be able to help us begin to answer these questions. fMRI is appealing in part because it can produce colorful images, which can be used visually to see and understand the location and source of differences in brain structures and processes. fMRI has recently been used in the leadership field to consider the basis of inspirational leadership (Boyatzis et al., 2012; Molenberghs et al., 2015).

qEEG represents a second neuroimaging technique that has become more widely used in recent years, especially in the area of leadership (e.g., Hannah et al., 2013; Waldman et al., 2011b). It uses electrodes positioned along the scalp to pick up electrical activity generated by the firing of the neurons in the brain. The advantage of qEEG is that it measures brain activity directly (contrary to fMRI which infers brain activity based on blood flow) and is relatively cheap and portable compared to expensive and cumbersome MRI machines. The latter makes it more practical for use in the work environment. The disadvantage of qEEG is that it is much less precise compared to fMRI. As a result, while qEEG can directly measure whether brain activity is or is not occurring, it is not as effective pinpointing where the activity is located. Researchers have used this method to consider differences in transformational leadership (Balthazard et al., 2012) and decision making effectiveness in complex situations (Hannah et al., 2013).

Neuroendocrinology

Neuroendocrinology focuses on the relationship between the endocrine system (that is, the glands that produce hormones) and the nervous system. Research in this area considers how the levels of certain neurotransmitters (for example, oxytocin, cortisol, and testosterone) influence domains such as affiliation, social cognition, emotion, aggression, stress, and anxiety. For instance, influencing oxytocin levels in humans through the use of nasal spray has become very popular recently as a method to increase trust (Kosfeld et al., 2005) and conformity to group norms (Stallen et al., 2012). Similarly, continual increases of cortisol levels have been shown to have detrimental effects on employee well-being and job performance (Lundberg, 2005) as well as risk-taking preferences (Carney et al., 2010).

Behavioral Genetics

Behavioral genetics is the study of how genetic markers influence ability and personality. The trait paradigm of leadership has long emphasized that certain individuals possess certain inherent characteristics that make them leaders. Traits such as dominance, confidence, intelligence, and masculinity are associated with leaders as opposed to followers (Bass, 1990; Lord et al., 1986). Researchers in the behavioral genetics field have helped increase the credibility of this paradigm by addressing this idea more objectively. For example, Li et al. (2012) found that 78 percent of certain aspects of leadership could be attributed to genetic factors, while only 22 percent were attributed to environmental factors. Studies in twins have also found genetic influences in relation to job satisfaction and work stress (Judge et al., 2012). Other studies have demonstrated that approximately 30 percent of leadership role occupancy can be explained by genetic factors (Arvey et al., 2006; Arvey et al., 2007).

AREAS OF GENDER AND LEADERSHIP RIPE FOR NEUROSCIENCE APPLICATIONS

Despite the increasing number of women being considered for leadership roles today, women experience unique challenges when seeking and operating in leadership positions. Some of these challenges have been attributed (fairly or not) to key differences between men and women such as differences in confidence, risk taking tendencies, and leadership style – all of which frequently have created a disadvantage for women from a perception and stereotype standpoint. This leads women not only to struggle to believe in their own abilities and experience, a phenomenon coined the "imposter syndrome" (Clance and O'Toole, 1987), but also to suffer from a deficiency in communicating confidence from a stylistic perspective. For instance, unconfident body language (for example, closed posture and lowered eye contact), qualifying statements (for example, "I think" or "I guess"), and apologizing (for example, "I'm sorry to bother you") can lead to negative perceptions of the woman's leadership ability (Eagly et al., 2003). Moreover, assumptions are sometimes made about women around risk taking, decision making, and emotions, all leading to challenging circumstance for women leaders. In this section, we reveal the neuroscience perspective on common challenges facing women: confidence, risk taking, and leadership style.

Confidence

In general, men are often characterized as more confident than women (Bengtsson et al., 2005), particularly women in leadership positions. Research suggests these women assume that others perceive them to be competent solely because of the position they hold rather than because of their skills and attributes. However, these women also doubt themselves and their own ability, so they feel like "imposters" because they may be misrepresenting themselves to their colleagues (Clance and O'Toole, 1987), leading to a downward spiral in confidence. Women who experience this impostor phenomenon rarely take credit for their successes, avoid self-promotion, and attribute their success to luck or mistakes. The opposite pattern is true for men.

Differences in confidence become even more pronounced when examining specific contexts and/or specific skills (Lundeberg et al., 1994). For example, in the context of leadership, women commonly report lower overall confidence in their leadership ability than men (Kay and Shipman, 2014). This is particularly striking since empirical evidence suggests there is not a significant difference in leadership ability between men and women (Yukl, 2002). More specifically, men in leadership positions are generally described as more confident when it comes to financial decisions (Barber and Odean, 2001; Correll, 2001). This idea is perpetuated by the fact that women who head businesses generally report lower levels of profitability (Robinson and Stubberud, 2011). As such, businesswomen have lower confidence in their financial acumen and decision-making abilities even when their role (for example, chief financial officer) suggests the competence to excel.

These findings spark interesting questions related to perception versus reality when it comes to confidence. Confidence associated with specific abilities or contexts is typically referred to as metamemory or metacognition in the cognitive psychology literature (e.g., Glenberg and Epstein, 1987; Pressley et al., 1990). Such literature suggests that an individual's confidence is a more accurate reflection of their skills after a similar experience than their confidence levels before ever engaging in that type of experience (Glenberg and Epstein, 1987; Lundeberg et al., 1994). For example, if a leader decides to make a large investment in a new technology and that investment was successful, that individual will typically express much more confidence in his or her ability to make similar investment decisions in the future. Research alludes that gender may play a key role here. It seems that men often display confidence in their abilities regardless of past success, whereas women tend to evaluate their confidence based on situational realities.

Therefore, do women actually possess lower confidence than men, or is it possible that men just assert confidence more quickly than women? One can imagine a situation where women and men are both asked to rate their confidence going into a meeting. Men may be more apt to report high confidence regardless of the situation, whereas women may under-report their confidence if they have little previous experience on which to base that confidence. This becomes an issue of whether we are measuring true confidence versus bravado or false or uninformed confidence. Similarly, social scientists have consistently found that men are more apt to display body language associated with confidence (Henley and LaFrance, 1984; LaFrance and Henley, 1994). "Masculine" body language includes taking up space, using directive gestures, and making more direct eye contact. Whether women are less confident or whether they simply display fewer markers of confidence is hard to say with psychological assessment.

On the other hand, given the lack of experience of women in leadership positions compared to men, it is plausible that they do possess inferior confidence levels compared to men. According to the work of Bandura (1997), confidence or self-efficacy in a particular domain (for example, leadership) is built from previous experience, feedback, and role modeling. Undoubtedly women, as a whole, have fewer past experiences upon which to build, fewer role models to watch, and little feedback to be shared. Similarly, if women do indeed possess fewer markers of confidence in their communication style, it is possible that this behavior signals how they are feeling on the inside. These are but a few of the questions that psychology has not been able to answer adequately in the area of gender differences in confidence.

play a key role in facilitating social relationships (Antonakis et al., 2009; Cherniss, 2010), and the ability to understand the emotions of others confers advantages to leaders (Côté et al., 2010; Walter et al., 2011). To a large extent, leaders achieve connections with their followers by possessing two interrelated capabilities, namely, empathy and emotional expression/regulation (Mayer and Salovey, 1997). These two capabilities work hand in hand to navigate social interactions, including those related to leadership. Other areas related to emotion and leadership that are worthy of discussion are ethical/moral behavior and stress.

Empathy

Much of the research on leadership style suggests that women are indeed more intuitive, sensitive, and empathetic (Park, 1996). Neurological evidence confirms this may be the case. Women are more perceptive to their environments and are more likely to be affected by context (Croson and Gneezy, 2009; Miller and Ubeda, 2012). This means that women are likely superior at navigating social situations and adapting their behavior accordingly, whereas men may "stay the course" regardless of contextual cues. This difference can be explained by inherent differences in the brain. While men generally favor the right brain (logic, detail, and linear) versus the left brain (holistic, intuitive, and abstract), women do not necessarily favor one side over the other. Instead, women's brains have a higher level of interconnectedness between the two hemispheres. Cunningham and Roberts (2006) argue that this increased interconnectivity can explain why women are better than men at recognizing facial expressions (Hoffmann et al., 2010) and picking up on an emotional climate within the work environment.

Additional neurological evidence is supportive of empathy differences between men and women. Specifically, there is evidence to suggest that the brain's mirror neuron system plays a significant role in the domain of social cognition, including empathy (Enticott et al., 2008). Mirror neurons fire or activate when people observe an action or emotion of another (Rizzolatti, 2005). In simple terms, mirror neurons work like seeing one's reflection in a mirror. When one individual experiences an emotion (for example, pain), those who witness that expression of pain (for example, facial expression or non-verbal communication) are able to mimic the same expressions and, in many cases, actually feel the pain of that individual. This idea suggests that a well-tuned mirror neuron system allows one to put oneself "in the shoes" of another. The ability to take the perspective of others is at the root of empathy and is important to key models of leadership, such as transformational leadership, which is predicated on the leader's ability to read and understand the experiences and needs of followers. To date, research has shown that women have increased mirror neurons activity when evaluating the emotions of others (Schulte-Rüther et al., 2008). This evidence suggests that women may indeed be more empathetic and, therefore, more relational leaders than men.

Emotional experience and expression

Research suggests that women respond to situations with more emotional intensity than men (Harshman and Paivio, 1987), especially when the situation is negative (Stevens and Hamann, 2012). An interesting question is whether women really feel with greater emotional intensity or whether the same emotion is just interpreted differently based on gender stereotypes. For instance, women are more apt to be labeled "emotional" when they feel strongly about something, while men may be coined "passionate" or some other term that carries a more positive connotation. Thus far, neuroscience suggests that women do feel emotions much more intensely and vividly than men (Hamann, 2003). Emotional intensity is directly related to the amygdala, which controls emotional information processing (Cahill, 2006). Research has found that the amygdala is larger for men than women (Goldstein et al., 2001), with the suggestion being that structural size differences may explain differences in emotional intensity. This idea suggests that women may react more emotionally than rationally in tense situations (for example, receiving negative feedback or peer conflict situations).

On the other hand, regardless of how women or men may actually feel, they can choose whether to express or suppress felt emotions. This concept is referred to as emotional regulation (Gross, 1999). The emotional intelligence literature suggests that effective leaders are often quite astute at managing and balancing their emotions (Mayer and Salovey, 1997). For instance, leaders may need to suppress fear or disappointment to protect followers in trying times, but they may be well served by overtly displaying enthusiasm or optimism about their vision for the future. According to brain imaging research, there are key differences between men and women in the prefrontal regions that are associated with reappraisal (that is, thinking before you emote) as well as differences in the amygdala, which are associated with emotional responding (that is, deciding whether to express or suppress) (McRae et al., 2008).

Ethical/moral behavior

Yet another stylistic difference that has been considered in the leadership literature is ethical leadership (Treviño et al., 2006). Ethical leadership remains a critical issue in today's society as few would argue against the importance of selecting and developing leaders who behave in an ethical manner for the good of followers, companies, and societies. Thus far, the research is mixed as to whether there are inherent gender differences in ethical or moral behavior. While some research suggests that women are more ethical than men, other work suggests that women are just more concerned with socially desirable and appropriate behavior (Dalton and Ortegren, 2011). Although there is no definitive neurological evidence that we know of to suggest obvious differences between men and women when it comes to ethical or moral behavior, research focused on the neurological link between moral judgment and emotion may prove useful. Research by Green and colleagues (Green and Haidt, 2002; Green et al., 2001) emphasizes the role of emotion versus rational thought in ethical decision making and moral reasoning. Using brain imaging technologies, they found that the emotional centers of the brain were more active when participants were asked to make certain moral decisions. To the degree that women may be more prone to certain emotional processes, such as emotional empathy (that is, feeling what another person is feeling), it would be interesting to consider neurological gender difference in this area. In contrast, other neuroscience work (e.g., Reynolds et al., 2010) highlights the role of cognitive processes when it comes to ethical judgments and decision-making, suggesting that men may have the advantage. Men are likely to have strengths in cognitive empathy (that is, imagining what one might feel but not actually feeling it). Whether ethical and moral behavior stems from emotion, cognition, or both is an important question with implications for individual differences in ethical and moral behavior.

CONCLUSIONS AND A WAY FORWARD

The goal of this chapter was to offer a basic understanding of the main concepts and methodologies associated with neuroscience research in order to offer a framework to compare gender differences in leadership. We recognize that it is not yet possible to use neuroscience methods to examine with total accuracy whether an individual will become an effective leader, a poor leader, or to tell us whether men or women are superior or different at leading. However, considering the rapid technological advancements in the field of neuroscience over the last couple of decades, it is not improbable that we may do so in the future.

We believe the future is particularly bright for neuroscience to contribute to our collective understanding of how we develop leaders in organizations. Leadership development represents a significant organizational investment that is focused on enhancing the effectiveness of leaders in areas such as communication, style and presence, decision making, relationships building, and team building. These are all areas in which gender differences have been discussed or suggested. As was alluded to above, women leaders are often perceived to be less powerful communicators with softer or more passive styles and body language, but they are better relationship and team builders when compared to their male counterparts. They may also be seen as less risk averse, more emotionally sensitive, and more prone to negative effects of stress. Although it is not definitive as to how much of this is perceptual or stereotypical versus reality, neuroscience is equipped to help psychology explore such ideas.

For example, neuroscience scholars have suggested that even the adult brain is somewhat malleable or "plastic" (e.g., Becker and Cropanzano, 2010). This means that the brain can change, based on the environment. This is good news for leaders in charge of training and development in organizations. The assumption of most training and development initiatives is that one can change behavior but cannot change people. To some degree this is certainly true. However, recent psychological evidence suggests that even personality may not be as stable as once thought (Judge et al., 2014). Neurological evidence corroborates this idea by suggesting that small interventions can drive big changes. For example, recent work found that envisioning success can engage the reward centers of the brain to help cultivate self-confidence (Finnerty, 2015). Similarly, a recent study demonstrated that brain activity could be changed based on short courses on kindness meditation (Klimecki et al., 2012).

Despite the interest in neuroscience methods to diagnose differences between employees or to develop leaders, we urge researchers and practitioners to proceed with caution and pragmatism. Certainly we are not suggesting that organizations should start scanning the brains of employees as a matter of course, nor should they monitor employee heart rates, distribute saliva tests, or pursue genetic testing. Such efforts would likely not be tolerated and would represent immense challenges for human resource and legal professionals due to concerns for privacy and confidentiality. Moreover, calls for neurological explorations of gender differences could prove particularly problematic given that such actions could serve to further highlight the divide between men and women in organizations.

When it comes to leadership, researchers and practitioners likely concur that we should be focused on distinguishing effective leaders from ineffective leaders regardless of gender. At the same time, neuroscience methods used willingly in certain samples (for example, the military) can be used to inform our thinking in organizations. For instance, soldiers have been asked to wear certain neurological devices during combat situations in hopes of understanding how leaders behave under stressful situations and how they make decisions under conditions of complexity. Moreover, recent research examined senior business leaders to determine whether there was a neurological basis for inspirational or visionary leadership. Using qEEG technology, researchers examined the brains of leaders while they articulated their company's vision for the future, and results indicated key differences in neurological activity between leaders labeled inspirational or visionary versus those that were not (Waldman et al., 2011a).

Overall, we believe the future is ripe for neuroscience as it applies to gender and leadership. In particular, neuroscience can shed additional light on the role of gender in understanding a leader's confidence level, risk taking propensities, and leadership style. We encourage researchers and practitioners to make additional advancements to theory and practice, and hope that this chapter inspires others to join the conversation.

REFERENCES

Antonakis, J., Ashkanasy, N.M., and Dasborough, M.T. (2009). Does leadership need emotional intelligence? *Leadership Quarterly*, 20(2), 247–261.

Arvey, R.D., Rotundo, M., Johnson, W., Zhang, Z., and McGue, M. (2006). The determinants of leadership role occupancy: Genetic and personality factors. *Leadership Quarterly*, 17(1), 1–20.

Arvey, R.D., Zhang, Z., Avolio, B.J., and Krueger, R.F. (2007). Developmental and genetic determinants of leadership role occupancy among women. *Journal of Applied Psychology*, 92(3), 693–706.

Balthazard, P.A., Waldman, D.A., Thatcher, R.W., and Hannah, S.T. (2012). Differentiating transformational and non-transformational leaders on the basis of neurological imaging. *Leadership Quarterly*, 23(2), 244–258.

Bandura, A. (1997). *Self-efficacy: The exercise of self-control*. New York, NY: Freeman.

Barber, B.M., and Odean, T. (2001). Boys will be boys: Gender, overconfidence, and common stock investment. *Quarterly Journal of Economics*, 116(1), 261–292.

Bass, B.M. (1990). *Bass and Stogdill's Handbook of Leadership*. New York, NY: Free Press.

Bass, B.M., and Avolio, B.J. (1994). Shatter the glass ceiling: Women may make better managers. *Human Resource Management*, 33(4), 549–560.

Becker, W.J., and Cropanzano, R. (2010). Organizational neuroscience: The promise and prospects of an emerging discipline. *Journal of Organizational Behavior*, 31(7), 1055–1059.

Bengtsson, C., Persson, M., and Willenhag, P. (2005). Gender and overconfidence. *Economics Letters*, 86(2), 199–203.

Bennis, W. (1984). The four compentencies of leadership. *Training and Development Journal*, 38(8), 14–19.

Bleidorn, W., Arslan, R.C., Denissen, J.J.A., Rentfrow, P.J., Gebauer, J.E., Potter, J., and Gosling, S.D. (2016). Age and gender differences in self-esteem – A cross-cultural window. *Journal of Personality Processes and Individual Differences*, 11(3), 396–410.

Boyatzis, R.E., Passarelli, A.M., Koenig, K., Lowe, M., Mathew, B., Stoller, J.K., and Phillips, M. (2012). Examination of the neural substrates activated in memories of experiences with resonant and dissonant leaders. *Leadership Quarterly*, 23(2), 259–272.

Byrnes, J.P., Miller, D.C., and Schafer, W.D. (1999). Gender differences in risk taking: A meta-analysis. *Psychological Bulletin*, 125(3), 367–383.

Cahill, L. (2006). Why sex matters for neuroscience. *Nature Reviews Neuroscience*, 7(6), 477–484.

Carney, D.R., Cuddy, A.J., and Yap, A.J. (2010). Power posing brief nonverbal displays affect neuroendocrine levels and risk tolerance. *Psychological Science*, 21(10), 1363–1368.

Charness, G., and Gneezy, U. (2012). Strong evidence for gender differences in risk taking. *Journal of Economic Behavior and Organization*, 83(1), 50–58.

Cherniss, C. (2010). Emotional intelligence: Toward clarification of a concept. *Industrial and Organizational Psychology*, 3(2), 110–126.

Clance, P.R., and O'Toole, M.A. (1987). The imposter phenomenon: An internal barrier to empowerment and achievement. *Women and Therapy*, 6(3), 51–64.

SUCCESS

The concept of a "career" can be defined as an "unfolding sequence of a person's work experiences over time," with a successful career focused on the "accomplishment of desirable work-related outcomes" (Arthur et al., 2005, pp. 178–179). Career success is traditionally measured against objective goals such as organizational promotion, financial reward, and status (Arthur et al., 2005; Kottke and Agars, 2015; Sturges, 1999). This assumes a linear career approach, where a person aspires to organizational advancement characterized by upwards mobility, greater responsibility, and increased pay, all of which are more consistent with the way the careers of men tend to develop (Vinkenburg and Weber, 2012). Organizations are generally structured around this traditional linear career path, with continuity of employment, demonstrations of organizational commitment through, for example, long hours of work, and a desire for hierarchical advancement rewarded (Mainiero and Sullivan, 2006; Sullivan et al., 2009). This is a more masculine approach to careers, with research demonstrating that men focus on objective factors such as position, status, and pay in their understanding of career success (Dyke and Murphy, 2006; Sturges, 1999).

Women's careers develop differently to those of men. They tend to be non-linear, more opportunistic, and more likely to be interrupted than the careers of men (Doherty and Manfredi, 2010; Lalande et al., 2000; Mainiero and Sullivan, 2005; Sullivan and Mainiero, 2008). Advancement to senior management positions is characterized by systematic upward progression and uninterrupted employment, which are much more difficult for women, given the way their careers tend to unfold (O'Neil et al., 2008). It also makes objective measures of success less relevant to many women.

While many organizations remain structured around conventional and objective notions of career and career success, there is an increasing focus on more subjective measures of success, which can include all aspects of life, rather than being bounded only by paid work (Heslin, 2005). These subjective success measures may include, for example, work–life enrichment, fulfilment, being challenged, and having an impact on the community (Ituma et al., 2011). Sturges (1999) explored the ways individual men and women described career success and was one of the first scholars to delve into more subjective elements. Using four different categories to identify how managers talked about their career success (climbers, experts, influencers, and self-realizers), she determined that women "were more likely than men to describe what success meant to them with reference to internal criteria, especially accomplishment and achievement, and intangible criteria, in particular personal recognition" (p. 247). Sturges (1999) also found that women were more likely to see career success as only one part of living a successful, balanced life. Interestingly, she suggested that the ways women conceptualize career success may be a response to the traditional, male-dominated nature of many organizations, concluding that:

> if women perceive that the traditional model of organizational success, based on hierarchical position and level of pay is not readily available to them, then they might choose to refocus their ideas of what success is on other less tangible and more internal criteria, which they believe to be more easily attainable. (p. 250)

Subsequent research has confirmed that, while external factors such as financial reward and promotion have relevance to women, career success is primarily determined by subjective factors, including achieving a balance between their work and personal lives, personal happiness and contentment, and having quality work and personal relationships (Dyke and Murphy, 2006; Lirio et al., 2007; Mainiero and Sullivan, 2005; Sullivan and Mainiero, 2008). Women are focusing on the concept of life success, of which a successful career comprises only one part.

In 2014, the University of Cambridge explored the meaning of success with 126 women from across the university, representing a diverse range of perspectives, ages, backgrounds, levels of seniority, and views on working lives, in a quest to become a more inclusive organization, committed to achieving gender equity (Bostock, 2014). This research was premised in the knowledge that success means different things to different people, but that this has not been recognized by organizations and reflected within their policies and structures. The book begins with a participant quote, "Be really hungry for success – but be brave enough to know that success can be measured in many different ways" (Bostock, 2014, p. 8), and it concludes by encouraging organizations to focus on ways of defining, measuring, and rewarding success more effectively, for the benefit of all employees, irrespective of factors such as gender or race (Bostock, 2014).

Women's understanding of career success is situated within their broader life context. Many women hold multiple identities, including those, for example, associated with ethnicity, race, class, religious beliefs, sexual orientation, and marital status. It is important to explore how these intersecting identities influence women's perceptions of career success. Research by O'Neill et al. (2013) on the impact of women's ethnic identities on career goals provides a very useful overview of the link between success and careers for women and the intersection of race and ethnicity. Using social cognitive career theory enabled them to take account of personal and contextual factors such as gender and ethnicity, social support, and perceived barriers on people's learning experiences (Ojeda and Flores, 2008). The researchers found that women's career goals are reflected differently across ethnic backgrounds. Using exploratory factor analyses, they categorized women's career goals as contemporary, balance, and conventional goals (see Table 16.1), and then they analyzed the order of importance of those three categories for white women and women of color generally, and then more specifically for black, Latina, and Asian women.

Table 16.1 Women's career goals

Goal types	Women's career goals
Contemporary goals	Intellectual challenge Passionate about work Positive impact on people and community Role modeling Self-actualization
Balance goals	Have children Location is important Time for personal relationships and outside interests
Conventional goals	Leadership position Measuring success by status Money

O'Neill et al. (2013) found that white women and women of color favored contemporary goals. However, balance was of a greater importance to women of color than white women. Within the broad grouping of women of color, there were also differences in the prioritization of career goals for black, Latina, or Asian women, highlighting the importance of examining the intersection between gender and ethnicity when seeking to understand the meaning women attribute to career success. Similarly, Lirio et al. (2007) examined the meaning ascribed to career and life success by women in Argentina, Canada, and Mexico. Women of all three cultures focused on subjective measures of success. They expressed little desire to climb the career ladder and emphasized specific elements, such as the importance of significant personal relationships and contributing to others. Career success was very much contextualized within the broader concept of living a successful life. However, there were notable cultural differences in areas such as the emphasis placed on balance, the importance of flexibility, a desire to influence change, and viewing career success as a shared or collective experience. Based on research within the Arab Middle East, Afiouni and Karam (2014) suggest that local realities for women in academia lead to a misalignment of responsibilities and expectations, based on what they term "mandated structures" of academia on the one hand, and societal gender expectations on the other. This tension is then "traversed" through agentic processes to create "modified structures" that are meaningful to the women (Afiouni and Karam, 2014, p. 550). Their research reinforces the fact that for women, irrespective of context, there is often a tension – particularly for ethnic minority women in Western cultures (Kamenou and Fearfull, 2006) but also, for example, for Muslim women in Pakistan (Syed and Ali, 2013) – among the societal expectations of being a good mother, and fulfilling other familial and community obligations, and having a career and being a strong and confident professional. It is essential, therefore, that researchers and practitioners alike look beyond gender to consider the socio-cultural context, the intersecting identities of women, and the ways those identities shape the meaning attributed to career success.

The ways women understand and conceptualize career success affect their career decisions. O'Neill et al. (2013) concluded that one of the reasons many women do not necessarily apply for CEO positions, but instead leave traditional organizations, and set up their own businesses, is due to a misalignment in terms of measuring success. Many women seek contemporary career goals, focused around subjective criteria such as a desire for balance; whereas most organizations focus on conventional goals, which focus on objective criteria such as promotion, status, and remuneration. O'Neill et al. suggest that, while some organizations are trying to redress this misalignment by providing, for example, more flexible work options to address the balance goal, women who take advantage of these flexible work arrangements are often perceived as less committed to the organization. Research suggests they are more likely to be assigned routine tasks and less likely to be considered for pay rises and promotions (Cahusac and Kanji, 2014; Eikhof, 2012; O'Neill et al., 2013; Sprung et al., 2014). O'Neill et al. (2013) suggest an alternative way for women to progress within organizations, while staying true to their career goals. Drawing on Fletcher's (1999) work on gender in the workplace, they suggest that women employ her four strategies – naming, norming, negotiating, and networking. "Naming" involves being clear about one's career goals and being able to articulate how they add value to the organization. "Norming" focuses on identifying and highlighting the need for a variety of reward practices that acknowledge the different interests and motivations of employees. "Negotiating" involves incremental change that challenges the inherent power structures of organizations and acknowledges the breadth of career goals that employees have. And "networking" ensures women have the support they need to remain true to their career goals.

The strategies suggested by O'Neill et al. (2013) are focused on agency. They require women to have the agency to make these changes, and imply that the responsibility rests with the women rather than with the structures that perpetuate bias toward conventional career paths and measures of success. While agency is undoubtedly part of the solution, structural change is also required to address this tension between the traditional under-standing of success, which rewards long hours of work and perceived organizational commitment, and the more contemporary career goals of women based on subjective factors and adopting a more whole-of-life approach. This must be combined with a greater understanding of the broader sociocultural, organizational, and personal contexts within which the career goals of women sit. Therefore, a combination of agency and structural change is required to understand and accommodate different conceptualizations of career success, and as one way to encourage greater diversity at the senior leadership and governance levels.

CHOICE

The concepts of meritocracy and choice are prevalent in organizational discourse, particularly as it relates to the careers of women (Broadbridge and Simpson, 2011). These concepts suggest that women have the same access to jobs and organizational advancement as men (Broadbridge and Simpson, 2011). The discourse of choice sug-gests that women are choosing to leave organizations rather than pursue leadership roles, primarily because they are choosing to prioritize relationships and family over their careers (Lewis and Simpson, 2015). In researching the choice discourse, Anderson et al. (2010) examined the experiences of 31 women partners in an international management consultancy firm who had left demanding roles in the organization in order to achieve greater balance and control over their lives. The women saw their decision to leave as their personal choice, rather than as a result of demanding and inflexible organizational roles and structures, which prevented them from achieving a balance between their work and personal domains. By presenting their decision to leave as one of personal choice, the organization avoided any responsibility for the significant demands placed on senior staff, which made it untenable for those women to continue working within that organ-ization (Lewis and Simpson, 2010). Similarly, research from Australia found that women frequently referred to "personal choice to justify their lower position in the organization as well as the slower career progress observed among female colleagues" (Simpson et al., 2010, p. 204). Organizations are therefore often exonerated from responsibility by failing to acknowledge the gendered environment within which they operate. Responsibility by default, therefore, falls to individual women.

The discourse of choice masks the organizational reality facing many women. Positional leadership is characterized by the notion of the "ideal worker," a gendered concept favor-ing men, and characterized by long hours of work, an ability to travel, and sacrifice of personal and family time (Cabrera, 2009; Rapoport, 2002; Sinclair, 2005; Sullivan and

access to networks and sponsors, the double bind of conventional expectations of what it means to be a woman, and those qualities thought necessary for leadership), as well as a lack of understanding around intersectionality. The assumption is that women are a homogeneous group, based on white, heterosexual, and middle-class norms. This further marginalizes, for example, women of color; women who identify as lesbian, gay, bisexual, trans, and intersex (LGBTI); and women from poor socio-economic backgrounds. The arrows suggest that we need to work to reduce these three areas in order to achieve gender equity and redress the gap between structure and agency.

The notion of choice is located within agency at the individual level. However, the notion of choice is not always real, as it is situated within a discourse that hides structural gender bias and is very much contextually bound. Leadership is represented at both the agency and the structural level, because it is understood and valued differently at each level. At the individual level it is represented as exercising leadership, which women do every day in a myriad of different contexts, although often invisible and not counted. Positional leadership is at the structural level where it is highly visible and can be counted. The curved arrow indicates that women can and do become part of the structure; this is where they can influence the change (in values and behaviors) to redress the gap in the middle represented by the arrows. However, there is evidence that women in leadership positions do not necessarily advocate to change existing structures (Coleman, 2011; Leberman and Palmer, 2009; Shaw and Leberman, 2015). This means that development programs aimed at agency need to ensure that women are made aware of both the wider structural and societal issues that impact gender equity, and the responsibilities associated with being a woman in leadership positions, in the quest for gender equity.

A WAY FORWARD

If we are going to make meaningful progress toward gender equity in the next 20 years, we need to work for change at both the individual and organizational level. Greater awareness is required at both levels, with a concomitant exploration and in-depth understanding of the discourse of choice, which, as highlighted above, is a contested space.

In recognizing women's differing career paths and interpretations of success, promoting alternate paths to senior leadership positions needs to be facilitated and valued. This will enable organizations to harness the expertise that women bring to the senior leadership table, drawing on their often diverse experiences developed over many years founded on interactions within the home, community, educational sector, and business. Given that both unpaid and paid work are equally part of a career and important to how many women understand success, organizations need to interpret time out of the paid workforce as part of a woman's career in the broadest sense, rather than seeing it as limiting.

Changing structures and disrupting traditional work practices benefits everyone, not only women. Increasingly, men are seeking alternative career paths, and overarching discussions about the sustainability of work and healthy work are becoming more prevalent. Across the world there are an increasing number of groups advocating for men to be part of the solution (see, e.g., Champions for Change, n.d.; HeforShe, n.d.; Male Champions of Change n.d.; NBA Lean in Together, n.d.). However, most of these initiatives are focused on having more women in senior positions, either as CEOs or on company boards.

For some women this is not a measure of success, and we therefore need to identify ways in which alternate markers of success are valued.

Women exercise leadership daily in a myriad of ways, making it difficult to "count." We argue that there is a need to celebrate this "hidden" leadership by redefining what leadership means to women. Most of the existing research has focused on women who are in positions of leadership that can be counted. This sends the message to women that to be successful one has to be in one of those "countable" roles, potentially devaluing the many women who exercise leadership in non-positional ways. Future research is therefore required on women's conceptualization of leadership, to provide a greater understanding of what leadership means to women more broadly, and how this is linked with notions of success and choice.

REFERENCES

Adler, N.J. (2015). Women leaders: Shaping history in the 21st century. In F. Ngunjiri and S. Madsen (Eds), *Women as Global Leaders* (pp. 21–50). Charlotte, NC: Information Age Publishing.

Afiouni, F., and Karam, C.M. (2014). Structure, agency, and notions of career success: A process-oriented, subjectively malleable and localized approach. *Career Development International, 19*(5), 548–571. doi:10.1108/CDI-01-2013-0007.

Anderson, D., Vinnicombe, S., and Singh, V. (2010). Women partners leaving the firm: Choice, what choice?. *Gender in Management: An International Journal, 25*(3), 170–183.

Arthur, M.B., Svetlana, N.K., and Celeste, P.M.W. (2005). Career success in a boundaryless career world. *Journal of Organizational Behavior, 26*(2), 177–202. doi:10.1002/job.290.

Barsh, J., and Yee, L. (2012). Unlocking the full potential of women at work. McKinsey & Company. Retrieved from http://www.mckinsey.com/business-functions/organization/our-insights/unlocking-the-full-potential-of-women-at-work.

Baruch, Y., and Vardi, Y. (2016). A fresh look at the dark side of contemporary careers: Toward a realistic discourse. *British Journal of Management, 27*(2), 355–372.

Bostock, J. (2014). *The Meaning of Success: Insights from Women at Cambridge.* Cambridge, UK: Cambridge University Press.

Broadbridge, A., and Simpson, R. (2011). 25 years on: Reflecting on the past and looking to the future in gender and management research. *British Journal of Management, 22*(3), 470–483. doi:10.1111/j.1467-8551.2011.00758.x.

Cabrera, E.F. (2007). Opting out and opting in: Understanding the complexities of women's career transitions. *Career Development International, 12*(3), 218–237. doi:10.1108/13620430710745872.

Cabrera, E.F. (2009). Protean organizations: Reshaping work and careers to retain female talent. *Career Development International, 14*(2), 186–201. doi:10.1108/13620430910950773.

Cahusac, E., and Kanji, S. (2014). Giving up: How gendered organizational cultures push mothers out. *Gender, Work and Organization, 21*(1), 57–70. doi:10.1111/gwao.12011.

Catalyst. (2007). The double-bind dilemma for women in leadership: Damned if you do, doomed if you don't. Retrieved from http://www.catalyst.org/knowledge/double-bind-dilemma-women-leadership-damned-if-you-do-doomed-if-you-dont-0.

Catalyst. (2013). Why diversity matters. Retrieved from http://www.catalyst.org/knowledge/why-diversity-matters.

Catalyst. (2016). Women's earnings and income. Retrieved from http://www.catalyst.org/knowledge/womens-earnings-and-income.

Champions for Change. (n.d.). Champions for change. Retrieved from http://www.globalwomen.org.nz/diversity-initiatives/champions-for-change/.

Coleman, M. (2011). *Women at the Top: Challenges, Choices and Change.* Basingstoke, UK: Palgrave Macmillan.

Derks, B., Ellemers, N., van Laar, C., and de Groot, K. (2011a). Do sexist organizational cultures create the Queen Bee?. *British Journal of Social Psychology, 50*(3), 519–535. doi:10.1348/014466610X525280.

Derks, B., van Laar, C., Ellemers, N., and de Groot, K. (2011b). Gender-bias primes elicit queen-bee responses among senior policewomen. *Psychological Science, 22*(10), 1243–1249. doi:10.1177/0956797611417258.

Derks, B., van Laar, C., Ellemers, N., and Raghoe, G. (2015). Extending the Queen Bee effect: How Hindustani workers cope with disadvantage by distancing the self from the group. *Journal of Social Issues, 71*(3), 476–496. doi:10.1111/josi.12124.

Dezsö, C.L., and Ross, D.G. (2012). Does female representation in top management improve firm performance? A panel data investigation. *Strategic Management Journal, 33*(9), 1072–1089. doi:10.1002/smj.1955.

Doherty, L., and Manfredi, S. (2010). Improving women's representation in senior positions in universities. *Employee Relations, 32*(2), 138–155. doi:10.1108/01425451011010096.

Dyke, L.S., and Murphy, S.A. (2006). How we define success: A qualitative study of what matters most to women and men. *Sex Roles, 55*(5–6), 357–371.

Eikhof, D.R. (2012). A double-edged sword: Twenty-first century workplace trends and gender equality. *Gender in Management: An International Journal, 27*(1), 7–22. doi:10.1108/17542411211199246.

Ellemers, N., Rink, F., Derks, B., and Ryan, M.K. (2012). Women in high places: When and why promoting women into top positions can harm them individually or as a group (and how to prevent this). *Research in Organizational Behavior: An Annual Series of Analytical Essays and Critical Reviews, 32*, 163–187. doi:10.1016/j.riob.2012.10.003.

Elliott, C., and Stead, V. (2008). Learning from leading women's experience: Towards a sociological understanding. *Leadership, 4*(1), 159–181. doi: 10.1177/1742715008089636.

Elsesser, K.M., and Lever, J. (2011). Does gender bias against female leaders persist? Quantitative and qualitative data from a large-scale survey. *Human Relations, 64*(12), 1555–1578. doi:10.1177/0018726711424323.

Ely, R.J., Ibarra, H., and Kolb, D.M. (2011). Taking gender into account: Theory and design for women's leadership development programs. *Academy of Management Learning and Education, 10*(3), 474–493. doi:10.5465/amle.2010.0046.

Fletcher, J.K. (1999). *Disappearing Acts: Gender, Power and Relational Practice at Work.* Cambridge, MA: MIT Press..

Fletcher, J.K. (2012). The relational practice of leadership. In M. Uhl-Bien and S. Ospina (Eds), *Advancing Relational Leadership Research: A Dialogue among Perspectives* (pp. 83–106). Charlotte, NC: Information Age Publishing.

Grant Thornton International. (2016). Women in business: Turning promise into practice. Retrieved from http://www.grantthornton.co.nz/2016-wib.pdf.

Grove, J. (2013). Gender still on the agenda. *Times Higher Education*, May 2, pp. 37–41.

HeforShe. (n.d.). Homepage. I want my voice to make a difference. Retrieved from http://www.heforshe.org/en.

Hegewisch, A., and DuMonthier, A. (2016). The gender wage gap by occupation 2015 and by race and ethnicity. Retrieved from http://www.iwpr.org/publications/recent-publications – sthash.xwwHA9St.dpuf.

Heslin, P.A. (2005). Conceptualizing and evaluating career success. *Journal of Organizational Behavior, 26*(2), 113–136.

Hewlett, S.A. (2007). Off-ramps and on-ramps: Women's nonlinear career paths. In B. Kellerman and D.L. Rhode (Eds), *Women and Leadership: The State of Play and Strategies for Change*, 1st edn (pp. 407–430). San Francisco, CA: Jossey-Bass.

Hurst, J., Leberman, S., and Edwards, M. (2016). Women managing women: Intersections between hierarchical relationships, career development and gender equity. *Gender in Management: An International Journal, 31*(1), 1–14. doi:10.1108/GM-03-2015-0018.

Ituma, A., Simpson, R., Ovadje, F., Cornelius, N., and Mordi, C. (2011). Four "domains" of career success: How managers in Nigeria evaluate career outcomes. *International Journal of Human Resource Management, 22*(17), 3638–3660.

Joecks, J., Pull, K., and Vetter, K. (2013). Gender diversity in the boardroom and firm performance: What exactly constitutes a "critical mass"? *Journal of Business Ethics, 118*(1), 61–72. doi:10.1007/s10551-012-1553-6.

Johnson, Z., and Mathur-Helm, B. (2011). Experiences with queen bees: A South African study exploring the reluctance of women executives to promote other women in the workplace. *South African Journal of Business Management, 42*(4), 47–55.

Kamenou, N., and Fearfull, A. (2006). Ethnic minority women: A lost voice in HRM. *Human Resource Management Journal, 16*(2), 154–172. doi:10.1111/j.1748-8583.2006.00010.x.

Kottke, J.L., and Agars, M.D. (2015). Creating and sustaining positive careers for women: A closer look at organizational context. In A.M. Broadbridge, and S.L. Fielden (Eds), *Handbook of Gendered Careers in Management: Getting In, Getting On, Getting Out* (pp. 275–289). Cheltenham, UK and Northampton, MA, USA: Edward Elgar Publishing.

Lalande, V.M., Crozier, S.D., and Davey, H. (2000). Women's career development and relationships: A qualitative inquiry. *Canadian Journal of Counselling, 34*(3), 193–203.

Leberman, S.I., and Palmer, F.R. (2009). Motherhood, sport leadership and domain theory: Experiences from New Zealand. *Journal of Sport Management, 23*(3), 303–334.

Lewis, P., and Simpson, R. (2010). Meritocracy, difference and choice: Women's experiences of advantage and disadvantage at work. *Gender in Management: An International Journal, 25*(3), 165–169. doi:10.1108/17542411011036374.

Lewis, P., and Simpson, R. (2015). Understanding and researching "choice" in women's career trajectories. In

A.M. Broadbridge and S.L. Fielden (Eds), *Handbook of Gendered Careers in Management: Getting In, Getting On, Getting Out* (pp. 44–60). Cheltenham, UK and Northampton, MA, USA: Edward Elgar Publishing.

Lirio, P., Lituchy, T.R., Ines Monserrat, S., Olivas-Lujan, M.R., Duffy, J.A., Fox, S., . . . Santos, N. (2007). Exploring career-life success and family social support of successful women in Canada, Argentina and Mexico. *Career Development International, 12*(1), 28–50. doi:10.1108/13620430710724811.

Litwin, A.H. (2011). Women working together: Understanding women's relationships at work. *CEO Insights,* Vol. 33, pp. 1–7.

Mainiero, L.A., and Sullivan, S.E. (2005). Kaleidoscope careers: An alternate explanation for the opt-out revolution. *Academy of Management, 19*(1), 106–123. doi:10.5465/AME.2005.15841962.

Mainiero, L.A., and Sullivan, S.E. (2006). *The Opt-Out Revolt: Why People are Leaving Companies to Create Kaleidoscope Careers,* 1st edn. Mountain View, CA: Davies-Black Publishing.

Male Champions of Change. (n.d.). Male champions of change. Retrieved from http://malechampionsofchange.com/.

Mavin, S. (2006a). Venus envy 2: Sisterhood, queen bees and female misogyny in management. *Women in Management Review, 21*(5), 349–364. doi:10.1108/09649420610676172.

Mavin, S. (2006b). Venus envy: Problematizing solidarity behaviour and queen bees. *Women in Management Review, 21*(4), 264–276. doi:10.1108/09649420610666579.

NBA Lean in Together. (n.d.). Pass it on with #LeanIn together. Retrieved from http://www.nba.com/2015/news/03/05/nba-leanin-org-official-release/.

New Zealand Women in Leadership. (2015). New Zealand Women in Leadership programme: Diversity in leadership, promoting better sector performance. NZWiL Steering Group, Wellington, New Zealand. Retrieved from http://www.universitiesnz.ac.nz/aboutus/sc/hr/women-in-leadership.

O'Neil, D., Hopkins, M., and Bilimoria, D. (2008). Women's careers at the start of the 21st century: Patterns and paradoxes. *Journal of Business Ethics, 80*(4), 727–743. doi:10.1007/s10551-007-9465-6.

O'Neill, R.M., Shapiro, M., Ingols, C., and Blake-Beard, S. (2013). Understanding women's career goals across ethnic identities. *Advancing Women in Leadership, 33,* 196–214.

Ojeda, L., and Flores, L.Y. (2008). The influence of gender, generation level, parents' education level, and perceived barriers on the educational aspirations of Mexican American high school students. *Career Development Quarterly, 57*(1), 84–95.

Pellegrino, G., D'Amato, S., and Weisberg, A. (2011). The gender dividend: Making the business case for investing in women. Retrieved from http://www2.deloitte.com/content/dam/Deloitte/global/Documents/Public-Sector/dttl-ps-thegenderdividend-08082013.pdf.

Prime, J.L., Carter, N.M., and Welbourne, T.M. (2009). Women "take care," men "take charge": Managers' stereotypic perceptions of women and men leaders. *Psychologist-Manager Journal, 12*(1), 25–49. doi:10.1080/10887150802371799.

Raelin, J. (2011). From leadership-as-practice to leaderful practice. *Leadership, 7*(2), 195–211. doi:10.1177/1742715010394808.

Raelin, J. (2016). Imagine there are no leaders: Reframing leadership as collaborative agency. *Leadership, 12*(2), 131–158. doi:10.1177/1742715014558076.

Rapoport, R. (2002). *Beyond Work–Family Balance: Advancing Gender Equity and Workplace Performance.* San Francisco, CA: Jossey-Bass.

Rhee, K.S., and Sigler, T.H. (2015). Untangling the relationship between gender and leadership. *Gender in Management: An International Journal, 30*(2), 109–134. doi:10.1108/GM-09-2013-0114.

Schein, V.E. (2007). Women in management: Reflections and projections. *Women in Management Review, 22*(1), 6–18. doi:10.1108/09649420710726193.

Shaw, S., and Leberman, S.I. (2015). Bringing the pieces of the puzzle together – using the Kaleidoscope Career Model to analyze female CEO's career experiences in sport. *Gender in Management: An International Journal 30*(6), 500–515. doi: 10.1108/GM-12-2014-0108.

Sheppard, L.D., and Aquino, K. (2013). Much ado about nothing? Observers' problematization of women's same-sex conflict at work. *Academy of Management Perspectives, 27*(1), 52–62. doi:10.5465/amp.2012.0005.

Simpson, R., Ross-Smith, A., and Lewis, P. (2010). Merit, special contribution and choice: How women negotiate between sameness and difference in their organizational lives. *Gender in Management: An International Journal, 25*(3), 198–207. doi:10.1108/17542411011036400.

Sinclair, A. (2005). *Doing Leadership Differently: Gender, Power, and Sexuality in a Changing Business Culture.* Carlton, VIC: Melbourne University Publishing.

Sinclair, A. (2007). *Leadership for the Disillusioned: Moving beyond Myths and Heroes to Leading that Liberates.* Crows Nest, NSW: Allen & Unwin.

Sprung, J.M., Toumbeva, T.H., and Matthews, R.A. (2014). Family-friendly organizational policies, practices, and benefits through the gender lens. In M.J. Mills (Ed.), *Gender and the Work–Family Experience: An Intersection of Two Domains* (pp. 227–249). New York, NY: Springer International Publishing. Retrieved from http://www.springer.com/us/book/9783319088907.

nize that our own backgrounds shape our interpretation (Creswell, 2009). We are both indigenous outsiders to our respective studies (Acker, 2001). Diehl has spent 21 years as a female leader of information technology in higher education, while Dzubinski spent 20 years working overseas in an evangelical mission organization. Yet we also brought our outsider, academic perspectives to the study of our environments (Acker, 2001). Additionally, we consider ourselves to be equalists; that is, we believe that all human beings regardless of any socially defined identity category are of equal value and deserve equal access, treatment, rights, opportunity, and freedom in all realms of society. In addition, like Fletcher and Ely (2003), we do not view gender as just a concern for women, but instead "as a central organizing feature of social life, with implications for men, women, and how we get work done" (p. 3). Qualitative research gave us the framework to understand ourselves as the research instrument and to recognize and value the knowledge that was co-constructed between us and our participants (Merriam, 2009).

To analyze our data, we started with a list of gender barriers discovered in literature and confirmed their existence in both studies. We discovered additional barriers inductively, by examining and comparing women's stories from both studies. We then confirmed that all barriers were internally consistent and did not overlap (Patton, 2002).

GENDER-BASED LEADERSHIP BARRIERS

We identified 27 gender-based leadership barriers, all of which existed in both the religion and the higher education studies. These 27 barriers are organized according to the level of society in which they generally operate most strongly: macro (societal), meso (organizational), and micro (individual), as shown in Figure 17.1.

Macro Barriers

Barriers operating in society as a whole prevent women from advancing or succeeding in leadership. These six barriers make it challenging for women leaders to contribute their leadership expertise and for both women and men to take women leaders seriously.

Control of women's voices
Women may be restricted in when and how they contribute to the conversation. One form of this control is low tolerance for women who express opinions that differ from the group. An academic leader explained, "The women . . . are consistently criticized for expressing any disagreement or dissent to what's been decided or what's been done." Women leaders may also find it challenging to communicate in ways accepted by men. A mission executive explained the conversational dynamics of her leadership team in which she was the only woman: "I found it hard to even be heard in this room full of strong guys. I almost had to be aggressive, and that's not who I was, in order to get my viewpoint heard . . . That was really difficult for a while. I almost gave up."

Cultural constraints on women's own choices
Women's choices regarding their field of study and career may be constrained by society. Some women in the higher education study found their choice of college major was

Figure 17.1 Gender-based leadership barriers by level of society*

affected by societal expectations. One had to overcome the assumption that she would go to a local junior college if she went to college at all. Her high school guidance counselor attempted to dissuade her: "Why do you want to go so far away? And why do you want to go to a college? Why don't you go to a community college?" Married mission executives were expected to raise their children before moving into leadership roles. One explained the viewpoint of her male colleagues: "[Married women] are busy being moms right now; we won't bother them."

Gender stereotypes
Women leaders may suffer negative consequences from relatively fixed and oversimplified generalizations held by society; as one university president stated: "In our society we still don't view presidents as women. Or even vice-presidents as women. And that must have

Personalizing

Sometimes women may assume personal responsibility for system or organizational problems. This happens partly because women see that the men around them do not have certain challenges, and therefore assume that the problems they encounter are due to something personal about them. The mission women in particular reported this challenge. One said:

> I just kept trying to please [my male colleague] and blamed myself for the situation. I grew up in a dysfunctional home and had some tolerance for abuse. I tried to talk with my boss about it and he dismissed me, [so] I was blaming myself more than the other person.

Similarly, an academic leader whose team was held accountable for audit findings attributable to her predecessor explained, "I personalize and feel responsible for my team [and] the permanent damage that they suffered." Neither woman was to blame for the events, but each took personal responsibility.

Psychological glass ceiling

When women internalize society's expectations for acceptable behavior, they may be unwilling to appear assertive and may undervalue their own abilities. Thus they are deterred from negotiating for what they want or need and may even advocate against themselves. One academic leader, now a university president, explained how she initially believed that executive leadership was beyond her capacity: "[The president] called me in and said, 'I want you to be provost.' And I said, 'Susan, you're bananas, that's stupid. There's other people that you should choose because I'm not big enough to do this.'"

Work–life conflict

Balancing professional responsibilities with personal or family responsibilities has long been discussed as a challenge for women. A mission executive explained, "It's hard if you're pulled in two directions, to try to give your best in two worlds at the same time." Conventionally, work–life conflict is considered an individual woman's problem, having nothing to do with the workplace. In reality, the roots derive from the gendered nature of organizations built on the male life norm and the assumption of someone at home caring for domestic responsibilities. In addition, this barrier can limit advancement, as an academic leader noted: "It can be quite a balancing act to raise your children while you're pursuing a career, and I think that is something that often impacts on a professional's ability to advance."

CROSS-SECTOR COMPARISON

The similarity in experiences of women leaders from the two sectors is striking, given that higher education has more women in top leadership than religious organizations (Lennon, 2013). One highly salient feature is the hidden and unconscious nature of these barriers. For women in both studies, the barriers were present and often tacitly accepted as par for the course. The main difference appeared in terms of barrier strength, in that seven barriers appeared more salient in the religious organization study, while only one appeared more salient in the higher education study. We determined the relative strength of each barrier based on both the number of participants who mentioned it and the extent to which it played a role in their leadership stories.

Similarities

Given inherent differences between higher education and religion, the barriers experienced by women in the two studies were unexpectedly similar. It is notable that examples of all 27 barriers were present in the interview data of both studies. For example, participants in both realms reported working with powerful but insecure women who exhibited bullying and marginalizing queen bee behaviors. Both studies had examples of conscious unconsciousness, women who chose not to notice or challenge gender disparities in the workplace. The reason may be for self-preservation and to not be perceived to align with groups opposing dominant organizational culture and power structures. Although it may seem that control of women's voices would not be as prevalent in higher education, it occurred in both environments.

Differences in Strength

While every barrier named in this study was present in both the higher education and mission organizations, the strength of some barriers differed. Seven barriers were more salient in the religious organization study, while only one seemed more salient in the higher education study.

First, cultural constraints on women's own choices were more salient in the religious organizations. While women from both studies found that societal expectations affected their choice of college major, the married mission executives were also expected to stay home to raise children. Such constraints appeared to be a central organizing principle of the mission executives' experiences. The combination of gender-role prescriptions from both society and their religious faith was an overwhelmingly powerful force that mission executives could not successfully resist or even articulate.

Second, gender unconsciousness was also more salient in the religious organization study. Many voices of authority in the evangelical faith tend to be suspicious of and even reject feminist thought, teaching women that their place is supporting, not challenging, male authority (Dzubinski, 2016). This may be why women executives in the mission organizations were unaware of gender disparities in the workplace.

Third, personalizing, or blaming themselves for organizational problems, existed in both studies but was particularly salient for women in the mission organizations. Although most mission executives understood that problems stemmed from their socialization as girls, they still took responsibility. The combination of organizational and religious pressure to comply with gender stereotypes may lead women to hold themselves personally responsible for organizational problems (Dzubinski, 2013; Scholz, 2010).

Fourth, the negative aspects of a two-person career structure were more frequently discussed in the religious organization study, as several participants began as the unpaid member of a two-person career. In the mission organizations, the women were expected to first support their husband's career and only later, once he was established and the children were grown, could they enter leadership.

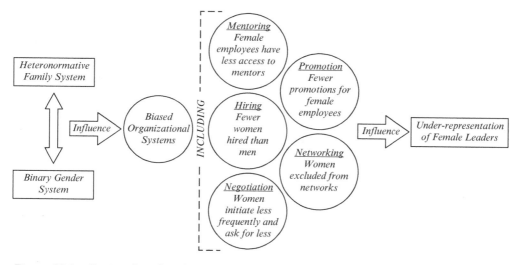

Figure 18.1 Sociocultural and organizational systems affecting the under-representation of female leaders

networking, mentoring, and promotion, that ultimately result in greater numbers of male leaders in most organizations. Finally, we consider the necessity of adopting a more balanced approach to attain gender equity in top leadership positions, and we discuss process-oriented questions and pose some tentative solutions that may support and create systemic change.

GENDERED ORGANIZATIONAL SYSTEMS: THE "MALE COMPETITIVE MODEL"

A major organizational system that affects women is the predominantly masculine corporate culture that continues to silently but essentially pervade organizational life. Although described in numerous ways, "culture" is defined as the assumptions, values, and norms that have been developed over time in order to solve problems of both internal integration and external adaptation, and that are taught to new employees as "the way we do things around here" (Schein, 2010, p. 15). Cross-culturally, most modern organizations have been developed and led by men in a way that has been adapted to their values and assumptions in predominantly gender-segregated societies (Granleese, 2004; Insch et al., 2008; Kark and Eagly, 2010; Liff and Ward, 2001; Lyness and Thompson, 2000; Meyerson and Fletcher, 2000; Neck, 2015; Reinhold, 2005).

As a result, a "male corporate culture" has become firmly entrenched in most industries, making it difficult for women to fit into the model of the "ideal" employee. In most companies, this ideal employee (and the most suitable for promotion to leadership positions) works long hours, is always available, is able to travel, and is willing to sacrifice for the organization should projects or events require additional efforts. All of these factors impact caregivers, who are disproportionately women, more negatively than their colleagues. Moreover, career advancement and leadership positions are often controlled via access to "old boys" networks, which remain crucial in terms of exchanging information, political influence, and mentoring. However, these networks are not easily accessed by women and other under-represented minorities because they tend to be homophilic. As a result, women struggle to fit into the model of the masculine ideal employee and experience pressure to adapt and prove themselves, often through working harder and finding creative solutions to access informal power networks in traditionally male-dominated domains, such as sports and social clubs (Marshall, 1995; Neck, 2015; Ragins et al., 1998; Reinhold, 2005).

Unfortunately, there is ample evidence that, rather than challenging and working to change these entrenched systems, women have been blaming themselves for not fitting into them more effectively (Meyerson and Fletcher, 2000). Numerous authors and practitioners have argued that women's "lack of confidence" and failure to "lean in" in order to navigate these systems are largely responsible for the under-representation of women in leadership positions. While these issues are important to address, according to O'Neil and Hopkins (2015) this "lack of confidence" viewpoint fails to challenge an organizational system in which men are often assumed to be natural leaders and women need to be "fixed" for their anomalies or failures to adapt (e.g., Kottke and Agars, 2005; Wittenberg-Cox, 2013). Thus, other authors highlight the necessity of questioning the nature of this gender-biased organizational system (Acker, 1991; Meyerson and Fletcher, 2000; Williams, 2000), which is also known as the "male competitive model" (Hewlett, 2007, p. 13).

Focusing on organizational processes and systems affecting women helps to highlight the ways in which this traditional organizational system is unsuitable for women and it fails to recognize the changing roles of men, including increasing paternal investments in child-rearing. On the contrary, it sustains the gender gap in leadership positions (O'Neil and Hopkins, 2015) and reinforces rigid gender roles. As a result, the glass ceiling is perpetuated (despite the increasing cracks in some domains and widening holes in others); women take more time to progress through leadership pipelines, and arguments that women are either not born leaders or that they lack the motivation and/or ability to lead are reinforced.

It is important to note that while numerous aspects of organizational systems advantage men, these systems have evolved over time (Acker, 1991; Budig and England, 2001; Correll et al., 2011; Martin, 2003). Sturm (2001) highlights that although laws have been enacted to ban so-called "first-generation" biases such as sexual harassment or discriminatory exclusions, these laws have not eradicated second-generation gender biases. As discussed elsewhere (for example, in Chapters 13, 23, and 25 of this *Handbook*), second-generation gender biases are defined as subtle forms of structural, relational, and situational biases that affect women (Sturm, 2001). These biases are reified in workplace processes that exclude women and under-represented minorities. Second-generation biases take the shape of informal norms, networking, mentoring, and evaluation processes that continue to favor men, yet are more subtle, multifaceted, and implicit than their predecessors. Despite the progress that has been made in minimizing explicit forms of first-generation gender discrimination, this progress has not been successful in addressing the less obvious forms of discrimination that continue to favor men, despite the appearance of legality and gender neutrality. An unfortunate side effect has often been a focus on the reasons why women need to change their behaviors, tactics, and styles in order to "play the game" more effectively, drawing needed attention away from how the game itself must be altered in order to support gender equality for both men and women. In the following sections, we explore how organizational systems that appear to be gender neutral continue to promote male leaders disproportionately.

WHY ARE ORGANIZATIONAL SYSTEMS BIASED?

The Heteronormative Family System

Organizational systems are not gender neutral in part because they are grounded in the traditional heterosexual family system that defines men as "breadwinners" and women as "homemakers." One significant reason why female leaders are under-represented in top positions is because organizational systems are embedded within heteronormative family system, where women frequently have both a professional career and more domestic responsibilities, giving rise to conflictual stereotypes (Eagly and Karau, 2002). These include the so-called "superwoman" who tackles both professional and family life with perfection, the "working mother" who sacrifices her family for work, and the "stay-at-home mom" who sacrifices her career ambitions for her family. Each stereotype has been cast alternately as ideal, unfortunate, or even shameful, with various groups of women and men privately and publicly casting aspersions on the chosen paths of others. Given the powerful influence of the heteronormative family system, gender equity within organizations is perhaps unrealistic without challenging the historical division of labor in the family system. Women have significantly more family responsibilities than men, impeding their ability to devote as much time, energy, and financial resources to their careers. In 2013, the average time per day spent on house chores by women was 2.6 hours, whereas men spent 2.1 hours (Bureau of Labor Statistics, 2015), leaving women 3.5 fewer working hours per week than their male colleagues. This gender inequity in the family infringes upon women's resources, perceived suitability, and motivation for leadership positions.

In addition, the heteronormative family system also perpetuates the implicit model of the ideal employee mentioned above, whose success fundamentally relies on the sacrifice of the female spouse's career. Schneer and Reitman (2002) found that individuals with the most successful careers in terms of earning were, first, married men with children and homemaker spouses, followed by married men with working spouses, and finally single men (Insch et al., 2008). In addition, married men with homemaker spouses were also the most satisfied with their careers. Pfeffer and Ross (1982) similarly found that wives acted as a critical resource for male managers' job performance, as spouses were instrumental in taking care of the household and providing counsel and assistance related to their husbands' jobs (see Judge et al., 1995). This research highlights one major source of the disproportionate career ascensions of married men, who are more likely to leave domestic responsibilities to their spouses, freeing them to focus on work responsibilities that involve working longer and more irregular hours, traveling frequently, and having informal networking opportunities outside of traditional working schedules, such as "happy hours," social events, and sports (Eagly and Carli, 2007a).

Female managers are not only less likely to benefit from these advantages experienced by male managers, but they are also more likely to face additional challenges. According to a Catalyst report (2004), men are more likely to leave domestic responsibilities to their spouses. Furthermore, female executives make more efforts to manage domestic responsibilities by hiring external help. Women are also more likely than men to delay or forgo having children to attain career success (Catalyst, 2004). Unfortunately, all of these factors, which serve to complicate women's ascension into leadership positions, are subsequently compounded as women have fewer role models for leadership – from sports to entertainment, politics, and business – and fewer female mentors who can support their career progression.

However, mounting evidence suggests that female managers can balance professional and domestic responsibilities effectively if organizations provide more support for family-friendly benefits such as equal paid parental leave. The United States (US) currently has no policy for paid parental leave. Only 21 percent of organizations currently offer paid maternity leave, and only 17 percent provide paid paternity leave (Society for Human Resource Management, 2015). However, in industries where competition for talented employees has become increasingly fierce, there is evidence that these policies are starting to shift. In the US, for example, many high-tech companies are now offering paid parental leave in hopes of retaining female employees after childbirth. Among some of the most innovative companies, Adobe now offers 26 weeks of paid parental leave, followed by Twitter with 20 weeks and Google with 18 weeks. Recently, Netflix made headlines with its offer of unlimited parental leave within a year following childbirth (Lachance Shandrow, 2015).

There are also some additional incentives for organizations to provide paid parental leave. Research suggests that paid parental leave helps to enhance gender equality within organizations, as the division of work between men and women becomes more balanced by involving men more significantly in childcare (Lanfranconi and Valarino, 2014; Rønsen and Kitterød, 2015). However, this research highlights that organizational systems are not only gender biased, but also heteronormative, underlying more complex silencing processes for under-represented minorities (see Priola et al., 2014).

Given all of these differences rooted in societal gender roles regarding child care, domestic work, spousal support, and parental leave, women continue to face challenges in attaining highly competitive top leadership positions rooted in systemic inequities. In the following section, we turn to additional organizational processes that reinforce, and in some cases exacerbate, these disadvantages for women.

PROCESSES THAT UNDERMINE WOMEN'S LEADERSHIP: HIRING AND PROMOTION

Previous research demonstrates that male-dominated corporate cultures create pervasive gender stereotypes that impact women leaders negatively. Women believe that they need to fit the values and behaviors of existing models to be perceived as good leaders. They believe that they need to be more effective and to work harder and faster than men (Ragins et al., 1998) in order to be successful. They also feel hyper-accountable for their successes and failures and remain largely unaware that organizational systems significantly impede their career advancement (O'Neil et al., 2011; O'Neil and Hopkins, 2015). Therefore, they often doubt their own capacities and are more likely to blame themselves

through social capital mobilization: help-giving behaviors are often discounted as not "exceeding expectations," and receiving help may reinforce stereotypes of dependency and incompetence.

INCLUSIVE LEADERSHIP AS A SOLUTION TO CHANGE ORGANIZATIONAL PROCESSES AND SYSTEMS

In sum, organizations must fundamentally change processes affecting hiring, networking, mentoring, and promotion by engaging in inclusive solutions involving everyone in the organization. Small changes at the organizational level can create a snowball effect that precipitates more radical changes (Meyerson and Fletcher, 2000). Several research and business cases have demonstrated that companies using diverse and inclusive strategies perform better than their peers (e.g., Desvaux et al., 2007). Thus, diversity and inclusion of women and under-represented minorities in leadership makes both moral and practical sense. Studies of the largest US companies reveal that the presence of women in executive roles leads to better financial outcomes (e.g., Carter et al., 2003; Erhardt et al., 2003; Krishnan and Park, 2005). McKinsey's research (Hunt et al., 2015) conducted in Canada, Latin America, the United Kingdom, and the United States, shows that gender-diverse companies in the top quartile are 15 percent more likely to perform above their respective national industry medians, and ethnically diverse companies are 35 percent more likely to perform above these respective medians. In addition, Deloitte Australia's research reveals that inclusive teams outperform their peers by 80 percent (Bersin, 2015).

American Express appears as one potential model of organizations using inclusive leadership (Clark, 2015). Of their 60,000 employees worldwide, 40 percent belong to an employee network of a special interest, such as women or under-represented minorities. American Express is aware that recruiting diverse individuals and supporting a workplace that is both lesbian, gay, bisexual, and transgender (LGBT)-friendly and women-friendly helps to attract and retain talented employees. Moreover, these under-represented minorities are more likely to support their brand and become potential customers. As such, American Express explicitly supports and promotes equity, which is visible in the eyes of the stakeholders. While there is no one best practice for fostering inclusion and valuing diversity, more and more companies are taking a similar approach to that of American Express.

Toward the end of creating sustainable change in organizational processes, researchers propose multiple inclusive solutions to tackle the problem from various sides. Specifically, Eagly and Carli (2007b) provide twelve solutions to change organizational processes and achieve a more gender-neutral system (see Table 18.1). In addition, training in self-promotion, negotiation, and politics; opening up informal networks; providing systemic developmental opportunities to women and under-represented minorities; benchmarking with organizations and industries that have made progress toward gender equality; and involving powerful men in change processes are all potential solutions. This research also highlights that small systemic changes in multiple domains can have larger and more visible impacts over time.

Other researchers focus exclusively on solutions that seek to involve powerful men by developing gender-inclusive leadership (Kelan, 2015a, 2015b). According to the "doing

Table 18.1 Solutions for changing organizational systems and practices

Changing organizational systems (Eagly and Carli, 2007b)	Gender-inclusive leadership practices (Kelan, 2015b)
Allow employees who have significant parental responsibility more time to prove themselves worthy of promotion.	Avoid sexually charged remarks and innuendos.
Avoid having a sole female member of any team.	Celebrate women's performance and give women credit.
Change the long-hours norm.	Challenge gendered language – use gender-sensitive metaphors.
Encourage male participation in family-friendly benefits.	Defend gender parity initiatives.
Ensure a critical mass of women in executive positions – not just one or two women – to head off problems that come with tokenism.	Develop constructive working practices.
	Encourage women to take developmental roles or apply for promotion.
Establish family-friendly human resources practices.	Identify with the dissimilar and search affirmatively (i.e., look outside personal networks for hiring and mentoring).
Help shore up social capital.	
Increase people's awareness of the psychological drivers of prejudice toward female leaders, and work to dispel those perceptions.	Make responsibilities in private life visible.
	Make sure that women are given a voice in meetings, and do not usurp speaking roles.
Prepare women for line management with appropriately demanding assignments.	Provide positive feedback to others who show gender-inclusive leadership.
Reduce the subjectivity of performance evaluation.	Show emotional competence in addressing fears associated with developing gender-inclusive practices.
Use open-recruitment tools, such as advertising and employment agencies, rather than relying on informal social networks and referrals to fill positions.	Take an active role in gender parity initiatives, such as attending women's network events and leading on gender parity initiatives.
Welcome women back.	

gender" perspective, gender is a social practice that creates gender differences, asymmetry, and hierarchy at work (Kelan, 2010). Therefore, to "undo gender," Kelan proposes solutions for male middle managers to engage in developing gender-inclusive leadership. The introduction of such leadership will not only support gender parity in the organizational systems and processes, but it might also lead to a gradual paradigm shift in which post-heroic leadership models will be celebrated (Fletcher, 2004). These leadership models do not rely on sex attributes, and they recommend a more androgynous leadership style and gender-neutral organizational systems by emphasizing the following skills: sharing vulnerability (Bligh and Ito, 2015; Brown, 2015; Fletcher, 1994), practicing empathy (Fletcher, 1994; Miller, 1986, 1991), and promoting mutual empowerment (Fletcher, 1994). Toward the end of accelerating this paradigm shift, we encourage additional

they are committed to work, and at the same time they feel guilty for not working when they are focused on caregiving and their children (Blair-Loy, 2003). Another primary source of strain is the workplace stigma associated with motherhood that can result in being penalized by co-workers and employers for using workplace flexibility policies designed to reduce work–family tensions (Leslie et al., 2012). Ultimately, these tensions require women to repeatedly negotiate and reconcile what it means to be a professional and what it means to be a parent.

To fully understand the experiences of women leaders within the gendered norms of leadership, we must understand the complexity and depth of these pressures as they are experienced by women in their ascent to leadership. To this end, we begin by discussing the current frames for understanding gendered expectations around work and caregiving. We consider the gendered division of labor at work and at home and the ideal worker norm. Next, we explore the work–family policies implemented by organizations and how using such policies affects employees; we focus on the flexibility bias and stigma that result from taking advantage of such policies. We then examine how women negotiate their professional identity along with their parental identity. While we focus on the stresses and strains experienced by professional women in their aspirations to climb the professional ladder, we also consider the tensions faced by men. Finally, we conclude with suggestions for further research on leadership and work–family balance as well as strategies for organizations and employees.

FRAMING AND REFRAMING WORK, FAMILY, AND GENDER

Despite increased numbers of women earning advanced degrees and participating in the labor force, as well as organizations' efforts at eliminating structural biases against women and implementing programs to increase the number of women in leadership ranks, women are still rare at the top echelons of both private and public sector organizations (Carter and Silva, 2010; Catalyst, 2008; Naff, 2001; Riccucci 2009). Research from Catalyst indicates that women MBA graduates still trail men at each career stage (Carter and Silva, 2010), and a recent survey of Harvard MBA graduates revealed that 57 percent of men but only 42 percent of women were in senior management positions (Ely et al., 2014). When considering why so few women occupy leadership positions, the discussion is often framed around the ideal worker norm, the gendered divisions of labor, and the private and public spheres of home and work life. Elite women in particular – white women in high-powered positions with a spouse in a comparable career – have been characterized as having the choice to opt out and assume the traditional women's role of caregiver (Stone, 2007). But reducing their dilemmas to such a simplistic framework avoids addressing or acknowledging the depth or complexity of their struggles as they negotiate work and family. In fact, a recent study conducted by the International Consortium for Executive Development Research suggests that the top two reasons both women and men leave organizations are compensation and opportunities for development, not parenthood responsibilities (as cited in Arscott, 2016).

One explanation long given for the disparity in the numbers of men and women at the top is that once women have children, the pull of being a mother exceeds that of their career aspirations (Ely et al., 2014). As such, "choice" is the rhetoric often applied in describing women's actions and decisions to veer away from the ideal worker norm and/ or leave the paid workforce altogether (Williams, 2000). Similarly, since Lisa Belkin's much-discussed 2003 *New York Times Magazine* article, considerable attention has been focused on the professional women who opt out of their high-level jobs to stay at home with children. But researchers have noted that this label is not accurate, and the "choice" and "opt-out" frames do not adequately capture the complexities and nuances of the decisions made by these women, or the tensions they experience whether they remain in the workforce or go home (Williams, 2000, 2010). In reality, many professional women who leave the workforce to assume full-time motherhood roles had not actually envisioned that they would do so (Blair-Loy, 2003; Stone, 2007; Williams, 2010). Studies of professional women who have left successful careers document organizational and employment circumstances that made it difficult or impossible for them to continue either in their previous roles or in roles with similar status (e.g., Blair-Loy, 2003). In fact, the actual numbers belie the impression that most professional women go home after having children; doing so is the exception, not the norm, and most women maintain employment after starting a family (Coltrane et al., 2013; Stone, 2007).

The gendered division of labor sees work and home as separate spheres where men are expected to be responsible for work (that is, the breadwinners) and women are expected to be responsible for home (that is, the caregivers) (Davies and Frink, 2014). Organizations themselves are gendered, structured around assumptions that workers are men, thus marginalizing women (Acker, 1990). Stemming from the gendered division of labor is the notion of the "ideal worker." Traditionally the ideal worker image is that of a white middle-class man with a family, a successful career, and a stay-at-home wife (Davies and Frink, 2014). The ideal worker is one who labors out of the home at least 40 hours per week, year round, and who has the support of a stay-at-home spouse (Williams, 2000; Williams et al., 2013). This ideal worker also takes little or no time off for child care (Galinsky and Matos, 2011). Alternately, this worker is depicted as the "zero drag" worker, embodied by both the man with a stay-at-home wife and the young, single, childless man eager to do well in his job and on call at all times (Hochschild, 1997). Today, employers often call for such dedication from both professional women and men (Reid and Ramarajan, 2016).

The norms of the ideal worker and the gendered division of labor manifest themselves into what Blair-Loy (2003) identifies as the "work devotion" and "family devotion" schemas. As an ideal type, the core assumption of the work devotion schema (the masculine schema) is that work deserves complete and total allegiance, that commitment to work should be a central tenet of one's life, and that one should devote an immense amount of time to working (Blair-Loy, 2003; Williams et al., 2013). Gendered expectations around caregiving responsibilities conflict with the assumptions inherent in the work devotion schema (Blair-Loy, 2003). What it means to be a good mother is drawn from a philosophy that emphasizes intensive parenting (Hays, 1996; Stone, 2007; Warner, 2005). Intensive parenting is marked by spending significant attention, time, energy, and financial resources on raising a child, with constant vigilance in meeting a child's every developmental need (Hays, 1996). Such a model describes the family devotion schema. In contrast to the work devotion ideal type, the family devotion schema assumes that a woman is in charge of home and family, motherhood is their primary allegiance, and women are fulfilled and find meaning through caregiving (Blair-Loy, 2003).

Women find themselves caught between the gendered expectations of allegiance to work and allegiance to family. As such, one of the primary strains felt by women is that of guilt. This tension is to some extent a "damned if you do, damned if you don't" situation. Professional women note feeling guilty regardless of what they do: for being committed to the family devotion schema or the work devotion schema (Blair-Loy, 2003). As Blair-Loy (2003) captured in one research participant's angst: "She cannot serve two masters. By being faithful to one devotion schema, she betrays the other" (p. 15).

Women may find themselves held back from career advancement and leadership positions because of the gendered expectations around work and caregiving (Blair-Loy, 2003; Leslie et al., 2012). Professional women with children may be viewed as warm but incompetent, leaving employers less interested in awarding them professional opportunities in hiring, promotion, and training (Cuddy et al., 2004). Employees seeking to ease tensions between work and family through the use of flexible work policies may inadvertently signal to employers that they are less committed to work, even if this is not the case, because of the motives employers may attribute to the use of such policies (Leslie et al., 2012). In turn, use of such policies can result in a career penalty. Next, we discuss workplace flexibility policies and the penalties, bias, and stigma related to their use.

WORK–FAMILY POLICIES AND FLEXIBILITY STIGMA

While many organizations officially offer policies and strategies to enable both women and men to balance work and life demands, in reality relatively few take advantage of these policies; often those who do can feel stigmatized, that they have slowed their careers, or have "fallen from grace" with their peers and the organization (Blair-Loy and Wharton, 2002; Blair-Loy et al., 2011; Stone, 2007; Stone and Hernandez, 2013; Williams et al., 2013). Even those organizations that have taken strides to support work–life programs and policies are still often not able to overcome gendered expectations of work and family life (Mescher et al., 2010; Williams et al., 2013). In today's environment where even the high-energy, intense Silicon Valley firms are beginning to embrace work–life flexibility for men and women alike, a flexibility bias and stigma still exists that negatively affects professionals, albeit in different ways (Reid and Ramarajan, 2016; Williams et al., 2013). In this sense, while the establishment of flexibility policies to reduce work and family tensions is one step forward, the negative effects to reputation and career may actually result in two steps back for professional women, especially those who are or aspire to be leaders.

Some studies have shown that work–life flexibility can be associated with increases in productivity, higher job satisfaction, and better overall mental health for employees (Gregory and Milner, 2009; McDonald et al., 2005; Theide and Ganster, 1995). Flexible work policies and practices that are often offered include flextime, telecommuting, part-time schedules, leave for caregiving, sabbaticals, and the ability to enter and exit the workforce over one's career (Galinsky et al., 2008). However, the existence of policies does not mean that employees are informed about the policies (Galinsky et al., 2008), that employees actually use the policies (Blair-Loy and Wharton, 2002; Blair-Loy et al., 2011), or that the culture of the organization is one that truly promotes and embraces flexibility (Galinsky et al., 2008; Mescher et al., 2010). Even when organizations offer flexibility policies, individual preferences for using these policies are embedded in the social context of the organization (Kossek and Lautsch, 2012). Furthermore, those at the upper echelons of the organizational hierarchy are even less likely to use work–life flexibility policies because cultural norms demand that those in leadership positions demonstrate organizational commitment by working long hours (Blair-Loy, 2001; Kanter, 1977).

Despite efforts by organizations to offer workplace flexibility policies, cultural and organizational norms often stigmatize the actual use of these policies. Implicit in this assumption is the expectation that any time spent on family and caregiving will be negatively interpreted by co-workers and superiors, lead to career penalties, and result in lower self-worth for the employee (Blair-Loy, 2003; Williams et al., 2013). For professionals, the use of flexibility policies violates the work devotion schema (Blair-Loy, 2003). Using workplace flexibility policies can reduce opportunities for interesting and meaningful work assignments, limit wage growth, and result in inferior performance evaluations and fewer opportunities for promotion (Cohen and Single, 2001; Glass, 2004; Schwartz, 1989; Stone and Lovejoy, 2004; Wharton et al., 2008). In sum, even if organizations attempt to support work–life fit by offering flexibility policies, employees who choose to use them may limit their opportunities to rise into leadership positions.

NEGOTIATING PROFESSIONAL IDENTITY AND PARENTHOOD

For professional women to advance their careers, they must continuously navigate the gendered assumptions that frame work and family, and deflect the stigma associated with using the very policies designed to reduce work–family tension. Ultimately, managing these tensions on the road to leadership is a process requiring constant reconciliation of professional identity with parental identity. Identity is the way we define our "self" or the way we answer the question "Who am I?" Identity is grounded in roles and the meaning we attribute to the different roles that we assume (Stets and Burke, 2000).

For many individuals, identity in the workplace is a balancing act. On the one hand, people seek to construct an identity that fits with their occupation or organization. At the same time, they wish to enact a workplace identity that is authentic to their own sense of self (Meyerson and Scully, 1995). Workplace identity construction may involve a bit of gaming: how much to surrender to fit in versus how much to claim (Meyerson and Scully, 1995). In part, this identity work stems from employees' attempts at managing the "tensions between organizational expectations that they be ideal workers . . . and the sort of workers they believe and prefer themselves to be" (Reid, 2015, p. 997). This tension is the stress felt between expected professional identities – often akin to the ideal worker norm – and experienced professional identities (Reid, 2015).

For women, the identity of being a good mother often clashes with the identity of being a good or ideal worker. The two roles appear to be incongruent by the terms of the gendered division of labor and the ideal worker norm. In their day-to-day interactions, professional women may find that their role of wife or mother overshadows that of their professional role. Even within a work context, women are often viewed first as a mother, then as a professional (Hatmaker, 2013). Women also frequently find that they must repeatedly prove themselves as professionals by outwardly demonstrating their devotion to work in order to advance; this only continues as they move up the career ladder and

REFERENCES

Acker, J. (1990). Hierarchies, jobs, bodies: A theory of gendered organizations. *Gender and Society*, *4*(2), 139–158.

Alderman, L. (2016). In Sweden, experiment turns shorter workdays into bigger gains. *New York Times*, May 20. Retrieved from http://www.nytimes.com/2016/05/21/business/international/in-sweden-an-experiment-turns-shorter-workdays-into-bigger-gains.html?_r=0.

Arscott, C.H. (2016). Why so many thirtysomething women are leaving your company. *Harvard Business Review*, March 15. Retrieved from https://hbr.org/2016/03/why-so-many-thirtysomething-women-are-leaving-your-company.

Belkin, L. (2003). The opt-out revolution. *New York Times Magazine*, October 26, pp. 42–47, 58, 85–86.

Berdahl, J.L., and Moon, S.H. (2013). Workplace mistreatment of middle class workers based on sex, parenthood, and caregiving. *Journal of Social Issues*, *69*(2), 341–366.

Blair-Loy, M. (2001). Cultural constructions of family schemas: The case of female finance executives. *Gender and Society*, *15*(5), 687–709.

Blair-Loy, M. (2003). *Competing Devotions: Career and Family among Women Executives*. Cambridge, MA: Harvard University Press.

Blair-Loy, M., and Wharton, A.S. (2002). Employees' use of family-responsive policies and the workplace social context. *Social Forces*, *80*(3), 813–845.

Blair-Loy, M., Wharton, A.S., and Goodstein, J. (2011). Exploring the relationship between mission statements and work-life practices in organizations. *Organization Studies*, *32*(3), 427–450.

Carter, N.M., and Silva, C. (2010). Women in management: Delusions of progress. *Harvard Business Review*, *88*(3), 19–21.

Casper, W.J., Bordeaux, C., Eby, L.T., Lockwood, A., and Lambert, D. (2007). A review of research methods in IO/OB work–family research. *Journal of Applied Psychology*, *92*(1), 28–43.

Catalyst (2008). 2008 Catalyst census of women board directors of the Fortune 500. New York, NY. Retrieved from http://www.catalyst.org/system/files/08_census_Women_Board_Directors.pdf.

Cohen, J.R., and Single, L.E. (2001). An examination of perceived impact of flexible work arrangements on professional opportunities in public accounting. *Journal of Business Ethics*, *32*(4), 317–328.

Coltrane, S., Miller, E.C., DeHaan, T., and Stewart, L. (2013). Fathers and the flexibility stigma. *Journal of Social Issues*, *69*(2), 279–302.

Cooper, M. (2000). Being the "go-to" guy: Fatherhood, masculinity, and the organization of work in Silicon Valley. *Qualitative Sociology*, *23*(4), 379–405.

Correll, S.J., Benard, S. and Paik, I. (2007). Getting a job: Is there a motherhood penalty? *American Journal of Sociology*, *112*(5), 1297–1338.

Crenshaw, K. (1991). Mapping the margins: Intersectionality, identity politics, and violence against women of color. *Stanford Law Review*, *43*(6), 1241–1299.

Cuddy, A.J., Fiske, S.T., and Glick, P. (2004). When professionals become mothers, warmth doesn't cut the ice. *Journal of Social Issues*, *60*(4), 667–865.

Davies, A.R., and Frink, B.D. (2014). The origins of the ideal worker: The separation of work and home in the United States from the market revolution to 1950. *Work and Occupations*, *41*(1), 18–39.

Dowd, N.E. (2000). *Redefining Fatherhood*. New York, NY: New York University Press.

Ely, R.J., Stone, P., and Ammerman, C. (2014). Rethink what you "know" about high-achieving women. *Harvard Business Review*, *92*(12), 100–109.

Galinsky, E., Bond, J.T., and Sakai, K. (2008). *2008 National Study of Employers: When Work Works*. New York, NY: Families and Work Institute. Retrieved from http://familiesandwork.org/site/research/reports/2008nse.pdf

Galinsky, E., and Matos, K. (2011). The future of work–life fit. *Organizational Dynamics 40*(4), 267–280.

Glass, J.L. (2004). Blessing or curse? Family responsive policies and mothers' wage growth over time. *Work and Occupations*, *31*(3), 367–394.

Gregory, A., and Milner, S. (2009). Work–life balance: A matter of choice? *Gender, Work and Organization*, *16*(1), 1–13.

Hatmaker, D.M. (2013). Engineering identity: Gender and professional identity negotiation among women engineers. *Gender, Work and Organization*, *20*(4), 382–396.

Hays, S. (1996). *The Cultural Contradictions of Motherhood*. New Haven, CT: Yale University Press.

Hekman, D.R., Johnson, S., Der Foo, M., and Yang, W. (forthcoming). Does diversity-valuing behavior result in diminished performance ratings for nonwhite and female leaders?. *Academy of Management Journal*. Advance on-line publication. doi: 10.5465/amj.2014.0538.

Hochschild, A.R. (1997). *The Time Bind: When Work becomes Home and Home becomes Work*. New York, NY: Henry Holt Company.

Humberd, B., Ladge, J.J., and Harrington, B. (2015). The "new" dad: Navigating fathering identity within organizational contexts. *Journal of Business and Psychology*, *30*(2), 249–266.

Ibarra, H., Ely, R.J., and Kolb, D.M. (2013). Women rising: The unseen barriers. *Harvard Business Review*, *91*(9), 60–66.
Kanter, R.M. (1977). *Men and Women of the Corporation*. New York, NY: Basic Books.
Kanter, R.M. (2010). Work pray love. *Harvard Business Review*, *88*(12), 38–38.
Kimmel, M. (2014). How can we help women? By helping men. *Huffington Post*, January 17. Retrieved from http://www.huffingtonpost.com/michael-kimmel/how-can-we-help-women-by-helping-men_b_4611523.html.
Kossek, E.E. (2016). Managing work–life boundaries in the digital age. *Organizational Dynamics*, *45*(3), 258–270.
Kossek, E.E. and Lautsch, B.A. (2012). Work–family boundary management styles in organizations: A cross-level model. *Organizational Psychology Review*, *2*(2), 152–171.
Kreiner, G.E., Hollensbe, E., and Sheep, M.L. (2009). Balancing borders and bridges: Negotiating the work–home interface via boundary work tactics. *Academy of Management Journal*, *52*(4), 704–730.
Leslie, L.M., Manchester, C.F., Park, T., and Mehng, S.A. (2012). Flexible work practices: A source of career premiums or penalties?. *Academy of Management Journal 55*(6), 1407–1428.
McDonald, P., Brown, K., and Bradley, L. (2005). Explanations for the provision–utilisation gap in work–life policy. *Women in Management Review*, *20*(1), 37–55.
Mescher, S., Benschop, Y., and Doorewaard, H. (2010). Representations of work–life balance support. *Human Relations*, *63*(1), 21–39.
Meyerson, D.E. (2003). *Tempered Radicals: How People Use Difference to Inspire Change at Work*. Boston, MA: Harvard Business School Press.
Meyerson, D. and J.K. Fletcher (2000). A modest manifesto for shattering the glass ceiling. *Harvard Business Review*, *78*(1), 126–136.
Meyerson, D.E., and Scully, M.A. (1995). Tempered radicalism and the politics of ambivalence and change. *Organization Science*, *6*(5), 585–600.
Naff, K.C. (2001). *To Look Like America: Dismantling Barriers for Women and Minorities in Government*. Boulder, CO: Westview Press.
Reid, E.M. (2011). Passing as superman: The ideal worker and men's professional identities. *Academy of Management Proceedings*, *2011*(1), 1–6.
Reid, E.M. (2015). Embracing, passing, revealing, and the ideal worker image: How people navigate expected and experienced professional identities. *Organization Science*, *26*(4), 997–1017.
Reid, E.M., and Ramarajan, L. (2016). Managing the high-intensity workplace. *Harvard Business Review*, *94*(6). Retrieved from http://ezproxy.lib.umb.edu/login?url=http://search.proquest.com/docview/1793343836?accountid=28932.
Riccucci, N.M. (2009). The pursuit of social equity in the federal government: A road less traveled?. *Public Administration Review*, *69*(3), 373–382.
Rudman, L.A., and Mescher, K. (2013). Penalizing men who request a family leave: Is flexibility stigma a femininity stigma?. *Journal of Social Issues*, *69*(2), 322–340.
Schwartz, F. (1989). Management women and the new facts of life. *Harvard Business Review*, *67*(1), 65–76.
Shellenbarger, S. (2016). Late-night work email: Blessing or curse?. *Wall Street Journal*, March 29. Retrieved from http://www.wsj.com/articles/late-night-work-email-blessing-or-curse-1459275326.
Smith, A.E., and Monaghan, K.R. (2013). Some ceilings have more cracks: Representative bureaucracy in federal regulatory agencies. *American Review of Public Administration*, *43*(1), 50–71.
Stets, J.E., and Burke, P.J. (2000). Identity theory and social identity theory. *Social Psychology Quarterly*, *63*(3), 224–237.
Stone, P. (2007). *Opting Out? Why Women really Quit their Careers and Head Home*. Berkeley, CA: University of California Press.
Stone, P., and Hernandez, L.A. (2013). The all-or-nothing workplace: Flexibility stigma and "opting out" among professional-managerial women. *Journal of Social Issues*, *69*(2), 235–256.
Stone, P., and Lovejoy, M. (2004). Fast-track women and the "choice" to stay home. *Annals of the American Academy of Political and Social Science*, *596*(1), 62–83.
Theide, T.L., and Ganster, D. (1995). Impact of family-supportive work variables on work. *Journal of Applied Psychology*, *80*(1), 6–15.
Townsend, N.W. (2002). *The Package Deal: Marriage, Work and Fatherhood in Men's Lives*. Philadelphia, PA: Temple University Press.
Vandello, J.A., Hettinger, V.E., Bosson, J.K., and Siddiqi, J. (2013). When equal isn't really equal: The masculine dilemma of seeking work flexibility. *Journal of Social Issues*, *69*(2), 303–321.
Van Maanen, J., and Schein, E.H. (1979). Toward a theory of organizational socialization. In B.M. Staw (Ed.), *Research in Organizational Behavior*, Vol. 1 (pp. 209–264). New York, NY: Wiley.
Warner, J. (2005). *Perfect Madness: Motherhood in the Age of Anxiety*. New York, NY: Riverhead Books, Penguin Group.

(Rivers and Barnett, 2013, p. 164). Christine Lagarde, chair of the International Monetary Fund, has opted for being overprepared. When asked if that was a problem, she acknowledged, "Well, it's very time consuming" (Shipman and Kay, 2014, p. 12).

Women can also benefit from the feedback available from executive coaches, mentors, and leadership development programs. Such sources of support and expertise can help aspiring leaders to identify biases that may impede advancement. Workplace affinity groups and professional women's organizations can similarly help individuals to find mentors and develop styles that will enhance their chances for success.

Those styles should strike the right balance between "too assertive" and "not assertive enough," and should combine warmth and friendliness with forceful approaches (Barsh et al., 2009, p. 231; Hoyt, 2010, p. 492). Ninety-six percent of Fortune 1000 female executives rated as critical or fairly important that they develop "a style with which male managers are comfortable" (Catalyst, 2001, p. 11). That finding is profoundly irritating to some women. At one national summit on women's leadership, many participants railed against asking women to adjust to men's needs. Why was the focus always on fixing the female? But as others pointed out, this is the world that women inhabit, and it is not just men who find overly authoritative or self-promoting styles offputting. To maximize effectiveness, women need ways of projecting a decisive and forceful manner without seeming arrogant or abrasive. Some experts suggest being "relentlessly pleasant" without backing down, and demonstrating care and competence (Babcock and Laschever, 2008, p. 252). Strategies include expressing appreciation and concern, invoking common interests, emphasizing others' goals as well as their own, and taking a problem-solving rather than a critical stance (Babcock and Laschever, 2008). Successful women leaders such as Sandra Day O'Connor, the first female Supreme Court Justice, have been known for that capacity. In assessing her prospects for success, one political commentator noted that, "Sandy. . .is a sharp gal" with a "steel-trap mind . . . and a large measure of common sense . . . She [also] has a lovely smile and should use it often" (Biskupic, 2009, p. 56). She did.

STRATEGIES FOR ORGANIZATIONS

The most important strategy for organizations in reducing gender stereotypes and bias is a commitment to that objective, which is reflected in organizational policies, priorities, and reward structures (Dobbin et al., 2007). That commitment must start at the top. An organization's leadership does not simply need to acknowledge the importance of equal treatment, but also to establish structures for promoting it, and to hold individuals accountable for the results. Supervisors need to be held responsible for their performance on gender equity issues, and that performance should be part of job evaluation structures (Bagati, 2009; Barsh and Yee, 2012; Ibarra et al., 2013; Kellerman and Rhode, 2007; Ridgeway and England, 2007). A commitment to leveling the playing field should figure in promotion and compensation decisions (Shellenbarger, 2012). Performance appraisals that include gender-related goals but that have no significant rewards or sanctions are unlikely to affect behavior (Dobbin and Kalev, 2007).

Successful approaches often involve task forces or committees with diverse members who have credibility with their colleagues and a stake in the results (Beiner, 2008; Dobbin and Kalev, 2007; Kalev et al., 2006; Prime et al., 2010). The mission of that group should be to identify problems, develop responses, and evaluate their effectiveness. Institutional self-assessment should be a critical part of all diversity initiatives (ABA Presidential Initiative Commission on Diversity, 2010). Leaders need to know how policies that affect inclusiveness play out in practice. That requires tracking progress on key metrics and collecting both quantitative and qualitative data on matters such as advancement, retention, assignments, satisfaction, and mentoring (Coffman and Neuenfeldt, 2014).

Periodic surveys, focus groups, interviews with former and departing employees, and bottom-up evaluations of supervisors can all cast light on problems disproportionately experienced by women. Monitoring can be important not only in identifying challenges and responses, but also in making people aware that their actions are being assessed. Requiring individuals to justify their decisions can help to reduce unconscious bias (Castilla, 2008). And requiring leaders to quantify their results can prevent complacency.

Well-designed voluntary training programs on bias can also be useful, although many existing programs fail to satisfy that description (Darden, 2009).[3] As sociologists Alexandra Kalev and Frank Dobbin (2015) note, "diversity training consumes the lion's share of the corporate diversity budget yet studies suggest that it may do little to change attitudes or behaviors" (p. 2). One review of close to 1000 published and unpublished studies of interventions designed to combat prejudice found little evidence that training reduces bias (Paluck and Green, 2009). In a large-scale review of diversity initiatives across multiple industries, training programs did not significantly increase the representation or advancement of targeted groups (Dobbin and Kalev, 2007; Dobbin et al., 2007). Part of the problem is that such programs typically focus only on individual behaviors, not on institutional problems; they also provide no incentives to implement recommended practices, and sometimes reinforce stereotypes and provoke backlash among involuntary participants (Darden, 2009; Kalev and Dobbin, 2015; Vaughan, 1998).[4] Other smaller-scale research offers a more optimistic picture. One survey of managing partners and general counsel of law firms reported largely positive responses to unconscious bias training. Many people "don't know what they don't know," and education can be helpful in "opening dialogue and making people aware" (Rhode and Ricca, 2015, p. 2483).

Another common strategy is networks and affinity groups for women and minorities. These vary in effectiveness. At their best, they provide useful advice, role models, and development of informal mentoring relationships (Kalev et al., 2006; Kellerman and Rhode, 2007). By bringing women together around common interests, these networks can also forge coalitions on gender-related issues and generate useful reform proposals (Yates, 2007). Yet the only large-scale study to address this issue found that networks had no significant positive impact on individuals' career development; they increased participants' sense of community but did not do enough to put people "in touch with what or whom they ought to know" (Dobbin et al., 2007, p. 25). Such research counsels against complacency. Organizations do not just need to establish a women's network; they need to monitor its effectiveness and devise strategies for improvement.

To make all these reforms possible, they must be seen not as "women's" issues, but as organizational priorities in which women have a particular stake. Men must be part of that struggle. As diversity experts note, "Inclusion can be built only through inclusion . . . Change needs to happen in partnership *with* the people of the organization not *to* them" (Miller and Katz, 2002, pp. 37–38). The challenge remaining is to create that sense of unity and to translate rhetorical commitments into organizational priorities.

contexts; contexts where women face gender stereotypes, can do gender well and differently simultaneously (Mavin and Grandy, 2013), and where homophily (Lazarsfeld and Merton, 1954), homosociality (Gruenfeld and Tiedens, 2005), women's intra-gender competition (Campbell, 2004), and female misogyny (Mavin, 2006a) operate as complex, dialectic, interlocking gendered practices and processes.

SETTING THE SCENE: QUEEN BEES, CATFIGHTS AND SISTERHOOD

Women leaders can find themselves operating outside a dominant social norm – on the boundaries within a dynamic interplay of holding power while simultaneously marginal – often out of place as women (Mavin and Grandy, 2016a). Women leaders in senior positions, at the top of organizational hierarchies, hold powerful positions in a masculine order and where leadership takes place in a context of competitive masculinity. They can also face an oxymoron in their social relations with other women (Mavin, 2008): expectations of positive solidarity behaviors from other women in the organization, while simultaneously being negatively evaluated for performing masculinities as queen bees (Mavin, 2008). Relationships between women take place within gendered contexts that limit potential for women's allegiances. Within these contexts women's intra-gender competition and female misogyny (Mavin, 2006a) emerge as processes that limit women's abilities to accept women's intra-gender differences. For us, women leaders are active agents in relationships with other women within gendered contexts where they can engage in gendering processes which both reinforce and challenge gender stereotypes.

We view gender as socially constructed rather than being the property of a person; gender is always being redefined and negotiated through everyday practices and situations (Poggio, 2006). All feminine and masculine subjectivities are jointly crafted in the larger context of gendered power (Mumby and Ashcraft, 2006). Gender is a "complex of socially guided perceptual and interactional and micropolitical activities that cast particular pursuits as expressions of masculine and feminine 'natures'" (West and Zimmerman, 1987, p. 126) and, as such, is a routine accomplishment (West and Zimmerman, 1987). Organizations reflect and shape society's gendered power structure where women are subordinate to men, where women who desire status and power in organizations are problematic, and where the relationship between power and resistance is dialectical and mutually defining (Mumby and Ashcraft, 2006). As women take up leader roles, they disrupt patterns of social homogeneous interactions and gender stereotypes that support associations of managers and leaders as male and men as "bosses," to which both men and women might negatively respond (Mavin, 2006a, 2006b). Within this dynamic there is room for agency; women have learned to resist and shape such normative expectations (Benschop, 2009; Connell and Messerschmidt, 2005; Mavin and Grandy, 2016a; O'Leary, 1988).

Within gendered organizations, men can experience greater opportunities for, and relationships with, others (men), which impact positively on their experiences (Collinson and Hearn, 2005). Contrary to the sisterhood stereotype, women in organizations are often not friends and do not always cooperate or support each other (Mavin and Grandy, 2012). Orbach and Eichenbaum's (1987) feminist psychoanalytical understanding is that women's relationships are grounded in emotional and psychological processes (that is, love, envy, and competition) that emerge when women perceive differences in each other. As the lack of women managers and leaders became a subject of research, women's relationships with each other became positioned either as a positive enabler to career capital through assumed sisterhood and solidarity (e.g., Legge, 1987), or as a key blockage through women in senior positions as "queen bees" (Abramson, 1975; Staines et al., 1973). Research into women's negative relationships at work has now emerged, which recognizes how women's perceived "catfights" (Tanenbaum, 2011) can be constructed as an explanation to legitimize women leaders' minority status (e.g., Camussi and Leccardi, 2005; Mavin, 2006a, 2006b). Recent research has begun to theorize female same-sex conflict (Sheppard and Aquino, 2013) and women leaders' intra-gender micro-violence and abject appearance (Mavin et al., 2014a; Mavin and Grandy, 2016a); however, the complexities women leaders experience within gendered organizational contexts facilitate a chasm in social relations between women that requires further exploration (Mavin and Williams, 2013).

Taking these complexities into account, we developed a theory of women's negative intra-gender relations as illustrated in Figure 21.1. This depicts complex, interlocking, and dynamic gendered practices and processes. In what follows, we begin by outlining what we propose is at the crux of the theory, that is, gendered contexts. Against a backdrop of gendered contexts, we explain the elements of doing gender well and differently, homophily and homosociality, intra-gender competition, and female misogyny.

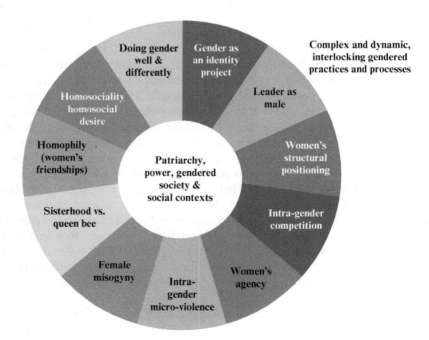

Figure 21.1   Women leaders: a theory of women's negative intra-gender relations

GENDERED CONTEXTS: GENDERED SOCIETY, PATRIARCHY, SOCIAL CONTEXTS, AND POWER

We begin with the heart of the theory, developing an understanding of gendered contexts in which negative intra-gender relations with other women occur. We propose that the gendered contexts of organizations and the prevalence of sex-role categorizations in assessing women leaders contribute to the backdrop of relations between women (Mavin, 2008) by encouraging and exacerbating differences between them (Mavin, 2006a). We focus upon the nexus of four considerations: (1) patriarchy as a societal system in which men hold power and from which women are largely excluded, is a backcloth to gendered organizational contexts; (2) masculine hegemony, which informs social relations; (3) the double-bind experienced by women leaders in organizations; and (4) the possibility of decoupling evaluations of men and women from the gender binary.

Men are normalized as doing management and leadership work, and this norm contributes to what we understand as a gendered order (Connell, 1987; Gherardi, 1994). Women have risen in numbers at management levels, yet they remain unusual as leaders, so that the "ideal leader" remains associated with masculinity and men (Acker, 1992); men are argued to be comfortable with organizational cultures as they perceive these as gender neutral (Simpson, 1997). Women's negative relations with other women take place within these gendered contexts, whereby patriarchy as sociostructural practices (Walby, 1989) shapes gendered social relations. Connell (1987) argues that "women are subjected to direct comparison with men, while being disadvantaged in the comparison from the start" (p. 228) through hegemonic masculinity. Hegemonic masculinity (Connell, 1987), understood as constructing a hierarchy of masculinities where some remain more "socially central, or more associated with authority and social power" (Connell and Messerschmidt, 2005, p. 846), continues to shape gender relations in organizations.

When women leaders engage with patriarchy they can find their femininities constrained by gendered stereotypes. This can result in women performing "emphasized femininities" (Connell, 1987, p. 228) to comply with hegemonic masculinity and orientate around "accommodating the interests and desires of men" (Connell, 1987, p. 183). This can close down possibilities of alternative femininities that do not comply with hegemonic masculinity. Yet, to accumulate competence and be promoted as leaders, women leaders face a double-bind dilemma (Gherardi, 1994). Women have to manage expectations of behavior appropriate to their perceived gender role, and behavior expected of leaders; the former associated with femininities, the latter with masculinities. This can lead to complexity for women in negotiating organizing contexts (see Eagly and Carli, 2007).

Recent research, however, argues that this double-bind is dissipating, in that gendered assumptions around the male norm are fragmenting; hence, women managers may experience congruence with the manager role if they have decoupled the male body (and masculinities) from competencies or values associated with management (Billing, 2011). We argue that while attempts may be made by some organizational members to decouple femininity and masculinity from particular behaviors and values, the gender divisions that shape expectations of what a manager and leader "do" and "look like" remain embedded in organizations. These gender divisions are based upon sex role categorizations (female/male) (Messerschmidt, 2009). This does not mean that gender binaries cannot be challenged or unsettled; rather, that the binary divide continues to constrain and restrict how men and women co-construct gender. In this way, undoing gender is redoing or doing gender differently (Messerschmidt, 2009; West and Zimmerman, 2009). These gendered contexts and assumptions provide a backdrop for women leaders' relations with other women and contribute to maintaining assumptions of masculine hierarchical superiority (Knights and Kerfoot, 2004) in organizing.

THE GENDER BINARY: DOING GENDER WELL AND DIFFERENTLY

Within gendered contexts women leaders can do gender well and differently (Mavin and Grandy, 2012, 2013), and this impacts their relations with other women in organizations. Of importance to us is recognition that the nexus of sex category and gender plays out in complex ways for women in self-and-other relations with women. Building on West and Zimmerman's (1987) work on doing gender, we have argued elsewhere (Mavin and Grandy, 2012, 2013) that perceived congruence (or lack thereof) between sex category and gender is illustrative of how the gender binary is still pervasive. Here we propose that this complexity translates into evaluations of women's social behaviors in organizations.

Doing gender is a micropolitical contextual activity accomplished through and in relations with others where the individual, consciously or otherwise, navigates what it is to enact being a man or woman, alongside normative expectations of what is understood to be appropriate for males or females (Messerschmidt, 2009; West and Zimmerman, 1987). Drawing on Goffman (1959), Mavin and Grandy (2013) argue that the "display and recognition of a socially regulated external mark of sex" (p. 234) results in sex categorization in that, due to some external "mark" of "sex," individuals are perceived to be male or female (Mavin and Grandy, 2013, p. 234). It follows then that if an individual is perceived to be "male" (sex category), he is expected to do gender in ways that align with being a man (and perform masculinity) (Mavin and Grandy, 2012). Otherwise, there is a perceived incongruence between sex category and gender; gender scripts are violated, and this can be used as a means to discredit or accept particular expressions of the doing of gender (Messerschmidt, 2009). To take into account the complexities of doing gender and how individuals might comply, resist, or bend alongside such normative expectations, we elsewhere propose (Mavin and Grandy, 2012, 2013) that gender can be done well and differently through simultaneous and multiple enactments of femininity and masculinity. Doing gender well involves doing gender appropriately in congruence with sex category; thus, "for a woman to do gender well or appropriately, as evaluated against and accountable to her sex category, she performs expected feminine behaviour through a body that is socially perceived to be female" (Mavin and Grandy, 2013, p. 234). Doing gender differently involves alternative expressions of femininity and/or masculinity, which may be incongruent with perceived sex category.

As it relates to our theory of women leaders' negative relations with other women, we propose that the use of "lazy" stereotypes (Elliott et al., 2016), such as the "queen bee" label given by both men and women, is a sexist evaluation of women leaders performing masculinities (Mavin, 2008). There is a perceived incongruence between the sex category of so-called women "queen bees" and how they enact leadership (for example, agentic rather than communal style) (Mavin et al., 2014a). Further, when women do gender well

interlinked with homophily when women "mark the social boundary" of friendship (Eve, 2002, p. 401).

The internalization of patriarchal values (Campbell, 2004) is one way of understanding women's intra-gender competition, as this can result in "raging misogyny" (or female misogyny) where women belittle "themselves and disassociate from other females" (Tanenbaum, 2011, p. 47). We extend this line of thinking to further understand women leaders' negative relations with other women. Despite women struggling with "being" competitive, Warning and Buchanan (2009) contend that women employ numerous strategies to gain competitive advantage at work. Our own work highlights more hidden intra-gender micro-violence illustrated through women leaders' accounts of intra-gender rivalry: competition, competitiveness, and competing with other women when they do gender well and differently (Mavin et al., 2014a).

Connell (1987) also explains this and argues how some femininities in different contexts, and constructed in a dynamic relationship with hegemonic masculinities, may result in complex resistance (that is, women performing masculinities by "doing competition," and/ or doing gender well and differently simultaneously) (Mavin and Grandy, 2013). When performing resistance in the shape of opposite behaviors to expected gender stereotypes, women can be responded to negatively by other women. Further, competition for scarce career opportunities and advancement for women contributes to negative assessment of other women in leader positions. For example, Ely (1994) studied women law partners where women were critical of other women's credentials as women and as lawyers.

Discussions of why there is competition between women in organizations are rare, and performing as a "competitive woman" remains a negative construction. Women leaders risk negative responses from men and women when they express that they are competitive and/or ambitious. Moreover, while there are unconscious and conscious competitive strategies between them, women are generally unaware of why this happens in gendered contexts, or of the implications. Including women's intra-gender competition into our theory of women leaders' negative social relations with other women, there is now a research agenda; this builds upon Campbell's (2004) call to further explore women's competition within alternative sites, and Orbach and Eichenbaum's (1987) feminist approach to reveal and deconstruct women's discomfort with competition. Further research is needed into how women's competition with other women emerges when gendered hierarchies are disrupted by women leaders who do gender well and differently simultaneously. As the final element in accounting for women leaders' intra-gender negative relations, we now turn to the concept of female misogyny (Mavin, 2006a, 2006b).

FEMALE MISOGYNY

Mavin (2006a, 2006b, 2008) originally conceptualized female misogyny in her research into experiences of academic women in United Kingdom business schools, and then she extended into studies exploring women's relationships with each other in organizations, management, and leadership. Her argument is that as women in powerful positions attempt to navigate the complexities of being both women and managers or leaders, they face female misogyny and negative assessments from other women in management whose expectations of solidarity and assistance in progression into senior roles are not met (Mavin, 2006a, 2006b). Female misogyny is understood as socially, culturally, and contextually constructed. It takes into account social processes, behaviors, and activities that women engage in – consciously or unconsciously – when they suppress, undermine, exclude, and stigmatize other women. In definitional form, female misogyny denotes women's "hatred," dislike, mistrust, or entrenched prejudice against other women as a sexually defined group.

Relational female misogyny (Mavin, 2006a, 2006b) between women in organizations is facilitated by gendered contexts. It is a means by which women are reminded of their subordinate positions. Mavin's (2006a, 2006b, 2008) thesis is that, as women disturb the gendered order by progressing up the organizational hierarchy or by expressing desire for power, they can invoke negative responses from both men and women who are enculturated to associate power with masculinities and men. Women who desire power then fail to live up to gendered feminine communal stereotypes associated with women generally (Okimoto and Brescoll, 2010). Female misogyny, therefore, emerges from the complex way in which gender order is embedded and the underlying assumptions and behaviors that socially construct and impact everyday experiences for women.

It is possible to see female misogyny in women's assessments of other women who perform as leaders counter-stereotypically (Mavin et al., 2014a). As successful women in men-dominated roles set a high benchmark for the assessment of other women within organizations, women can strategically reject these women to prevent unfavorable assessments of themselves (Parks-Stamm et al., 2008). Women become "socially unattractive" to other women (Rudman and Phelan, 2008) when they engage in activities with women where the outcomes have implications for their own evaluations at work. Rudman and Phelan (2008) argue that this is unconscious self-oppression, in that even when women are seen as competent, they are unattractive to other women. Competition between women, therefore, restricts possibilities for women leaders' friendships and solidarity behavior, and it constrains women's social attractiveness to other women.

We have argued previously (Mavin et al., 2014b) that female misogyny emerges when successful women are perceived to be unlikeable "norm violators" (Parks-Stamm et al., 2008, p. 245) and thus become an identity threat to other women (Parks-Stamm et al., 2008), threatening the status quo and gendered order. Women, rather than finding themselves attractive in organizations, distance themselves from each other through competitive strategies and intra-gender micro-violence (Mavin et al., 2014b) and/or reject other women as threatening their identities. These social processes can also inter-relate with a friendship boundary marking highlighted earlier (Eve, 2002), facilitating distances between women and constraining women leaders' opportunities for positive relationships with other women.

Integrating female misogyny into a theory of women's negative relations with other women enables a richer understanding of how women negotiate organizations and leadership. Female misogyny is dynamically interconnected with women's doing of gender well and differently, intra-gender friendships, homosocial relations, and competition. It is constructed and reproduced within the prevailing patriarchal social order. Therefore, female misogyny offers a further contribution in understanding women's negative relations with each other.

WHY THE DARK SIDE OF WOMEN LEADERS' RELATIONSHIPS?

The elements we have discussed in explaining women's negative relations are interlinked, fluid, simultaneous, and at times contradictory. The elements highlight the ambiguity, ambivalence, and struggle women leaders experience in gendered contexts. When women leaders attempt to secure self-coherence, women can engage in negative social relations with each other and recast traditional gendered norms (for example, "queen bee," and women as unsuitable for leadership) (Mavin et al., 2014a). Our theory of women leaders' negative intra-gender relations is grounded in women's relational, socially constructed experiences within complex, dynamic, interlocking gendered practices and processes.

Through the interlocking elements of our theory, we begin to see how threats to women's identity constrain and facilitate negative intra-gender behavior between women as active subjects. Differences and fragmentation between women, which threaten women's identity, have emerged throughout the elements we have discussed. This fragmentation between women and divisions in social relations constrains challenges to the status quo (Mavin, 2006a) and critically constrains normalizing processes for women leaders. For example, women engage in female misogyny when they respond negatively toward women leaders who do not meet expectations of the gender binary (for example, through emphasized femininity or solidarity behavior), and they are unaware of or fail to acknowledge the complexities of the gendered organizing context. These relations overly emphasize individual women's behavior or non-behavior (for example, naming women as "queen bees") as the root of the problem (Mavin, 2006a, 2006b, 2008). In doing so, women contribute to the maintenance of the "individual woman as problem," which perpetuates gendered hierarchies in organizations.

Such negative relations between and among women leaders can also facilitate intra-gender micro-violence as they negotiate elite leadership in competitive masculine contexts (Mavin et al., 2014a). A further example is how women's embodiment in elite leader roles can be constrained in a context of intra-gender relations (Mavin and Grandy, 2016a). Thus, explaining why women's negative relations occur in gendered contexts also helps us to understand how, as a consequence of the reproduction of gender, women are reminded of their subordinate position by themselves, by men, and by their women colleagues (Fotaki, 2011). Women fragment and separate from each other through processes of negative social relations, which can limit positive allegiances between women and reaffirm women's alliance with men in gender dynamics. Yet, dialectically, as women develop a sense of self in relation with others, the threat of their separation from other women also facilitates negative relations between them. This highlights how subjectivity is fragmented, unstable, and constructed dynamically through relations (Mumby and Ashcraft, 2006). From our theorizing, we argue that knowing more about women leaders' social relations with other women at the nexus of friendships, solidarity behaviors, competition, and collaboration is a fruitful research agenda to progress women leaders' normalization in senior positions.

A further contribution in theorizing women's negative intra-gender relations is to talk of the "dark side" of women leaders' relationships with each other at work. If, despite complexities in relations between men, their intra-gender relations can be characterized by competition, cooperation, friendship, and support – albeit potentially instrumentally

(Collinson and Hearn, 2005) – then the academy could usefully explore women's intra-gender relations in organizations and raise consciousness of gendered contexts possibly strengthening women's agency. Raising consciousness of men and women as to why women's negative intra-gender relations emerge can also circumvent the ways in which these relations are subsequently used against women to legitimize their minority status as leaders (Sheppard and Aquino, 2013).

We acknowledge that women leaders' negative intra-gender relations are not experienced by every woman or in the same way. We also recognize that power is intertwined with the construction and enactment of the consequences of these social relations as part of the gendering of organization. This theory gives regard to the gendered contexts within which social processes and co-constructed experiences take place, including agency, structure, culture, patriarchy, and hegemonic masculinity. Our theory also accounts for ambiguity, instability, and fluidization of gender roles; the doing of gender well and differently simultaneously; and the continued evaluation of men and women against gender binaries. Power is positioned as key to gendered contexts in that women leaders' structural positioning, and the power they hold and ways of doing gender they perform, influence the differential social relations between women. These gendered contexts are salient in how women's socially constructed intra-gender experiences are shaped, constructed, and constrained within them.

CONCLUSION

Women leaders' negative intra-gender relations are an under-researched area worthy of exploration. We acknowledge that, in speaking the unspeakable, we run the risk of perpetuating practices that blame women for these relations. However, in taking into account the complex and dialectical gendered contexts, practices, and processes through which these relations unfold, we offer an opportunity to raise consciousness and challenge ways of being, knowing, and doing. We are aware how these negative relations can be used against women to legitimize their minority status as leaders. Through our theory we see: (1) how women work to negotiate, resist, and comply with dialectical experiences; and (2) how women's negative intra-gender relations take place within gendered contexts that exacerbate differences between women.

As researchers we recognize that social constructions are neither arbitrary nor the product of consensus among social groups; rather, they are grounded in power and "reflect the ability of the powerful to 'fix' meaning in ways that privilege those forms of reality that serve the interests of the powerful" (Mumby, 1998, pp. 167–168). Our contribution is a theory of women leaders' negative intra-gender relations that offers new insights into gendered organizing processes, and it explains these social relations as grounded within gendered contexts where women engage in a dynamic interplay: a nexus of doing gender well and differently, homophily, homosociality, intra-gender competition, and female misogyny.

leaders, and women in film and television. The collection's contributing authors recognized the important role that the media plays in the socialization and construction processes that lead to a narrow range of representations of women as leaders; texts and imagery are considered as socially constitutive in shaping our understanding of what leadership is and who can or should be a leader. For example, Rippin et al. (2016), in their examination of women professionals, draw attention to how media creates a "performative heritage" of gender, where men and women are seen to produce and reproduce particular forms of leadership. This, in turn, has an effect on both men's and women's perceptions of women professionals, which leads to either the reinforcement or the development of stereotypes. The idea of a performative heritage of gender supports established research that points to women professionals' marginalization, such as a propensity for women to be maneuvered into roles with caring responsibilities that limit women's career choices and association with professional work (Kanter, 1977). This marginalization and the framing of women through gender is in contrast to the representation of men as genderless (Pantti, 2005); this is evident in the professional lives of women in the media, where only 37 percent of stories across newspapers, radio, and television are reported by women professionals (Macharia, 2015). The media as a workplace, therefore, contributes to and reinforces limited representations of women in professional roles (Elliott et al., 2016).

The volume (Elliott et al., 2016) also points to gendered media constructions of women executive leaders developed through dominant discourses that are effective in signaling the unacceptability and lack of credibility of women as leaders. Although more women are being appointed to company boards, women executives continue to be trivialized in the media through a focus on their visibility as token women and, conversely, their invisibility as leaders (Mavin et al., 2010). Panayiotou's (2016) examination of popular Hollywood films from the last 30 years explores the portrayal of executive women in organizational spaces. This research draws on Butler's (1990) concept of gender performativity, illustrating that gender is not something we are, but it is something we do. The doing of gender (West and Zimmerman, 1987) – how we perform gender as individuals and are in turn collectively informed by broader hegemonic discourses – influences who is given legitimacy to occupy particular organizational spaces. Collectively, the volume chapters highlight how a media spotlight on women leaders' appearance and their personal relationships serves to establish powerful discourses where women are positioned as "other" to the male norm and evaluated against their gender rather than their leadership potential. These dominant discourses (re)produced by the media through specific representations of women are therefore seen to perpetuate gendered stereotypes. In the next section we examine stereotypical representations and their effects in more depth.

THE MEDIA: GENDER, STEREOTYPES, AND METAPHORS

Stereotypes and metaphors used in the depiction of women's leadership and how they inform our understanding of women's leadership as a social, cultural, and political phenomenon remain relatively unexamined. In this section we are concerned with highlighting how metaphors and stereotypes act as verbal imagery. We do this as a means to examine the relationship between mundane micro-level everyday social practices, such as leadership, and "macro-level institutional processes of reproduction and transformation"

(Ashcraft and Mumby, 2004, p. 115), including media representations. Attending to the relationship between the communication of particular representations through imagery and the broader socio-cultural landscape, we view images of women's leadership as social representations and "complex sites of social interaction and struggle over meaning" (Guthey et al., 2008, p. 4). Thus, as Guthey et al. (2008) observe, such leadership imagery proposes "unarticulated theory" that shapes how "researchers 'see' leaders, followers, and organizations" (p. 4). We therefore ask: what can the stereotypes and metaphors used to depict women's leadership in the media reveal to us about understandings of women's leadership?

Stereotypes of gender have been defined as the "widely shared cultural beliefs about men and women" that act in society as "cultural instructions or rules for enacting gender" (Ridgeway, 2011, p. 57), "learned early in life" (Rudman and Phelan, 2010, p. 192), and which have emerged from traditional divisions of labor between men and women. The tenacity and pervasiveness of stereotypes in shaping social understandings of women's ability and suitability for certain occupations and roles is documented in a number of experimental studies in social psychology. Steinpreis et al. (1999), for example, asked research participants to rate the resumes of two fictitious applicants – one male and one female – for a tenured academic post. Apart from the name of the applicant, the CVs were identical; however, only around one-fourth of research participants deemed the woman worthy of the job (Steinpreis et al., 1999). Other studies have identified the concept of stereotype threat (Steele, 1997), where individuals stigmatized by the stereotype's negative associations are aware that they may be judged or treated "in terms of those negative stereotypes" (Davies et al., 2002, p. 1616). The role played by the environment, including media images (Davies et al., 2002; Davies et al., 2005), in priming gender roles has illustrated how stereotypes threaten the increase of women in leadership positions. The significance of gender stereotypes in understanding women's leadership, including barriers to their career progression and the ways in which women are positioned as leaders, is debated in Chapters 3, 17, and 28 of this *Handbook*. In relation to the media, Davies et al.'s (2005) study, for example, confirmed that, when exposed to commercials that stereotyped women, subsequent participation in a leadership task "undermined women's aspirations" (p. 276). In a meta-analysis of three research paradigms – Schein's (1973) "think male, think manager" paradigm, Powell and Butterfield's (1979) agency–communion paradigm, and the masculinity–femininity paradigm (Shinar, 1975) – Koenig et al. (2011) concluded that "the descriptive aspects of stereotyping make it difficult for women to gain access to leader roles" (p. 637). Their research observes how the "prescriptive aspects of stereotyping could produce conflicting expectations concerning how female leaders should behave – that is they should be agentic to fulfil the leader role but communal to fulfil the female gender role" (p. 637). This supports studies that demonstrate how stereotypes in the media are influential in forming social expectations of how women in business and organizational leadership roles should conduct themselves (Czarniawska and Rhodes, 2006).

Gendered stereotypes evoke "constraining role traps" (Lewis and Simpson, 2012, p. 6). Ridgeway (2011) observes how people use gender as a way to understand ourselves and others. Adopting this frame can fuel "powerful confirmation biases that help sustain gender stereotypes in the face of disconfirming experiences" (Ridgeway, 2011, p. 161). Even prior to Kanter's (1977) *Men and Women of the Corporation*, which identified metaphors of gendered stereotypes of women in the workplace (that is, "seductress," "pet," and "iron maiden,"), the metaphor of the "queen bee" was used to describe women who felt they had achieved success without women's liberation (Abramson, 1975; Staines et al., 1973). Research calls for such labels to be challenged to change negative perceptions of women in leadership roles and the gendered structures of organizations (Mavin, 2008).

Recent textual studies of the discursive construction of feminism in 998 United Kingdom and United States news items between 1968 and 2008 (Mendes, 2012) and discourses of feminism from a corpus of German and British newspapers from 1990 to 2009 (Jaworska and Krishnamurthy, 2012), draw our attention to the contemporary problematization of women in the media. Feminism, according to Jaworska and Krishnamurthy (2012), is regularly positioned as "outdated, and no longer relevant" (p. 423); it is marginalized in both the British and German press with a "climate of negativity surrounding the term" (p. 424). While optimistic that women's increasing involvement in the media will draw attention to feminist issues, Rhode (1995) nevertheless identifies persistent gender-related concerns, including the absence of women in the press, their "underrepresentation," and the "not-so-benign neglect of women's issues" (p. 686). She goes on to note four ways in which feminism is often caricatured and characterized. The first is through "demonization" of feminism as a cause (p. 692), and the second is through "personalization and trivialization" (p. 696) where feminist causes are portrayed as trivial and tied to particular individuals. The third is through "polarization" (p. 701), which establishes feminism in opposition to the mainstream. And finally, the fourth way that feminism is caricatured and characterized is by "blurring the focus" (p. 703), where the media seems to undermine feminist causes and objectives to focus on what individuals should do rather than advocating social change.

Equally, metaphors mobilized to symbolize women leaders' struggle to attain and maintain leadership roles can also reinforce stereotypes of women leaders' competence (see Chapter 3 of this *Handbook* for additional details about metaphors). Ryan and Haslam (2005), for example, have been forced to respond to misinterpretations of the "glass cliff" metaphor. Responding to Judge's (2003) view of a correlation between a company's lower share performance and the number of women on its board, Ryan and Haslam (2005) illustrate that a drop in a company's share price and overall performance often led to a woman's appointment to a leadership position. Defending the metaphor of the glass cliff to describe evidence of the precariousness of women's leadership roles, they emphasize the need to pay attention to the broader context of women's leadership appointments – such as social, organizational, and psychological processes – and not solely financial data (Ryan and Haslam, 2009). These social processes include the perpetuation of stereotypical images of leadership by the media.

As we noted in earlier work (Stead and Elliott, 2009), a number of metaphors and stereotypes have been used to symbolize women and leadership, and these are regularly referred to and reproduced in the media. In this previous examination, we argued that stereotypes and metaphors can both help and hinder women's achievements and can exclude more detailed considerations of women leaders' workplace context. This analysis illuminated two aspects. First, it highlighted how metaphors are used in the media to characterize the nature of women's leadership, including glass ceilings, glass walls, and glass cliffs. And, second, the analysis illustrated the stereotypical ways in which women leaders are categorized in the media. These categorizations include how women are portrayed as having to be like (or tougher than) men (for example, queen bee, iron maiden), and how the ideal women leader can also be positioned as one who surrenders herself in the name of the greater good (selfless heroine). We debate the implications and effects for our understanding of women as leaders from the use of such metaphors and, in particular, we draw attention to how associated imagery excludes important considerations of social, political, and cultural context. We therefore aim to illuminate the relationship between everyday micro-level social practices of representing women's leadership through metaphor, stereotype, and macro-level processes that (re)produce and transform assumptions and views (Ashcraft and Mumby, 2004). These include organizational and institutional processes and practices that operate within perceptions of leadership as a male activity (Wajcman, 1998) and which are reproduced and represented through media imagery.

IMAGERY CHARACTERIZING THE NATURE OF WOMEN'S LEADERSHIP: GLASS CEILINGS, GLASS WALLS, AND GLASS CLIFFS

An enduring metaphor developed to explain why women remain under-represented in organizational leadership roles and the extent to which gender discrimination is embedded in organizations (Meyerson and Fletcher, 2000) is that of the glass ceiling, sometimes referred to as the glass wall (Eriksson-Zetterquist and Styhre, 2008). While studies that examine the notion of the glass ceiling largely recognize a substantial increase in the number of women working in leadership positions since the 1960s (Davidson and Cooper, 1992), there is also acknowledgement that despite women's increasing participation in the workforce, the glass ceiling holds value as a metaphor worthy of empirical investigation, as noted earlier in this *Handbook*, and in particular in Chapter 3. For example, in the United Kingdom (UK) the Cranfield School of Management's *Female Financial Times Stock Exchange (FTSE) 100 Report* (Vinnicombe et al., 2015) observes that in 2015 women still hold fewer than 25 percent of board roles in the top 100 Financial Times Stock Exchange (FTSE 100) companies. Noting some progress in the number of women on FTSE 100 boards, the UK Equality and Human Rights Commission (2016) observes that this progress masks the failure of companies outside the top 100 to increase women's board representation partly, they suggest, due to widespread use of "old boys'" networks when appointing to board positons (Tutchell and Edmonds, 2015).

Although a well-established metaphor frequently used by the media to draw attention to how women face more career barriers than men (Simpson and Altman, 2000), the glass ceiling as a metaphor is nonetheless critiqued for its simplification of the barriers that women face. Connell (2006), for instance, argues that the glass ceiling approach is an insufficient, "categorical" approach to gender that assumes "two fixed categories of persons – men and women – defined by biology" (p. 838). This approach, Connell suggests, ignores gender as a "dynamic system," and obscures the gendering of organizations including the "patterns of interactions and relationship" (p. 838) that stand above differences – perceived or otherwise – between individuals. The frequent adoption of the glass ceiling metaphor in the media to draw attention to continuing gender inequality at leadership levels in organizations is therefore risky. Although it highlights the difficulties

expected to teach, enable, and empower others without getting anything in return, expected to work interdependently while others do not adopt a similar stance, expected to work mutually in non-mutual situations, and expected to practice less hierarchical forms of interacting even in traditionally hierarchical contexts. (p. 655)

Women leaders viewed as selfless heroines are equated with the organization's caregivers (Elliott and Stead, 2008), and stand in danger of being exploited. What might be regarded as post-heroic leadership characteristics, such as enabling and empowering others, might then be seen as "natural" to women and therefore not worthy of reward or leadership status.

IMPLICATIONS AND CONSEQUENCES

Implications arising from the resilience of stereotypes and metaphors associated with women's leadership are multilayered. Discussions regarding the images of glass ceilings and glass cliffs draw attention to the challenges women face in achieving leadership positions (Stead and Elliott, 2009). They highlight the low number of women in leadership roles and also direct our attention to an uncomfortable environment for women leaders where gender stereotyping leads to persistent metaphors that continue to pervade the media and popular culture; if we had gender equity we would be less likely to hear of queen bees (Gatrell and Cooper, 2007). The stereotypes we examine here are important barometers of how women enact and negotiate leadership and how women's leadership is perceived and received. Images associated with the selfless heroine stereotype highlight positive aspects of "feminine" leadership such as empathy. The iron maiden stereotype illustrates that women can be assertive and competent. The consequences arising from these representations in the media are significant in drawing attention to the very different experiences that women leaders encounter in addition to the difficulties they face in achieving equality with men leaders. However, the principal utility of such representations and their casual everyday articulation is how they communicate and reflect wider social understandings of gender.

By adopting a view of gender that recognizes how it operates in different ways at a number of levels (Wharton, 2005), we can study the effects of such stereotypes. The implications of stereotypical images that are used in the media are powerful; the visual imagery they invoke communicates expectations regarding women leaders' performances and identities.

One level at which gender might be understood is as residing in personalities, characteristics, and attributes. Here, gender operates at an individual level and in relation to particular traits or attributes that individuals possess (for example, women as caring and men as assertive) (Wharton, 2005). Research demonstrates how men are often advantaged if they take on female qualities (Swan, 2006), while women who take on masculine qualities – as represented by the iron maiden stereotype – are not similarly advantaged. For women, displaying masculine qualities can be highly problematic (Knights and Kerfoot, 2004). This may bolster male domination through the use of masculine behaviors to assert leadership. It also may serve to reinforce the gender binary as women risk being labeled as untrue to their gender if they do not display qualities associated with femininity.

Portrayed as selfless heroines in the media, women leaders might also be considered in relation to women who put post-heroic leadership approaches into practice (Fletcher, 2004). Post-heroic leadership practices, including the sharing of power and working to develop environments that facilitate collective learning, are, Fletcher (2004) argues, relational practices conflated with femininity and associated with the selflessness of mothering. This raises difficulties for women leaders in relation to post-heroic practices in several ways. First, the expectation that women behave in a selfless way can render their leadership practice invisible; they are, after all, "doing what they always do," and this is a form of leadership that does not generally receive media coverage. Men who perform relational leadership practice, however, may be recognized and rewarded as attempting to do something new. The association of the post-heroic with mothering renders the reciprocity of relational practice invisible or makes it "disappear" (Fletcher, 2004, p. 655). The principles upon which understandings of post-heroic leadership are based – the interaction and mutuality of engagement and empowerment – are constrained in their social attribution to either men or women. In enacting such principles, men leaders may be seen therefore to be doing leadership. Women performing such principles, on the other hand, may be viewed as just doing what is natural to their sex category.

If we take a view of gender as a "master identity" with associated cultural meanings, which cuts across all situations and "has no specific site or organizational context" (West and Zimmerman, 1987, p. 128), we are encouraged to analyze how roles, such as leadership, are constituted through interaction. This draws our attention to where and how men and women interact in a way perceived as appropriate to their gender (that is, how they "do gender") (Wharton, 2005). Seen through this prism, the image of women in leadership in the media as selfless heroine might be considered appropriate in that selfless giving is seen as doing (feminine) gender. Images of women leaders as either queen bees or iron maidens are, by contrast, more disruptive as women are deemed not to be "doing gender" appropriately. Queen bees, who are depicted as selfish and ambitious, do not do their gender due to their ambition and perceived lack of selflessness. Iron maidens do not do gender as they seek to play men at their own game by adopting masculine traits in their leadership practice and interactions with men. Stereotypes of women leaders may either disrupt or confirm particular leadership constructions. In assigning these stereotypes to women leaders they are often assessed as "out of place" (West and Zimmerman, 2005, p. 77), as they are operating outside the restricted range of what is regarded as appropriate behavior for their sex. The image of a woman dressed in traditional male office attire holding a whip serves to highlight her otherness. This reinforces a view that regards women leaders as unnatural inhabitants of leadership roles, unless they interact in ways that are viewed as traditionally feminine, which of themselves are not seen as leaderful. This, then, has the effect of maintaining the view of women as different and deficient (Wajcman, 1998).

Gender can also be understood as embedded in and reproduced through social practices and structures as well as organizational and institutional cultures (Wharton, 2005). Wajcman (1998) argues that "the dominant symbolism of corporations is suffused with masculine images" (p. 49). Ideas of success, therefore, equate to being "tough, forceful leaders" (p. 49). Wajcman's study demonstrates how gender is reproduced in the workplace by formal and informal organizational decision-making processes (for example, recruitment and promotion procedures), based on assumptions which perceive managers and leaders as male.

With work and organizational life dominated by masculine archetypes, the metaphors of glass ceilings and glass cliffs can have the effect of keeping women from achieving leadership roles. Used in the media, these metaphors reinforce that women have to be tougher, work harder, and overcome more obstacles to prove themselves more competent than their male counterparts. Although many women leaders would recognize this as close to their experience, we suggest that we need more positive representations and images that reflect women's leadership experiences in a deeper, more nuanced way (Stead and Elliott, 2009).

Negative stereotypes reinforced in the media draw attention to the lack of acknowledgement given to the complexity faced by women in leadership roles. Stereotypical representations commonly ignore the social identity (that is, sex, race, class, and organizational role) of the leader and the social setting (for example, social, cultural, historical, and organizational environments) in which women are practicing leadership (Fletcher, 2004). Some media representations are pointed in their reference to social identity and setting, such as the example of Margaret Thatcher as the Iron Lady. Nevertheless, such representations remain broad generalizations. As an example of verbal imagery that conjures the vision of a woman in man's clothing, the suggestion is that only a man – or, at a stretch, a woman who acts like a man – can lead a nation.

CONCLUSIONS AND FUTURE CHALLENGES

In this chapter we have suggested that a media focus on women leaders combined with limited in-depth research on women's practice of leadership leads to individualistic and stereotypical representations. Drawing on previous analyses (Stead and Elliott, 2009), we have shown how metaphors that explain organizational barriers provide the context for recurring and persistent stereotypes of women leaders present in the media, including those of queen bee, iron maiden, and selfless heroine. Our critical exploration of these metaphors points to a resilient leadership norm associated with being male and maintaining women as "out of place" (West and Zimmerman, 2005, p. 77). Women are not perceived to be as credible as male leaders, and in taking on a leadership role they are also seen to be operating beyond the bounds of acceptable female behavior. In order to be recognized and accepted as leaders, women must then "negotiate their femininity and sexuality" (Hughes, 2002, p. 41). The recurrent metaphor of iron maiden illustrates well how women are in a double-bind situation. By displaying feminine characteristics, they do not fit the perceived leadership norm, yet by exhibiting masculine characteristics they do not fit the perceived female gender role that defers to male authority (Powell and Butterfield, 2003). The media's reproduction of these stereotypes, therefore, sustains women's leadership as outside of the norm, continuing to represent women as subordinate to men (Knights and Kerfoot, 2004) and affirming an understanding of leaders as men with associated "male" characteristics (Indvik, 2003).

Our analysis illustrates the need to develop research that can more accurately reflect the complexities of women's leadership practice, the socio-cultural context in which women lead, which includes the media's representation of women leaders. We suggest two strands of further research. First, we observe a lack of research that examines women's experiences of being a leader and of doing leadership. Exploring the mundane and the everyday can provide fresh insight into the ways women negotiate leadership and their femininity in order to advance as leaders and to be seen and accepted as authoritative and credible. Providing detailed qualitative research of women's doing of leadership offers the potential for understandings that may disrupt and unsettle traditional stereotypes. Second, the emerging literature on women's leadership and the media illuminates the media and popular culture as a rich site for further research. Investigating the ways in which women's leadership is constructed and represented through newspapers, magazines, television, and film enables exploration of how women are envisaged, positioned, and framed as leaders. This may provide a contextual and contemporary map of how women's leadership is perceived and understood. These two strands of research are not necessarily distinct, but they offer the opportunity to integrate and contrast women's everyday doing of leadership with social representations. In this way, we create the possibility of presenting more nuanced understandings of women's leadership practice and the sociocultural environments in which they enact leadership.

NOTE

*   Earlier versions of some sections of this chapter have appeared in Stead and Elliott (2009).

REFERENCES

Abramson, J. (1975). *The Invincible Woman: Discrimination in the Academic Profession.* London, UK: Jossey-Bass.

Ashcraft, K.L., and Mumby, D.K. (2004). *Reworking Gender: A Feminist Communicology of Organization.* Thousand Oaks, CA: Sage.

Billing, Y.D., and Alvesson, M. (2000). Questioning feminine leadership. *Gender, Work and Organization, 7*(3), 144–157.

Butler, J. (1990). *Gender Trouble: Feminism and the Subversion of Identity.* New York, NY: Routledge.

Coleman, L., and Pinder, S. (2010). What were they thinking? Reports from interviews with senior finance executives in the lead-up to the GFC. *Applied Financial Economics, 20*(1/2), 7–14.

Connell, R. (2006). Glass ceilings or gendered institutions? Mapping the gender regimes of public sector worksites. *Public Administration Review, 66*(6), 837–849.

Czarniawska, B., and Rhodes, C. (2006). Strong plots, popular culture in management practice and theory. In P. Gagliardi and B. Czarniawska (Eds), *Management Education and Humanities* (pp. 195–218). Cheltenham, UK and Northampton, MA, USA: Edward Elgar Publishing.

Davidson, M., and Cooper, C. (1992). *Shattering the Glass Ceiling: The Woman Manager.* London, UK: Sage.

Davies, P.G., Spencer, S.J., Quinn, D.M., and Gerhardstein, R. (2002). Consuming images: How television commercials that elicit stereotype threat can restrain women academically and professionally. *Personality and Psychology Bulletin, 28*(12), 1615–1628.

Davies, P.G., Spencer, S.J., and Steele, C. (2005). Clearing the air: Identity safety moderates the effects of stereotype threat on women's leadership aspirations. *Journal of Personality and Social Psychology, 88*(2), 276–287.

Davies-Netzley, S.A. (1998). Women above the glass ceiling: Perceptions on corporate mobility and strategies for success. *Gender and Society, 12*(3), 339–355.

Dundes, L. (2001). Disney's modern heroine Pocahontas: Revealing age-old gender stereotypes and role discontinuity under a façade of liberation. *Social Science Journal, 38*(3), 353–365.

Elliott, C., and Stead, V. (2008). Learning from leading women's experience: Towards a sociological understanding. *Leadership, 4*(2), 159–180.

Elliott, C., Stead, V., Mavin, S., and Williams, J. (2016). *Gender, Media, and Organization: Challenging Mis(s) representations of Women Leaders and Managers.* Charlotte, NC: Information Age Publishing.

Equality and Human Rights Commission. (2016). Inquiry warns "inexcusable and unacceptable" variation in progress for women on boards in FTSE companies. April 15. Retrieved from http://www.equalityhumanrights.

23. Advancing women through developmental relationships

Wendy M. Murphy, Kerry Roberts Gibson, and Kathy E. Kram

The business case for greater representation of women in leadership roles has been steadily accumulating evidence, with several studies finding that organizations perform better (Curtis et al., 2014; Lublin, 2015; Noland et al., 2016) and are more innovative when they have more women at the top (Østergaard et al., 2011; Talke et al., 2010). Performance benefits are particularly striking, as Dezsö and Ross (2012) explain:

> We find that, ceteris paribus, a given firm generates on average 1% (or over $40 million) more economic value with at least one woman on its top management team than without any women on its top management team, and enjoys superior accounting performance. (p. 1084)

However, women face difficult odds for advancement compared to men, who are five times more likely to reach chief executive officer (CEO) from the executive committee level (Devillard et al., 2012).

Research suggests that the accumulation of both human capital (that is, individual knowledge, skills, and abilities) and social capital (that is, those resources embedded in work relationships) are necessary for leadership development (Bunker et al., 2010; Day, 2001). A primary challenge for women is a lack of access to informal networks, which includes those developmental relationships that provide the mentoring and sponsorship needed to propel women to the upper echelons (Hewlett, 2013; Ibarra, 1997; Ibarra et al., 2013). Over the past 30 years, mentoring scholarship has shifted from focusing on the traditional, dyadic mentor–mentee relationship to demonstrating the need for a developmental network: a set of people who take an active interest in and action to advance focal individuals' careers and personal growth (Higgins and Kram, 2001). Studies have shown that support from a developmental network improves outcomes for protégés beyond that of a single mentor, including heightened compensation and promotions (Higgins and Thomas, 2001; Murphy and Kram, 2010; Seibert et al., 2001), personal learning (Lankau and Scandura, 2002), performance (Yip, 2015), and work satisfaction (Higgins, 2000). Developmental networks can provide an array of support functions including career and psychosocial support (Kram, 1985) as well as holding behaviors that can offset and mitigate the challenges preventing high-potential women from reaching top leadership roles (Chandler and Murphy, forthcoming).

Individual leadership skills are honed through on-the-job experience (Yip and Wilson, 2010), which includes internalizing a leadership identity (DeRue and Ashford, 2010). Leaders must have the intrapersonal competence to form an accurate model of themselves (Gardner, 1993) and to engage in identity development (Hall, 2004). In order for women to ascend successfully to leadership roles, they must be able to envision themselves as leaders

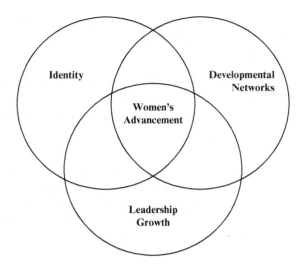

Figure 23.1   Conceptual map for women's advancement through relationships

and to experiment with provisional selves as they move up the hierarchy (Ibarra, 1999). The leader identity construction process is fundamentally social. Identities are claimed and sustained through relational role requirements that form a set of behavioral expectations giving purpose and meaning to the role (Sluss and Ashforth, 2007). Furthermore, a leader's identity is tied to her purpose (Ibarra et al., 2013). High-quality relationships with developers can support this process of leadership identification; however, women often lack access to intra-organizational role models who can help them develop an authentic style that is accepted by others (Ely and Rhode, 2010).

In this chapter, we integrate the literatures on leadership, identity, and positive relationships at work to provide a foundation for understanding how to advance women through developmental relationships (see the conceptual map, Figure 23.1). We suggest that five specific types of relationships within a developmental network are critical for growing women leaders: mentors, sponsors, peers, executive coaches, and learning partners. This set of developmental relationships facilitates the complex individual and relational learning women require to build human and social capital as leaders in organizations. We discuss strategies for individual women crafting these developmental relationships and how organizations can create a climate that fosters these connections.

CHALLENGES FOR WOMEN'S LEADERSHIP GROWTH

The unique challenges women leaders face in their efforts to reach the upper echelons in organizations (e.g., Catalyst, 2007; Devillard et al., 2012; Hewlett et al., 2010) explain why women are still significantly under-represented in top management teams and on boards. The reality is that women face both structural and perceptual barriers that exclude them from consideration for top roles and from the sponsorship that gains them the necessary visibility and access (Ibarra, 1997; Ibarra et al., 2013; McPherson et al., 2001; Whitely et al., 1991). However, support from developers in their network can assist them in overcoming these challenges (Chandler and Murphy, forthcoming).

Structural barriers include exclusion from informal networks at work, a lack of sponsors, and a lack of role models, all contributing to work practices that have unintended negative consequences for women. For example, studies on informal social networks in the workplace highlight that women have limited access to key networks and therefore create different network structures that are less able to provide the benefits gained by their white male counterparts (Ibarra, 1993, 1995). Women are less likely than men to report having sponsors, who are critical for raising their visibility and advocating for promotions (Hewlett et al., 2010). In addition, women lack role models to help them own a style that is authentically theirs and accepted by others (Ibarra et al., 2013), and whose style and behaviors they can emulate or learn from. Indeed, studies show that women of color face a "double disadvantage" that leads to the greatest amount of exclusion in organizations (Bell, 1990; Murrell, 2000). Finally, second-generation gender bias identifies these as subtle, often "invisible barriers for women arising from cultural assumptions as well as organizational structures, practices, and patterns of interaction that inadvertently benefit men while putting women at a disadvantage" (Ibarra et al., 2013, p. 64). Included among this list is that career paths are often gendered, designed to fit men's lives when women were a very small portion of the workforce. Examples include formal rotations in sales or operations that are more likely to be held by men, or international assignments assuming a "trailing spouse."

Perceptual challenges include being evaluated against a white, male leadership standard, the double-bind dilemma, and a lack of interpersonal comfort in cross-gender relationships (Chandler and Murphy, forthcoming). In work settings, the two primary interpersonal dimensions of warmth and competence are competing stereotypes; a particular challenge for women leaders when women are expected to be warm, whereas leaders are expected to be competent but not warm (Fiske et al., 2002). Research on this "double-bind" for women leaders suggests that women who are evaluated on the basis of a masculine standard face unappealing choices in determining how to act as leaders. Catalyst (2007) identified three such choices, all of which can damage women's ability to move toward the C-suite: being either too tough or too soft; being perceived as either likeable or competent, but not both; and receiving fewer rewards and experiencing tougher standards vis-à-vis men. Lastly, research on interpersonal comfort suggests that diversified mentoring relationships between dissimilar individuals have less identification and rapport due to lack of shared social identities (e.g., Allen et al., 2005). In particular, cross-gender relationships often lack closeness due to fear of sexual innuendos and rumors that may result (Hurley, 1996).

Overcoming these structural and perceptual barriers, as discussed in Part III of this *Handbook*, is critical for women's growth and development enabling them to advance as leaders. Leadership development means helping people learn from their work (Day, 2001), and since developmental relationships are by definition learning relationships that enable career growth and advancement (Kram, 1985; Murphy and Kram, 2014), these relationships are essential for advancing women leaders.

IDENTITY AND IDENTIFICATION AS A LEADER

Relationships play an integral role in the formation of an individual's identity. Scholars identified the importance of relationships in individual identity development in the early 1900s, with the concept of the "looking glass self," where those around us reflect who we are (Cooley, 1902). This phenomenon still occurs today as women (and men) define themselves based on how those around them tell them who they are. Given this reality, the developmental network plays a critical role in shaping how an individual crafts her identity.

One of the key reasons that relationships are so important to identity formation is the underlying need to belong. The need to belong is a fundamental human motivation that details how individuals need to be part of "lasting, positive and significant relationships" (Baumeister and Leary, 1995, p. 497). As a result of this inherent need to belong, researchers have found that relationships change how we process information (Reis et al., 2000). That is, how behavior is interpreted and how attributions are assigned often depends upon the specific relationship in which it occurs rather than an objective assessment (Eberly et al., 2011; Reis et al., 2000). As a result, the feedback and cues a woman receives from key relational others plays a significant role in how she crafts her own identity (Ashforth et al., 2015).

To further explain this process, the level of relational identification within each developmental relationship must be considered. Relational identification is "the extent to which one defines oneself in terms of a given role-relationship" (Sluss and Ashforth, 2007, p. 11). Whether a woman chooses her level of relational identification consciously or subconsciously, the degree to which a woman incorporates a given relationship into her identity will determine how much influence the relationship has on her personal identity (Ashforth et al., 2015; Humberd and Rouse, 2015). As such, to create strong identities as leaders, women need a plethora of relationships where the relational other portrays (that is, projects back) a view in which the woman is able to see herself as a leader. Since one of the largest obstacles to the development of women is the internalization of a leadership identity, relationships that reflect back versions of themselves that include leadership identities are essential in supporting this process.

The individuals that women include in their developmental networks are important for all of the reasons delineated above; in addition, a rich body of literature shows that past relationships impact the future. That is, who women surround themselves with today plays a critical role in the determination of who women are, the way they process information, and their expectations of themselves in the future (Madsen, 2008; Reis et al., 2000). The impact of relationships today on future versions of one's self is one of the most overlooked areas of relationship research. Earlier research has described how individuals create both relational schemas and relational scripts in which patterns of interactions and expectations evolve (Andersen and Chen, 2002; Baldwin, 1992). These earlier relational schemas and scripts serve to guide future interaction patterns. As a result, our future actions and behaviors are determined by our current experiences, making early developmental relationships critical in whether or not women will ultimately rise to higher levels of leadership. In light of this, women may be in particular need of strong developmental networks, as compared to men, depending upon cultural and social expectations from childhood that may hinder the development of women as leaders (Eagly, 1987).

Peers

Peer relationships were first identified in Kram's (1985) research as an important source of developmental support. These relationships are by definition between equal colleagues in terms of age, status, or work role in the organization, though external peers may also be important (see the "Learning Partners" section below). A peer relationship can provide career functions including information sharing, career strategizing, and job-related feedback, as well as psychosocial functions including friendship, confirmation, emotional support, and personal feedback (Kram and Isabella, 1985). The quality of peer relationships range from purely instrumental – those providing informational resources only – to high-quality peers who are capable of providing the full range of support. High-quality or "special" peers offer a safe relational space in which to share dilemmas and vulnerabilities (Kram and Isabella, 1985; Ragins and Verbos, 2007). Though peers are less often studied, they are the most available and accessible developmental relationships (Murphy and Kram, 2014; Parker et al., 2008) and should be considered a critical part of a developing leader's network.

Peer developers are often colleagues in an individual's immediate work team, in equivalent roles within a different functional or geographic area, or in roles that are a step ahead or a step behind in the organizational hierarchy. Peers are more accessible than other potential developers in a hierarchical organization because other relationships may involve complicating power dynamics, such as supervisory authority or task interdependencies (Parker et al., 2014). Because they are at the same level, peers also tend to be more approachable and available. Within developmental networks, the existence of one peer relationship that provides psychosocial support significantly improves work satisfaction (Higgins, 2000). Peer colleagues who are also friends create stronger ties over time, reinforcing the value of the relationship and providing efficiency when women have developmental needs.

One specific type of peer, the "step-ahead mentor," may be uniquely positioned to meet women leaders' developmental needs. Step-ahead mentors are peers who are more experienced or in a position one level ahead of the focal woman in the organization. Research shows that step-ahead mentors provide more career support and role modeling than equivalent peers (Ensher et al., 2001). Thus, step-ahead peers can be essential in teaching protégés the necessary skills, getting them access to resources, and connecting them to key people to get their job done (Murphy and Kram, 2014). Because of the lack of role models for women in most organizational hierarchies, high-quality step-ahead mentors (of either gender) may play a critical role in assisting women to see themselves as leaders and imagine themselves succeeding at a higher level in the workplace.

Executive Coach

The coaching relationship can be an important developmental relationship for advancing one's career, particularly for women. Coaching can be described as a dialogue in which the woman receiving coaching is able to reflect on her own process and actions in such a way that enables her to see how she can improve her own effectiveness (Hunt and Weintraub, 2011). This dialogue is established through strategic questions from the coach to enable effective self-reflection on the part of the woman leader and, when necessary, may include appropriate feedback in the form of observations of the woman's behavior as observed by the coach (Hunt and Weintraub, 2011). Because the job of the coach is to focus exclusively on the development of the employee, the normal reciprocity necessary for effective workplace relationships is removed, yet the relationship can still offer an important high-quality connection for the focal woman (e.g., Dutton and Heaphy, 2003). With this singular focus on the individual woman, the time invested with the coach is more efficient than with other potential members of the woman's developmental network.

Perhaps most importantly, coaches offer a safe environment in which women can focus on either acquiring or improving a particular skill set or cultivating the self-reflection skills necessary for their own growth and development (Murphy and Kram, 2014). Good coaches can help both current and future women leaders self-reflect through the use of strategic questions so that the women can identify what is preventing them from moving forward in their leadership development. As addressed earlier in this chapter, women often struggle the most with their own identity as a leader, making the coaching relationship a particularly safe place for them to explore these challenges. That is, because the coach represents an objective third party, an executive coach provides the focal woman with a new lens through which to view herself as a leader.

Because the coaching relationship centers on honest, authentic self-reflection, trust with the coach becomes one of the most important attributes of an effective coaching relationship. The necessity of trust hinges on the self-disclosure inherent to self-reflection. Self-disclosure occurs when an individual shares personally relevant information about herself (Cozby, 1973). As previous research has shown, self-disclosure is a critical mechanism for relationship development and can increase liking between relationship members (Collins and Miller, 1994). However, other research has highlighted the risks of self-disclosure, especially in light of status differences or the presence of stigmas (Phillips et al., 2009; Ragins, 2008). Given this, woman leaders need to be especially cognizant of the coach's willingness to keep the information shared between woman leader and coach as confidential. Without this sense of safety, that what is shared within the coaching relationship will remain within the coaching relationship, the potential to enhance the focal woman's leadership development will never be realized.

The benefits of the coaching relationship can vary depending on whether the coach is internal to the organization or external. If the coach is internal to the organization, then the coach's insights into the culture of the organization – the accepted norms of how work is done within the specific organization – can be essential, especially for newcomers (e.g., Rollag, 2004). Having a specific individual internal to the organization to guide a woman leader in the "ins and outs" of the internal procedures and the customs unique to the given organization can be invaluable. Assuming the internal coach is well-respected within the organization, they will have the ability to help teach the woman leader how to navigate the nuances and unwritten expectations of the organization that are critical to internal advancement.

If the coach is external to the organization, then the focal woman has the opportunity to explore concerns and challenges she is facing without any fear of repercussions for not already knowing the answer to the questions she is asking, or for not having all the necessary skills (technical or interpersonal) expected at her level. Having a coach external to the organization offers the same exclusive focus on the development of the focal woman without any of the risks of self-disclosure inherent within an internal coaching relationship. In other words, an external coach has less ability to harm the focal woman's reputation within the organization, simply because the external coach is not part of the organization. Any bias or status loss that could occur following self-disclosure would not be relevant to the advancement of the woman leader because presumably the external coach would not have any role in determining promotions or advancement for the focal woman.

Regardless of whether the coach is external or internal to the organization, the coaching relationship offers a specific opportunity for women to focus exclusively on their own development. As such, the coaching relationship offers a unique and important role in the developmental network for current and future women leaders.

Learning Partners

Learning partners represent an often overlooked component of the focal woman's developmental network. Learning partners represent individuals in the woman leader's network that are focused on learning and growing together (Murphy and Kram, 2014). As a result, these members of the developmental network often originate from life outside of work: relationships with a spouse, neighbor, friend, or even parents. Earlier research has shown that developmental relationships from outside of work contribute to increased levels of life and career satisfaction (Murphy and Kram, 2010). One of the reasons that learning partners play such a critical role in the development of women is that they contribute psychosocial support.

Psychosocial support occurs when the leader receives counseling, friendship, and validation (Kram and Isabella, 1985). Receiving psychosocial support from relationships outside of work is critical for women because of the objectivity and external perspective that relationships outside of work provide. These different viewpoints can often help women to reframe the challenges they are facing within the workplace. Furthermore, knowing that the focal woman is appreciated and validated regardless of what happens at work can help fulfill her innate need to belong, especially when facing particularly challenging times at work (Baumeister and Leary, 1995). By having the need to belong fulfilled outside of the workplace, women are in a better position to act purposefully at work, which can lead to better decision-making.

As such, we encourage women to seek relationships with learning partners outside their workplace. When the learning partner is in a similar life-stage as the focal woman, they offer camaraderie and empathy as well as an outsider's perspective on experiences from within the organization. Even if the learning partner works in a different industry or is at a somewhat different level within the organizational hierarchy of the learning partner's respective organization, finding commonality in the struggles shared with her learning partner can offer the necessary validation and courage to take action on her own behalf.

PRACTICAL IMPLICATIONS

This chapter integrates literature on women in leadership, identity, mentoring, and positive relationships at work to propose advancing women through developmental relationships. We describe how a robust developmental network can be critical for women to overcome the structural and perceptual challenges in ascending to leadership roles (Murphy and Kram, 2014). Developers help women to improve skills, form an authentic leadership identity, and connect with other key senior leaders. Specifically, we utilize current scholarly research to highlight five developmental relationships – mentors, sponsors, peers, executive coaches, and learning partners – who together provide the full range of career support, psychosocial support, and role modeling essential for helping women navigate into leadership positions. Developmental networks must be responsive to the needs of the focal individual and the organization in which they are embedded, requiring regular attention to the composition of this critical support system.

Our view is that women must be strategic in creating their own developmental network to ensure the necessary personal growth and development that advancing their career requires (Murphy and Kram, 2014; Shen et al., 2015). That is, women must carefully select who is in their development network, not just simply have a developmental network. By being intentional and strategic in building developmental relationships, women can ensure they connect with individuals who will enable them to grow into the leaders they want to be. Though it is possible for a woman to become a leader without such relationships, research consistently shows that the likelihood of success is great if they do (Dobrow et al., 2012).

Women need to continually reassess the health of the relationships within their developmental network. As addressed earlier, women can choose how intently to identify within a relationship, or how much a given relationship defines them (Sluss and Ashforth, 2007). These varying levels of relational identification determine how much influence a given relationship can have on the focal woman. The danger occurs when women choose higher levels of relational identification with unhealthy or dysfunctional developmental network relationships. To mitigate this risk, women will benefit from continually evaluating which developmental relationships give them energy, versus cost them energy (Dutton and Heaphy, 2003). Developmental relationships that do not provide support, encouragement, or leadership identity are not healthy. As such, women should consider disengaging from any developmental relationship that is not enhancing their growth as leaders.

Above all, women need to prepare now for the leadership level they want in the future by crafting a developmental network that will help get them there. That is, it is critical for women to spend time today considering the future-self they desire. By reflecting on their future-self, women will have a clearer understanding of who they are looking for when seeking individuals to be part of their developmental network. Women who surround themselves today with people similar to who they want to be in the future will have the greatest chance of becoming the leader they want to be.

Women are more likely to be able to create and sustain developmental relationships in a workplace with a developmental culture. A developmental culture is one that combines challenging, meaningful work with support and caring for employees (Hall and Mirvis, 1996). Organizations that foster a developmental culture design jobs that provide learning opportunities, value employees' efforts to coach and develop others, and allocate resources to training and initiatives that enable individuals to form collaborative relationships with others (Murphy and Kram, 2014). In order to cultivate a developmental culture, leaders must recognize the critical role that networks play in developing women leaders, and shift their mindset such that development is an important part of everyday interactions. Regular assessment of current human resource and people development practices, as

Scandura, T.A., and Ragins, B.R. (1993). The effects of sex and gender role orientation on mentorship in male-dominated occupations. *Journal of Vocational Behavior, 43*(3), 251–265. doi:10.1006/jvbe.1993.1046.

Seibert, S.E., Kraimer, M.L. and Liden, R.C. (2001). A social capital theory of career success. *Academy of Management Journal, 44*(2), 219–237.

Shen, Y., Cotton, R.D., and Kram, K.E. (2015). Assembling your personal board of advisors. *MIT Sloan Management Review, 56*(3), 81–92.

Sluss, D.M., and Ashforth, B.E. (2007). Relational identity and identification: Defining ourselves through work relationships. *Academy of Management Review, 32*(1), 9–32. doi:10.5465/amr.2007.23463672.

Stephens, J.P., Heaphy, E. and Dutton, J. (2012). High quality connections. In K. Cameron and G. Spreitzer (Eds), *The Oxford Handbook of Positive Organizational Scholarship* (pp. 385–399). New York, NY: Oxford University Press.

Talke, K., Salomo, S., and Rost, K. (2010). How top management team diversity affects innovativeness and performance via the strategic choice to focus on innovation fields. *Research Policy, 39*(7), 907–918. doi:10.1016/j.respol.2010.04.001.

Thomas, D.A. (1990). The impact of race on managers' experiences of developmental relationships (mentoring and sponsorship): An intra-organizational study. *Journal of Organizational Behavior, 11*(6), 479–492. doi:10.1002/job.4030110608.

Turban, D.B., Dougherty, T.W., and Lee, F.K. (2002). Gender, race, and perceived similarity effects in developmental relationships: The moderating role of relationship duration. *Journal of Vocational Behavior, 61*(2), 240–262. doi:10.1006/jvbe.2001.1855.

Whitely, W., Dougherty, T.W., and Dreher, G.F. (1991). Relationship of career mentoring and socioeconomic origin to managers' and professionals' early career progress. *Academy of Management Journal, 34*(2), 331–350. doi:10.2307/256445.

Yip, J. (2015). Lonely at the top? How organizational position shapes the developmental networks of top executives. Unpublished doctoral dissertation. Boston University, Boston, MA.

Yip, J., and Wilson, M.S. (2010). Learning from experience. In E.V. Velsor, C.D. McCauley, and M.N. Ruderman (Eds), *The Center for Creative Leadership: Handbook of Leadership Development* (pp. 63–95). San Francisco, CA: Jossey-Bass.

24. Gender differences in developmental experiences
Cathleen Clerkin and Meena S. Wilson

In all countries in which benchmarking studies have been conducted, research on trends shows slow or stagnant rates of progress in the percentages of women reaching senior, top, and director-level positions (Catalyst, 2014; KPMG International et al., 2016; Soares et al., 2013). In this chapter, we argue that one of the reasons for the dearth of women in top positions is that women have a hard time obtaining what is considered the "right" experiences, in the "right" context, at the "right" career juncture. We offer a review and analysis of the most salient similarities and differences between women's and men's experiences as an important entry-point for expanding our understanding of gender and leadership.

We conducted our review using EBSCO host research databases and Google Scholar to search by keywords and academic thought leaders related to this work. Additionally, we reviewed and incorporated reports on women's leadership development experiences in business-oriented media outlets and by relevant consulting groups.

In general, we found gendered variation in access to and use of the typical developmental experiences considered vital for becoming effective top-level leaders. We explore these gender differences in regard to quantity, quality, and specific type of experiences provided to women and men. Our analysis leads us to put forward two propositions: on the one hand, women miss out on critical job experiences that would prepare them for senior management roles; and on the other hand, the life experiences and capabilities that prepare women to be outstanding senior leaders do not carry gravitas in the circles in which organizational selection and promotion decisions are made. We conclude by mapping the way forward and outlining implications for future research and practice.

THE LESSONS OF EXPERIENCE FRAMEWORK

We used the Center for Creative Leadership (CCL)'s *Lessons of Experience* (LOE) research as our basic framework for examining leadership development experiences in this chapter. LOE is based on interviews with hundreds of executives who were asked to reflect on key experiences and events that led to a lasting change in how they lead and manage, and what they learned from those experiences and events (McCall et al., 1988). We chose this framework for several reasons. Firstly, it is one of the few which compares experiences of men and women at the executive level. Secondly, this framework has been used and validated across cultures and generations. Finally, this framework is based on real leaders' retrospectives, not on lab studies.

The LOE framework proposes that there are five broad categories of experiences that provide leadership lessons: challenging assignments, developmental relationships, coursework and training, hardships, and personal life experiences (McCall et al., 1988;

Yip and Wilson, 2010). Each of these categories includes many different types of specific experiences (see Table 24.1 for descriptions of common types of experiences within each category). This categorization is based on stories of memorable events told by more than 800 executives, in more than 200 different organizations, in 36 different countries, over the past 30 years (Lindsey et al., 1987; McCall et al., 1988; Van Velsor et al., 2013; Wilson and Chandrasekar, 2014; Yip and Wilson, 2010).

The first three categories, challenging assignments, developmental relationships, and coursework, respectively, make up the "70-20-10 rule" commonly used by talent management practitioners. Challenging assignments are difficult tasks people must perform within their job that requires pushing themselves beyond their comfort zone or previous training (Wilson and Chandrasekar, 2014). Examples of challenging assignment experiences include being promoted, being relocated to a different country or department, being asked to create something new, or fixing a current problem in the organization. Developmental relationships describe growth through workplace-related interpersonal interactions, such as working with bosses and superiors, getting feedback and coaching, and working with difficult co-workers (Van Velsor et al., 2013). The third category, coursework and training, refers to official programs designed to develop leadership skills, such as courses at executive leadership institutions or leadership workshops run by human resources (HR) departments of organizations.

Two additional categories of developmental experiences typically fall outside the realm of organizational facilitation. The first is hardships, which include unfortunate events that require leaders to rise to the occasion. Examples of hardships include unforeseen career setbacks, organizational crises, mistakes, or ethical dilemmas (Wilson and Hoole, 2011). The final category is personal experiences, which encompasses experiences that leaders might have had outside their current career, such as family situations, early life experiences or jobs, spiritual encounters, or personal traumas (Van Velsor et al., 2013). Because organizations generally cannot – or should not – create personal experiences and hardships as interventions, these categories are not usually included in HR-led leadership development initiatives.

While the LOE research originated in the United States (US), cross-cultural research studies suggest that these five main categories of development experiences are fairly consistent globally (Van Velsor et al., 2013; Wilson and Chandrasekar, 2014; Wilson and Hoole, 2011; Wilson and Van Velsor, 2010). However, there is cultural variation in regard to how common and how central different developmental experiences are. For instance, in a recent study, managers in India reported personal experiences as the most common way to gain developmental leadership experience; in China, managers most often mentioned challenging assignments (specifically, turnarounds); and in the US, managers most often mentioned developmental relationships (specifically, bosses and superiors) (Van Velsor et al., 2013). These disparities are a reminder that continuing comparative analysis of the relationship between experiences and leadership development across gender and culture is important to our understanding of leadership development.

Table 24.1   *Leadership development from lessons of experience*

Categories	Experience types	Description
Challenging assignments	Cultural crossing	Regular, direct contact with co-workers who have different cultural and societal norms (e.g., relocation to different region, country).
	Horizontal move	Transitioning to another function, business unit, organization, or industry sector with new types of work or work culture that did not involve a promotion.
	Increase in job scope	Significant increase in budget, number of direct reports, resources, and/or complexity of tasks. May involve promotion, expansion of responsibilities, and visibility.
	New initiative	Developing or launching new products or services to set up new units, enter new markets, embark new lines of business, or create new business.
	Stakeholder engagement	Experiencing high-level interactions that called for reconciling competing points of view and working out solutions without formal authority.
	Turnaround/ fix-it	Fixing/stabilizing a failing or underperforming business/unit through restructuring, downsizing, closing, or implementing an organizational culture change.
Developmental relationships	Bosses and superiors	Interacting with higher-level leaders who were positive or negative role models, coaches, teachers, or catalysts to development.
	Difficult people	Working with individuals who provoked tension, resentment, and disputes due to differing working styles, preferences, and opinions.
	Feedback and coaching	Job-related, formal or informal conversations, advice or mentoring concerning situations, abilities, or traits related to leading.
Courses and programs	Coursework and training	Attending a development/training class or program to advance learning, growth, or career progress.
Hardships	Career setbacks	Unforeseen, unwanted blocks to career progression, caused by another person or event (e.g., being fired, demoted, passed over, or placed in a poor-fitting role).
	Crisis	Unexpected, uncontrollable or shocking events (e.g., product recall, ethics violation, scandal, natural disaster). May damage publicity, reputation, or cause injuries.
	Ethical dilemmas	Observing fraudulent, illegal, or immoral behavior by a senior leader.
	Mistakes	Technical, ethical or strategic errors that result in failure to meet goals (e.g., product malfunction, a poor hiring decision, a loss of credibility or face, or a collapsed venture).

Harvard Business School received bad press over an advertisement for their executive training program which featured a picture of a classroom full of men, and not a single woman (Noyes, 2015). Moreover, a recent study showed that mixed-gender, general leadership development programs predominantly focused on masculine approaches to leadership (for example, autonomous, agentic, and transactional behaviors), which may be less relevant to women participants (Sugiyama et al., 2016).

Trends also suggest that the pay-off from these programs is not the same for women and men. Despite the fact that MBAs give a quick return on investment and MBA graduates report high levels of job satisfaction and career growth, within a few years of graduation women with MBAs earn lower salaries, manage fewer people, and are less pleased with their progress than men with the same degree (Kitroeff and Rodkin, 2015). Similarly, research on high potential leadership programs show gender differences in enrollment and outcomes: compared to men, a greater percentage of women enroll in leadership development courses early in their careers, and stay in them for a greater length of time, leading some experts to question whether women are "developed to death," while men more quickly move on to the next big role (Silva et al., 2012).

Finally, men and women may be given access to different types of leadership development coursework and training. As mentioned above, women tend to be the minority in developmental programs, especially executive development. Additionally, mixed-gender leadership development programs tend to show a preference for male styles of leadership. Hence, these programs may not hold the same amount of relevant leadership information for women. Because of this, many training institutions offer female-only leadership development programs. Research shows that such programs can offer transformational learning opportunities for women, through creating a safe environment that affirms women's gendered experiences and by using pedagogy that is relational and identity-based (Debebe et al., 2016; Sugiyama et al., 2016). Moreover, some experts argue that women need fundamentally different types of leadership training in order to obtain successful careers as leaders (Ely et al., 2011). (See Chapter 25 of this *Handbook* for more on women-only leadership programs.)

Hardships

Hardships ensue from unfortunate and unforeseen situations that are beyond the control of the organization and individuals (Wilson and Hoole, 2011; Wilson and Van Velsor, 2010; see Table 24.1). In general, hardships are regarded as transformative. They give rise to feelings of loss of control, meaning, or identity, and force introspection which can redefine values, commitments, and purpose (Moxley and Pulley, 2004). Broad descriptions of how hardships can push leaders to their next level of development include terms such as "defining moments" (Badaracco, 1997), "leadership crucibles" (Bennis and Thomas, 2002) and "life's curveballs" (Moxley and Pulley, 2004). Personal limitations come to the surface and the need to change one's behavior or pay better attention to people and technical issues becomes apparent. Adverse situations can teach resilience and integrity, compassion for others, and a more balanced approach to life.

However, unlike the first three categories of experiences, hardships are not typically desired or planned. As such, there are few objective well-designed studies available, and less is known about whether these lessons are learned in the same way and to the same extent by women and men. For instance, there is next to no research demonstrating empirically whether gender impacts the amount of hardship leaders face; although a few reports suggests that women identify more leadership lessons from hardships compared to men (Douglas, 2003; Van Velsor and Hughes, 1990) and African American women identify more hardships than white American women (Douglas, 2003). This relative dearth of research is not surprising, considering that hardship is such a nebulous, subjective, and context-dependent category. Nevertheless, there is evidence that many leaders undergo hardships along their leadership journey, and that gender can influence the quality and types of hardship experienced.

Our literature review revealed trends in the nature of hardships reported by men and women. Specifically, hardships described by men more often relate to general organizational or group-level challenges and failure to achieve business outcomes. In comparison, women's hardships seem to be more personal, largely involving individual-level struggles to climb the corporate ladder. Take, for example, hardship experiences described primarily by male managers from China, India, Singapore, and the US (Van Velsor et al., 2013; Wilson, 2008; Yip and Wilson, 2008; Zhang et al., 2009). Chinese managers gave examples of technical and professional mistakes that resulted in failure to meet performance targets or derailed business goals. In India, managers talked about strategic and operational mistakes, incidences of business or personal failure, and errors of judgment in the way people and situations were handled. Singapore's senior public service leaders described crises such as health epidemics and threats to security. Finally, US senior executives cited ethical dilemma and business mistakes. Few examples across these four countries involved personal career difficulties.

In contrast, women's examples of hardships tend to be more pointed and overwhelmingly tied to gender-based experiences. Although evidence is largely anecdotal and examples are culture- or country-specific, the type of hardships discussed are largely universal. Stories are told of how women's voices are silenced (Heath et al., 2014). Women are expected to perform "office housework" (for example, upgrading office decor, coordinating social events, fetching coffee, taking notes), which demean women and damage their career prospects (Frankel, 2004). Too often, traditional views of women cross from benevolent to hostile sexism (Glick and Fiske, 1997), which manifest as mild or virulent sexual harassment. Sexual advances can often come from top- and senior-level males who see themselves as immune to censure (Elsesser, 2015). And throughout these trials, women struggle to meet work and family responsibilities or dual-career obligations (Fredriksen-Goldsen and Scharlach, 2001; Hochschild and Machung, 2012). (See Part IV of this *Handbook* for more about gender-based challenges and barriers.)

It remains unclear whether these gender differences are accurate reflections of the most common hardships experienced by men and women, or whether they are simply the types of gendered hardships focused on in the literature and/or by leaders themselves. We found little empirical evidence regarding systematic gender differences in how each type of hardship is handled and how insights are gained. We surmise that women and men may learn different lessons from hardship, and that these lessons could impact their leadership effectiveness and career choices in different ways; however, more research is needed before conclusions can be drawn.

Personal Experiences

Personal experiences encompass incidents in early life, roles involving youth leadership, family situations, early job experiences, spiritual encounters, and mid-life transitions, that influence a person's principles, attitudes, and behaviors (Van Velsor et al., 2013). They involve transformative learning (Mezirow, 1991) in which opinions, beliefs, values, perceptions, and role expectations change. Personal experiences are times in life when values are formed, an approach to life or work is sorted out, or life direction is re-formed (Wilson and Chandrasekar, 2014). While personal life experiences are not typically cultivated as part of organizations' formal leadership development efforts, research shows that many leaders learn important leadership lessons outside of the workplace (Van Velsor and Hughes, 1990). Unfortunately, for both women and men, these experiences are often discounted by organizations. In this section, we depart slightly from our previous analytic approach, since it does not make sense to discuss the quantity and quality of personal life experiences.

The overall LOE literature on personal experiences focuses predominantly on men's early life experiences that taught them resilience or the ability to recover from setbacks (Yip and Wilson, 2010). Stories are told of growing up in poverty, of lessons learned as Boy Scouts, and of first jobs as check-out clerks. In contrast, much of the literature on women's personal experiences focuses on the concept of work–life balance and how women can (or cannot) manage a career while maintaining traditional gender role obligations.

Historically, women in many parts of the world have prioritized contributions to their family over their workplace and placed their careers on hold when they married or became mothers. Our review suggests that these women find such personal experiences to be a source of profound leadership learning. For example, many women run households and/or support their spouses and family businesses, and these roles facilitate perspective taking, decision making, managing crisis and change, and negotiating across generations (Llopis, 2014). In-depth research on leadership development in the lives of US women governors (Madsen, 2008a) and women university presidents (Madsen, 2008b) have found that these highly successful women leverage experiences from their personal lives throughout their careers.

Ruderman and colleagues assert that friendships, community initiatives, volunteering, parenting, and spousal roles build extensive knowledge, skills and perspectives, and develop leadership talent (Ruderman et al., 2002). Leadership competencies acquired in such environments include learning to work with different people; adjusting to others' personalities and working style; communicating and negotiating in ways that reach different ages, genders, and cultures; and handling and recovering from mistakes. According to their research, non-work activities and relationships help women to cultivate psychological strength and confidence; access networks for feedback and support; and take advantage of multiple opportunities for new, practical learning. Women in the study report professionally benefitting from having multiple life roles, including attaining the psychological rewards, social support, and skills needed to excel in the workplace (Ruderman et al., 2002).

This important overlap in skills and knowledge acquired in career leadership and personal leadership is not restricted to women. Research shows that family role commitment is related to positive family-to-work spillover and reduced psychological strain for both men and women (Graves et al., 2007). Moreover, scholars have argued that understanding self-relevant meanings from leaders' personal lives is an important part of authentic leadership for both men and women (Shamir and Eilam, 2005). Personal life experiences can also impact people's willingness to follow others. Managers' intentions to quit have been linked to their leaders' negative work–family spillover (O'Neill et al., 2009).

However, although life at home and in the community offers opportunities for learning and practicing leadership, organizations do little to capitalize on the value accrued from these off-the-job experiences, often assuming that experiences outside of the workplace "deplete" work resources rather than enhancing them (Ruderman et al., 2002). This depletion argument has been disproportionately leveled against women, as women more often take time out of their career to attend to their personal lives, and are presumed to be more focused on the home. In fact, research on "the motherhood penalty" shows that many organizations are reluctant to hire or promote mothers equally, because they are seen as less dedicated workers; yet comparative analyses demonstrate that mothers perform no lower on work effort, intensity, engagement, or enhancement compared to fathers and non-parents (Kmec, 2011). An argument can be made that women's personal experiences expand their leadership capacities in ways that would make the workplace more humane and honest (Ruderman et al., 2002), and that organizations cannot afford to ignore or not utilize women as powerful and talented resources.

LOOKING FORWARD: IMPLICATIONS FOR PRACTICE AND RESEARCH

Our literature review suggests that women have some significant disadvantages when it comes to obtaining key leadership development experiences. Many of the "ideal" experiences (for example, well-funded challenging assignments, positions abroad, high-level sponsorships) still seem to disproportionately go to men. This is perhaps not surprising, considering that modern leadership development pathways were largely constructed by men, with men in mind. As such, when people think of these types of developmental experiences and opportunities, they may implicitly and automatically consider men more readily than women. This has broad, long-term consequences for women, who may be passed over for leadership later in their careers due to having missed these types of experiences earlier in their careers. In short, the experiences that are seen as vital for leadership are often seen as a poor fit for women and, subsequently, women are seen as a poor fit for leadership.

Moreover, the types of leadership development experiences that women do acquire tend to be undervalued and ignored or risky and harrowing. For instance, women's challenging assignments tend to be lateral moves, have smaller budgets, or are glass cliff situations that men have passed over. Women also tend to encounter more difficult relationships in the workplace and have more hardships related to career setbacks. Finally, while many women feel that they have learned valuable leadership lessons from their personal lives, these experiences are often not acknowledged in the workplace. This combination of circumstances can make women burn out or become frustrated with a system that feels stacked against them.

McClelland, D. (1979). *Power: The Inner Experience.* New York, NY: Irvington.

Mezirow, J. (1991). *Transformative Dimensions of Adult Learning.* San Francisco, CA: Jossey-Bass.

Mohr, T. (2014). Why women don't apply for jobs unless they're 100% qualified. *Harvard Business Review*, August. Retrieved from https://hbr.org/2014/08/why-women-dont-apply-for-jobs-unless-theyre-100-qualified.

Morrison, A., White, R., and Van Velsor, E. (1987). *Breaking the Glass Ceiling: Can Women Make It to the Top of America's Biggest Corporations?.* Reading, MA: Addison Wesley.

Moss-Racusin, C.A., and Rudman, L.A. (2010). Disruptions in women's self-promotion: the backlash avoidance model. *Psychology of Women Quarterly, 34*(2), 186–202.

Moxley, R., and Pulley, M. (2004). Learning from hardships. In C.D. McCauley and E. Van Velsor (Eds), *The Center for Creative Leadership Handbook of Leadership Development* (pp. 183–203). San Francisco, CA: Jossey-Bass.

Noyes, K. (2015). What's missing from executive education: Women. *Fortune*, April 6. Retrieved from http://fortune.com/2015/04/16/executive-education-women/.

O'Brien, K.E., Biga, A., Kessler, S.R., and Allen, T.D. (2010). A meta-analytic investigation of gender differences in mentoring. *Journal of Management, 36*(2) 537–553.

O'Neill, J.W., Harrison, M.M., Cleveland, J., Almeida, D., Stawski, R., and Crouter, A.C. (2009). Work–family climate, organizational commitment, and turnover: Multilevel contagion effects of leaders. *Journal of Vocational Behavior, 74*(1), 18–29.

Ohlott, P.J., Ruderman, M.N., and McCauley, C.D. (1994). Gender differences in managers' developmental job experiences. *Academy of Management Journal, 37*(1), 46–67.

Petrilla, M. (2016). Women entrepreneurs are "more ambitious and successful" than men. *Fortune.* Retrieved from http://fortune.com/2016/02/29/women-entrepreneurs-success/.

Ragins, B.R., Townsend, B., and Mattis, M. (1998). Gender gap in the executive suite: CEOs and female executives report on breaking the glass ceiling. *Academy of Management Executive, 12*(1), 28–42.

Rivers, C., and Barnett, R.C. (2013). *New Soft War on Women: How the Myth of Female Ascendance is Hurting Women, Men and our Economy.* New York, NY: Penguin.

Ruderman, M.N., Ohlott, P.J., Panzer, K., and King, S.N. (2002). Benefits of multiple roles for managerial women. *Academy of Management Journal, 45*(2), 369–386.

Rudman, L.A. (1998). Self-promotion as a risk factor for women: The costs and benefits of counterstereotypical impression management. *Journal of Personality and Social Psychology, 74*(3), 629–645.

Ryan, M.K., and Haslam, S.A. (2005). The glass cliff: Evidence that women are over-represented in precarious leadership positions. *British Journal of Management, 16*(2), 81–90.

Ryan, M.K., Haslam, S.A., and Postmes, T. (2007). Reactions to the glass cliff: Gender differences in the explanations for the precariousness of women's leadership positions. *Journal of Organizational Change Management, 20*(2), 182–197.

Shamir, B., and Eilam, G. (2005). "What's your story?" A life-stories approach to authentic leadership development. *Leadership Quarterly, 16*(3), 395–417.

Silva, C., Carter, N.M., and Beninger, A. (2012). Good intentions, imperfect execution: Women get fewer of the "hot jobs" needed to advance. New York, NY: Catalyst.

Soares, R., Mulligan-Ferry, L., Fendler, E., and Kun, E.W.C. (2013). 2013 Catalyst census: Fortune 500 women executive officers and top earners. Report. New York, NY: Catalyst.

Sugiyama, K., Cavanagh, K.V., van Esch, C., Bilimoria, D., and Brown, C. (2016). Inclusive leadership development drawing on pedagogies of women's and general leadership development programs. *Journal of Management Education, 40*(3), 253–292.

Van Velsor, E., and Hughes, M.W. (1990). Gender differences in the development of managers: How women managers learn from experience. Technical report. Greensboro, NC: Center for Creative Leadership.

Van Velsor, E., Wilson, M., Criswell, C., and Chandrasekar, A. (2013). Learning to lead: A comparison of developmental events and learning. *Asian Business and Management, 12*(4), 455–476.

Wilson, M. (2008). *Developing Future Leaders for High-Growth Indian Companies: New Perspectives.* Greensboro, NC: Center for Creative Leadership.

Wilson, M., and Chandrasekar, A. (2014). *Experience Explorer Facilitator's Guide.* Greensboro, NC: Center for Creative Leadership.

Wilson, M., and Hoole, E. (2011). Developing leadership: India at the crossroads. *Vikalpa: The Journal for Decision Makers, 36*(3), 1–8.

Wilson, M., and Van Velsor, E. (2010). The new terrain of leadership development: An Indian perspective. In Verma, S. (Ed.), *Toward the Next Orbit: A Corporate Odyssey* (pp. 269–284). New Delhi, India: Sage Publications India.

Woodall, J., Edwards, C., and Welchman, R. (1997). Organizational restructuring and the achievement of an equal opportunity culture. *Gender, Work and Organization, 4*(1), 2–12.

Yip, J., and Wilson, M. (2008). Developing public service leaders in Singapore. White paper. Greensboro, NC: Center for Creative Leadership.

Yip, J., and Wilson, M.S. (2010). Learning from experience. In E. Van Velsor, C.D. McCauley, and M.N. Ruderman (Eds), *The Center for Creative Leadership Handbook of Leadership Development* (pp. 63–95). Greensboro, NC: Center for Creative Leadership.

Zhang, Y., Chandrasekar, A., and Wei, R. (2009). *Developing Chinese Leaders in the 21st Century.* Greensboro, NC: Center for Creative Leadership.

25. Women-only leadership programs: a deeper look
Mary Ellen Kassotakis

As the leadership development industry has grown and proliferated across the globe, so too have programs that are focused on diverse audiences. In many countries women have been entering the workforce in the same numbers as men; however, they have not attained similar parity in leadership roles. As has been discussed in previous chapters in this *Handbook*, women are greatly under-represented in senior positions in almost all industries; men continue to far outnumber women in these upper echelons (Adler, 2015). In the face of anti-discrimination laws existing in many countries, this disparity is both ironic and discouraging. Given the information explosion, the world of work is increasingly complex and constantly changing. Yet, despite Sheryl Sandberg's (2013) admonition that women "lean in" to opportunities, which spawned renewed focus and public attention in this arena, and compelling research that suggests women bring unique qualities to global leadership roles (Ngunjiri and Madsen, 2015), the most recent research still affirms that women are under-represented at every level in the corporate pipeline, with the greatest disparity at the senior leadership level (Leanin.org and McKinsey, 2015).

As a practitioner in the high-technology industry of "Silicon Valley," I have observed that employee talents required to remain competitive and viable in the global workplace are obsolescing at ever-faster rates. One of the primary ways that organizations attempt to address skill gaps is by investing in the "know-how," knowledge, and abilities of their employees. Recently the Association for Talent Development (ATD) (2016) found that closing skills gaps was one of the top priorities for talent development functions across all countries, and the learning element continues to be critical. The learning and development industry (that is, the training industry) began in earnest in the United States in the 1950s and quickly gained (and maintains) global enthusiasts. Today, companies are investing more resources in developing leaders than ever before, spending more than $100 billion on leadership development annually (American Society of Training and Development, 2014; Bersin by Deloitte, 2016). Yet, surprisingly, close to 90 percent of business and human resources leaders still see leadership shortfalls as a top issue, while only 37 percent of companies studied actually believe the leadership programs they have implemented for men and women are effective (Bersin by Deloitte, 2016).

The opportunity for strengthening the impact of women in organizations today is great. In fact, McKinsey & Company noted that advancing women's equality in societies across the globe could add $12 trillion to global growth by 2025 (Woetzel et al., 2016). Some educational and professional service firms are meeting the demand for leadership development opportunities that are designed specifically for women in senior roles; however, there is a need for more research that is focused on exploring whether these efforts have value. Kellerman (2012) agreed when she said that, given the investment in a thriving and decades-old leadership development industry and the proliferation of programs uniquely designed for women, it is difficult to understand whether there is value in women-only programs since the representation of women at the upper echelons of power remains so low.

The purpose of this chapter is to explore the topic of leadership development programs for senior women leaders, excluding programs targeted at skill development for board of director positions. Sections on both university-sponsored and non-university-based women's leadership programs are included. Specific attention is then given to the pedagogical methods used in leadership development programs (that is, coaching, mentoring, and sponsorship), common subject matter included in leadership development for women (executive education programs and options offered by professional service firms), and the advantages of women-only programs. The definition of "women in senior positions" is rather subjective; consequently, for the purposes of this chapter it is defined as mid-level to senior-level executives in corporate organizations who aspire to higher levels of responsibility, compensation, and influence, including the role of chief executive officer (CEO).

BACKGROUND

There is a growing assortment of educational organizations from business schools, corporate universities, executive coaches, commercial training institutions, and online platforms vying to meet the learning and development demand with "executive education" programs that hold the promise of providing keys to career advancement in short bursts of structured learning activities. These programs attract senior leaders for many reasons, including the promise of interaction with renowned faculty who represent marketplace thought leadership, a prestigious academic affiliation, and the opportunity to network with other industry professionals. In addition to mixed-gender programs, there is a particular market demand for women-only learning experiences. While the registration fees for university-based programs for women augment the revenue stream for their executive education programs, other organizations are also seeing the opportunity to garner increased revenues by meeting the demand for women-only workshops and programs.

Given the enormous sums being spent on programs, Ibarra et al. (2013) noted that "companies spend time, money, and good intentions on efforts to build a more robust pipeline of upwardly mobile women, and then not much happens" (p. 62). Furthermore, observers have noted that the investment in developing female leaders is inconsistent (Bersin by Deloitte, 2016). Some studies report that women get professional development but do not necessarily get promoted into higher positions. The Bersin by Deliotte (2016) research did not reveal any quantifiable evidence that addresses the efficacy of the learning investment (that is, the return on investment) for both mixed-gender and women-only programs.

UNIVERSITY-SPONSORED CURRICULA

For this chapter, I reviewed executive development programs (March through May of 2016) that target corporate women in senior positions across the globe. The programs in this dataset include leadership development programs designed and delivered by business schools, as well as a number of programs offered by suppliers who specialized in the delivery of women-only leadership development programs. I discovered that program

many organizations have implemented peer-mentoring circles to reach greater numbers of females. Interestingly, Tolar (2012) stated that high-achieving women described the role of mentors as both a help and a hindrance. In her qualitative study, the participants noted that the absence of mentors was at times a benefit and also a deficit. The majority of women in this study found mentoring to be a career development advantage; however, a minority had concerns about the selection of mentors: being matched with those mentors who may wield "undue influence," impede "personal development," and "perpetuate systemic norms that these women encountered as barriers" (p. 181). Overall, providing women the opportunity to listen to and learn from others' experiences, particularly as they make choices concerning mentoring relationships, can be an effective strategy to determine who is best enabling self-selection in or out of formal mentoring relations. More details on the research around mentoring can be found in the other chapters in this part of the *Handbook*.

On the other hand, challenging the value of mentoring, Hewlett (2013) used research to argue that top-talent senior women leaders would be better served finding sponsors instead of mentors, and she delineated the key differences between mentoring and sponsorship. Mentors serve as a sounding board and can offer advice, support, and guidance as requested, with little or no expectation in return. In contrast, sponsors are more invested in the advancement of their protégés. Sponsors offer guidance and critical feedback; they can connect their protégés with senior executives. Hewlett suggests that sponsors can serve as levers to move women into senior ranks. Sponsors can offer the opportunity to rise above some of the intrinsic gender inequities in the workplace by facilitating stretch assignments and by creating upward pressure on pay and visibility.

To summarize, the pedagogical methods used in contemporary executive education programs are primarily used for both genders (for example, lectures, experiential learning, action learning, case studies, simulations, gaming and badging, mentoring, feedback assessments, and coaching). Although it is purported that there are some pedagogical differences between mixed-gender and women-only programs, the literature does not provide this evidence. The one exception is the use of gender-sensitivity practices. Debebe (2011) noted that a distinction can be made for the use of gender-sensitive teaching and learning practices that include:

> articulating a leadership dilemma, receiving and giving feedback, receiving and giving coaching, transmitting knowledge, teaching with intentionality, candor, giving support, participating in collaborative learning, engaging in deep reflection, making a commitment to change, sustaining relationships, and reawakening conviction through meaningful artifacts. (p. 692)

WOMEN-ONLY PROGRAM ADVANTAGES

Since many universities are extending their executive education platforms to meet the demand for programs targeted specifically to women-only participants, a key question remains: What are the advantages for women-only programs? First, the most obvious advantage is that of "safety." With the freedom to speak one's mind in workshops – without the concern of being perceived as defensive or dimwitted – participants are more likely to share opinions without the concern of possibly being judged by males. Debebe

(2011) explored what could be done to create safety for women-only participants so that they could experiment with breaking comfortable patterns with the assumption "that deep individual change is necessary for fundamental organization change" (p. 680). This study included instructional designs for gender-sensitive pedagogical practices, and ultimately Debebe noted that "for many women, being in an all-female environment is both rare and affirming, immediately putting them at ease" (p. 687). An environment for transformational learning could, indeed, produce favorable results through the coalescing of two primary elements: (1) a women-only learning environment; and (2) the use of gender-sensitive teaching and learning methodologies. These methodologies include enabling participant interactions that both challenge and support, as well as enabling participants to self-reflect and become open to self-disclosure. Researchers (Debebe, 2011; Ely et al., 2011) argue that in an all-female environment, women can discuss shared experiences without the need for broaching gender-related concerns, possible power plays, or fear of rejection. Safety is created in these environments because of the affirmation of women's experience and the provision of both challenge and support.

Another study also affirmed the validity of a women-only development setting because the programs "provide a safe and supportive environment for improving self-confidence, learning new skills, and learning from the experiences of successful role models" (Clarke, 2011, p. 498). Clarke observed that women can assist each other in building social capital via networking and mentoring, and they can encourage each other to take risks. Women-only development programs are uniquely suitable to enable participants to learn new skills, to learn from others, and to develop enhanced self-confidence. In supportive women-only environments, the viewpoints of women are heard and not overshadowed by those of men. In a review of women's leadership development programs, the gender composition of leadership programs was noted as a key theme that contributed to psychological safety for the female participants (Debebe et al., 2016; Vinnicombe et al., 2013). As an example, one program's internet description noted:

> One very important benefit of The Women's Leadership Forum is the opportunity to exchange ideas with a group of highly experienced businesswomen who face similar challenges in their professional lives. Through this program, many participants develop lasting relationships and are able to draw on a valuable network of peers who can offer ongoing advice and support. (Women's Leadership Forum, n.d., para. 3)

An assumption is that women will support each other in a workshop setting; however, being in a learning environment of only women certainly does not ensure the feeling of "safety." According to Kaiser and Spalding (2015), promoting "identity safety" within organizations can reduce the identity threat that some women experience. Indeed, it is not a given that safety will be found in a women-only environment; Mavin and Williams (2013) reviewed the literature of the negative inter-relations of some women and the lack of solidarity behaviors that undermine expectations of safety (for example, "queen bee" behaviors). Much of the safety is dependent on the skill and expertise of facilitators and agreement by the participants to shared norms regarding disclosure. With the assistance of skilled facilitators, these norms can foster trust and make it safe for participants to feel vulnerable.

A second advantage for women-only programs is that of more effectively assisting women in finding their leadership "identity." The actual learning environment helps to shape the forms of identity that participants assume (DeRue and Ashford, 2010). An understanding of the role of identity takes different situations into account so that learners construct and work within multiple identities, as these identities might be rooted in various cultural nuances (Debebe and Reinert, 2014; Kark et al., 2016). For example, with a virtual workplace it is helpful to understand how to influence others in different contexts when English is a second language. Women can become "savvy" about cultural differences and identify ways to use their strengths to influence powerfully (Brandon and Seldman, 2004). In this manner they can hopefully avoid major pitfalls and sidestep possible gaffes by embedding real work in leadership development efforts.

In a qualitative examination of leadership development initiatives for women, Debebe (2009) specifically explored the critical role that the environment plays in learning and sought to understand the transformational learning experiences women may have, specifically in women-only classrooms. She concluded that transformational learning can, indeed, take place in the context of leadership development training. The key to fostering personal leadership growth for women is internal change. Stead and Elliott (2013) encouraged that consideration be given to the impact of social norms that women experience with different leadership learning designs. The importance of personal identities is influenced by the organizational context in addition to social identities that can pose a challenging dichotomy for participants. Work on identity should be carefully considered, as participants may adhere to negative stereotypes (Ely et al. 2011; Stead and Elliott, 2013).

Beyond theory and design of programs for women's leadership development, Debebe et al. (2016) noted that the opportunity for relevant evaluation and impact data and the importance of embedding learning and development experiences in the real work of organizations are also important. They also noted the importance of studying the "intersectionality" in women's leadership programs. Intersectionality refers to "the complex of reciprocal attachments and sometimes polarizing conflicts that confront both individuals and movements as they seek to 'navigate' among the raced, gendered, and class-based dimensions of social and political life" (Center for New Racial Studies, n.d., para. 1). Debebe et al. (2016) noted that there is currently little empirical and theoretical evidence as to how intersectional issues impact women's leadership experiences. Future studies may reveal the full complexity of women's leadership when the interaction of multiple identities is taken into account, producing a powerful learning experience beyond gender identity. Chapter 27 in this *Handbook* provides more details on this construct.

Lastly, the ability to network with women representing a wide variety of industries, ages, and backgrounds can be a catalyst for improved career satisfaction. In 2006, van Emmerik et al. found that men were able to use their networks more effectively than women. Since that time, conferences for women and learning programs have proliferated. According to Kolhatkar (2016), women are certainly taking advantage of attending women-only leadership development programs and women's conferences in record numbers, even though there is no empirical evidence to demonstrate that women's ability to use their networks is more or less effective than that of men. Recently, general leadership development programs were compared specifically with women's leadership development programs to understand the extent to which inclusive leadership practices (particularly those that draw on relational skills) are common to both (Sugiyama et al., 2016). This study observed that women-only programs focus more attention on relational practices. Additionally, the study raised the question of pedagogical approaches that could address diverse identities, the intersectionality of identities, and inclusive behaviors toward these identities. The efficacy of these approaches presents an opportunity for further research. Because the pedagogical methods for mixed-gender and women-only executive development programs are similar, as discussed previously, gender-sensitive practices might be the significant differentiator.

The key question then becomes: How do the topics differ among various universities and for-profit organizations for women-only leadership development programs that enable safety, networking, and a focus on identity? Grounded in theories of both gender and leadership, researchers Ely et al. (2011) categorized principles for approaching leadership development programs targeted for women, and they discussed three principles: "(1) situate topics and tools in an analysis of second-generation gender bias, (2) create a holding environment to support women's identity work, and (3) anchor participants on their leadership purpose" (p. 486). They suggested a framework that also included many of the common learning methods described earlier (for example, assessments, feedback, coaching, and networks). As has been noted, these are methods that have experienced rapid adoption in the leadership development programs in the workplace and in education offerings. More empirical evidence to demonstrate the efficacy of these methods is needed.

For those seeking advancement via exposure to academic experts and both industry experts and peers, mixed-gender executive education programs can serve as a cornerstone experience. However, until gender equity is pervasive, women-only programs provide a valuable experience for those who seek a supportive environment to ponder and discuss deeply personal issues that impact their career choices. If well designed, these programs offer women the opportunity to reflect upon specific factors that may impede ascension into more senior roles, such as unconscious bias. Additionally, these programs enable participants to cultivate expanded professional networks that can help to catapult them to new leadership opportunities and experiences.

DISCUSSION AND RECOMMENDATIONS

The review of literature in the previous section identified distinct advantages for women-only programs: (1) participants' sense of safety; (2) structured reflection on identity and factors related to intersectionality; and (3) building social capital via networking. These are important for everyone, and there should be no stigma attached to these advantages.

As the organizational "war for talent" continues to escalate across the globe, companies are focusing on the leadership capabilities of employees. The quest for development has propelled the opportunity for universities and professional development firms to garner increasing profits through their various workshops and programs, including women-only programs. Since organizations have not broken the "glass ceiling" to date, further research is needed to understand the causes of disparity in leadership ranks between the genders. Is the root problem unconscious bias or the lack of incentives that foster true change? Is it a difference of ambition in genders due to perceptions of acceptable leadership behaviors, gaps in specific leadership competencies or capabilities, perceived ambition and motivation, the influence of the corporate culture, or even the agenda and whims of an organization's current CEO? Previous chapters in this book have addressed these topics in depth.

Clarke, M. (2011). Advancing women's careers through leadership development programs. *Employee Relations*, *33*(5), 498–515. doi:101108/01-425451111153871.

Debebe, G. (2009). Transformational learning in women's leadership development training. *Advancing Women in Leadership*, *29*(7), 1–12.

Debebe, G. (2011). Creating a safe environment for women's leadership transformation. *Journal of Management Education*, *35*(5), 679–712. doi:10.1177/1052563910397501.

Debebe, G., Anderson, D., Bilimoria, D., and Vinnicombe, S.M. (2016). Women's leadership development programs: Lessons learned and new frontiers. *Journal of Management Education*, *40*(3), 231–252. DOI: 10.1177/1052562916639079.

Debebe, G., and Reinert, K.A. (2014). Leading with our whole selves: A multiple identity approach to leadership development. In M.L. Miville and A.D. Ferguson (Eds), *Handbook of Race-Ethnicity and Gender in Psychology* (pp. 271–293). New York, NY: Springer.

DeRue, D.S., and Ashford, S.J. (2010). Who will lead and who will follow? A social process of leadership identity construction in organizations. *Academy of Management Review*, *35*(4), 627–647. doi:10.5465/AMR.2010.53503267.

Dinolfo, S., and Nugent, J.S. (2010). Making mentoring work. Retrieved from http://www.catalyst.org/system/files/Making_Mentoring_Work.pdf.

Ely, R.J., Ibarra, H., and Kolb, D.M. (2011). Taking gender into account: Theory and design for women's leadership developmental programs. *Academy of Management and Education*, *10*(3), 474–493.

Harvard Business Review. (2015). *HBR Guide to Coaching Employees*. Boston, MA: Harvard Business Review Press.

Hewlett, S.A. (2013). *Forget a Mentor, Find a Sponsor: The New Way to Fast-Track your Career*. Boston, MA: Harvard Business School Publishing Corporation.

Ibarra, H., Ely, R., and Kolb, D. (2013). Women rising: The unseen barriers. *Harvard Business Review*, *91*(9), 60–66.

Jue, A.L., Marr, J.A., and Kassotakis, M.E. (2010). *Social Media at Work: How Networking Tools Propel Organizational Performance*. San Francisco, CA: Jossey-Bass.

Kaiser, C.R., and Spalding, K.E. (2015). Do women who succeed in male-dominated domains help other women? The moderating role of gender identification. *European Journal of Social Psychology*, *45*(5), 599–608.

Kark, R., Preser, R., and Zion-Waldoks, T. (2016). From a politics of dilemmas to a politics of paradoxes: Feminism, pedagogy, and women's leadership for social change. *Journal of Management Education*, *40*(3), 293–320.

Kellerman, B. (2012). *The End of Leadership*. New York, NY: Harper.

Knowles, M.S., Holton, E.F., and Swanson, R.A. (2011). *The Adult Learner*, 7th edn. Oxford, UK: Elsevier.

Kolb, D.A. (2014). *Experiential Learning: Experience as the Source of Learning and Development*. Upper Saddle River, NJ: Prentice Hall

Kolhatkar, S. (2016). The female solidarity have-it-all, feel-good machine. *Bloomberg Businessweek*, February (4462), 48–55.

Korn Ferry Institute. (2013). Career playbook: Practical tips for women in leadership. Retrieved from www.kornferry.com/institute/627-career-playbook-practical-tips-for-women-in-leadership.

Leanin.Org and McKinsey & Company. (2015). Women in the workplace. Retrieved from www.mckinsey.com/business-functions/organization/our-insights/women-in-the-workplace.

Linehan, M., and Scullion, H. (2008). The development of female global managers: The role of mentoring and networking. *Journal of Business Ethics*, *83*(1), 29–40. doi:10.1007/s10551-007-9657-0.

Mavin, S., and Williams, J. (2013). Women's impact on women's careers in management: Queen bees, female misogyny, negative intra-relations and solidarity behaviors. In S. Vinnicombe, R.J. Burke, S. Blake-Beard, and L.L. Moore (Eds), *Handbook of Research on Promoting Women's Careers* (pp. 178–195). Cheltenham, UK and Northampton, MA, USA: Edward Elgar Publishing.

McCall, M.W., Jr. (2010). Recasting leadership development. *Industrial and Organizational Psychology*, *3*(1), 3–19. doi:10.1111/j.1754-9434.2009.01189.x.

McCall, M.W., Jr., Lombardo, M.M., and Morrison, A.M. (2008). *The Lessons of Experience: How Successful Executives Develop on the Job*. New York, NY: Free Press.

Neal, S., Boatman, J., and Miller, L. (2013). Women as mentors: Does she or doesn't she? A global study of businesswomen and mentoring. Pittsburgh, PA: Development Dimensions International. Retrieved from http://www.ddiworld.com/resources/library/trend-research/women-as-mentors-does-she-or-doesnt-she.

Ngunjiri, F.W., and Madsen, S.R. (Eds). (2015). *Women as Global Leaders*. Women and Leadership: Research, Theory and Practice. Charlotte, NC: Information Age Publishing.

O'Neil, D.A., Hopkins, M.M., and Bilimoria, D. (2015). A framework for developing women leaders: Applications to executive coaching. *Journal of Applied Behavioral Science*, *51*(2), 253–276.

Ortiz-Walters, R., Eddleston, K., and Simione, K. (2010). Satisfaction with mentoring relationships: Does gender identity matter?. *Career Development International, 15*(2), 100–120.

Sandberg, S. (2013). *Lean In: Women, Work and the Will to Lead.* New York, NY: Alfred A. Knopf.

Scott, J.C., and Reynolds, D.H. (Eds). (2010). *Handbook of Workplace Assessment: Evidence-Based Practices for Selecting and Developing Organizational Talent.* The Professional Practice Series. San Francisco, CA: Jossey-Bass.

Segers, J., Vloeberghs, D., Henderickx, E., and Inceoglu, I. (2011). Structuring and understanding the coaching industry: The coaching cube. *Academy of Management Learning and Education, 10*(2), 204–221. doi:10.5465/AMLE.2011.62798930.

Stead, V., and Elliott, C. (2013). Women's leadership learning: A reflexive review of representations and leadership teaching. *Management Learning, 44*(4), 373–394. doi:10.1177/1350507612449504.

Sugiyama, K., Cavanagh, K.V., van Esch, C., Bilimoria, D., and Brown, C. (2016). Inclusive leadership development: Drawing from pedagogies of women's and general leadership development programs. *Journal of Management Education, 40*(3), 253–292. doi: 10.1177/1052562916632553.

Tippins, N.T., and Adler, S. (Eds). (2011). *Technology-Enhanced Assessment of Talent.* The Professional Practice Series. San Francisco, CA: Jossey-Bass.

Tolar, M.H. (2012). Mentoring experiences of high-achieving women. *Advances in Developing Human Resources, 14*(2), 172–187. doi:10.1177/1523422312436415.

van Emmerik, I.J.H., Euwema, M.C., Geschiere, M., and Schouten, M. (2006). Networking your way through the organization: Gender differences in the relationship between network participation and career satisfaction. *Women in Management Review, 21*(1), 54–66. doi:10.1108/09649420610643411.

Van Velsor, E. (1998). Assessing the impact of development experiences. In E. Van Velsor (Ed.), *Assessing the Impact of Development Experiences* (pp. 262–288). San Francisco, CA: Jossey-Bass.

Van Velsor, E., McCauley, C.D., and Ruderman, M.N. (2010). Center for Creative Leadership Handbook of Leadership Development. In E. Van Velsor, C.D. McCauley, and M.N. Ruderman (Eds), *Assessing the Impact of Development Experiences* (pp. 262–288). San Francisco, CA: Jossey-Bass.

Vinnicombe, S., Moore, L.L., and Anderson, D. (2013). Women's leadership programmes are still important. In S. Vinnicombe, R.J. Burke, S. Blake-Beard, and L.L. Moore (Eds), *Handbook of Research Promoting Women's Careers* (pp. 406–419). Cheltenham, UK and Northampton, MA, USA: Edward Elgar Publishing.

Wankel, C., and Blessinger, P. (2012). *Increasing Student Engagement and Retention Using Immersive Interfaces: Virtual Worlds, Gaming, and Simulation.* Cutting-Edge Technologies in Higher Education. Bingley, UK: Emerald Group Publishing.

Wharton's Women's Executive Leadership: Business Strategies for Success (n.d.). University of Pennsylvania. Retrieved from http://executiveeducation.wharton.upenn.edu/for-individuals/all-programs/womens-executive-leadership-business-strategies-for-success.

Woetzel, J., Madgavkar, A., Ellingrud, K., Manyika, J., Hunt, V., and Krishnan, M. (2016, May). Realizing gender equality's $12 trillion economic opportunity. McKinsey Global Institute. Retrieved from www.mckinsey.com/global-themes/employment-and-growth/realizing-gender-equalitys-12-trillion-economic-opportunity.

Women's Leadership Forum. (n.d.). Harvard Business School. Retrieved from http://www.exed.hbs.edu/programs/wlf/Pages/participants.aspx.

26. Supporting women's career development
Ronald J. Burke*

Women continue to enter the workforce in increasing numbers, so it should come as no surprise that more attention is being paid to their career development and advancement. Organizations need to attract and retain the best talent available. The nature of work and organizations has changed, as has the definition of careers. Careers are now seen as "boundaryless" (Arthur and Rousseau, 1996), "protean" (Hall, 1996), and "kaleidoscopic" (Mainiero and Sullivan, 2006). Women's careers unfold differently from men's, as men and women develop differently (Gallos, 1989), and the genders are treated differently in workplaces and in society at large (Burke, 2014; Ragins et al., 1998). Researchers have called for different career theories for women and men (Gallos, 1989; Larwood and Gutek, 1987), and women's careers are seen as more complicated (O'Neil and Bilimoria, 2005a, 2005b; Powell and Mainiero, 1992).

Researchers have found both benefits to organizations from having more women in executive roles and barriers that individual women face in advancing. For example, Tarr-Whelan (2009) noted several organizational benefits that included greater profits, stronger ability to weather financial downturns, policies that contribute to individual and societal health, increased commitment to corporate social responsibilities, and management that reflects twenty-first-century teamwork and participative decision making. Yet, even with the strong business case toward including women in top leadership boards and teams, women sometimes feel like travelers in a foreign land (Burke, 2014). Morrison (1992) listed six important barriers to women's career advancement: (1) prejudice (that is, treating differences as weaknesses); (2) poor career planning and development and a lack of opportunities for women; (3) a lonely, hostile, and unsupportive work environment; (4) lack of organizational savvy on the part of women; (5) the "old boys' network," and the greater comfort men have in interacting with other men; and (6) difficulty in balancing work and family (for example, overload, conflict, and stress). There is evidence that these barriers continue to exist today (Burke, 2014). Hundreds of other scholars have discussed a host of additional barriers as well (Phillips and Imhoff, 1997; Mattis, 1994). A more detailed discussion of barriers can be found in Part IV of this *Handbook*.

The purpose of this chapter is to present a variety of issues surrounding the support of women in the workplace through career development. White et al. (1992) define career development as "a successive and systematic sequence of attitudes and behaviors associated with work-related experiences, which acknowledges the individual's personal life across the entire span of the life cycle" (p. 13). Using this definition as the foundation for this chapter, I discuss women's career models and types, values of managerial women at work, initiatives supporting women's career development, and finally, implications and conclusion.

WOMEN'S CAREER MODELS AND TYPES

Historically, writing and research on careers has focused on men and the work role. In the current post-industrial period, careers of women (and men) now involve more job changes and the constant interplay of multiple roles across the life-span. Careers of both women and men have become "boundaryless" (Hall, 1996). Career development has become a more self-guided and self-directed process; one's life and occupational career are connected, individuals increasingly search for a balance in their lives, and career development has become a journey toward fulfillment and happiness. Overall, Betz and Fitzgerald (1987) and Larwood and Gutek (1987) argued in past decades that women's career development was different from men's. If this is the case, then it is important to explore career models and types created specifically for women.

Powell and Mainiero (1992) argued that women's careers are viewed very differently from men's careers. They developed a model of women's careers that included both work and non-work factors; subjective and objective indicators of career and life success; personal, organizational, and societal factors; and the notion that women's careers may not go through a predictable series of stages over time. Moen (2001) stated that women, compared to men, have more complex career patterns or career histories. In addition, Lee (1994) identified three important sex differences: (1) women's careers are affected by child-rearing; (2) women give birth at different ages, giving greater variability in career-related events; and (3) women and men differ in the time and involvement they devote to work and family-related activities. There is ample evidence that women's career patterns have been and continue to be varied (Huang et al., 2007).

Gender-focused career research through the years has clarified some themes and trends (see O'Neil and Bilimoria, 2005a). For example, the focus on the following three themes has emerged in a number of studies: the intersection of work and family, the management of multiple responsibilities, and the differential treatment of women and men in organizations (Burke, 2014). Two related patterns within these themes include the idea that women's careers are shaped by their relational and contextual experiences, while male careers are shaped by male-defined constructions of work and careers. Thus women's patterns were more likely to be protean and kaleidoscopic, given their development and circumstances (Gersick and Kram, 2002; Lyness and Thompson, 2000). Goffee and Nicholson (1994) also noted increasing variability in career patterns among both women and men. The career patterns of younger women are being recognized as very different from the career patterns of older women, and the career patterns of both women and men are slowly becoming more similar over time.

O'Neil et al. (2008) identified four patterns in the literature on women's careers. First, women's careers were embedded in larger life contexts. Second, families and careers were central to women's lives. Third, women's career paths reflected a wide range and variety of patterns. And fourth, both human and social capital were critical factors for women's careers. Yet, male-defined constructions of work and career success continued to dominate both research and practice. These scholars found that organizations required the separation of career and life. In their research, families were seen as liabilities to women's career development and success in the workplace.

In a sample of 133 women participating in MBA and executive education seminars, O'Neil et al. (2004) examined women's career types and their effects on personal satisfaction with their career success, as well as the sources to which they attributed this success. Two dimensions were used to identify their career types and the nature of their career pattern: ordered or emergent (that is, linear, sequential, and ladder-like versus emergent or reactive) and an internal versus external career locus (that is, self-directed versus organizationally directed). O'Neil et al. (2004) identified three clear career types: "achievers," "navigators," and "accommodators." Achievers (30 percent of the sample) had ordered careers and an internal locus; navigators (39 percent of the sample) had ordered careers and an external career locus; and accommodators (27 percent of the sample) had emergent careers with a career locus midway between internal and external. Navigators held highly positive views of their careers, achievers had mildly negative views of their careers, and accommodators had highly negative views of their careers. Accommodators were significantly less satisfied with their careers than women having both navigator and achiever career types. This study suggests that women, to be success-ful, need to seek guidance for their career direction and advancement, and they also need to develop their human capital, as these factors contributed greatly to their satisfaction with career success.

In another study, O'Neil and Bilimoria (2005b) undertook interviews with 60 women (ages ranging from 24 to 60, with an average age of 42), dividing them into three age cohorts: early, middle, and late career phases. The data showed distinct patterns in how women's careers developed over time. Three phases were noted: the idealized achieve-ment phase, the pragmatic endurance phase, and the reinventive contribution phase. The middle phase indicated lower levels of engagement, commitment, and enthusiasm, repre-senting a less than full utilization of their talents. Women regrouped by finding other ways of contributing. The researchers argued for improved organizational efforts to provide women with coaching and mentoring, supervisors who encouraged their development, challenging job assignments, appreciation for non-traditional work histories and learned abilities, and recognition of unique talents. Additional information about these and other potential efforts can be found in other chapters of Part V of this *Handbook*.

Another model to consider in studying women's careers includes one that emerged from White's (1995) interviews with 48 successful women in business, industry, and public life using a life-span developmental perspective. The interviews covered their childhoods, personalities, work histories, and non-work family issues. White developed an age-linked stage model of women's career development including eight stages: (1) early adult transi-tion, 17–25 years (exploration); (2) entering the adult world, mid-twenties (crystallization and implementation); (3) established, 25–33 years; (4) early thirties transition, 33–35 years; (5) settling down, 35 years (advancement); (6) late thirties transition, 38–40 years (achievement); (7) 40–50 years (rebalancing); and (8) maintenance, fifties onward. The majority of these women had high career centrality and worked continuously and full-time (only five took career breaks, fitting home and family responsibilities around their work). Interestingly, these women exhibited a male model of career success, as all demon-strated high levels of career centrality and commitment (often the result of early career challenge); several mentioned having mentors, and most exhibited a low homemaking commitment. About one-third exhibited high career commitment at an early age.

The frameworks outlined above provide a sampling of career models and types that have emerged from a number of studies throughout the last few decades, and they inform discussions of career development. It is important to note that career development takes place at the intersection of the individual and the organization. Organizational initiatives are therefore needed to support women's career development opportunities. Women benefit from coaching and mentoring, working for managers who support their development and advancement, accessing resources and opportunities to develop their skills, receiving challenging and visible assignments, and gaining recognition for their accomplishments. Women at different phases of their careers will need different combinations of these factors.

For example, women often leave the workforce on a temporary basis to have children or take care of an aging parent. Those women who plan to return or actually do return to the workforce find the jobs available usually have less pay and prestige. Work satisfaction is reduced and organizations fail to utilize their talents (Hewlett and Luce, 2005). There are things that organizations can do in order to retain their talent and help "off-ramping" women. These include reducing the stigma of employees using non-traditional work arrangements, maintaining relationships with these women while on leave, creating reduced-hours jobs, and offering flexible work days and work-at-home possibilities.

Smith et al. (2012), in a sample of 258 Australian women (about one-third in middle or senior management), studied the relationship of "glass ceiling" beliefs (denial, resilience, acceptance, resignation) to their happiness, work engagement, career satisfaction, and psychological and physical well-being. Denial was positively correlated with levels of work engagement and career satisfaction; resignation was negatively related to happiness and to levels of both emotional and physical well-being; resilience had positive relationships with both happiness and work engagement; and acceptance was negatively related to work engagement. Thus, organizations that address concerns about the glass ceiling and make efforts to successfully reduce these perceptions and beliefs are likely to have more engaged women managers and professionals.

Organizations have continued to create policies and practices to develop and reward upwardly mobile career paths; hence women's human and social capital have not resulted in their career advancement. Women benefit from organizational structures that support them in integrating many life roles successfully, yet the typical hierarchical organization does this poorly.

VALUES OF MANAGERIAL WOMEN AT WORK

To further understand women's career experiences, a number of studies have explored what managerial women value at work. First, McKeen and Burke (1994) asked 245 women MBA graduates – typically early in their career, and working in a number of different organizations – how important each of 19 organizational initiatives were in helping them develop a more satisfying and productive career with their organizations. Factor analysis yielded four elements: (1) family-friendly policies (for example, time off work, flexible hours, and corporate child-care centers); (2) career development programs; (3) training; and (4) challenging work assignments. Researchers found that the most important initiatives were challenging work assignments, flexible working hours, flexible vacation arrangements, family emergency days off, and computer technology facilitating work at home. These organizational initiative factors were correlated with work outcomes such as job and career satisfaction, future career progress beliefs, and the intent to quit.

Flexible Work Arrangements

There are numerous flexible work arrangements that companies are now implementing to assist their employees in integrating their work–life commitments and roles. Studies have shown that these initiatives (for example, reduced-load work arrangements, job sharing, teleworking or telecommuting, compressed work week, flexible work hours, parental leave policies) have resulted in, among other benefits, employee retention and improved performance. For example, Lee et al. (2002) reviewed effects of part-time work among professionals, which they termed reduced-load arrangements, in a variety of professions, including law, accounting, engineering, computer science, medicine, and management. They also presented data from their own study of 86 managers and professionals working in 42 different organizations; 82 participants worked on reduced-load arrangements, and four were involved in job-sharing. Most were women (77 percent), married (78 percent) with children (80 percent). The respondents worked 32 hours a week, about 17 hours less than a full-time employee. Respondents reported a high level of success with their reduced workload. Managers and human resource professionals in these workplaces were also very positive about this experiment. Communication between all relevant actors proved to be a significant factor in this success. Many more recent studies (e.g., Nugent et al., 2013) have found similar results in implementing flexible work arrangements that can positively impact the careers of women (and men).

Addressing Barriers

Through policy changes and implementing strategic and targeted initiatives, organizational leaders must also be engaged in addressing barriers that are unique to women. Although there are many (see Part IV of this *Handbook*), three will be briefly mentioned here: networking, employment gaps, and dealing with the "maternal wall."

First, Ibarra (1992) used an intergroup analysis to study differences in men's and women's access to informal networks at work. Men had greater centrality and homophily (relationships with same-sex others) in their network relationships than did women. Women's networks were differentiated in that they sought social support from women and instrumental support from men. Ties to women reduced women's centrality but increased men's. Thus, informal networks in this advertising agency were different for women and men, with men's networks seeming to have advantages. Strategic interventions must be developed – through building capacity in individual women and by changing existing structures and processes – to strengthen career development for women through networking.

Second, the backlash that results from women's employment gaps has been a concern through the decades and continues today. Burke and McKeen (1996), in a study of 792 MBA graduates of a Canadian university, many in early career stages, considered the effects of employment gaps on their levels of work and career satisfaction. They found that 384 women had no gaps (49 percent), 240 had one gap (30 percent), 149 had two gaps (14 percent), 43 had three gaps (5 percent), and 14 women had four or more gaps (2 percent). Thus, in this sample, slightly more than half the women studied had one or more career gaps (51 percent). Women reporting more gaps differed from those having fewer gaps on both personal demographics (for example, age, marital status, number of children) and work situation characteristics (for example, size of organization). Women reporting more employment gaps also indicated less current job and career satisfaction, less job involvement, lower future job prospects, and lower incomes. Men and women who have employment gaps get "punished" in various ways, but significantly more women than men have gaps in their careers (Judiesch and Lyness, 1999). Organizations must find ways to address this barrier.

Third, Williams (2004) wrote that women face a "maternal wall" of biases and stereotypes when they announce that they are pregnant. McIntosh et al. (2012) reported that motherhood remained a barrier to career progression, even in a female-dominated profession such as nursing. Mothers, for example, were rated less competent than fathers or people without children (Cuddy et al., 2004). Field research (e.g., Hebl et al., 2007) has also shown that pregnant women faced subtle discrimination. However, Morgan et al. (2013) found that it is possible to reduce this bias. They found that pregnant women fared better in job interviews when they indicated their competitive nature, availability, and work and career commitment; demonstrated that they had already developed child care arrangements; and were available to work when needed. In addition, pregnant women who saw their supervisor as more supportive of families were more willing to announce their pregnancies; supportive supervisors can be strong allies of pregnant women and new mothers (Jones et al., 2013). Finally, when women discuss their current and future employment status and plans for maternity leave with their supervisors before they take leave, they can establish an important contract with their supervisors. If these expectations are realized upon return to work, all is well; if these expectations are breached following return from maternity leave, dissatisfaction results. Thus, training supervisors as to how best to deal with women who become pregnant can not only support such women, but can also increase their retention.

IMPLICATIONS AND CONCLUSION

Burke (2005), using Catalyst's case study evidence of best practices, listed the following characteristics of successful organization initiatives supporting the career advancement of women:

- motivation and rationale linked to business goals, strategies, and profitability;
- support from the highest organizational levels;
- development of communication plans clearly stating that these best practices are associated with business issues;
- built-in accountability mechanisms so responsibility is associated with managerial efforts;
- monitoring progress and making adjustments as needed; and
- introducing a number of change initiatives simultaneously.

Other researchers (e.g., Holton, 2002) have identified the following as elements of a successful and systematic women's career development initiative: assessments and evaluations of career development for women, career development audits, mentoring and sponsorship programs, development of a women's network, work–life balance and flexibility initiatives, a leadership development program, other training and development opportunities, the identification and development of high-potential women, cross-functional training, support for women to obtain line experience, and succession planning that identifies women in the process.

In summary, there are clear and important benefits to women, men, families, and organizations in supporting women's career development. There is also a need to appreciate that women and men are socialized differently, to acknowledge the unique needs of women, and to recognize that organizations were designed by men for men. This means that women are disadvantaged as a result, which should guide the initiatives that organizations implement moving forward. Yet, it is important to note that there is great variability in the needs of women; just like men, all women are different. As outlined earlier in this chapter, work experiences are critical in the career development of women and men, and there are different career models and types of career patterns existing for women that can be helpful in strategically designing work experiences in the future. In addition, it is important to remember that supporting women's career development does not involve "fixing the women." Instead, advancing women's careers requires organizational changes starting at the executive level to achieve a gender-balanced workplace. And finally, as noted previously, it is also important to enlist more men as allies in women's advancement.

There is reason for optimism, as changing times have resulted in more talented women in managerial and professional jobs, younger women may have more female role models, more men have experience working with capable women, younger men may be more supportive of women's aspirations, more men want to spend time with their families, and organizations are facing a "war for talent." Companies are realizing that using the talents of women has become a business imperative.

Organizations need to legitimate a variety of career paths, including career breaks, in order to acknowledge the many responsibilities of women outside of their work roles, and the differing needs of women and men at various life and career stages (for example, early-career women may need challenge, support, recognition, and mentoring; whereas mid-career women may desire flexible work arrangements or a job redesign to help them be more successful in all their life and career roles). In addition to offering a variety of career path opportunities, and in order to make full use of women's talents, organizations should provide formal and informal mentors and networking opportunities for women, examine their human resource management policies and practices for bias, have senior executives support and lead work–life balance initiatives, and model cultures of inclusion.

NOTE

*   Preparation of this chapter was supported in part by York University, Canada.

REFERENCES

Arthur, M.B., and Rousseau, D. (1996). *The Boundaryless Career*. Oxford, UK: Oxford University Press.
Betz, N.E., and Fitzgerald, L.F. (1987). *The Career Psychology of Women*. New York, NY: Academic Press.
Burke, R.J. (2005). High-achieving women: Progress and challenges. In R.J. Burke and M.C. Mattis (Eds),

Supporting Women's Career Advancement: Challenges and Opportunities (pp. 13–30). Cheltenham, UK, and Northampton, MA, USA: Edward Elgar Publishing.

Burke, R.J. (2014). Organizational culture, work investments, and the careers of men: Disadvantages to women? In S. Kumra, R. Simpson, and R.J. Burke (Eds), *The Oxford Handbook of Gender in Organizations* (pp. 371–392). Oxford, UK: Oxford University Press.

Burke, R.J., Burgess, Z., and Fallon, B. (2006). Benefits of mentoring to Australian early career women managers and professionals. *Equal Opportunities International*, 25(1), 71–79.

Burke, R.J., Divinagracia, L.A., and Mamo, E. (1998). Training and development activities and career success among Filipino managerial women. *Career Development International*, 3(6), 260–265.

Burke, R.J., Koyuncu, M., and Wolpin, J. (2012). Work experiences, satisfactions and psychological well-being among women managers and professionals in Turkey. *European Journal of Psychology*, 8(1), 95–111.

Burke, R.J., and McKeen, C.A. (1990). Mentoring in organizations: Implications for women. *Journal of Business Ethics*, 9(4), 327–337.

Burke, R.J., and McKeen, C.A. (1994). Training and development activities and career success of managerial and professional women. *Journal of Management Development*, 13(5), 53–63.

Burke, R.J., and McKeen, C.A. (1996). Employment gaps and work and career satisfaction of managerial and professional women. *International Journal of Manpower*, 17(1), 47–58.

Catalyst. (1998). *Advancing Women in Business: The Catalyst Guide*. San Francisco, CA: Jossey-Bass.

Cuddy, A.J., Fiske, S.T., and Glick, P. (2004). When professionals become mothers, warmth doesn't cut the ice. *Journal of Social Issues*, 60(4), 701–718.

Fiksenbaum, L., Koyuncu, M., and Burke, R.J. (2010). Virtues, work experiences and psychological well-being among managerial women in a Turkish bank. *Equality, Diversity and Inclusion: An International Journal*, 29(2), 199–212.

Filsinger, C. (2012). How can maternity coaching influence women's re-engagement with their career development. *International Journal of Coaching and Mentoring*, 6(1), 46–56.

Fulmer, R.M., and Conger, J.A. (2004). *Growing your Company's Leaders: How Great Organizations Use Succession Management to Sustain Competitive Advantage*. New York, NY: AMACOM.

Gallos, J. (1989). Exploring women's development: Implications for career theory, practice and research. In M. Arthur, D.T. Hall, and B. Lawrence (Eds), *Handbook of Career Theory* (pp. 110–123). Cambridge, UK: Cambridge University Press.

Gersick, C., and Kram, K.E. (2002). High achieving women at midlife: An exploratory study. *Journal of Management Inquiry*, 11(1), 104–127.

Gino, F., Wilmuth, C.A., and Brooks, C.A. (2015). Compared to men, women view professional advancement as equally attainable but less desirable. *Proceedings of the National Academy of Sciences*, 112(40), 12354–12359.

Goffee, R., and Nicholson, N. (1994). Career development in male and female managers – convergence or collapse. In M.J. Davidson and R.J. Burke (Eds), *Women in Management: Current Research Issues* (pp. 80–92). London, UK: Paul Chapman.

Hall, D.T. (1996). *The Career Is Dead: Long Live the Career*. San Francisco, CA: Jossey-Bass.

Harrington, B., Van Deusen, F., and Humberd, B. (2011). *The New Dad: Caring, Committed and Conflicted*. Boston, MA: Boston College Center for Work and Family.

Hebl, M.R., King, E.B., Glick, P., Singletary, S.L., and Kazama, S. (2007). Hostile and benevolent reactions toward pregnant women: Complementary interpersonal punishments and rewards that maintain traditional roles. *Journal of Applied Psychology*, 92(6), 1499–1514.

Hewlett, S.A., and Luce, C.B. (2005). Off-ramps and on-ramps: Keeping talented women on the road to success. *Harvard Business Review*, March, pp. 43–54.

Holton, V. (2002). Training and development: Creating the right environment to help women succeed in corporate management. In R.J. Burke and D.L. Nelson (Eds), *Advancing Women's Careers* (pp. 119–138). Oxford, UK: Blackwell.

Huang, Q., El-Khouri, B.M., Johansson, G., Lindroth, S., and Sverke, M. (2007). Women's career patterns: A study of Swedish women born in the 1950s. *Journal of Occupational and Organizational Psychology*, 80(3), 387–412.

Ibarra, H. (1992). Homophily and differential returns: Sex differences in networks structure and success in an advertising firm. *Administrative Science Quarterly*, 37(3), 422–447.

Jones, K.P., King, E.B., Gilrane, V., McCausland, T., Cortina, J., and Grimm, K. (2013). The baby bump: Managing a dynamic stigma over time. *Journal of Management*. Advance online publication. doi:10.1177/0149206313503012.

Judiesch, M.K., and Lyness, K.S. (1999). Left behind? The impact of leaves of absence on managers' career success. *Academy of Management Journal*, 42(4), 641–651.

Koyuncu, M., Burke, R.J., and Fiksenbaum, L. (2006). Work engagement among women managers and professionals in a Turkish bank: Potential antecedents and consequences. *Equal Opportunities International*, 25(4), 299–310.

Kram, K.E., and Isabella, L.A. (1985). Mentoring alternatives: The role of peer relationships in career development. *Academy of Management Journal, 28*(1), 110–132.

Larwood, L., and Gutek, B.A. (1987). Working towards a theory of women's career development. In B.A. Gutek and L. Larwood (Eds), *Women's Career Development* (pp. 15–27). Thousand Oaks, CA: Sage.

Lee, M.D. (1994). Variations in career and family involvement over time: Truth and consequences. In M.J. Davidson and R.J. Burke (Eds), *Women in Management: Current Research Issues* (pp. 242–258). London, UK: Paul Chapman.

Lee, M.D., MacDermid, S.M., and Buck, M. (2002). Reduced-load work arrangements: Response to stress or quest for integrity of functions. In D.L. Nelson and R.J. Burke (Eds), *Gender, Work Stress and Health* (pp. 169–190). Washington, DC: American Psychological Association.

Luthans, F., Avey, J.B., Avolio, B.J., and Peterson, S.J. (2010). The development and resulting performance impact of positive psychological capital. *Human Resource Development Quarterly, 21*(1), 41–67.

Lyness, K.S., and Thompson, D.E. (2000). Climbing the corporate ladder: Do female and male executives follow the same route? *Journal of Applied Psychology, 89*(1), 86–101.

Mainiero, L.A., and Sullivan, S.E. (2006). *The Opt-Out Revolt: Why People Are Leaving Companies to Create Kaleidoscope Careers*. Mountain View, CA: Davies-Black Publishing.

Mattis, M.C. (1994). Organization initiatives in the USA for advancing managerial women. In M.J. Davidson and R.J. Burke (Eds), *Women in Management: Current Research Issues* (pp. 241–275). London, UK: Paul Chapman.

McIntosh, B., McQuaid, R., Munro, A., and Dabir-Alai, P. (2012). Motherhood and its impact on career progression. *Gender in Management: An International Journal, 27*(5), 346–364.

McKeen, C.A., and Burke, R.J. (1991). Work experiences and career success of managerial and professional women: Study design and preliminary findings. *Canadian Journal of Administrative Sciences, 8*(4), 251–258.

McKeen, C.A., and Burke, R.J. (1994). The women-friendly organization: Initiatives valued by organizational women. *Employee Counselling Today, 6*(1), 18–25.

McKinsey. (2013). *Lessons from the Leading Edge of Gender Diversity*. New York, NY: McKinsey.

Moen, P. (2001). The gendered life course. In L. George and R.H. Binstock (Eds), *Handbook of Aging and the Social Sciences*, 5th edn (pp. 179–196). San Diego, CA: Academic Press.

Morgan, W.B., Walker, S.S., Hebl, M.R., and King, E.B. (2013). A field experiment: Reducing interpersonal discrimination toward pregnant job applicants. *Journal of Applied Psychology, 98*(5), 799–809.

Morrison, A.M. (1992). *The New Leaders: Guidelines on Leadership Diversity in America*. San Francisco, CA: Jossey-Bass.

Morrison, A.M., White, R.P., and Van Velsor, E. (1987). *Breaking the Glass Ceiling*. Reading, MA: Addison-Wesley.

Morrison, A.M., White, R.P., and Van Velsor, E. (1992). *Breaking the Glass Ceiling: Can Women Reach the Top of America's Largest Corporations?* Reading, MA: Addison-Wesley.

Nugent, J.S., Dinalfo, S., and Giscombe, K. (2013). Advancing women's careers: A focus on strategic initiatives. In S. Vinnicombe, R.J. Burke, S. Blake-Beard, and L.L. Moore (Eds), *Handbook of Research on Women's Careers* (pp. 391–405). Cheltenham, UK, and Northampton, MA, USA: Edward Elgar Publishing.

Ohlott, P.J., Ruderman, M.N., and McCauley, C.D. (1994). Gender differences in managers' development job experiences. *Academy of Management Journal, 37*(1), 46–67.

O'Neil, D.A., and Bilimoria, D. (2005a). Women's career development phases: Idealism, endurance and reinvention. *Career Development International, 10*(3), 168–189.

O'Neil, D.A., and Bilimoria, D. (2005b). *Women and Careers: A Critical Perspective on the Theory and Practice of Women in Organizations*. Cleveland, OH: Case Western Reserve University.

O'Neil, D.A., Bilimoria, D., and Saatcioglu, A. (2004) Women's career types: Attributions of satisfaction with career success. *Career Development International, 9*(4), 478–500.

O'Neil, D.A., Hopkins, M.M., and Bilimoria, D. (2008). Women's careers at the start of the 21st century: Patterns and paradoxes. *Journal of Business Ethics, 80*(4), 727–743.

Phillips, S.D., and Imhoff, A.R. (1997). Women and career development: A decade of research. *Annual Review of Psychology, 48*(1), 31–49.

Powell, G.N., and Mainiero, L.A. (1992). Cross-currents in the river of time: Conceptualizing the complexities of women's careers. *Journal of Management, 18*(2), 215–237.

Prime, J., Otterman, M., and Salub, E.R. (2014). Engaging men through inclusive leadership. In R.J. Burke and D.A. Major (Eds), *Gender in Organizations: Are Men Allies or Adversaries to Women's Career Advancement* (pp. 365–384). Cheltenham, UK, and Northampton, MA, USA: Edward Elgar Publishing.

Ragins, B.R., and McFarlin, D.B. (1990). Perceptions of mentor roles in cross-gender mentoring relationships. *Journal of Vocational Behavior, 37*(3), 321–339.

Ragins, B.R., Townsend, B., and Mattis, M.C. (1998). Gender gap in the executive suite: CEOs and female executives report on breaking the glass ceiling. *Academy of Management Executive, 12*(1), 28–42.

Ruderman, M.N., and Ohlott, N.J., (2002) *Standing at the Crossroads: Next Steps for High-Achieving Women*. San Francisco, CA: Jossey-Bass.

Rutherford, S. (2003). Different yet equal. In R.J. Burke and M.C. Mattis (Eds), *Supporting Women's Career Advancement: Challenges and Opportunities* (pp 332–346). Cheltenham, UK, and Northampton, MA, USA: Edward Elgar Publishing.

Skinner, S. (2014). Understanding the importance of gender and leader identity formation in executive coaching for senior women. *Coaching: An International Journal of Theory, Research and Practice, 7*(1), 102–114.

Smith, P., Caputi, P., and Crittenden, N. (2012). How are women's glass ceiling beliefs related to career success? *Career Development International, 17*(5), 458–474.

Tarr-Whelan, L. (2009). *Women Lead the Way: Your Guide to Stepping Up to Leadership and Changing the World.* San Francisco, CA: Berrett-Koehler.

Vinnicimbe, S., Moore, L.L., and Anderson, D. (2013). Women's leadership programmes are still important. In S. Vinnicombe, R.J. Burke, S. Blake-Beard, and L.L. Moore (Eds), *Handbook of Research on Promoting Women's Careers* (pp. 406–419). Cheltenham, UK and Northampton, MA, USA: Edward Elgar Publishing.

White, B. (1995). The career development of successful women. *Women in Management Review, 10*(1), 4–15.

White, B., Cox, C., and Cooper, C.L. (1992). *Women's Career Development: A Study of High Flyers.* Oxford, UK: Blackwell.

Williams, J.C. (2004). The maternal wall. *Harvard Business Review, 82*(1), 26–32.

Wittenberg-Cox, A. (2013). Stop fixing women and start building managerial competences. In S. Vinnicombe, R.J. Burke, S. Blake-Beard, and L.L. Moore (Eds), *Handbook of Research Promoting Women's Careers* (pp. 106–116). Cheltenham, UK, and Northampton, MA, USA: Edward Elgar Publishing.

27. Future strategies for developing women as leaders
Faith Wambura Ngunjiri and Rita A. Gardiner

As women continue to be under-represented in positions of authority across diverse sectors and locations, there are efforts at the individual, organizational, and societal levels toward increasing their numbers and access to leadership. Leadership development efforts are aimed at growing the numbers of women available to take on leadership positions in organizations. These leadership training and development programs cost organizations billions of dollars annually (Gurdjian et al., 2014; Kassotakis and Rizk, 2015). However, few of those leadership development programs are directed at women only. This is surprising, given recent statistics demonstrating that women are not obtaining leadership positions at a significant level (Ely et al., 2011; Hopkins et al., 2008; Sugiyama et al., 2016). It seems that previous assumptions that filling the pipeline would produce gender parity in leadership have been proven incorrect (Ely et al., 2011).

Leadership development is complicated in that not only does it involve different individuals, but it is also focused on adult learning. This type of development is "multilevel and longitudinal" (Day et al., 2014, p. 64). Day et al. argue that leadership development occurs within a relational context involving peers, subordinates, supervisors, and others. Further, leadership development occurs over time (Day et al., 2014), through a mixture of progressively challenging work assignments and the necessary relational growth. Unfortunately, women often do not have access to those necessary growth experiences and relational capitals that would help them to develop a leadership identity (Ely et al., 2011).

This chapter unfolds as follows. First, we review key issues in leadership development as postulated in the other four chapters within this part of the *Handbook*. Second, we provide a succinct critical review of recent literature on women's leadership development, before turning to consider how an intersectional approach to leadership development is necessary to ensure that diversity issues are an integral component of programming. We concentrate on women-only leadership development programs because we believe these programs would be strengthened by an intersectional approach, especially because, as others have argued (e.g., Ely et al., 2011; Chapter 12 of this *Handbook*), leadership development for women involves a process of identity development (Moorosi, 2013). Such an approach could help women to recognize the complexity of identity, even as it could help to problematize what it means to be a woman and a leader in different contexts (Hernandez et al., 2015; Ospina and Foldy, 2009). Although gender bias is a problem, so too are other forms of prejudice, such as racism, classicism, and ageism, to name a few. If we want to tackle the serious issues regarding the continued under-representation of women in leadership positions and the unfair practices that women face in organizations, we need to look at this problem through a wider lens. Hence, we advocate for an intersectional approach to women's leadership development, with a focus on women-only programs. However, before we propose our intersectional approach, below we provide a summary of the four preceding chapters, focusing on developing women leaders.

Murphy, Gibson, and Kram argue in Chapter 23 that although mentoring is important, a developmental network needs to be more diverse to provide a range of supports needed for women to advance their leadership careers. First, Murphy and colleagues posit that individual leadership skills are gained through work experience. Second, it is necessary for women to see themselves as leaders if they wish to be seen by others as leaders. Further, research shows that women are often evaluated based on a masculine standard. Murphy and colleagues contend that negative cues from others may adversely affect a woman's perception of herself as leadership material. Women need to see themselves as leaders, to internalize a leadership identity; failure to do so may impede their leadership development. The authors suggest that what this means is that we need to begin building women's confidence as children and teenagers.

In Chapter 24, Clerkin and Wilson explore the difference gender makes when it comes to the types and quality of developmental experiences available to men and women to help them learn to become leaders. They argue that women have less access to the kinds of developmental experiences that are perceived as most influential on the path to leadership. Specifically, women get qualitatively and quantitatively fewer challenging assignments than men. Further, their literature review found that because women need more supportive relationships to help them gain both confidence and credibility as leaders, it is particularly important for them to have sponsors – those who can open doors, rather than merely mentors – who offer emotional and psychological support. Another important area that contributes to leadership development is coursework and training. Clerkin and Wilson found that most programs are still designed with men in mind, an idea we shall develop further as we propose more women-only leadership development programming.

In her review of both the scholarly and practitioner literature in Chapter 25, Kassotakis argues that, at least for now, there is need for both women-only and mixed-gender leadership development programming. Her review further exposes how many of the women-only programs available focus on fixing the deficiencies that women have, such as the need for personal branding, building stakeholder networks, developing assertiveness and executive presence, and building women's confidence. Kassotakis proffers that women-only programs are particularly necessary to provide a safe learning environment where women can learn from each other, engage both their gender and leadership identities, unpack second-generation bias and institutional bias issues, learn about their own unconscious prejudices, and create supportive networks to help them as they move up career ladders. We will pick up on many of these themes in our review of the literature below and our recommendation for an intersectional framework for women's leadership development.

To support women's career development, Burke contends in Chapter 26 that women are often disadvantaged because many organizations were designed by men, for men. To be successful, Burke argues, women need male allies to help them advance through the leadership hierarchy. But there are some reasons for optimism. First, he asserts that there are many talented female leaders who act as role models for younger women. Second, because men are more used to working with capable women leaders than in the past, prejudice is lessened. Finally, because companies are experiencing challenges in hiring top executives, hiring women leaders is now a business imperative. To take full advantage of the diverse potential of women's talents, Burke contends that corporations need to examine their human resource management policies and practices.

The preceding chapters provide rich resources for thinking about ways to enhance women's leadership. In this chapter, we propose an intersectionality perspective on leadership development for women. By recognizing the need to engage critically with the positionality of women at the nexus of their various identities and roles (Ngunjiri et al., 2017), together with the place of identity in leadership development for women (Chapter 12 in this *Handbook*), we may discern new strategies for women's leadership development. These strategic efforts can potentially help women to overcome the institutional barriers in their ascent to positions of authority.

Despite policy initiatives and political rhetoric surrounding gender parity, there is still a long, long way to go. Although progress in women's leadership has been made, much remains to be achieved (Adler, 2015; Madsen, 2012). Indeed, significant barriers to women's advancement in the workplace are still in place in most countries. Not only do masculine workplace cultures have a negative effect on women's upward mobility (Clark, 2011; Debebe et al., 2016; Trefalt et al., 2011), but it is also clear that changing policies without concomitant alterations in social and organizational practices will not change the gender imbalance in leadership.

Further, despite significant changes in societal beliefs around family responsibilities over the last few decades, it is still the case that women often bear the greater responsibility for child and elder care. This responsibility may, in turn, translate into many women having lower career expectations because they put their family responsibilities ahead of their careers. For this situation to change, more recognition is needed regarding how women's careers evolve differently from men's. Scholars advocate for diverse strategies to enable women to build their social capital and obtain the confidence necessary to succeed (Clark, 2011), and this also makes focusing on women-only leadership development programs an urgent imperative.

To advance women leaders, leadership development efforts are essential, right alongside cultural changes supportive of women's roles in organizations and the public arena. If women are to advance through leadership hierarchies, enhanced programming is needed that focuses on women, in addition to those programs already focusing on both men and women. In particular, women-only leadership development programs are an avenue for women to learn new skills, realize their leadership potential, enhance the development of their identity as leaders, and develop strategic networks necessary to become successful leaders (Debebe et al., 2016).

THE CASE FOR WOMEN'S LEADERSHIP PROGRAMS

Recent research by Sugiyama et al. (2016) indicates that general leadership development programs tend to draw more from a masculine approach to leading. However, studies demonstrate that women-only development programs can help women to develop their leadership capacity (Vinnicombe et al., 2013). These gender-specific programs can help women to build the necessary confidence, self-awareness, and understanding to lead others successfully. Programs that offer coaching and mentoring also aid women leaders' success (Clark, 2011; Sugiyama et al., 2016; Vinnicombe et al., 2013). One of the key learnings from women-only leadership programming is the ability to become more agentic in dealing with workplace issues (Ely et al., 2011). Furthermore, these programs help women to build supportive networks, a key factor in leadership success. Successful leadership programs must not only provide a supportive enviroment, but also include topics such as conflict and risk management as well as business ethics (Ely et al., 2011). Program organizers should help women to find suitable mentors and sponsors. This will help participants to learn how successful women leaders dealt with setbacks and overcome barriers. This knowledge can help aspiring women leaders to increase their self-efficacy.

Yet women's leadership programs are still perceived as controversial, even within some companies looking for greater gender diversity among leaders (Vinnicombe et al., 2013). One argument leveled against women's leadership programs is that they may stigmatize those who participate in them. But because women often have different ways of knowing and life experiences (Belenky, 1986), these programs can be extremely beneficial in contributing to women's development as leaders (Vinnicombe et al., 2013).

Empirical research shows that, generally, women have a more participative leadership style and lead in a transformational rather than directive manner (Eagly and Carli, 2003; Vinnicombe et al., 2013). Moreover, although male leaders receive higher ratings from employees for their ability to handle stress and confidence, women leaders excel at empathy and interpersonal skills. These gender differences influence organizational practices and workplace dynamics. Therefore, leadership programming needs to resonate with women's different gendered experiences. Sugiyama et al. (2016) found that women's leadership programs in their sample conceptualized leadership in relational terms – that a leader's role is to manage inter-relationship performance – whereas the same institutions conceptualized leadership in terms of driving business performance in their general leadership programs that were open to men and women. In their study sample of 20 women's leadership development programs (WLDPs), they found that many provided developmental support to participants. When "women are able to focus on their own development and challenges in a room full of people with similar issues and experiences" (p. 273), their leadership knowledge and personal confidence is enhanced. This is even more critical when one considers the intersecting roles women play, and the intersections of identities with which they have to contend. Before proceeding with our recommendations for an intersectional perspective, we highlight various recommendations and suggestions found in the literature on women's leadership development.

What Makes for a Successful Program?

Leadership scholars have identified various elements that contribute toward effective women's leadership development programs. Ely et al. (2011) begin with the recommendation that programming must first situate topics and tools in an analysis of second-generation gender bias. Second, programs must create a supportive environment for women's identity work. This is important to help participants recognize how they may internalize gender bias. Third, programs must help participants comprehend their individual leadership purpose. Furthermore, seeing gender from a broader, structural perspective helps to comprehend how normative ways of thinking about masculinity and femininity negatively impact ideas about leadership. For example, teaching women "the rules of the game" may be counterproductive, since leading in a masculine way violates gender norms (Ely et al., 2011). As such, leading like a man can be a negative thing for most women to do.

Vinnicombe et al. (2013) identify three different aspects that women's leadership programs must put in place to be successful. First, women and management must share responsibility for organizational change. When there is a lack of shared responsibility, women can become disillusioned about the purpose of leadership training (Jarvis et al., 2013). Second, Vinnicombe et al. (2013) argue that there needs to be a safe space for women to build their leadership development capacities. Finally, the authors identify the need for self-efficacy in women's leadership development. An important objective, therefore, is for leadership development practitioners to help women become more agentic in their leadership.

Focusing on women-only programming allows leadership development practitioners to create a safe space where female participants are able to share stories and learn from their mistakes and triumphs (Debebe, 2011). As such, learning in a women-only environment helps women leaders to validate their experiences. For programming to be most effective, therefore, trainers and facilitators need to provide a supportive environment with plenty of feedback and coaching. Creating a women's only environment is but one component; facilitators also need to develop "gender-sensitive teaching and learning practices" (Debebe, 2011, p. 704). One huge benefit of women-only programs is that these programs enable participants to learn to navigate gender issues in organizational contexts (Debebe, 2011). Yet development programs can only do so much; organizations must also be willing to change to allow more women to see themselves as leaders. If more women leaders are desired, then organizational barriers to success must also be lifted.

One aspect that may interfere with a woman's ability to move up the career ladder is integrating the various roles that women play in the workplace, at home, and in their communities; that is, finding work–life balance or integration. The conflict between work and life may result in women refusing to take on senior leadership roles if they privilege their life (that is, familial) responsibilities over "climbing up" the proverbial career ladder (Debebe, 2011). But there are other barriers to women's leadership, such as second-generation bias, which we discuss next.

Overcoming second-generation bias

Researchers explain that second-generation bias is different from the overt discrimination of women (that is, first-generation bias) experienced in earlier years. In concert with Ely et al. (2011), Trefalt et al. (2011) argue that gender equity in leadership is curtailed by organizational gender bias. This bias is deeply entrenched in many organizational cultures, negatively affecting women's leadership success. Trefalt et al. state that:

> sustainable progress can only be achieved when we surface, understand, and address the subtle ways that gender dynamics shape women's paths to leadership and the relationships women develop to advance their careers. These dynamics, often called second generation gender bias, are deeply embedded in the culture, norms and work practices in organizations, playing out below the surface of formal systems of hiring, promotion, and compensation. (p. 1)

Trefalt et al. argue that these second-generation biases are a powerful hindrance to women's progress into leadership in organizations.

Although women participants are, in general, positive about single-sex leadership programming, progress in women's leadership continues to be stalled by second-generation gender bias (Ely et al., 2011). This bias exists because of the "masculinization" of organizational cultures and the pressure women feel to do business "like a man" (Ely et al., 2011; Vinnicombe et al., 2013). Additionally, second-generation bias may overlook those workplace practices that seem gender-neutral but, in reality, negatively affect women's career prospects (Trefalt et al., 2011). The fact that these practices are subtle and operate below the surface makes them all the more difficult to uproot within organizational cultures, structures, and processes, impacting the effectiveness of leadership development efforts. But these gender biases in organizational culture speak to broader societal issues, as we now demonstrate.

Sexuality and gender bias

Today, there is an overwhelming focus on the sexualized body (Kelan, 2013). Media images influence societal attitudes regarding women leaders (Kelan, 2013; Mavin and Grandy, 2012). Leaders' bodies are often read in a way that privileges and reinforces heterosexual male leadership norms. But women also act to "police" other women's bodies, leading to a restricted idea of what the ideal women leader should look like (Mavin and Grandy, 2012). Chapter 22 of this *Handbook* has a more detailed discussion of the effect of media on women and leadership.

The idea that women leaders must hide their sexuality also points to a gender bias in terms of how professional femininity is constructed. Kelan (2013) argues that the way women dress reinforces normative readings of gender. She explores how her MBA students interpreted leadership ability through media representations of leaders. Although women students liked the way that some women leaders dressed for power, male students viewed any image they judged "sexy" as dismissive of women's capabilities. What this suggests is that women must dress conservatively and carefully if they want to be seen as successful. Gender is normalized and anesthetized through our clothes, revealing how gender norms are reproduced in the workplace. Kelan (2013) argues that leadership development is about changing how we perceive ourselves. Current leadership practices often encourage a way of thinking that reinforces dominant gender narratives. Tactically, using images in leadership development may help us to understand how gender norms are reproduced, and serve to reinforce a particular kind of leadership (Kelan, 2013). An intersectional perspective can also help us to be more attentive to what we see, as we will argue in a later section.

Responding to networking challenges and opportunities

Leadership development programs must teach women strategies to learn how to expand networks by deepening and widening their relationships. Ely et al. (2011) argue that men and women use their networks differently. It appears that men are more willing to use networks in a multipurpose fashion and be willing to ask others for career advice, whereas women shy away from doing this because it seems inauthentic. In addition, women need to learn how to develop strategies for connecting with potential sponsors. Although some women are reluctant to network, they need to recognize how the skills and personal attributes that helped them obtain their current career may not help them rise further. Clark (2011) argues that networking and mentoring are key to building social capital and enhancing future career prospects. There is still, however, a gender gap in terms of building enough social capital to tap into networks successfully (Trefalt et al., 2011). The challenge of networking is further complicated when race, ethnicity, national origins, and other identity markers intersect in individual women's lives (Hernandez et al., 2015). Therefore, leadership development practitioners must challenge themselves to create leadership programming that serves to enhance women's "power and decision-making authority" and recognizes cultural differences, as detailed in the *Asilomar Declaration and Call to Action on Women and Leadership* (Madsen and Rosser-Mims, 2015, p. 6).

Rethinking negotiation and change management

It is commonly assumed that most women are not good at negotiation (Ely et al., 2011). But Ely et al. (2011) argue that women are just as competent at negotiation, but that they negotiate for different things. For instance, women may prefer to negotiate matters such as time off for family. Leadership developers need to encourage women to improve their negotiation skills by focusing on specific situations, rather than concentrating on deal-making. Having exercises where women practice their negotiation tactics will also help them to gain confidence in their ability to negotiate. Not only will this expand an understanding of what negotiation means, but it will also serve to increase women's agentic capacities. However, leadership development practitioners would be well advised to recognize that the intersection of gender with other identities, such as race, further complicates negotiation and change efforts by women of color. The fear of being branded an angry black woman, for example, may discourage a black woman from engaging in agentic behavior (Hernandez et al., 2015).

Leading change requires persuasive skills and the ability to inspire others. Yet because some women leaders are hired when companies are in trouble – that is, the "glass cliff" experience – these skills many need further development (Haslam and Ryan, 2008). Case studies that show different women who have transformational and transactional skills can help women to build confidence in their own leadership style (Ely et al., 2011). Sharing stories can also help women to understand how others are similarly affected by organizational gender bias, and that getting ahead is not just about individual merit.

Making career transitions

Sometimes, it can be difficult to move to the next level if a woman is good at her job. According to Clark (2011), "learned behaviours can be just as detrimental to career progress as contextual barriers. Women-only programs help participants become aware of these self-limiting behaviours and to explore strategies for overcoming them" (p. 508). Participants should reflect on how the talent for one job may not work for another. Spending too much time problem-solving, for example, while male colleagues "do" impression management, may not be a wise strategy (Ely et al., 2011). Furthermore, women who want to move up the corporate ladder need to engage in self-reflection to understand that senior leadership positions require personal sacrifices. Taking on a senior leadership role requires a person not only to be willing to take on greater responsibilities, but also to learn how to become more politically savvy, something that some women find difficult.

Other women engage in masculine models of leadership because they think this is what they need to do to get ahead. Yet such an approach may be counterproductive. Mavin et al. (2014) argue that those women in senior leadership positions must not only do gender well, but they must also do it differently. Senior women leaders are held to a normative gender standard and, hence, they must possess feminine characteristics such as empathy. Moreover, the commonplace assumption is that heterosexual gender homogeneity is the norm across most senior levels of an organization (Atewologun and Sealy, 2014) and, as Mavin et al. (2014) explain, "it is well established that these positions are 'masculinized' and constructed around male norms" (p. 440). At the same time, to be a good leader, women must be willing to do the difficult work to obtain results. Yet when women leaders act in a way that is perceived as unfeminine, they are often castigated for their action.

To mitigate this problem, facilitators need to develop a holistic approach to leadership development. Such an approach encompasses not only the content and teaching methods, but also how women's experiences and core values are respected (Debebe, 2011). Creating these conditions enables women to recognize their shared experiences and to explore ethical dilemmas in a non-confrontational manner. This frees women to talk about gender-related concerns, many of which participants may feel uncomfortable sharing when men are present. Programs that offer training for women only, and sometimes for women of color only, are necessary to deal with the intersecting roles women play, and the identities women occupy, in an environment that is safe for engaging in identity work. Thus, for more women to see themselves as leaders, it is necessary for leadership development programs to create safe spaces to encourage sharing of positive and negative workplace experiences.

Creating safe spaces
For participants to feel safe enough to share their experiences, they must experience a sense of belonging and a caring environment. Creating safe space is crucial for women to feel able to speak frankly about the challenges in the workplace. Such frank talking may well not take place if someone feels that they are in the minority (Hernandez et al., 2015; Rosette et al., 2016). Those who create and develop leadership programming must be alert to how "horizontal violence" between women is perpetuated (Madsen, 2012). Acknowledging gendered micro-practices of violence in the workplace (Mavin et al., 2014) may make some participants uncomfortable. However, negative workplace interactions must be addressed if we are to develop programming that speaks to the realities of women's lives.

Alongside a supportive environment, women must be willing to engage in difficult conversations (Jarvis et al., 2013). These conversations are necessary to allow for different voices to be heard. Having space to engage in difficult conversations about how we communicate and when we show empathy to others is crucial (Lugg and Tooms, 2010). Exchanges need to be open-ended, since it is in wrestling with difficult questions from diverse perspectives that we encourage greater empathy and the ability to lead successfully in complex situations, a process that is more likely when an intersectional framework is utilized in developing leadership development programming that is cognizant of the intersections of race with gender, sexuality, and other identities (Jarvis et al., 2013; Lugg and Tooms, 2010).

Identity work
Identity work reveals that individuals construct their identity in relation to the norms of their environment. In adopting the term "intersectional identity salience," Atewologun (2014) counters the "essential assumptions about social identities" (p. 280) by illustrating how organizations influence which identity factors are perceived as meaningful. A leader's agentic ability, for example, may be constrained by which identities are regarded as "leaderly" in a particular workplace. Additionally, Lugg and Tooms (2010) suggest that

there is little discussion of how workplace bullying negatively affects queer individuals. Identity work may be important for reconceptualizing leadership development programs, but it has to be conceived in a robust way. Next, we argue that an intersectional lens may be beneficial in developing future leadership programs that take seriously the roles and identities that may be salient for emerging women leaders.

AN INTERSECTIONAL APPROACH TO WOMEN'S LEADERSHIP DEVELOPMENT

The term "intersectionality" was conceptualized to reference the idea that, for women and people of color, gender intersects with race and other identities to complicate their experiences in organizations. Categories that are socially constructed impact the experiences of women and people of color in a matrix of domination or oppression at the intersections of gender, race/ethnicity, national origins, and other difference markers in specific societies (Collins, 2004; Crenshaw, 1991; Hernandez et al., 2015). An intersectional framework helps to uncover the challenges and opportunities, the moments of oppression, as well as those that demonstrate privilege, in the experiences of women as leaders in various organizational contexts (Livingston et al., 2012; Ngunjiri et al., 2017, Rosette et al., 2016). Ngunjiri et al. (2017) identify three critical contributions of intersectionality relating to women and leadership: (1) intersectionality exposes the hierarchical discourse in women's leadership studies; (2) intersectionality foregrounds the complexities of women leaders' identities; and (3) intersectionality problematizes the fluidity and global nature of women leaders' experiences. Thinking through these three inter-related contributions allows for a rethinking of leadership development programming in a more inclusive manner. We discuss each aspect in turn below.

Intersectionality Exposes Hierarchical Discourse

Using an intersectional framework helps to expose the hierarchical discourse in women's leadership studies that often privilege gender over other identities, particularly in Western countries (Holvino, 2010; Ospina and Foldy, 2009; Livingston et al., 2012). Further, an intersectional perspective reveals that gender is often ignored in leadership development theory and practice. For example, in the seminal literature review of 25 years' worth of leadership development literature from the *Leadership Quarterly*, there is only one significant mention of women and leadership: Eagly's (2005) argument that it is challenging for women to demonstrate relational authenticity due to the interactions of gender role and leadership role requirements (Day et al., 2014). Twenty-five years' worth of studies from the pre-eminent leadership journal, and only one reference with a significant focus on gender, is very telling. Similarly, Madsen and Scribner (2017) examined 15 management journals, and found that five of them did not publish any studies with female-only participants in the period January 1, 2010 to March 1, 2016 (see Madsen and Scribner, 2017, for a comprehensive analysis of the management journals).

Identities are far more complex than any one category can illuminate (Collins, 2004; Dill and Zambrana, 2009). Hence, women's leadership programs that focus exclusively on gender may not offer participants a nuanced understanding of how power and privilege operate in the workplace. Instead, these programs may unwittingly act to silence voices of dissent. For example, it might be uncomfortable for a black woman to contradict the white trainer in a room full of other white women. Similarly, it might be difficult for a lesbian to discuss how she feels discriminated against because of her sexuality if the examples that the facilitators provide are always about heterosexual encounters. Whether implicitly or explicitly, leadership programs that focus exclusively on women's experience may perpetuate social inequality by ignoring the effect of other identity characteristics (Holvino, 2010). This is why, Debebe and Reinert (2014) maintain, we need a more holistic approach to leadership development that recognizes the diversity of women's lived experiences. Adopting an intersectional approach can allow for the effects of workplace diversity to be better understood and appropriate measures crafted to uproot oppressive policies, structures, and cultural norms. Such an approach requires new ways of thinking, not only about how we deliver programming, but also about how trainers and participants need to be mindful of difference.

Intersectionality Foregrounds the Complexity of Identity

Despite decades of activism and policy changes, it is still the case that a relatively small number of women hold senior leadership positions (Gardiner, 2015). If we look at these senior women leaders, on average, we find commonalities – in the Western world at least – in that these women are more likely to be white, middle-class, able-bodied individuals. If we focus just on gender, we will not obtain the kind of inclusive leadership that is so fundamental to the well-being of organizations, especially those interested in social justice. An intersectional framework may help us to develop leadership programming, mindful of how multiple axes of identity inter-relate (Ngunjiri et al., 2017). It is our view that an intersectional framework can help leadership development practitioners to engage in new, creative approaches (Davis, 2008).

Programming that gives space for thinking about ethical problems and providing potential solutions could be one way that deep learning occurs. Developing problems or case studies that tease out intersectional workplace dilemmas could be another method. Sharing stories regarding participants' experiences of workplace marginalization might also help participants to consider a problem from different perspectives. These practical examples can assist participants to learn to blend leadership theory and organizational practice. In turn, this may enable leaders to become more aware of how power and privilege operate in workplace situations.

An intersectional framework can help us to better comprehend how women and men perpetuate injustices, both structural and individual (Mavin et al., 2014). White privilege is a significant injustice; working with an intersectional framework can assist programmers to become more sensitive with regard to privilege. Atewologun and Sealy (2014) argue that an intersectional perspective can help us to understand the complexities and fluidity of white privilege. Thus, examining privilege in conjunction with disadvantage serves to illuminate the complexities of identity. But these conversations are not discussed in leadership training literature, perhaps because they reveal that women leaders do not always act in a manner that supports other women (Mavin et al., 2014) (see Chapter 21 of the *Handbook* for an in-depth discussion). Yet difficult conversations in a supportive environment may lead to the kind of breakthrough learning that can help to advance a more inclusive and, thus, socially responsible leadership. Although participants may feel uncomfortable, it is necessary to move beyond a comfortable place if we are to develop ethical leaders who are willing to recognize their own prejudices so as to be better able to respond in a respectful way.

Thus, adopting an intersectional framework can help us to better understand the complexities of power and privilege in the workplace. Recognizing that privilege is "contextual, conferred and contested" (Atewologun and Sealy, 2014, p. 427) also helps us to comprehend how marginalized individuals face daily struggles. Atewologun and Sealy (2014) describe how senior executive leaders from ethnic minorities are often "hyperaware of privilege" (p. 427). This hyperawareness is something that may be lacking from those who fit the dominant white heteronormative leadership stereotype. But learning from those who have experienced being marginalized in the workplace may help leaders to understand how privilege operates. As a result of this greater knowledge, leaders may become better able to effect positive organizational change that is respectful of difference.

Engaging in uncomfortable conversations could provide the impetus and space for leadership training to invoke deep learning. Jarvis et al. (2013) suggest that there needs to be space for participants to engage with "everyday" events so that what is taking place locally can be shared and better understood. It may also be through sharing anxieties in the workplace that change can occur. For the trainer, this requires being willing to articulate and listen to a myriad of viewpoints, since it is through contradiction and tension that the deepest learning may take place.

Yet, because leadership development programs are often evaluated based on narrow criteria set up by employers ahead of time, it can mean that this kind of deep learning may be stymied (Jarvis et al., 2013). This is why it is important that leadership development facilitators understand their responsibility not just to the employer, but also to the participants. For example, it may be that those who voice their dissent are not wanted in particular workplaces. By encouraging women to speak out, programs may make it harder for some to be satisfied with their employer (Jarvis et al., 2013). In theory, one could argue that such dissatisfaction may prove useful because the would-be leader may discover the confidence to look for a new role in a different workplace. In the short term, however, programming that encourages agentic behavior may lead to employee disatisfaction with her current employer. Moreover, what an employee regards as productive change in the workplace may be regarded in a very different light by an employer. Thus, it is important that leadership development programs offer women support for occasions when their agentic views may be out of step with their organization. But to do so would require a long-term commitment, from both the leadership trainer and the employer. Often, this is not how these programs operate. This might suggest that it would be better to run more leadership programs in-house. The danger here, however, is that participants may feel even more unwilling to share their opinions honestly, because they are wary of organizational backlash should they not toe the corporate line.

Intersectionality Problematizes Women Leaders' Experiences

Until recently, little has been written about how intersectionality can provide us with a theoretical lens through which to problematize women's experiences of leadership (Choo and Ferree, 2010; Gardiner, 2015; Hernandez et al., 2015; Purdie-Vaughns and Eibach,

2008). Not only can intersectionality provide conceptual richness, but adopting an intersectional approach to women's leadership development may also help us to better understand how global complexities affect how women become leaders. Identities may change in different locales and cultures (Blackmore, 2009; Corlett and Mavin, 2014; Hernandez et al., 2015). What works well in one cultural milieu may be inappropriate in another. For example, an individualistic approach to leading that is common in the West may be inappropriate in cultures that have a more collective understanding of leadership. Taking a leadership development program aimed at women in North America and applying it to women in Africa or Asia may not only be ineffective, but may also perpetuate the Western cultural hegemony that postcolonial feminist scholars have long argued against. We suggest that an intersectional approach can help researchers and practitioners to develop leadership programming that is more responsive to different, culturally appropriate ways of leading.

CONCLUSION AND MOVING FORWARD

In this chapter, we have made the case for women-only leadership development programming supported by relevant recent literature, including the other four chapters in this part of the *Handbook*. Our argument is that women-only leadership development programs are necessary because of the continued under-representation of women in senior leadership positions, in addition to the tendency for general leadership programs to be designed with men in mind (Sugiyama et al., 2016). We argue that an intersectional framework enables us to develop women's leadership programming that speaks to the complexity of lived experience. There are many positive aspects of women-only leadership programming, as we show. We agree with many scholars that creating safe spaces where women can talk honestly about their leadership experiences is a positive step (Debebe, 2011). However, a focus on gender alone may sometimes be to the detriment of other axes of identity. Lived experience tells us that identities change. What is most salient in one situation will be different in another (Hernandez et al., 2015). It is necessary to ensure that leadership development programs are cognizant of the intersecting roles women play, and the identities women occupy, in an environment that is safe for engaging in identity work.

It is imperative that those scholars and practitioners engaged in leadership development programming reflect upon their core goals. Although we agree with suggestions that future programming focuses on helping women feel more comfortable in using their networks to enhance their careers and to access mentors (Clark, 2011), it is also important for scholars and practitioners to engage in reflection with regard to what they perceive as most essential to their leadership programs. That is, what is the specific purpose of the leadership development program? Is programming specifically for women to gain leadership positions on a par with their male counterparts? Or is programming aimed at broader equity and social justice goals? We would argue that it is unlikely that programming can succeed in these two aims at the same time, since an approach founded on social justice may well have different aims from one focused on developing individual women leaders.

Leadership development occurs over time and involves many individuals (Day et al., 2014). An intersectional framework recognizes that women have different career obstacles.

Some may lack social capital and networks. Others may find that being agentic or assertive is counterproductive. Many may not have access to the powerful relationships that can lead to advancement. All these women are potential leaders. As such, we need leadership development programs that help diverse women to succeed. An intersectional framework urges scholars and practitioners to pay attention to the impacts that race, gender, ethnicity, national origins, and sexual identities might have on women, and to appropriately mitigate against any disadvantages that minority identity bestows upon them. In this regard, ensuring that women, especially those further minoritized by other identity markers, are getting the necessary relational, social, cultural, and organizational resources to level the playing field for accessing leadership development becomes an imperative.

Finally, adopting an intersectional approach to leadership training, we believe, would enrich any leadership development programming. Such an approach to leadership development helps to recognize the nuanced ways in which identity matters to leadership. And this is good not just for women, but for all those who work in organizations.

REFERENCES

Adler, N.J. (2015). Women leaders: Shaping history in the 21st century. In F.W. Ngunjiri and S.R. Madsen (Eds), *Women as Global Leaders* (pp. 21–50). Charlotte, NC: IAP.

Atewologun, D. (2014). Sites of intersectional identity salience. *Gender in Management: An International Journal, 29*(5), 277–290. doi: 10.1108/GM-12-2013-0140.

Atewologun, D. and Sealy, R. (2014). Experiencing privilege at ethnic, gender and senior intersections. *Journal of Managerial Psychology, 29*(4) 423–439.

Belenky, M.F. (1986). *Women's Ways of Knowing: The Development of Self, Voice, and Mind.* New York, NY: Basic Books.

Blackmore, J. (2009). International response essay leadership for social justice: A transnational dialogue. *Journal of Research on Leadership Education, 4*(1), 1–10. Retrieved from http://files.eric.ed.gov/fulltext/EJ875405.pdf.

Choo, H., and Ferree, M. (2010). Practicing intersectionality in sociological research: A critical analysis of inclusions, interactions, and institutions in the study of inequalities. *Sociological Theory, 28*(2), 129–149.

Clark, M. (2011). Advancing women's careers through leadership development programs. *Employee Relations, 33*(5), 498–515.

Collins, P.H. (2004). Learning from the outsider-within: The sociological significance of Black feminist thought. In S. Harding (Ed.), *The Feminist Standpoint Theory Reader: Intellectual and Political Controversies* (pp. 103–126). New York, NY, USA and London, UK: Routledge.

Corlett, S., and Mavin, S. (2014). Intersectionality, identity and identity work. *Gender in Management: An International Journal, 29*(5), 258–276. doi: 10.1108/GM-12-2013-0138.

Crenshaw, K. (1991). Mapping the margins: Intersectionality, identity politics, and violence against women of color. *Stanford Law Review, 43*(6), 1241–1299.

Day, D.V., Fleenor, J.W., Atwater, L.E., Sturm, R.E., and McKee, R.A. (2014). Advances in leader and leadership development: A review of 25 years of research and theory. *Leadership Quarterly, 25*(1), 63–82. doi. org/10.1016/j.leaqua.2013.11.004.

Davis, K. (2008). Intersectionality as buzzword. *Feminist Theory, 9*(1), 67.

Debebe, G. (2011). Creating a safe environment for women's leadership transformation. *Journal of Management Education, 35*(5), 679–712. doi: 10.177/1052562910307501.

Debebe, G., Anderson, D., Bilimoria, D., and Vinnicombe, S.M. (2016). Women's leadership development programs: Lessons learned and new frontiers. *Journal of Management Education, 40*(3), 231–252. doi:10.1177/10 52562916639079.

Debebe, G., and Reinert, K.A. (2014). Leading with our whole selves: A multiple identity approach to leadership development. In M.L. Miville and A.D. Ferguson (Eds), *Handbook of Race-Ethnicity and Gender in Psychology* (pp. 272–293). New York, NY: Springer.

Dill, B.T., and Zambrana, R.E. (Eds). (2009). *Emerging Intersections: Race, Class, and Gender in Theory, Policy, and Practice.* New Brunswick, NJ: Rutgers University Press.

Eagly, A.H. (2005). Achieving relational authenticity in leadership: Does gender matter?. *Leadership Quarterly, 16*(3), 459–474. doi.org/10.1016/j.leaqua.2005.03.007.

Eagly, A.H., and Carli, L.L. (2003). The female leadership advantage: An evaluation of the evidence. *Leadership Quarterly*, *14*(6), 807–834.

Ely, R.J., Ibarra, H., and Kolb, D.M. (2011). Taking gender into account: Theory and design for women's leadership development programs. *Academy of Management Learning and Education*, *10*(3), 474–493. doi: 10.5465/amle.2010.0046.

Gardiner, R. (2015). *Gender, Authenticity and Leadership: Thinking with Arendt*. London, UK and New York, NY, USA: Palgrave Macmillan.

Gurdjian, P., Halbeisen, T., and Lane, K. (2014). Why leadership development programs fail. McKinsey & Co. Retrieved from http://www.mckinsey.com/global-themes/leadership/why-leadership-development-prog rams-fail.

Haslam, S.A., and Ryan, M.K. (2008). The road to the glass cliff: Differences in the perceived suitability of men and women for leadership positions in succeeding and failing organizations. *Leadership Quarterly*, *19*(5), 530–546. doi:10.1016/j.leaqua.2008.07.011.

Hernandez, K.C., Ngunjiri, F.W., and Chang, H. (2015). Exploiting the margins in higher education: A collaborative autoethnography of three foreign-born female faculty of color. *International Journal of Qualitative Studies in Education*, *28*(5), 533–551. doi:10.1080/09518398.2014.933910.

Holvino, E. (2010). Intersections: The simultaneity of race, gender and class in organization studies. *Gender, Work and Organization*, *17*(3), 248–277.

Hopkins, M.M., O'Neil, D.A., Passarelli, A., and Bilimoria, D. (2008). Women's leadership development strategic practices for women and organizations. *Consulting Psychology Journal: Practice and Research*, *60*(4), 348–365. doi: 10.1037/a0014093.

Jarvis, C., Gulati, A., McCririck, V., and Simpson, P. (2013). Leadership matters: Tensions in evaluating leadership development. *Advances in Developing Human Resources*, *15*(1) 27–47. doi: 10.1177/1523422312467138.

Kassotakis, M.E., and Rizk, J.B. (2015). Advancing women's leadership development: Effective practices for the design and delivery of global women's leadership programs. In F.W. Ngunjiri and S.R. Madsen (Eds), *Women as Global Leaders* (pp. 163–185). Charlotte, NC: IAP.

Kelan, E.K. (2013). The becoming of business bodies: Gender, appearance, and leadership development. *Management Learning*, *44*(1), 45–61.

Livingston, R.W., Rosette, A.S., and Washington, E.F. (2012). Can an agentic Black woman get ahead? The impact of race and interpersonal dominance on perceptions of female leaders. *Psychological Science*, *23*(4), 354–358. doi: 10.1177/0956797611428079.

Lugg, C.A., and Tooms, A.K. (2010). A shadow of ourselves: Identity erasure and the politics of queer leadership. *School Leadership and Management*, *30*(1), 77–91.

Madsen, S.R. (2012). Women and leadership in higher education: Learning and advancement in leadership programs. *Advances in Developing Human Resources*, *14*(1), 3–10. doi: 10.1177/1523422311429668.

Madsen, S.R., and Rosser-Mims, D. (Compilers). (2015). *Asilomar Declaration and Call to Action on Women and Leadership*. Women and Leadership Affinity Group, International Leadership Association. Retrieved from http://www.ila-net.org/Communities/AG/Asilomar_Declaration2015.pdf.

Madsen, S.R. and Scribner, R.T. (2017). A perspective on gender in management: The need for strategic cross-cultural scholarship on women in management and leadership. *Cross Cultural and Strategic Management*, *24*(2).

Mavin, S., and Grandy, G. (2012). Doing gender well and differently in management. *Gender in Management: An International Journal*, *27*(4), 218–231. doi:10.1108/17542411211244768.

Mavin, S., Grandy, G., and Williams, J. (2014). Experiences of women elite leaders doing gender: Intra-gender micro-violence between women. *British Journal of Management*, *25*(3), 439–455. doi:10.1111/14 67-8551.12057.

Moorosi, P. (2013). Constructing a leader's identity through a leadership development programme: An intersectional analysis. *Educational Management Administration and Leadership*, *42*(6), 792–807. doi: 10.1177/17411 43213494888.

Ngunjiri, F., Almquist, J., Beebe, M., Elbert, C., Gardiner, R., and Shockness, M. (2017). Intersectional leadership praxis: Unpacking the experiences of women leaders at the nexus of roles and identities. In J. Storberg-Walker and P. Haber-Curran (Eds), *Theorizing Women and Leadership: New Insights and Contributions from Multiple Perspectives*. (pp. 249–263). Charlotte, NC: Information Age Publishing.

Ospina, S., and Foldy, E. (2009). A critical review of race and ethnicity in the leadership literature: Surfacing context, power and the collective dimensions of leadership. *Leadership Quarterly*, *20*(6), 876–896.

Purdie-Vaughns, V., and Eibach, R. (2008). Intersectional invisibility: The distinctive advantages and disadvantages of multiple subordinate-group identities. *Sex Roles*, *59*(5), 377–391. doi: 10.1007/s11199-008-9424-4.

Rosette, A.S., Koval, C.Z., Ma, A., and Livingston, R. (2016). Race matters for women leaders: Intersectional effects on agentic deficiencies and penalties. *Leadership Quarterly*, *27*(3), 429–445. doi:http://dx.doi.org/10.1016/j.leaqua.2016.01.008.

Sugiyama, K., Cavanagh, K.V., van Esch, C., Bilimoria, D., and Brown, C. (2016). Inclusive leadership development: Drawing from pedagogies of women's and general leadership development programs. *Journal of Management Education*, 40(3), 253–292. doi:10.1177/1052562916632553.

Trefalt, S., Merrill-Sands, D., Kolb, D., Wilson, F., and Carter, S. (2011). Closing the women's leadership gap: Who can help? CGO Insights – Center for Gender and Organizations Briefing Notes 32. April. Retrieved from http://www.simmons.edu/~/media/Simmons/About/CGO/Documents/INsights/Insights-32.ashx?la=en.

Vinnicombe, S., Moore, L.L., and Anderson, D. (2013). Women's leadership programs are still important. In S. Vinnicombe, R.J. Burke, S. Blake-Beard, and L.L. Moore (Eds), *Handbook of Research on Promoting Women's Careers* (pp. 406–420). Cheltenham, UK and Northampton, MA, USA: Edward Elgar Publishing.

Afterword
Susan R. Madsen

I want to share a few final thoughts as I conclude my work on this book. Although there are many women and leadership books published, this one is truly unique, as it digs deeply into some areas of inquiry that have not yet been articulated and discussed in a single volume. In the Introduction to this *Handbook* I asked the question, "Why do we need another book focused on gender and leadership research?" I then answered that although some progress has been made, what we are currently doing is not working. This book offers more answers, more theory, and more research. It suggests ideas for more strategic change interventions that are based on rigorously tested women and leadership theory and research. It offers new findings that can get us all thinking more "outside the box" for solutions. It can, if we use it in the way that it is intended, help us to shake things up as theorists, scholars, researchers, and practitioners so that we can work to change the status of women globally.

I believe that this *Handbook* is a gift to the field of women and leadership, and I hope you agree. First, you have read some chapters that set the stage (that is, the current status of women leaders, women and leadership declarations and calls to action, and some overarching themes and metaphors that seem to guide current thinking). Next, you reviewed a series of chapters that presented theoretical lenses that frame (or should frame) our current scholarship. Third, the *Handbook* then deeply explored the range of women's individual motivators to lead (that is, aspirations, ambition, identity, purpose and calling, power, neuroscience, and women's understandings of success and choice). Fourth, you read the latest literature on gender-based leadership challenges and barriers; and finally, the book concluded by focusing on the most up-to-date research on how to develop women leaders.

I do want to note that I intentionally decided not to have specific chapters that addressed critical elements or variables that should never be overlooked. These have included, but were not limited to, different contexts (for example, community, country, global), various sectors (for example, corporate, government, non-profit), and a range of demographic differences (for example, race, ethnicity, age, marital status, family situation). Instead of requesting separate chapters on each, I asked all the authors to address these constructs within their chapters throughout the book. This book definitely does not cover everything within the women and leadership arena, but it does move the field forward, and, in doing so, brings to light more questions. I have always said to my students: the sign of a strong scholarly dialogue is when individuals leave the interaction or experience with more questions than answers.

To conclude, I want to highlight an important point that has not been discussed enough in this book. In order to truly understand women and leadership, we must first actually do more research on a variety of precursors that fall under the gender equality umbrella. Without more theory, research, and strategic initiatives around the most basic elements of strengthening the impact of women, we cannot make substantial and sustainable changes in the upper echelons of leaders. Unequal opportunities and poor treatment of women remain concerning in nearly all countries, contexts, and sectors (Madsen et al., 2015). As quoted previously, the McKinsey Global Institute's (2015) "The power of parity: How advancing women's equality can add $12 trillion to global growth" stated that "gender inequality is a pressing global issue with huge ramifications not just for the lives and live-lihoods of girls and women, but more generally, for human development, labor markets, productivity, GDP [gross domestic product] growth, and inequality" (p. ii). Foundational areas of inquiry that provide a stronger footing for women to become leaders include, but are not limited to, the following topics (see McKinsey Global Institute, 2015):

- child marriage;
- digital inclusion for women;
- female education levels;
- female labor-force participation rate;
- female political representation;
- financial inclusion for women;
- legal protections for women;
- maternal mortality;
- representation of women in professional and technical jobs;
- sex ratio at birth;
- unmet needs for family planning;
- unpaid care work;
- violence against women;
- wage gap for similar work.

To me, all of the work we do as theorists, scholars, and practitioners that focuses on any of the above list of critical areas related to gender inequality – directly or indirectly – serves to strengthen the impact of women in formal and informal leadership roles around the world. For example, working to enhance female education levels has a direct relationship to women becoming leaders. When women feel safe, they are more likely to find their voices and their confidence; they are more likely to influence others positively. In short, they are more likely to become leaders.

My friend Meg Wheatley (2010) introduced me to a prophecy from the Elders of the Hopi Nation, said to be given in Oraibi, Arizona, on June 8, 2000. It was addressed, "To my fellow swimmers":

Here is a river flowing now very fast.
It is so great and swift that there are those who will be afraid,
who will try to hold on to the shore.
They are being torn apart and will suffer greatly.

Know that the river has its destination.
The elders say we must let go of the shore.
Push off into the middle of the river,
and keep our heads above water.

And I say see who is there with you and celebrate.
At this time in history, we are to take nothing personally,

least of all ourselves,
for the moment we do, our spiritual growth and journey come to a halt.

The time of the lone wolf is over. Gather yourselves.
Banish the word struggle from your attitude and vocabulary.
All that we do now must be done in a sacred manner and in celebration.
For we are the ones we have been waiting for.

Although much work remains to be done, as we do our part in whatever way we choose –
researching, publishing, speaking, mentoring, coaching, teaching, educating, motivating,
and inspiring – life will change for one girl or woman at a time, for one family or group
at a time, for one entity or organization at a time, for one village or community at a time,
and even for one country or region at a time.

And that is what matters most.

REFERENCES

Madsen, S.R., Ngunjiri, F.W., Longman, K.A., and Cherrey, C. (Eds) (2015). *Women and Leadership around the World*. Charlotte, NC: Information Age Publishing.
McKinsey Global Institute. (2015). The power of parity: How advancing women's equality can add $12 trillion to global growth. September. Retrieved from http://www.mckinsey.com/global-themes/employment-and-growth/how-advancing-womens-equality-can-add-12-trillion-to-global-growth.
Wheatley, M. (2010). *Perseverance*. San Francisco, CA: Berrett-Koehler Publishers.

Index

language and leadership 113
value of 125
sociological theory 79, 100–101
  classical perspectives 103
  cultural reproduction tradition 102–3
  elites 100
  institutional tradition 101–2
  modern conflict tradition 102
  social structures 100
  women and leadership theory 103–4
    Acker's gender/inequality regimes 108–9
    barriers to women's access to leadership
      roles 104
    Kanter's token theory 106–8
    social network theory 109
    status characteristic theory 105–6
    unconscious bias 104–5
    women's experience of leadership 108
soft power 43
speaking time *see* talking time
special peers 414
speech styles 118
sponsors/sponsorship 39, 40, 228
  developmental experiences 383, 424
  developmental relationships 367, 368
  difficulties for women securing 368
  lack of 277, 363
  role and purpose of 368
  women only leadership programs 401
spousal contributions 285
stakeholders 31, 35, 38, 41
standards, unequal 279–80
status 102
  beliefs 105–6
  biases 106, 110
  characteristic 105
  hierarchy and 123
  power and 226
  token theory 106–7
status characteristic theory 105–6
stay-at-home mom stereotype 291
Stead, V. and Elliott, C. 166–7
step-ahead mentors 369
stereotype threat 92–3, 346
stereotypes 36, 50, 51
  criticisms of research on 231–2
  desired beliefs 232
  gender 274–5
  Kanter's tokens 116
  lazy 332
  media 346–7, 347–8
    imagery 349–53
  minority status 229
  prevailing and changing 169–70
  purpose of 350

racial 91–2
shaping women's behavior and beliefs 92–4
sociohistorical context 350
women and lack of fit 87
women's power behaviors 225–6
see also gender stereotypes
stigma
  flexibility 307–8, 309–10
  workplace, associated with motherhood 305
strain *see* stress
stress 245–6
  flexibility stigma 307–8
  future research and practice 310–12
    changing gendered cultural assumptions
      312
    intersectionality 311
    small wins 312
    work–life balance strategies 311
  gendered division of labor 306
    ideal worker concept 306
  guilt 304–5, 306–7
  negotiating professional identity and
    parenthood 308–310
      multiple identities, tensions caused by 309
  opting out of elite leadership roles 305–6
  workplace stigma associated with
    motherhood 305
structural behavior 169
structural theory 224
subjective assessments 238
subjective task value 176
success 109
  agency 258
  alternative paths 263
  career 255
  conceptual framework with choice and
    leadership 261–3
    structure and agency 262–3
  as defined for men 310
  definition 184
  factors in women's advancement 413
  research on 256
  strategies for progression 257–8
  subjective measures 255–6
  women's career goals 256–7
  women's perception of 255–6
  see also career development
succession management 416
superwoman stereotype 291
symbolic interactionism 195, 201

talking time 225, 226
  competition for 116
task-oriented leadership 246
team effectiveness theory 131